CRITICAL ISSUES IN CRIME AND JUSTICE

CRITICAL ISSUES IN CRIME AND JUSTICE

Albert R. Roberts
editor

Foreword by
Roslyn Muraskin

SAGE Publications
International Educational and Professional Publisher
Thousand Oaks   London   New Delhi

29314880

For information address:

SAGE Publications, Inc.
2455 Teller Road
Thousand Oaks, California 91320

SAGE Publications Ltd.
6 Bonhill Street
London EC2A 4PU
United Kingdom

SAGE Publications India Pvt. Ltd.
M-32 Market
Greater Kailash I
New Delhi 110 048 India

Printed in the United States of America

Library of Congress Cataloging-in-Publication Data

Main entry under title:

Critical issues in crime and justice / [edited by] Albert R. Roberts.
  p. cm.
  Includes bibliographical references.
  ISBN 0-8039-5497-2 (cl).—ISBN 0-8039-5498-0 (pb)
  1. Criminal justice, Administration of—United States. 2. Law enforcement—United States. 3. Corrections—United States.
  I. Roberts, Albert R.
  HV9950.C77 1994
  364.973—dc20   93-41637

94 95 96 97 98   10 9 8 7 6 5 4 3 2

Sage Production Editor: Diane S. Foster

Brief Contents

Detailed Contents

PART IV: THE COURTS

PART V: CORRECTIONAL SYSTEMS

Foreword

Many textbooks have been known to induce sleep with detailed accounts of theoretical information, voluminous statistical reports, and reams of historical facts that students are required to memorize and give back during examinations. This volume is different. It is a very practical, up-to-date, how-to book written in a style responsive to the learning needs and interests of all criminal justice students. The authors of the various chapters focus on what are considered the *real problems* and most pressing controversies in the criminal justice system of today.

In recent years, a new set of policies, program innovations, and professional roles have evolved at federal, state, and county criminal justice agencies. As a result of changing crime trends—growing numbers of violent juveniles, growing numbers of residential burglaries, rapid increases in violent carjackings, and increased arrests and convictions of drug dealers, increased convictions of repetitive and chronic sex offenders, battered women applying for restraining orders, and corporate criminals being indicted—new legislation has been enacted with several innovative programs having emerged. This book, *Critical Issues in Crime and Justice*, describes the latest policies and program developments. This writer was particularly impressed with the comprehensive and timely coverage the 24 contributors give to each component of the criminal justice process and the most critical issues of the 1990s.

Critical Issues in Crime and Justice is an outstanding and comprehensive work. Chapter 1 provides an important overview to the study of criminal justice. Dr. Albert Roberts provides the reader with a well-written orientation to the scope of the problems, primary sources of crime data trends, costs of each component of the justice system, and current sentencing options. Dr. Roberts predicts an end to new prison construction nationwide and an expansion of intermediate sanctions such as intensive probation supervision and boot camps. If criminal court judges and state and county commissioners of corrections do not lessen the warehousing of prison inmates, it is most likely that extensive prison riots will occur by the twenty-first century in many of the larger state prisons.

The case exemplar, written by Donald Sears (a criminal defense attorney who has worked as a police officer) provides an additional overview and integrative framework to the book. Sears provides a highly realistic and penetrating view on how the criminal justice system works (or fails to work) at each stage of processing, from arrest to maxing out or parole. The author's use of a detailed case example throughout his article will be especially appealing to students.

Twenty-four prominent criminal justice experts from all regions of the United States have written chapters for this book. Each contributing author has many years of experience in the criminal justice field, e.g., as a law enforcement administrator, criminal justice professor, attorney, social worker, forensic psychologist, police officer, detective, F.B.I. Special Agent, or probation supervisor. The total number of years of criminal justice experience of the authors added together is almost 500.

Criminal justice educators and their students have been searching for a textbook that thoroughly reviews the critical issues, controversies, and practices in the administration of justice today. *Critical Issues in Crime and Justice*, comprised of all original chapters, meets this need. This textbook is highly recommended as the primary or secondary textbook for the following courses: Introductory Criminal Justice, Critical Issues in Criminal Justice, Justice in American Society, and Special Topics in Criminal Justice.

As a former chair of Criminal Justice at the C.W. Post Campus of Long Island University and in my present capacity of Associate Dean of Public Service, it is my pleasure to review many textbooks. As a result of many years as a professor, administrator, and editor of *The Justice Professional*, I feel confident in evaluating the quality of Professor Roberts' latest work. *Critical Issues in Crime and Justice* is the most timely, readable, thought-provoking, criminal justice text published in the past 10 years. This exceptionally practical and well-written text will provide the serious student with an in-depth understanding of the critical issues, policy reforms, and promising remedies to crime and justice.

It is my expectation that this book will rapidly become valuable not only as a college textbook, but also as a reference book in college libraries, law schools and law office libraries, public libraries, as well as county criminal justice agency libraries. This work promises to become an indispensable reference for personnel in numerous criminal justice professions, including attorneys, probation officers, correctional counselors, police training instructors, social workers, forensic experts, psychologists, researchers, and chemical dependency counselors. This is an exciting work, and I am proud to play a role in it.

Roslyn Muraskin, Ph.D.
Associate Dean
School of Public Service
College of Management
C.W. Post Campus of Long Island University

Preface

This book has been prepared for introductory and advanced courses on the American criminal justice system and its interrelated components. It includes a comprehensive examination of the current critical issues and policy dilemmas within the system of criminal justice affecting local communities throughout the United States. Each contributing chapter author examines the dilemmas confronting the police, prosecutors, defense attorneys, judges, legislators, juvenile justice officials, and probation and correctional administrators.

There is a growing realization that law enforcement and judicial agencies need to safeguard the legal rights of both the accused and the crime victim. While attempting to balance the rights of the accused with those of the innocent victim, the criminal justice system is plagued by a shortage of staff resources, increased numbers of violent crime victims, a low percentage of arrests for serious crimes, repeated cases of police use of excessive force, tremendous court backlogs, severely overcrowded jails and prisons, a high percentage of charges dismissed or reduced, and skyrocketing costs of white-collar as well as property-related crime. Several promising and cost-effective strategies to crime control, offender rehabilitation, and juvenile aftercare have been developed. This volume will provide an extensive background and discussion of the critical issues, policy reforms, and model program developments.

Critical Issues in Crime and Justice will be useful as the primary or supplementary text for Introduction to Criminal Justice and related overview courses. This timely book, entirely made up of originally written chapters by leading experts in the criminal justice field, will provide students with comprehensive readings on critical and controversial issues, policies and legal reforms, and the key components of the criminal justice system. This book includes chapters on the following important critical issues:

- motivation and career patterns of burglars
- the advantages and disadvantages of the penile plethysmograph testing for convicted sex offenders
- the reasons why carjacking has become so prevalent and when it becomes a crime of opportunity
- defining the three major types of white-collar crime and finding the best way to estimate the number and costs of white-collar crime
- higher education versus training for police officers
- police use of excessive force and emerging social control measures
- the failure of determinate sentencing policies
- drug treatment programs for juvenile offenders that work
- jail overcrowding and jail reform litigation
- newly developed model juvenile aftercare programs

In contrast to the traditional textbooks, this book includes detailed information and specific chapters on the above topics.

Integration and synthesis of the individual chapters is accomplished through the Chapter Summaries, which briefly reviews the focus of each chapter. In addition, this book provides standard use of timely case illustrations and trend data in most chapters, policy and model program examples from many of the 50 states, and end of chapter summaries. Each chapter also ends with a series of five to eight review and discussion questions included as a guide to further the student's comprehension of the chapter.

Albert R. Roberts

Chapter Summaries

The chapter authors share several beliefs about the field of criminal justice, critical issues and policies, and the nature of college textbooks. First, we have attempted to provide an intensive analysis of the major issues, problems, and remedies rather than a superficial presentation of every issue and problem confronting the criminal justice system. Second, we believe that students can better understand the key justice issues, concepts, and policies if these are presented in clear, nontechnical language. Third, we are convinced that a comprehensive understanding of the most current issues related to the components of the criminal justice system and the treatment of offenders is necessary for all students of criminal justice and criminology. Without an understanding of the organizational structure and policies that lead, for example, to jail and prison overcrowding or to police use of excessive force, students find it very difficult to suggest improved policies or new programs. Finally, each chapter provides detailed information on current trends, policies, and programs as well as the problems that must be addressed. Awareness of current conditions and programs is requisite to understanding the ways in which changes can be implemented and injustices eliminated.

Violent crime and property-related crime are most pronounced in our highly populated cities. The administration of justice and the processing of suspected offenders in felony cases vary from one jurisdiction to the next. Despite the wide variation in handling offenders and periodic injustices in the overburdened criminal justice systems, large cities seem to be very similar in the critical justice issues they frequently encounter. Chapter 1 provides an overview of the patterns and trends in official crime rates.

Annual sources of data on the nature and extent of the different types of crime are discussed. Also examined are the phenomenal costs of operating the criminal justice system. The Case Exemplar that follows Chapter 1 reviews each stage in the criminal justice process with a typical case. It is important for students to understand that the process frequently begins when an arrest is made and ends with parole or maxing out. This article examines how the system works with regard to enforcing the criminal law, discretion and decision making, delays in the process, and outcomes.

Chapter 2 reports on the findings from a field study of burglars and burglary. The subjects of the study were active burglars who reconstructed burglaries previously committed and evaluated sites previously burglarized by others. The study explored several issues critical to the understanding of burglary. Among these are (a) How do residential burglars choose targets? and (b) What determines a burglar's perception of a particular site as a vulnerable target? Burglars were found to be more opportunistic than previously thought, yet the study concluded that rational processes were at work in the decision-making strategies of burglars. Drug use affected the rational decision process in various ways. Professor Cromwell concluded that a crime prevention strategy that does not take into account the large percentage of burglars who use drugs is doomed to failure.

Chapter 3 examines specialized model programs for the treatment of sex offenders in separate facilities and as part of a county probation department in Arizona. The apprehension, prosecution, and disposition of sex offenders have added huge numbers to the criminal justice system in the last 10 to 15 years, yet responses to this population have often been ill informed and inconsistent. Risk assessments for these offenders are necessary to determine who can be supervised in the community and who needs long-term incarceration. Recidivism studies generally show less recidivism if the offender has participated in a structured cognitive-behavioral program that specifically addresses his sexual deviancy. Significant cost savings can be realized, but surveillance must be strict. The greatest impact on reducing the number of victims can be made by focusing more effort on juvenile offenders. Good assessment and treatment are vital.

"More money is stolen each year with a pencil than with a gun." Although this is true, the public usually thinks of crime as robbery, burglaries, and so forth ("street crimes"), not fraud, tax conspiracy, or price fixing ("suite crimes"). Chapter 4 explores white-collar crime—a term used by social scientists to describe crimes committed by businesses and "successful" citizens that are not usually the focus of law enforcement efforts. The development of this concept in research and practice is traced and analyzed. It is observed that white-collar crime is too broad a concept to be useful for research or practitioners. A tripartite definition of white-collar crime is suggested as more useful to guide research and law enforcement efforts. The chapter concludes with a call for a national program to estimate the number, types, and impact of white-collar crime.

Part II of this volume focuses on three critical issues in law enforcement: (a) Should college degrees be required of all new police recruits? (b) What types of police administrative structures and policies are likely to lead to regular police use of excessive force? (c) What is a realistic definition of community policing, and can it work only in suburban police departments? Chapter 5 begins with consideration of the distinction between police *training* and *collegiate education* for police officers. Simply defined, training is the practical and applied side of education. It is designed to convey skills, attitudes, and general information necessary to carry out the day-to-day operations of policing. Education is the more theoretically based knowledge, values, and attitudes one gains from formal exposure to substantive written material or comprehensive lecture and debates on issues. Instructors should be aware that the question of how much formal education entry level police officers actually require is a longstanding one among police policy makers and police administrators.

Additionally, financial support has been made available intermittently by federal and state scholarships. More recently, in 1993, President Clinton announced to the nation a crime bill that would provide federal funding for more than 925,000 new law enforcement officers throughout the country. Whether or not national efforts and educational incentives are successful, it is clear that the police are moving in the direction of increased numbers of college-educated line officers. This chapter will explore the merits and drawback of having police officers possess college levels of education.

Various institutional mechanisms are available to control the use of excessive force by police officers. Chapter 6 begins by defining what is meant by "excessive police force" and outlining the scope of this problem. This is followed by an examination of the limitations inherent in a number of proposed external controls (e.g., criminal prosecution, civilian review boards, municipal control) that seek to address this concern. The potential for controlling excessive force through internal means is explored. Finally, a contrast is presented between the experiences of two police agencies that have responded to acts of brutality in very different ways.

The law enforcement community has attempted to deal with crime through a variety of strategies. Most experts will acknowledge, however, that few of these efforts appear to have been successful in dealing with crime. Chapter 7 focuses on a new strategy that is taking hold, namely community policing. As part of a research grant from the National Institute of Justice, Professor Joseph Ryan attempted to define community policing by determining the goals of policing. The research revealed that police cannot readily translate their daily activities into goals, which in reality makes it difficult to assess whether they are succeeding at what they hope to accomplish. Further, community policing is not yet definable as a concrete police strategy, but the underlying theme that emerges is one in which the police are recognizing the need to be accountable to those they serve.

Chapter 8 focuses on the crime wave of the 1990s: armed vehicle theft, better known as carjacking. FBI Special Agent Beekman begins her chapter by reporting on the estimated number of carjackings in 1991 and 1992. The number increased from approximately 19,000 in 1991 to over 25,000 in 1992. The next section of the chapter explains why this random and violent type of crime has become so prevalent and why it is viewed as a crime of *opportunity*. The final section of the chapter identifies and discusses federal and local countermeasures as well as carjacking prevention strategies.

Part III explores critical issues and problems in the juvenile justice system. Chapter 9 briefly describes the history of data collection on juvenile offenders and juvenile offenses, explains major policy shifts in juvenile justice over the last 50 years, and traces recent trends in the processing of juvenile offenders. The trends reviewed include intake, detention, adjudication, and disposition decisions by the courts. Trends in offense patterns, referrals to court, and characteristics of juvenile offenders are also examined. Particular attention is paid to the interaction of race, gender, and offense. The most disturbing trend noted is the dramatic increase in the most severe dispositions for male, nonwhite drug offenders. Waivers of nonwhite juveniles to adult court more than doubled during a recent 4-year period. Implications of these trends are discussed, and suggestions for improving equity in the processing of juvenile offenders are offered.

Chapter 10 examines the problems of adolescent drug abuse and drug dealing, which are very serious issues especially in poor and minority communities in large urban areas. The incidence of drug-related violence and its impact on the courts, law enforcement agencies, the school system, families, and whole communities are documented almost daily in the media. This chapter discusses the apparent attractions of the lifestyle of the drug dealer and the risks and some of the underlying causes that motivate young men in particular to become drug dealers. It also delineates how courts handle such cases, and the treatment programs that are available for both addicts and nonusing dealers. The chapter ends with a plea for the development of effective programs to prevent an increase in addiction and criminal behavior.

The past several decades have witnessed substantial failure on the part of youth corrections nationwide to reduce the reoffending rate for a substantial number of juveniles released from secure confinement. Responding to this widespread and persistent problem, the Office of Juvenile Justice and Delinquency Prevention (OJJDP) of the U.S. Department of Justice issued a request for proposals entitled "Intensive Community-Based Aftercare Programs" in 1987. This research and development initiative was designed to assess, test, and disseminate information on intensive juvenile aftercare program prototypes/modes for chronic serious juvenile offenders who initially require secure confinement. Chapter 11 documents the progress of this project (from 1988 to 1993) to develop a promising prototype of intensive juvenile aftercare. The assumptions, goals, and strategies defining this programming effort are discussed in the context of an emerging intensive supervision movement that is increasingly being used as a major point of reference in the design and implementation of community-based interventions for high-risk juvenile offenders.

Part IV of this volume focuses on criminal and family courts as well as trends in determinate sentencing. Chapter 12 introduces the reader to sentencing policy, which is viewed as one of the most difficult tasks of government. Establishing equity in sentencing while protecting society from the criminal is a balancing act of diverse elements that often leads to apparent inequities. Structuring sentencing policy to eliminate such disparities has led increasingly to determinate sentencing systems where uniformity of outcomes is the goal. Unfortunately, even these systems have not resolved the disparity problem so that subsequent reforms have emphasized sentencing guidelines as the solution. But systems using sentencing guidelines have also encountered difficulties, so the search for the optimal solution goes on even today. Making effective sentencing policy has proven to be a much more difficult process than many reformers imagined in the beginning. The process of reform is continuous, and this chapter describes one phase in that process.

Chapter 13 focuses on plea bargaining and the problems inherent in this judicial dilemma. The courts have their hands full in their attempt to preserve a fair yet expeditious system of justice. Attorneys are the "playmakers" in that they face constant pressure to achieve justice through compromise and negotiated settlements. Professor Payne discusses whether there are any solutions to the problems surrounding plea bargaining.

Responsive prosecutors, judges, and legislators have begun to recognize family violence as a serious crime. All 50 states have passed civil and/or criminal statutes to protect battered women. Chapter 14 examines programs aimed at reducing and eventually eliminating woman battering. Navigating the court system is generally a time-consuming and overwhelming ordeal for victims of violent crime. But for a woman who has survived repeated physical abuse and terroristic threats by a spouse or boyfriend, the thought of going to court may be so intimidating that she never does go there.

Part V of this book examines the most critical issues in corrections today. These timely issues include the reasons for jail overcrowding, the potential of prison-based industries and private sector partnerships with correctional agencies, and the trends and the utility of parole and intensive parole systems. Overcrowding is often viewed as the primary jail problem, largely because most other difficulties stem directly from the booming jail population. Whereas state prison populations have more than doubled over the past decade, the number of jail inmates in such cities as New York has tripled. Chapter 15 examines the pattern of jail overcrowding in New York City, Miami, Chicago, Houston, and Los Angeles. It provides a critical examination of overcrowding in the context of social sanitation: that is, warehousing those members of the urban underclass whom society finds offensive. Remedies, solutions, and alternatives to jail are also discussed as they relate to social and correctional reform.

In Chapter 16, Professors McNally and Dwyer present an extensive review of the role of prison industries in American corrections from a historical and contemporary perspective. Discussion focuses on the description and analysis of several models of prison work programs. Special attention is given to the loss of business to foreign markets and the potential for using prison-based industries as an alternative to offshore competition. Legislative and policy issues are considered and alternatives proposed.

Chapter 17 examines the changing patterns of parole supervision nationwide. The historical origins of parole, its relationship to the rehabilitative ideal, and the forces shaping parole supervision over the past 20 years are addressed in order to gain an understanding of state-level adaptations to a fluctuating parole supervision environment. The forces examined are (a) changing sentencing and correctional philosophies, (b) altered organizational structures for the delivery of correctional services, (c) increasing correctional populations, resulting in fiscal and workload constraints, and (d) critical evaluations of parole supervision effectiveness. State-level release-supervision strategies are discussed for various states (California, Florida, Illinois, Maine, New York, and Texas), illustrating how states that have or have not abolished discretionary parole release and parole supervision undertake postrelease supervision in the 1980s and 1990s.

PART I

OVERVIEW OF
CRIMINAL JUSTICE

1

Crime in America

Trends, Costs, and Remedies

ALBERT R. ROBERTS

The critical issues surrounding the criminal justice system and its subsystems have evoked strong emotions and debate. Public outcry and legislative support for change are often prompted by the media coverage and the public's fear about youth violence, drug abuse, and victimization. As a result, the components of the criminal justice system often seek ways to maximize the efficiency of law enforcement agencies, remodel the court system, create effective juvenile offender treatment strategies, and implement correctional rehabilitation programs.

This text focuses on the critical and controversial issues within the organizations and agencies administering justice services in American society. The American justice system is made up of lawmaking bodies, such as state legislatures, as well as county, state, and federal law enforcement agencies. These governmental agencies include county prosecutors, the police, the courts, corrections, and probation and parole. Police officers detect crime, investigate citizen complaints, attempt to control crime by making arrests, and provide emergency services to crime victims and the community. The courts handle defendants. The court has the legal responsibility of enforcing the state criminal code against alleged defendants who have been indicted for specific criminal acts. The court is also empowered to protect the same defendants from the violation of their constitutional rights by criminal justice practitioners. Jails and short-term county correctional institutions confine pretrial detainees and sentenced misdemeanants. Corrections professionals supervise convicted offenders in county, state, and federal prisons as well as community correctional centers. County and city probation officers are responsible for supervising juvenile and adult offenders in the community. State parole officers supervise juvenile and adult offenders in the community. In the federal system, the functions of probation and parole are combined. As a result, we have federal probation and parole agents monitoring, supervising, and checking up on offenders in the community.

The Nature and Extent of Violent Crime

Violent crime is one of the most serious social problems facing American society. The two most comprehensive statistical sources of crime data in America are the annual FBI Uniform Crime Reports (UCR) and the National Crime Survey (NCS). The UCR includes a nationwide view of crime data based on "crimes known to the police" and "arrests" made by over 16,000 city, county, and state law enforcement agencies. The National Crime Survey (NCS) conducts massive victimization surveys with approximately 45,000 to 60,000 households every 6 months. Household members are interviewed in order to determine whether they have been the victims of the major crimes of rape, robbery, assault, burglary, personal and household larceny, or motor vehicle theft. The NCS discloses the extent to which specific crimes are not reported to the police and the reasons victims give for not reporting crimes.

Figure 1.1 depicts an alarming crime clock based on an aggregate representation of data from the UCR. The crime clock indicates that in 1990 there was one murder every 22 minutes, one forcible rape every 5 minutes, one robbery every 49 seconds, one burglary every 10 seconds, one larceny-theft every 4 seconds, and one motor vehicle theft every 19 seconds. The FBI report cautions the reader that the crime clock display should not be interpreted to imply regularity in the commission of crimes in all 16,000 (approximately) police agencies contributing crime data; rather, it represents the annual ratio of crime to fixed time intervals.

The data reported by the FBI provide estimates of the extent of criminal activity known to law enforcement agencies. In 1991, there were over 1.9 million violent crimes reported to the police. This includes 106,000 reports of forcible rape, 1.08 million assaults, and over 24,000 murders. Murders

FBI Crime Clock

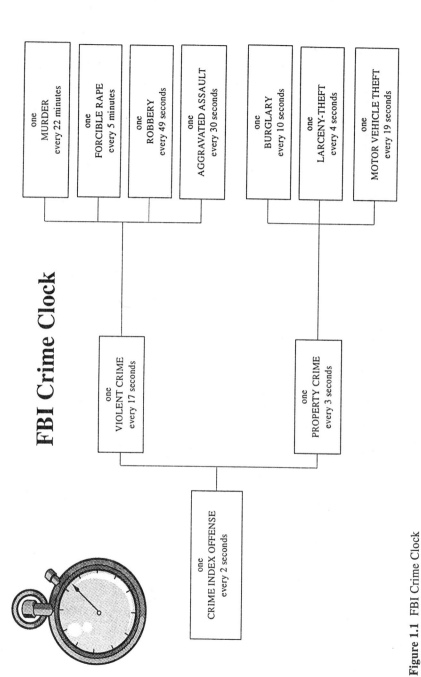

one
CRIME INDEX OFFENSE
every 2 seconds

one
VIOLENT CRIME
every 17 seconds

one
PROPERTY CRIME
every 3 seconds

one
MURDER
every 22 minutes

one
FORCIBLE RAPE
every 5 minutes

one
ROBBERY
every 49 seconds

one
AGGRAVATED ASSAULT
every 30 seconds

one
BURGLARY
every 10 seconds

one
LARCENY-THEFT
every 4 seconds

one
MOTOR VEHICLE THEFT
every 19 seconds

Figure 1.1 FBI Crime Clock

SOURCE: Uniform Crime Reports for the U.S., 1990 by the Federal Bureau of Investigation, 1991, Washington, DC: Government Printing Office.

increased dramatically between 1981 and 1991, from 13,315 to 24,074. This is particularly disturbing because a growing number of the murders in the 1990s are committed by teenagers against other teenagers. According to the National Center for Health Statistics, in 1990 alone 4,200 teenagers were killed by bullets. This alarming figure shows a sharp increase from 1985, when there were 2,500 gun-related teen deaths. Across America, there is a growing trend of juveniles arming themselves with illegally obtained handguns and semiautomatic weapons. More and more youths in populated cities like Miami, New York, Newark, Baltimore, Los Angeles, Houston, and Omaha are carrying 9 mms, .357 Magnums, MAC-10s, and 12-gauge sawed-off shotguns.

Table 1.1 compares crime figures and rates of the UCR and the NCS. Together these two major sources of crime statistics offer a more accurate annual estimate of crime rates than either would separately. Even though the NCS bases its measures of crime on the number of victimizations rather than the number of incidents, it does reveal the main weakness of the UCR. NCS crime figures are larger than UCR crime figures because a number of crimes are not reported to the police. The UCR include only "incidents"—crimes reported to the police. In addition, because more than one person can be involved in a crime incident, the number of victimizations is usually greater than the number of incidents.

The National Crime Survey (NCS) uses the panel survey method to collect information on personal and household victimizations. A representative sample of households is interviewed seven times at 6-month intervals. This method is called a "panel survey" because the same people are interviewed again. For example, 16,000 people over 12 years of age are interviewed in February. In the next month (March), and in each of the four successive months, an independent probability sample of the same sample size is interviewed. In August, the apartment dwellers and home-owners first interviewed in February are revisited and interviewed again. Similarly, the original March subsample is revisited in September, the April units in October, and so on.

The NCS conducted its first victim surveys in 1972. The NCS is conducted annually by the Bureau of Justice Statistics (BJS) in cooperation with the U.S. Bureau of the Census. This national victimization database has documented a large amount of unreported crime. In some cities the disparity between unreported crime and "crimes known to the police" is as high as 4 to 1. According to the NCS, the main reasons given by respondent victims for not reporting victimization incidents were general apathy and their belief that there was really nothing the police could do about the crimes.

TABLE 1.1 Crimes of Violence: National Crime Survey and Uniform Crime
            Reports, 1990

Crime	National Crime Survey		Uniform Crime Reports	
	Number	Rate	Number	Rate
Total	2,458,00	1,420	1,820,130	731.8
Forcible Rape	130,000	60	102,560	41.2
Robbery	1,150,000	570	639,270	257.0
Aggravated Assault	1,601,000	790	1,054,860	424.1

SOURCE: *Criminal Victimization, 1990* by the Bureau of Justice Statistics, 1991 (October), Bureau of Justice
Statistics Bulletin, Washington, DC: Department of Justice; *Uniform Crime Reports for the U.S., 1990* by the
Federal Bureau of Investigation, 1991, Washington, DC: Government Printing Office; *National Crime Victim-
ization Survey* (p. 6) by the Bureau of Justice Statistics, 1991, Washington, DC: Department of Justice.

During 1991 approximately 95,000 individuals (in a sample of 48,000
nationally representative households) were interviewed regarding crimes
they recalled experiencing during the preceding 6-month period. The
summary findings are as follows:

The estimated number of personal crime victimizations in the nation rose from
34.4 million in 1990 to 35.1 million in 1991, a 1.9% increase.
  In 1991, unreported victimizations were estimated at 22 million personal
crimes (rape, robbery, assault, and larceny) and household victimizations (burglary, household larceny, and motor vehicle theft).
  In 1991, over 6.42 million persons survived a violent crime such as rape,
robbery, or assault, while 12.99 million persons were victims of theft.
  About 37% of all victimizations and 49% of all violent victimizations were
reported to law enforcement authorities in 1991, almost identical to the percentage for 1990. (Bureau of Justice Statistics, 1992 [April], p. 5)
  Crime and delinquency permeate all segments of American society. However,
young black and Hispanic males living in low-income neighborhoods are more
likely to be victims of violent crimes and burglary.
  Men have higher rates of victimization for personal crimes than women, except
for the crime of rape [the NCS includes homosexual as well as heterosexual rape].
  With the exception of purse snatching, elderly persons have substantially
lower victimization rates than do younger persons.
  African Americans are more frequently victims of violence than whites.
  In general, Hispanics have higher rates of victimization for household burglary and larceny than do non-Hispanics. In general, the higher a person's
income, the more likely he or she is to be a victim of theft. (Bureau of Justice
Statistics, 1991b, pp. 4-5)

The Cost of Crime

Crime costs billions of dollars each year. There are two major costs: monetary and human costs. Monetary costs can be estimated by identifying criminal justice system operating costs and offender processing costs. Human costs refer to the lost lives and unused human potential of the thousands of homicide victims each year.

The total annual cost of crime has been estimated at between $110 and $136.9 billion. Several component costs of the criminal justice system can be fairly accurately measured. These include police, corrections, and court budgets. Other component costs are very difficult to measure accurately. These include net losses from robbery, burglary and larceny; credit card fraud; computer crime; automated teller machine fraud; federal income tax evasion; and counterfeit notes and currency.

Monetary costs to crime victims are astronomical! They include cash and property replacement costs for victims of robbery, burglary, personal and household larceny and motor vehicle theft. In 1991, the FBI estimated the following national costs for people who were victimized in 1990: robbery victims, $501 million; burglary victims, $3.5 billion; larceny-theft victims, $3.8 billion; and motor vehicle theft, in excess of $8 billion (Federal Bureau of Investigation, 1991, pp. 19, 28, 33, 39). In 1988, the BJS listed the following economic costs of crime: $37 billion net loss from robbery, burglary, and larceny of banks; almost $60 billion from drug abuse costs, plus an additional $2 billion for health care related to drug abuse and drug treatment services; $500 million for credit card fraud; $13.2 billion for drunk driving costs resulting from DWI motor vehicle crashes; $21.7 billion for private security costs; and over $81 billion for federal income tax evasion. These cost estimates do not include the billions of dollars lost as a result of white-collar crime.

The American correctional system is the most populated prison system in the world. By the end of 1991, the total number of prisoners confined in federal or state correctional facilities reached a record of 823,414 inmates (Bureau of Justice Statistics, 1992 [July], p. 8).

The annual cost of incarcerating over 1.2 million individuals in our prisons and jails is estimated at $20 billion. Prisons are expensive to build and operate. As states and counties have tried to handle the growing prison populations, prison budget allocations have also grown. During the past decade state legislatures have appropriated $30 billion to build new prisons and additional units (Methvin, 1992, p. 28).

The annual operating and capital expenditures budget for adult and juvenile correctional institutions is $16.06 billion for adult corrections and $1.74 billion for juvenile corrections (American Correctional Association, 1993).

As noted by Dr. Michael Welch in Chapter 15, the majority of inmates in most county and city jails are pretrial detainees. Most of these pretrial detainees are too poor to make bail. Jails are populated by a disproportionate number of black, Hispanic, poor, uneducated, and unemployed men. More than half have drug and alcohol problems.

Unlike the huge investment in state and federal prisons costing over $30 billion dollars in the past decade, the government's investment in victim services has been relatively small. Between 1984 and 1992 only $620 million was allocated by the U.S. Department of Justice's Office for Victims of Crime and by state attorney generals to aid crime victims and witnesses (Roberts, 1992, p. 14). Federal and state funding of victim service and witness assistance programs has been minimal when compared to expenditures for prisons and the costs of personal/residential security.

The victims movement has made slow and steady progress since 1975, when a federal agency, the Law Enforcement Assistance Administration (LEAA), allocated funding for just 14 projects geared to helping crime victims and witnesses. With the demise of LEAA in 1981, many cities and counties did not have the funds to continue the victim assistance projects. Therefore the majority of the prosecutor-based witness assistance programs ended in the late 1970s and early 1980s. However, in the mid-1980s, two important events led to increases in funding to help crime victims. They were:

1. The passage of the Victims of Crime Act (VOCA) of 1984, funded by federal criminal penalties.
2. The enactment of legislation in 28 states to fund new programs to aid crime victims and witnesses (Roberts, 1990). The majority of these states fund victim services through penalty assessments and fines.

There are two major types of local programs designed to aid crime victims and witnesses. The first type is under the auspices of a city or county prosecutor and is located in a prosecutor's office, a county office building, or the local courthouse. The major goal of these victim/witness assistance programs is to alleviate the stress and trauma for victims and witnesses who testify in court. For example, prior to the court date, program staff accompany the victim to an empty courtroom to orient the individual to the physical layout and the courtroom procedures. Other services may include transportation to court, child care while the victim or witness is appearing at the court, apprising the victim of the progress of the court case, and referral to social service agencies.

The second major type of program operates under the auspices of a nonprofit social service agency, a city or county police department, or a county probation department. These types of programs often provide victims with concrete services (e.g., emergency food vouchers) as well as crisis intervention at the crime scene, in the program office, or in the person's home. Victim service programs sometimes provide a range of additional services such as accompaniment to and advocacy in court, repair or replacement of broken locks, and emergency financial aid (Roberts, 1990).

The federal VOCA funding was distributed to the states in order to fund prosecutor-based witness assistance programs, sexual assault programs, and battered women's shelters. By 1992, VOCA was funding close to 2,500 victim-oriented programs. When compared to the almost complete lack of support services given to victims during the 1960s and 1970s, victim services have certainly improved. However, there is still a long way to go. Only a dozen police departments have either 24-hour crisis intervention units or victim service programs. Finally, whereas most state prisons employ an average of 350 correctional officers, most prosecutor-based witness assistance programs have only two to four full-time staff. Each victim/witness assistance program has the potential to serve thousands of violent crime victims in its area, but most states and counties refuse to allocate the funds for critically needed staff positions to treat crime victims.

Characteristics of Offenders

In Chapter 15 of this book, Professor Michael Welch characterizes the inmates in our city jails as the growing underclass: a group of people who have the misfortune of populating our jails as pretrial detainees because they do not have the money to post bail. Cole (1992) estimates that about 5 million of the 33 million Americans with incomes below the official poverty line are members of this new group. This group tends to be overrepresented by minorities: African Americans and Hispanics. Being part of this underclass is more a way of life than a social or economic condition. Their behavior patterns typically include antisocial behavior, habitual criminality, chemical dependency, out-of-wedlock births, very erratic work histories and long periods of unemployment, welfare dependency, school failure, and illiteracy. For the most part, this group lacks hope for leading a productive life. Their lives have been filled with pain and despair as they see their friends and relatives incarcerated, addicted to drugs, dealing in drugs, sick or dying from AIDS, or victims of brutal crimes. The inner city youths that get caught up in the criminal justice system are usually products of decaying urban neighborhoods and families where the primary role model is a parent or older sibling who is either dealing drugs or serving time in a state prison for a violent crime.

Almost 20 years ago, the author identified and discussed the five most prevalent handicaps among prison inmates: (a) character disorder: an antisocial defect resulting from undersocialization and inappropriate acting-out responses to the stresses of daily living; (b) unemployability: lack of motivation to work as well as marketable vocational skills; (c) relationship hangups: lack of close interpersonal ties with family and friends; (d) social stigma: being labeled a felon; and (e) immaturity: lack of the capability to take responsibility for one's actions and a general inability to make socially acceptable decisions (Roberts, 1974, p. 6). Many of the above handicaps characterize today's juvenile and adult offenders. However, with the phenomenal increase in drug abuse since the early 1980s, the typical offender has become increasingly prone to violence.

The most critical concerns among criminal justice professionals in the 1990s are the chronic use of drugs by juvenile and adult offenders and the increased spread of infectious and deadly diseases (i.e., AIDS and tuberculosis). The rates of AIDS and drug abuse in the criminal justice system continues to rise each year. As increased numbers of sex offenders are sentenced to probation and other community-based alternatives, the threat of transmission of the HIV virus to victims of sexual assault intensifies. In Chapter 3, Scott reports a steep increase in reported and investigated sex crimes over the last decade and the mostly inadequate management of these crimes by the criminal justice system to date. In Chapter 10, Robertson and Waters discuss the increased use of drugs by inner city adolescents. They examine drug arrests and drug-related homicides in Newark, New Jersey, and California and find a statistical association between violent crime and possession and/or distribution of illicit drugs.

Most convicted offenders do not possess the academic or vocational skills for legitimate employment. Unfortunately, with only limited opportunities to earn money legally, they turn to illegal activity at an early age. It is extremely difficult to convince youthful offenders that it is better in the long run to stay in school and prepare for a law-abiding career when they see their peers making $1,000 a week trafficking in illegal drugs. Their future is dismal, many die before they reach the age of 30, and many more spend their most productive years in jail or state prison.

Recent surveys of American jails and state correctional facilities indicate the disproportionate number of black and Hispanic inmates. In June of 1991, 65% of state prison populations "belonged to racial or ethnic minorities" (Beck et al., 1993, p. 3). In large city jails such as Los Angeles, Miami, Chicago, and New York City, the overwhelming majority of inmates are either black or Hispanic. For example, in New York City's nine jails the inmate population is almost 55% black and 34% Latino (Mack, 1993, p. 39). According to Cole (1992), "Nearly one out of every four black males between the ages of 20 and 29 is under some type of correctional supervision—probation, prison or parole" (p. 21).

The majority of crimes are committed by repeat offenders. Generally, these individuals have no respect for others and are unable to maintain normal relationships of love, respect, and trust with a significant other. In 1991, only one third of the inmates in state prisons had completed high school, and 19% had dropped out in the eighth grade or earlier (Beck, 1993).

The profile of the typical offender is that he is a young black or Hispanic male, has grown up in poverty, and has not received the nurturance of a close family. His values and morals are typically learned from television or the street (Coffen, 1989). The career in crime usually begins at an early age. He tends to be a drug user and a heavy drinker who takes no responsibility for his unlawful actions and shows no remorse (Livingston, 1986).

Remedies

The criminal justice system consists of the formal governmental agencies and personnel who are empowered with the responsibility of enforcing the criminal code. These agencies or components of the system include the police, prosecutor's office, public defender's office or legal aid, the courts, and corrections.

Basically, criminal justice practitioners and policy makers hold one of three philosophies with regard to the criminal law, crime, and offenders: (a) punishment, (b) rehabilitation and treatment, or (c) a combination of punishment and rehabilitation. During the 1960s and 1970s, the prevailing popular view of administrators and practitioners was that criminal behavior patterns could be treated by rehabilitation, that is, a combination of education and counseling. Probation and community alternatives such as work-release and pretrial diversion were the preferred option in many jurisdictions. Incarceration was usually used as a last resort after probation had been tried several times and failed. However, the crime rate climbed, drug-related crime skyrocketed, and communities became fearful of their safety. Newspaper and magazine reports repeatedly stated that correctional treatment wasn't working because of the increase in crime, especially violent crime.

According to Dr. Merlo (1992), during the 1980s and early 1990s corrections became a political issue, both nationally and in many states. The Willie Horton incident during the 1988 presidential campaign illustrates the power of a media campaign focusing on one individual failure. Horton escaped from a Massachusetts work furlough program, went to Maryland, broke into a home, violently raped the woman residing in the home, and assaulted her fiancé with a knife. The Bush campaign staff made prison furloughs an emotionally charged issue and a symbol that the governor was soft on crime and coddled violent offenders (Merlo, 1992, p. x). Although Governor Michael Dukakis had never been the Massachusetts Commissioner of Corrections, and although most offenders (approximately 200,000 per year) do well in furlough programs, Dukakis was hurt politically because of this one case. A few months after the Bush campaign thrust it into the spotlight, Governor Dukakis signed legislation that prevented all inmates serving life sentences from obtaining a furlough. Due to the intensified public fears of chronic offenders as well as drug- and gang-related violent offenders, we have witnessed a "trend toward punitiveness among policy makers, a punitiveness founded on feelings of frustration, anxiety and loss of control" (Fairchild & Webb, 1985, p. 9).

As a result of tougher and determinate sentencing laws administered by judges, primarily in response to public outcries, the number of inmates under the jurisdiction of federal or state correctional agencies climbed to a record high of 883,593 at the end of 1992. Since 1980 the number of prisoners confined in correctional facilities nationwide has increased an astounding 168%. The imprisonment rate rose from 329,821 in 1980 to 502,752 in 1985 to 883,593 at the end of 1992 (Gilliard, 1993).

From 1991 to 1992, prison populations increased the most in four states from 1991 to 1992. The largest gain in the number of prisoners took place in Texas with an increase of 9,501 inmates, followed by California with 7,688, New York with 3,874, and Michigan with 2,596 additional prisoners.

Examining the trend in the offense composition of state prison admissions reveals a significant increase in offenders convicted of drug offenses and offenders violating probation or parole conditions. In 1980, drug offenses accounted for only 1 out of every 15 court-committed admissions to state correctional facilities. However, by 1990 approximately 1 in 3 newly sentenced offenders had been convicted of drug offenses (Gilliard, 1993). During the same 12-year period, probation and parole violators committed by the courts to state prisons increased from just under 17% to approximately 30% of the total admissions.

Jails and prisons are human warehouses for the new underclass: the thousands of drug-abusing, unemployed, and repeat offenders. Prisons are overpopulated and recidivism rates are high. We have learned that building more prisons is not the solution. Many of our nation's prisons have become schools for crime, places where offenders become more incorrigible and violent as a result of the unsanitary, degrading, and inhumane conditions in many prisons.

The determinate sentencing experiments of the 1980s have not worked. Chapter 12 in this book focuses on the outcomes created by determinate sentencing schemes. In a number of states determinate sentencing laws and guidelines have resulted in increased prison time for drug and sex offenders. One of the underlying problems is that most jurisdictions have not developed comprehensive treatment programs in the community for drug or sex offenders. Chapter 3 discusses several model programs for effectively treating sex offenders.

During the past 20 years courts have found a number of American jails to be in violation of the 8th Amendment (banning cruel and unusual punishment) and the 14th Amendment (guaranteeing due process rights) of the Constitution. In Chapter 15, Professor Michael Welch documents the fact that about 30% of America's large city jails were under court order to reduce overcrowding or improve general conditions of confinement in 1991. Professor Welch provides a comprehensive analysis of court-ordered reforms, changes in institutional conditions, and policy alternatives. He underscores the paramount importance of carefully weighing options and developing optimal policy plans based on a well-coordinated approach to problem analysis and policy design.

By 1993 there were close to 900,000 inmates in our nation's state and federal correctional facilities. How do they typically spend their time each day? Usually in one or two ways: (a) "hanging out" in the prison yard or recreation area or locked in their cells, or (b) working a full day in prison factories that are joint ventures with private companies. Productivity standards are comparable to those of manufacturers on the outside. The inmate workers receive minimum wage. They are required to turn over their wages to the state or federal prison in order to provide monetary restitution to their victims and to send payments to the inmates' dependents. A small sum of money is put aside each week in a "going home" savings account in preparation for the inmates' release.

Twenty years ago the author called for the "building and operating of modern factories within correctional facilities" in order to transmit marketable job skills to inmates while paying them minimum wages (Roberts, 1974, pp. 33-34). The author's recommendation on instilling a solid work ethic and good work habits to inmates stemmed from his awareness of the successful industrial prison in Coldingly, England where 80% of the prisoners were working for civilian foremen in the early 1970s (Roberts, 1974).

Putting inmates to work in labor intensive manufacturing and production jobs is a realistic alternative to inmate idleness and potential prison riots. Several different organizational models of prison industries have emerged in the 1990s:

1. The state government model in which the prison industries produce products solely for state and local governmental agencies use, such as desks, chairs, and file cabinets or laundry for the state hospitals.
2. The joint venture model in which prison industries contract with a private corporation to produce products that the corporation will market and distribute.
3. The corporate model is similar to a private sector business and accordingly inmates are hired, trained, and transported daily (work-release) to a manufacturing facility near the prison.

In Chapter 16, Professors McNally and Dwyer provide a comprehensive examination of new and expanded prison industries for the 1990s. This chapter begins with a detailed description of inmates' work assignments at Zephyr Products, Inc. in Kansas. Then it thoroughly discusses the past, present, and future of prison industry alliances with the private sector. McNally and Dwyer aptly document the development of prison industry partnership programs with private sector companies on a limited basis in 23 states. They conclude their chapter by enumerating the specific benefits of prison industry enhancement programs to taxpayers, corporations, prisons, labor, and the offenders themselves. In sharp contrast to the federal correctional institutions where the overwhelming majority of inmates work in prison industries (Unicor), the majority of inmates in state prisons are locked in their cells and taking naps, "hanging out" in the prison yards, or "pumping iron" in the weightlifting rooms. Hopefully, correctional administrators will follow the recommendations of Professors McNally and Dwyer.

Building prisons has been extremely expensive. The prison and jail construction boom of the 1980s has failed to solve the worsening crime problem. While state and federal budgets were being cut back, 62 new correctional institutions were opened across the United States during 1990 at a cost of over $1.7 billion (Camp & Camp, 1991, p. 40). In addition, in excess of $441 million was allocated to renovate or expand older institutions (Camp & Camp, 1991, p. 43). Clear and Cole (1990) documented the exorbitant cost of maximum security prisons as ranging from $70,000 to $300,000 per cell to build. They further estimated that it costs close to $12,000 per cell for adequate staffing. In sharp contrast, cost estimates of traditional probation and parole range from $300 to $1,200 annually per offender (Clear & Cole, 1990, p. 433).

The remedies that will be used increasingly during the 1990s include juvenile aftercare programs, prison industry, private sector partnership programs, and intermediate sanctions such as intensive probation and parole supervision, shock incarceration-boot camps, community residential centers, community service, fines, and restitution.

Conclusion

Community-based correctional alternatives such as probation and parole are considerably less costly than incarceration. For example, traditional probation supervision costs about $584 annually per offender (McDonald, 1989). However, with approximately 3.2 million persons under the jurisdiction of adult probation and parole agencies in 1992, the personnel costs add up (American Correctional Association, 1992). Intensive probation supervision is also less costly than incarceration. Recent estimates of the cost of intensive probation supervision range from $6,000 to $8,000 annually per offender (McShane & Krause, 1993, pp. 168-172) compared to annual prison costs ranging from $15,000 to $23,000 per offender.

During the 1980s the United States witnessed phenomenal growth in the number of nonviolent offenders sentenced to community supervision, particularly probation. The number of offenders on probation or parole skyrocketed from more than 1 million persons to 3.1 million persons (American Correctional Association, 1992). Due to the constant pressures of prison overcrowding, traditional probation and intermediate sanctions are becoming the sentence of choice for most judges with all but the most violent and chronic adult offenders.

Several recent surveys confirm that a geographically and demographically representative sample of citizens in Pennsylvania, Delaware, and Alabama firmly support alternatives to prison sentences. The three preferred sanctions for nonviolent offenders are boot camps, carefully monitored probation plus restitution, and intensive probation supervision (IPS) plus community service. The public is beginning to realize that mandating the offender to a work assignment or to give money back to the victim is less expensive than prison and more likely to rehabilitate the offender (Farkas, 1993, pp. 1, 15).

The underlying philosophy rooted in all intermediate sanctions is that convicted offenders can be punished fairly, consistently, and humanely in the community. Offenders in IPS are required to maintain employment or attend school, abide by a strict curfew, be available for routine drug testing, and provide community service or restitution to victims. Offenders committing infractions are quickly punished with additional fines, restitution, or incarceration.

Therefore these sanctions are much more stringent than traditional probation, and they provide necessary daily surveillance and drug testing of offenders. At the same time that the offender is being held accountable, he or she is allowed the opportunity to act responsibly in the community. Intermediate sanctions are usually less costly than prison, and they offer the offender a chance for rehabilitation in a less restrictive environment than a correctional institution. For a detailed examination of the trends and changes in routine parole as well as intensive parole supervision, see Chapter 17 by Professors Ringel, Cowles, and Castellano.

IPS, day fines, and restitution offer much promise for the future. The main problem is that without adequate funding to hire needed staff, these programs can become the failures of the 1990s. With adequate planning, program development, and increased monitoring and accounting, intensive probation surveillance programs and restitution programs for certain types of offenders could save states and counties billions of dollars.

Discussion Questions

1. Compare and contrast the data collection methods used in compiling the Uniform Crime Reports and the National Crime Survey.
2. According to the National Crime Survey (NCS), which race(s) and gender are most likely to be victimized by personal crimes?
3. List the major monetary cost estimates of crime and the official sources of these estimates.
4. Identify and discuss common characteristics and behavior patterns of adult offenders.
5. Discuss the reasons why tougher and determinate sentencing laws for drug-related offenders have led to a crisis in corrections in a number of our most populated states.

References

American Correctional Association. (1992). *Directory of probation and parole agencies in the U.S., 1992-1994*. Laurel, MD: Author.

American Correctional Association. (1993). *ACA directory of juvenile and adult correctional departments, institutions, agencies and paroling authorities*. Laurel, MD: Author.

Beck, A., Gilliard, D., Greenfeld, L., Harlow, C., Hester, T., Jankowski, L., Snell, T. T., Stephan, J., & Morton, D. (1993, March). *Survey of state prison inmates, 1991*. Washington, DC: Department of Justice, Bureau of Justice Statistics.

Bureau of Justice Statistics. (1988, March). *Report to the nation on crime and justice* (2nd ed). Washington, DC: Department of Justice.

Bureau of Justice Statistics. (1990). *Drugs and crime facts*. Washington, DC: Department of Justice.

Bureau of Justice Statistics (1991a). *Probation and parole 1990*. Washington, DC: Department of Justice.

Bureau of Justice Statistics. (1991b). *Violent crime in the United States*. Washington, DC: Department of Justice.

Bureau of Justice Statistics. (1992, April). *BJS national update*, Vol. 1, No. 4. Washington, DC: Department of Justice.

Bureau of Justice Statistics. (1992, July). *BJS national update,* Vol. 2, No. 1. Washington, DC: Department of Justice.

Camp, G. M., & Camp, C. G. (1991). *Corrections yearbook—1991, adult corrections.* South Salem, NY: Criminal Justice Institute Inc.

Coffen, T. (1989, May 15). Violent crime: Causes and cure. *Washington Spectator,* pp. 1-3.

Clear, T. R., & Cole, G. F. (1990). *American corrections.* Pacific Grove, CA: Brooks/Cole.

Cole, G. (1992). *The American system of criminal justice.* Pacific Grove, CA: Brooks/Cole.

Fairchild, E. S., & Webb, V. (Eds.). (1985). *The politics of crime and criminal justice.* Newbury Park, CA: Sage.

Farkas, S. (1993, April). Pennsylvanians prefer alternatives to prison. *Overcrowded Times, 4,* pp. 1, 13-15.

Federal Bureau of Investigation. (1991). *Uniform crime reports for the U.S., 1990.* Washington, DC: Government Printing Office.

Gilliard, D. K. (1993). *Prisons in 1992.* (Bureau of Justice Statistics Bulletin). Washington, DC: Department of Justice.

Lindgren, S. A. (1992). *Justice expenditure and employment, 1990.* (Bureau of Justice Statistics Bulletin). Washington, DC: Department of Justice.

Livingston, M. (1986, May 4). Criminal cancer: Is there a cure? *State* [New Jersey], p. 1B.

McDonald, D. (1989). "The cost of corrections: In search of the bottom line." *Research in Corrections,* 2(a), 1-25.

McShane, M. D., & Krause, W. (1993). *Community corrections.* New York: Macmillan.

Merlo, A. (1992). *Corrections in the U.S.* Cincinnati: Anderson.

Methvin, E. H. (1992, February). Doubling the prison population will break America's crime wave. *Corrections Today, 54,* 28-40.

Roberts, A. R. (1974). *Correctional treatment of the offender.* Springfield, IL: Charles C Thomas.

Roberts, A. R. (1990). *Helping crime victims.* Newbury Park, CA: Sage.

Roberts, A. R. (1992). Victim/witness programs: Questions and answers. *FBI Law Enforcement Bulletin, 6,* 12-16.

Walker, S. (1989). *Sense and nonsense about crime.* Pacific Grove, CA: Brooks/Cole.

Case Exemplar on
Criminal Justice Processing

DONALD J. SEARS

The criminal justice system is grounded in a number of fundamental principles that guarantee to all citizens certain rights that cannot be denied. It is these rights that our criminal justice system seeks to preserve and protect.

Whether these rights are protected is a function of how the criminal justice system operates. In order to fully understand and appreciate the dynamics of the system, a detailed look at how one case is processed is most appropriate. What follows, therefore, is a step-by-step walk through the criminal justice process, from arrest to parole.

Saturday night, March 23, a report of gunshots is received by the dispatch officer in Precinct #505. She broadcasts the report to officers on patrol in the area, who approach the scene of the call with caution. As they arrive, they see and hear no indication that a crime has been committed. The ranking officer on the scene directs the others as they take up positions around the house.

After several knocks at the door, one of the officers manages a glimpse through a partially opened bedroom window. He sees the body of a black female, lying face down on the floor. No movement is detected. Nor does there appear to be anyone else in the house. Another officer radios that he has found the back door open.

Gathering this information, the ranking officer on the scene determines that probable cause exists to enter the house, and he orders that the officers enter the house to investigate.

Inside, they find signs of an argument. Overturned furniture and broken china are strewn throughout the living room. Attending to the woman on the floor, they find three gunshot wounds to the chest. There is no sign of life. She has apparently been killed with a small caliber handgun, fired at close range. Inside the drawer of a nightstand they find ammunition for a .38 caliber revolver. This is taken as evidence. The murder weapon, however, is not recovered.

A further search of the house reveals the woman's handbag, found in the hall closet. Police find her driver's license inside and identify her as Joanne Brown.[1] They also find a photograph of her and a black male inside the purse. Detectives are called to the scene, as is the medical examiner. As the coroner's officers photograph the body and document the crime scene, detectives begin to canvass the area, questioning neighbors about Joanne. Many indicate that she was separated from her husband and was seeking a divorce. Her husband, Rodney Brown, had left the home approximately 10 days ago, after Joanne had filed some type of legal papers with the family court. They positively identify Rodney as the man in the photograph with Joanne. Although several of the neighbors heard the gunshots, none saw anyone run from the scene.

At this point, homicide detectives believe that Rodney Brown is the prime suspect in the killing of Joanne. Paystubs found in a desk drawer of the house indicate that Rodney works as a meat packer in a downtown meat-packing plant. The following morning, detectives speak to the foreman of the plant. He advises that Rodney has not shown up for work for the last several days. The personnel manager advises police that Rodney filled out a change of address card about one week ago and that his paychecks are now mailed to an apartment on West Clover Avenue.

An arrest warrant is drawn up for Rodney, charging him with the murder of Joanne. Police also contact a judge in order to secure a search warrant for the apartment on West Clover. In a detailed affidavit, homicide detectives outline the information that has been gathered so far and assert that this leads to the conclusion that there is probable cause to believe that Rodney killed Joanne. In response to the judge's questions, the detectives assert that Rodney may be hiding out in his apartment and may still be armed with the murder weapon. In light of all of the circumstances presented to her, the judge agrees that there is probable cause to believe that Rodney is the murderer. She also agrees that there is probable cause to believe that evidence of the crime may be found in the West Clover apartment. As a result, she signs the search warrant.

Several hours later, police surround the apartment building on West Clover. Detectives knock on the door of Rodney's apartment, only to find that he is not home. They contact the manager, who unlocks the apartment door after seeing the search warrant. Police scour the apartment, looking for evidence of the crime. Inside a bedroom closet, they find a fully loaded .38 caliber handgun, which is immediately seized as evidence.

Believing that Rodney will eventually return to his apartment, police set up a surveillance of the building. At approximately 11:30 a.m., they see Rodney get out of a taxicab in front of the building. Not wanting a confrontation on the street, which would provide more opportunity for Rodney to escape, they allow him to enter the building and arrive at his apartment door. Just as he unlocks the door, police move in. They seize him and immediately place him under arrest. He is handcuffed and forced to sit at his own dining room table until a patrol car arrives to transport him to the precinct house. One of the detectives asks why he killed Joanne. Rodney replies that he never meant to, the gun just went off while they were struggling.

Rodney is placed into the rear of the patrol car and transported to the station. On the way, he is advised that he has the right to remain silent and the right to an attorney. He has the right to refuse to answer questions and, if he does answer questions, he can stop answering at any time. He is also told that if he does make any statements, they can be used against him. When asked at the station if he wants to make a confession, he refuses.

Rodney is taken to the booking room, where he is told to empty his pockets. The booking officer takes an inventory of Rodney's belongings and places them in a locker for safekeeping. An arrest report is filled out, recording information such as name, address, telephone number, date of birth, height, weight, descriptive markings (i.e., scars, tattoos, etc.), nicknames and social security number. The crime charged, name of the victim, date of arrest, and police file number are also recorded on this form. At first Rodney does not want to tell police this information. When they advise that he cannot refuse, he reluctantly furnishes these details. His photograph is taken, first from the front and then from the side, with the police file number recorded on the photographs. He is then fingerprinted.

The officer first takes prints of each individual finger, rolling each one from side to side. He then prints the four fingers of each hand as a group. Next, the thumbs are printed without rolling—each is simply pressed flat. Finally, the officer takes the prints of Rodney's palms. This process is repeated four times because the local department retains one set of prints, the federal government requires one set, and the state government must have two. Rodney is allowed to wash his hands and is then placed in an interview room to await the arrival of a detective.

Before attempting to take a statement from Rodney, the detective in charge of the investigation types out an investigation report, detailing all of the events leading up to Rodney's arrest. After approximately one hour, he is ready to take a statement from Rodney. He advises Rodney again of his constitutional rights and asks him if he would like to talk about the incident. Rodney indicates that he first wants to speak to a lawyer and asks the detective to contact the public defender's office for him. The officer refuses, advising that he is not required to provide an attorney. Nor will he tell Rodney the phone number for the public defender's office.

Not wanting to speak with the detective without first talking to a lawyer, Rodney refuses to give a statement. He is placed in a holding cell while the desk officer contacts a judge to determine bail. The judge considers the crime charged, Rodney's family support and ties to the community (how long he has lived in the area, employment history, etc.), and any prior convictions that exist. He is trying to determine if Rodney poses a danger to society and if there is a risk that he will flee the jurisdiction if released. After considering all of these factors, the judge sets bail at $100,000. Because Rodney cannot afford this and there are no family members he can turn to for help, he is remanded to the county jail until his initial appearance on Monday.

Police transport him to the county facility that evening, where his clothes are taken away and he is given a uniform and assigned to a cell. The jail is very crowded and noisy. The guards seem oblivious to the noise and the uncomfortable conditions and indifferent to Rodney's well-being. He must share a cell with five other inmates, all of whom are awaiting trial for committing violent crimes. He is told that he has just missed dinner and thus must wait until breakfast for something to eat. He is also told that he will be taken to the county courthouse in the morning for his initial appearance. This will require him to get up at 5:00 a.m. so that he can eat breakfast, be shackled to other prisoners, be placed in a transport van, and arrive at the courthouse by 8:30 a.m.

On Monday, March 25, Cynthia Durham, an attorney with the county public defender's office, picks up her caseload for the day. It consists of 17 new cases, representing just a portion of those persons arrested over the weekend. One of these new cases is *State v. Rodney Brown*. She glances through the police reports as she walks through the hallway to the criminal courtroom. The judge is already on the bench, calling the list for the day. He will take care of the initial appearances first. In the jury box sit all of the prisoners brought from the county jail, including Rodney. When his name is called, he is instructed to stand up.

Cynthia advises the judge that she has been assigned to the case. The judge in turn tells Rodney that Ms. Durham will be his lawyer. He then reads the charges to Rodney. They include murder, unlawful possession of a weapon, and possession of a weapon for an unlawful purpose. Cynthia enters a not guilty plea on behalf of Rodney and asks the judge to reduce the bail, arguing that Rodney is not likely to flee. The prosecutor opposes her request and advises the judge that this matter will be presented to the grand jury within the next 10 days. The judge denies Cynthia's request and sends Rodney back to the county jail, where he will stay for the next 3 weeks without hearing anything from his attorney or the court.

Shortly after Rodney's initial appearance, the assistant county prosecutor assigned to handle Rodney's case schedules a time to present the case to the grand jury. He subpoenas the homicide detective who had the main responsibility in the investigation and arrest of Rodney. No other witnesses are necessary.

On April 8 the grand jury considers the case of *State v. Rodney Brown.* This group of 23 citizens from the community listens as the homicide detective describes the details of the investigation. He is allowed to tell the jurors what other people said and did because hearsay evidence is allowed at the grand jury hearing. The prosecutor is also allowed to ask leading questions in an effort to make the process move more quickly. The defendant is not present, nor is his attorney. Indeed, no evidence as to the defendant's version is given to the grand jury.

After the detective testifies, the prosecutor advises the members of the grand jury what the law is regarding the crimes that have been charged. He also advises that they can indict the defendant for any lesser included offenses or they can originate new charges that they feel are warranted. He then dismisses them to their deliberation room, where they consider whether there is probable cause to indict the defendant for the crimes charged.

After 2 hours of deliberation, the grand jury determines that there is sufficient evidence upon which to base an indictment, and they return a three-count indictment against Rodney Brown, charging him with murder in the first degree, unlawful possession of a weapon, and possession of a weapon for an unlawful purpose. The indictment is delivered to the prosecutor, where it will remain secret for 2 days. This waiting period is designed to allow the prosecutor time to arrest the defendant if he is free on bail. Because Rodney is still in jail, this is of no consequence. Eventually the indictment is released to the public, and the court schedules an arraignment date.

On April 18 Rodney is brought back to court for his arraignment. Once again, he sits in the jury box with a number of other inmates from the jail. He has not seen or spoken to his attorney at all. When his name is called, he stands up and his attorney approaches counsel table. The judge advises that the grand jury has indicted him and describes the crimes charged and the penalties he is exposed to, which include the death penalty if he is convicted of first degree murder. Cynthia advises the judge that Rodney is pleading not guilty to all charges and once again asks the judge to lower bail. This request is denied.

The prosecutor provides Cynthia with discovery in the case, consisting of all of the police reports, the autopsy report, and a list of all of the witnesses that the state may call at trial. The prosecutor also advises the judge that he will make a decision within the next 10 days whether he will seek the death penalty in this case. The judge then signs an order to that effect, which also provides that any defense motions that Cynthia wishes to make on behalf of her client must be filed within 30 days. Finally, the judge schedules a plea bargaining session, called a pretrial conference, for June 5. Without speaking to his lawyer at all, Rodney is taken back to the courthouse holding cell, where he remains until transported back to the jail later that day.

One week after the arraignment, Cynthia visits Rodney at the jail. This is the first time the two actually meet to speak about the case. They are placed in an attorney interview room where they can speak in private, although a guard waits right outside the door.

Rodney tells her his version of what occurred between him and Joanne on March 23. Their marital problems had been ongoing for several months, and Joanne filed a domestic violence complaint against him with the family court. Without hearing Rodney's side of the story, the family court judge issued a restraining order against Rodney, forbidding him from staying in their home. He stayed several nights with friends, but then needed to get clean clothes and some personal belongings. Although he tried to get the police to accompany him to the house (which was a requirement of the restraining order), the local officers told him they were too busy and could not spare the manpower. He thereafter took it upon himself to go to the house alone.

When he got there, Joanne at first let him in. They began to talk, and he asked why she was doing this to him. An argument erupted, and the two began to throw things at each other. Joanne ran into the bedroom and tried to get the revolver that they kept in the nightstand. He grabbed it and the two struggled for the weapon. It eventually went off, killing Joanne. Frightened, Rodney fled out the back door with the gun.

Although Cynthia listened intently, she was somewhat skeptical about Rodney's story. She already knew that the domestic violence complaint was signed by Joanne because Rodney had a history of violent behavior. Three prior domestic violence complaints had been signed against him, and he had even been convicted of criminal assault on one of those occasions. In addition, the autopsy report showed three bullet wounds to the chest with no powder burns on the clothing. This told Cynthia that the gun was fired repeatedly from at least five feet away and thus could not have gone off accidentally while the two were struggling for it. Although she confronted Rodney with these discrepancies, he maintained his version of the incident.

When she returned to her office, Cynthia drafted up a number of motions for filing with the court. These included various suppression motions (designed to prevent the state from using or referring to any evidence seized as a result of an illegal search), a *Miranda* motion (designed to prevent the state from using or referring to any statements made by Rodney after he was placed in custody), and a motion to prevent the application of the death penalty in this case. The latter was rendered unnecessary because, in her mail, she found a letter from the prosecutor indicating that he would not seek the death penalty in this case. Finally, she asks her investigator to interview neighbors of Rodney, to see if anyone saw or heard anything that might help in his defense.

On June 5, the date of his pretrial conference, Rodney is brought to the courthouse early. Cynthia meets with him in the holding cell of the courthouse to discuss the case. Her investigator has found nothing that will help. Cynthia's plan for his defense is that it was not an intentional act but rather an accidental shooting. In this way, Rodney would be guilty of the lesser included offense of manslaughter rather than murder. Although he would still be sentenced to prison, it would be for much less than the life sentence he is facing for first degree murder.

She explains to Rodney that there are some problems with pursuing this line of defense. Because no other witnesses have been found to corroborate Rodney's version of a struggle, Rodney is the only witness who can tell the jury of the fight with Joanne. If he testifies, however, the prosecutor can tell the jury about his prior conviction for assault as well as his history of domestic violence. If he never takes the stand to testify, this information cannot be brought out. Thus there is a danger in testifying in his own behalf. She also emphasizes again that the physical evidence does not support his version of the killing. Nevertheless, it is the only defense that Rodney has.

When court begins, the prosecutor presents the plea bargain he is willing to offer to Rodney. He will amend the charge from first degree to a second degree murder in exchange for a guilty plea. The weapons charges will thereafter be "merged" into the murder conviction, and Rodney will only be sentenced on the murder charge. In addition, the prosecutor will agree not to seek an enhanced prison term. Because Rodney has a prior record, the prosecutor could seek to increase the mandatory term of incarceration that Rodney is facing. If he accepts the plea offer, the prosecutor will not ask for this.

Cynthia discusses this with Rodney, who tells her that he cannot agree to any time in prison. If he has to go to prison, he would rather take his chances with a jury. Cynthia rejects the offer on behalf of Rodney, and the judge sets out a scheduling order for the trial. Because there are a number of pretrial motions to be decided, he schedules a pretrial hearing for July 17. The trial will take place on August 21.

On July 17, the prosecutor is ready to proceed with the pretrial motions. Even though the defendant has asserted that the police procedures used in the investigation were improper, it is the prosecutor's burden to prove that everything the police did was correct. Thus the prosecutor must present witnesses to explain to the judge the procedures that were used. In this regard, the prosecutor must show that *every* search was legal and that the questioning of Rodney at the scene was constitutionally proper.

Cynthia points out that there are actually seven searches that must be reviewed by the judge: five at the scene of the crime and two at Rodney's apartment. At the scene of the crime, these include the initial entry into the house; opening of the nightstand drawer; opening of the hall closet; opening of the handbag found inside the closet; and opening of the desk drawer where Rodney's paystubs were found.

Cynthia is trying to convince the judge that these searches are unconstitutional because the officers did not have probable cause to conduct the search. Therefore any evidence found as a result must be suppressed, including the body of Joanne, the ammunition from the nightstand, the handbag from the closet, the photograph of Rodney found inside the handbag, and Rodney's paystubs.

As to Rodney's apartment, Cynthia's approach is that there was not enough evidence for the initial judge to issue the search warrant. As a result, the warrant was defective, and therefore the search was improper. The revolver found in Rodney's bedroom would thereafter have to be suppressed.

Finally, Cynthia believes that any statement made by Rodney at the scene of the crime must be suppressed because Rodney was not advised of his constitutional rights prior to making the statement.

After hearing the testimony of the officers involved in the investigation, the judge finds that the police were justified in entering Joanne's house. The information available to the officers at the time clearly indicated that a crime had been committed. The officers knew that gunshots were heard just moments before they arrived, they saw an apparent victim on the floor, and there was evidence that the assailant had escaped out the back door. Taken in the totality of the circumstances, these facts were sufficient to establish probable cause to believe that a crime had occurred within the house. This alone would be enough to justify a search of the house.

Because it appeared that Joanne was injured, it was critical that they enter immediately. Moreover, there was a likelihood that the suspect could be fleeing the jurisdiction. Because time was critical, it was appropriate for the officers to act immediately rather than seek a written search warrant from a judge. Thus all of the evidence found at the scene of the crime would be admissible at the trial.

Next, the judge addresses Cynthia's motion to suppress the evidence found at Rodney's apartment. He states that there was more than enough evidence to find that Rodney was a likely suspect in the murder, that he lived at the apartment identified in the search warrant, and that he could still be armed with the murder weapon. Once inside the apartment, the police had the right to conduct a search of the premises, including the closet where the revolver was found. Thus this evidence would not be suppressed.

Finally, the judge hears the argument on whether Rodney's statement at the scene should be suppressed. The prosecutor tries to convince the judge that Rodney's statement was voluntary. Cynthia argues that because Rodney was in custody at the time, police were required to advise him of his rights before any questioning. Because they did not, any statements given by Rodney should be suppressed. The judge agrees with Cynthia and rules that the prosecutor may not use Rodney's statement against him.

Although both sides are ready to begin the trial on August 21, the judge informs them that he is still in the middle of another trial, which will last for several more days. Thus Rodney's trial will have to be adjourned. After three more adjournments, the trial is ready to begin on October 9.

The actual trial begins with jury selection. Each side attempts to obtain jurors who will be more sympathetic to their side. Fourteen people will ultimately be chosen to sit as jurors on Rodney's case. These 14 are chosen from a panel of almost 100 prospective jurors.

The judge advises all of the prospective jurors that this is a criminal case involving the death of a woman. He introduces the attorneys and Rodney and reads a list of the expected witnesses. If any of the jurors know any of these individuals, they will be excused. The clerk then picks 14 names at random, and these people are seated in the jury box. The judge asks all of them their name, occupation, and marital status, if they have ever been involved in any type of lawsuit (civil or criminal), if they have ever served on a jury before, if they have ever been the victim of a crime, and if they have any affiliation to any law enforcement agencies. Ultimately, the judge is looking for people who can be fair and impartial and decide the case based on the evidence that is presented to them.

If a juror indicates that he or she cannot be fair and impartial, the judge will excuse him or her from service in this case "for cause." Even if the juror indicates that he or she can be fair and impartial, each attorney has a number of peremptory challenges. These challenges can be used in order to excuse jurors from service when the attorney feels that the juror might not be sympathetic to his or her side. Conversely, when a challenge is used, it is hoped by the attorney that the next prospective juror chosen will be more likely to find in their favor.

Eventually, 14 people are chosen as acceptable jurors to both sides, and the jury is sworn in. Opening statements now take place.

The prosecutor delivers his opening statement first. He tells the jurors what he hopes to prove in order to obtain a conviction of the crimes charged. In this regard, he reads the indictment to the jury so they know exactly what the defendant is facing. He then relates to the jury a summary of what he thinks the testimony will be. He assures them that at the conclusion of the case they will be convinced that the defendant is guilty.

Cynthia emphasizes in her opening statement that the defendant is not required to prove his innocence. On the contrary, the prosecutor has the heavy burden of proving Rodney guilty beyond a reasonable doubt. She urges them to listen carefully to the testimony and to ask themselves a critical question throughout the case—Where are the eyewitnesses who saw Rodney? She advises that at the conclusion of the case they will be left with so many questions that they will have a reasonable doubt as to the guilt of Rodney and will have to find him not guilty.

After a short recess, the prosecutor begins his case. His first witness is a neighbor who heard the gunshots. Although she did not see the killer, she sets the stage for the rest of the witnesses' testimony. The next witness is the chief investigating detective. He testifies about the chronology of events leading up to the arrest of Rodney, including arrival at the scene, discovery of the body, questioning of neighbors, and the search of Rodney's apartment. He is prevented from telling the jury what the neighbors told him, however, because this constitutes impermissible hearsay testimony. It is prohibited because it would be unfair to allow the prosecutor to present evidence that could not be probed for accuracy, by way of cross-examination, when the person who actually made the statement is not present in court. Thus the matrimonial problems that neighbors related to police are never revealed to the jury.

The personnel manager from Rodney's job testifies about his unexplained absence from work and his change of address. Finally, the medical examiner testifies. He details the injuries received by Joanne, and how they resulted in her death. He is allowed to give his opinion, as a medical expert, that the cause of death was definitely the gunshot wounds. On cross-examination, Cynthia tries to establish that the wounds could have been inflicted accidentally during the course of a struggle. He is adamant, however, that the shots were fired from several feet away.

The prosecutor introduces into evidence the revolver found in Rodney's closet, the picture found in Joanne's handbag, the ammunition found in the nightstand, Rodney's personnel records, and the bullets that were removed from Joanne's body. At that point, the prosecutor advises the judge that he will rest, indicating that he has presented all of the evidence that he feels is relevant to the case.

Cynthia makes a motion, asking the judge to dismiss the charges against Rodney because the prosecutor has failed to meet his burden of proof. The judge denies her request, indicating that, at this stage of the case, the prosecutor is entitled to the benefit of all of the favorable evidence, as well as all of the reasonable inferences that can be drawn from the evidence. In this light, the jury could possibly find Rodney guilty of the crimes charged.

It is now time for Cynthia to present her witnesses. She advises the judge that she has no witnesses other than perhaps Rodney. No one can force Rodney to testify, however, and thus she asks for some time to discuss this with him. A short recess is taken so that Cynthia can discuss with Rodney whether he should testify in his own behalf. They review the evidence presented by the prosecutor so far. He has shown that neighbors heard gunshots and police thereafter found Joanne dead. No one saw who did it. Nor did anyone see the murderer running from the scene. The house showed signs of a struggle prior to the murder, and Rodney was identified. Neighbors told how Rodney had left the house several days prior to the murder and the jury knew that Rodney was absent from work during this same time. They also knew that Rodney had rented an apartment and that a revolver was found inside. Because Rodney's statement was suppressed, however, the jury does not know about his confession.

Cynthia and Rodney decide that the prosecutor's case seems weak. The prosecutor has not even shown that Rodney was there that night. If Rodney testified, his past history could be exposed, and this could convince the jury to convict him. Indeed, the jury might believe that Rodney has a tendency to violence, and is therefore the type of person who could kill, simply because of his past record. In addition, there is no evidence to corroborate Rodney's story that the shooting was accidental. Thus they decide that Rodney will not testify in his own behalf. Cynthia will simply argue that the prosecutor has not proven his case beyond a reasonable doubt. She therefore advises the judge that the defense rests as well.

Closing arguments are given, but in reverse order of the opening statements. Because it is the prosecutor's burden to prove the case, he is allowed to go last so that he can rebut the arguments of the defense.

Cynthia argues that there is a lack of evidence to prove that Rodney is guilty. Although she expresses sadness at the death of Joanne, she implores the jury not to convict Rodney for a crime that he did not commit. She reminds the jury that Rodney has a Constitutional right to remain silent and that they should not hold it against him simply because he did not testify. Finally, she reiterates that the evidence must show that Rodney is guilty beyond a reasonable doubt and that if they have a "reasonable doubt" as to whether he is guilty, they *must* find him not guilty.

The prosecutor reviews all of the evidence and argues that it all points to Rodney as the guilty party. He infers for the jury that Rodney and Joanne had a fight that culminated in her death. Why else would Rodney leave his home and his job without explanation? He tells the jury that although he must prove Rodney's guilt beyond a reasonable doubt, he is not required to prove the case beyond *all* doubt, or beyond *a shadow of a doubt,* but merely beyond a *reasonable* doubt. He maintains that he has done so.

After closing arguments, the judge instructs the jury on the applicable law that they are to consider in their deliberations. This includes the elements of the crimes charged, definitions of key terms in criminal law, certain rights of the defendant, and the prosecutor's burden of proof. He advises that the jury's verdict must be unanimous and that they are to deliberate until they reach a verdict or until they are hopelessly dead-locked. The two alternates are then chosen at random by the clerk. These two will not participate in the deliberations but will remain in the court-house just in case they are needed.

Because it is late in the day, the judge tells the jury that they must return in the morning for their deliberations. He advises them not to speak to anyone about the case and not to start their deliberations until they are all together again. The next morning, they begin deliberations, and after four hours they reach a verdict.

The foreman of the jury announces that they have found Rodney not guilty of first degree murder but guilty of the lesser included offense of murder in the second degree. They have found him not guilty of unlawful possession of a weapon and possession of a weapon for an unlawful purpose. The jury is "polled" and each juror confirms that this is the unanimous verdict. The judge excuses the jurors, and thanks them all for their service.

Cynthia requests that the verdict be set aside because it is against the weight of the evidence and because it is inconsistent. On this latter point, she asserts that it is inconsistent for the jury to find Rodney guilty of murder by shooting but find him not guilty of ever possessing a weapon.

The judge denies her request. He explains that it is not his function to substitute his view of the evidence for the jury's. Rather he must only determine whether there is enough evidence for the jury to believe that

Rodney was guilty of second degree murder. In this regard, the judge feels that although there was no direct testimony that placed Rodney at the scene of the crime, there was enough circumstantial evidence to find him guilty of the murder. He also believes that although the verdict may appear to be inconsistent, the jury is allowed to consider each count of the indictment separately and reach an independent conclusion as to each. He is not allowed to probe into the rationale of the jury as to why they may have convicted on one count while acquitting on another.

The judge advises Rodney that he will have to return to court on November 20 for sentencing. In the interim, he will order the probation department to prepare a presentence report. In this regard, a probation worker reviews the police reports and statements of witnesses, may question those involved, evaluates the impact of the crime on the victim's family as well as society, and interviews the defendant. The worker then makes a recommendation to the judge as to what the appropriate sentence should be. The judge is not bound by the recommendation but quite often finds it helpful in arriving at an appropriate sentence.

On November 20, Rodney returns to court to be sentenced. The judge, prosecutor and Cynthia have reviewed the presentence report, which recommends incarceration in state prison for 7½ years, with a parole ineligibility period of 2½ years (one third of the sentence). The prosecutor argues that Rodney should be given the maximum sentence allowable for a second degree crime and urges the judge to sentence him to 10 years, with a 3⅓ year parole ineligibility period. Cynthia, on the other hand, tries to convince the court that the minimum sentence would be sufficient to punish Rodney and deter him and others like him from committing similar crimes in the future. She requests that the sentence be 5 years, with no parole ineligibility period at all.

Considering the aggravating and mitigating circumstances of both the crime and Rodney's background, including his prior history of violence, the judge imposes the sentence recommended in the presentence report and commits Rodney to state prison for 7½ years, with a parole ineligibility of 2½ years. He is given credit for the time he has already served awaiting trial and is thereafter turned over to the custody of the commissioner of corrections for processing into the state prison system.

Rodney is taken back to the county jail, where he has spent the last 8 months of his life. In early December, a decision is made to transfer him to the state's medium security prison upstate. Shortly before Christmas, he is shackled and placed on a transport bus with other prisoners for the long ride upstate.

As they approach the prison, he is surprised to find that it does not have the high stone walls, barbed wire, and guard towers he envisioned. Although it does have walls surrounding it, they are not ominous looking but rather smooth and brightly painted. Passing through the gate, he enters a central compound where prison guards are waiting. He files off the bus with the other prisoners, and they are directed to the intake area of the prison.

When it is Rodney's turn, he sits at a desk and a prison intake official fills out the necessary paperwork for admitting him into the prison. Information about Rodney's background, family, medical history, employment history, and details about the crime are discussed. He is assigned a prisoner number, given a uniform to wear, and led to a two-man cell. His cell mate is already there, having arrived one week ago. He is serving time for armed robbery.

As the weeks and months pass, Rodney spends most of his time either in his cell or hanging around the compound. Occasionally he receives word on the progress of the appeal filed by the public defender's office. Fourteen months after his conviction, he is advised that the appellate court has denied his appeal, affirming both the conviction and the sentence imposed by the trial judge.

Boredom is a way of life here because there are few programs to occupy the prisoners' time. What few programs exist are overcrowded and uninteresting. Eventually, he works at the prison laundry. Although it is a menial job, it at least gives him something to do during the day.

A social worker from the probation department visits him about once a month. She seems genuinely interested in his welfare and how he is getting along in prison. She tries to arrange stimulating outlets for Rodney that will pass the time and also provide some type of vocational as well as social retraining for when Rodney eventually leaves prison. At first he resists her efforts but eventually begins to participate in a variety of programs.

After 20 months at state prison, he is advised that his case is being reviewed by the parole board for release in another 2 months, which coincides with the expiration of his parole ineligibility period. The process includes a review of the facts of the crime, any opposition to release filed by the victim's family, and an interview with Rodney. The latter is sometimes the most critical because the parole board is very interested in seeing whether Rodney has made an adequate readjustment of his life to the point where he will not be a danger to himself or others if he is released. They are also interested in seeing that Rodney is remorseful for what he did and has been reformed by the process.

On the day of the hearing, the parole board seems somewhat sympathetic to Rodney, noting that he has made a good adjustment to prison life and has been a model prisoner. No response has been received from any of

Joanne's family members regarding his release. Nevertheless, the board denies his parole, reasoning that he has not served enough time in prison. The crime, they state, was a very serious one, and if they let him out now, the deterrent effect of the justice system will be undermined. He will be eligible for another parole review in 6 to 8 months.

Rodney passes the next 6 months in much the same manner as before. He merely "exists," trying to find ways to pass the endless hours of idleness. When he again comes up for review, the parole board grants his application for release. In total, he has served almost 3 years.

Upon his release, he is given the name of his parole officer and advised to contact him within two weeks. He eventually makes an appointment to see the parole officer, and the two discuss some of the requirements of parole. Rodney must obtain a steady job or attend school full time. He must avoid any opportunity for criminal behavior and cannot be arrested for anything. He must even avoid associating with "criminal types." He is not allowed to leave the state. If he finds that he must leave, he must first seek permission from the parole officer. The parole officer will require him to report once a month so that the officer can monitor Rodney's progress in society. If Rodney fails to comply with these requirements, his parole can be revoked and he can be sent back to prison to serve out the remainder of his term.

Finding a job is difficult for Rodney, but eventually he locates a small grocery store that is willing to hire an ex-convict. He works for minimum wage, sweeping floors and doing general cleanup work. He abides by his parole requirements and faithfully reports once a month. After being under the control of his parole officer for 2½ years, he is released completely. This finally concludes his involvement with the criminal justice system, a process that has taken almost 5½ years to complete.

Note

1. All of the names in this case study are fictitious, and any resemblance to real persons, either living or deceased, is purely coincidental.

2

Burglary

The Burglar's Perspective

PAUL CROMWELL

Burglary is easy, man. I've done about 500 [burglaries] and only been convicted one time. That time it was just stupid. . . . I smoked some dope before I went into this place. I was already half drunk. I found this comic book inside one of the kid's bedrooms and started reading it. I must have gone to sleep man, 'cause the next thing I remember this cop was standing there shaking me and telling me to wake up.

Billy, a juvenile burglar

Why am I a burglar? It's easy money. . . . Beats working!

Robert, a 20-year-old burglar

I can make good money when I want to. I usually get $12 an hour [as a roofer] and all the overtime I want. But, shit man, I can make $1,000 a day doing houses [burglaries] and nobody tells me when to get up, or when to eat, and there ain't no money taken out for tax.

Ramon, a career burglar

AUTHOR'S NOTE: This research was supported by National Institute of Justice Grant No. 88-IJ-CX-0042. The opinions expressed are those of the author and do not necessarily represent the position or policies of the United States Department of Justice. Portions of this material have been published previously in Paul Cromwell, James N. Olson, and D'Aunn W. Avary, *Breaking and Entering: An Ethnographic Analysis of Burglary,* Newbury Park, CA: Sage, 1991. Reprinted with permission of Sage Publications.

These burglars are essentially correct in their appraisal of the benefits and risks associated with burglary. Burglary constitutes one of the most prevalent predatory crimes, with an estimated 5.1 million burglary offenses committed in 1990 (Bureau of Justice Statistics [BJS], 1991), resulting in monetary losses estimated to be over $3.4 billion annually. Yet only about one half of all burglaries are even reported to the police (BJS, 1991).[1] More alarming still, U.S. Department of Justice statistics reveal that less than 15% of all reported burglaries are cleared by arrest (Sessions, 1991). Consequently, burglary has been the subject of a great deal of research in the hope that understanding would lead to the development of effective prevention measures and ultimately to reduction in the incidence of burglary (Lynch, 1990).

Focus of This Chapter

This chapter reports findings from a study of burglars and burglary—from the perspective of the burglars themselves. Several issues critical to the understanding of burglary and the consequent development of burglary prevention and control strategies are addressed. Among these are (a) How do residential burglars choose targets? (b) What determines a burglar's perception of a particular site as a vulnerable target? Increasing interest is being focused on the role of environmental cues that may indicate situational vulnerability. Recent crime prevention efforts have centered on identifying these factors and utilizing the knowledge to develop schemes to reduce the potential for burglary. However, the assessments from research in this critical area have been mixed. The purpose of this study is to test the validity of the assumptions upon which such environmental crime prevention programs are based by explicating the target selection decision-making process. Knowledge of how burglars evaluate potential target sites would allow effective burglary prevention strategies to be developed and implemented.

Theoretical Perspective

One approach to understanding how burglars choose targets and make other decisions relevant to the crime of burglary views criminal decision making as primarily a product of opportunity. Several researchers have concluded that the majority of burglaries are the result of exploitation of opportunity rather than careful, rational planning (Cromwell, Olson, & Avary, 1991; Rengert & Wasilchick, 1985, 1989; Scarr, 1973). This perspective argues that offenders develop a sensitivity to the opportunities in everyday life for illicit gain and that burglars and other "motivated" individuals see criminal opportunity in situations where others might not. This "alert opportunism" (Shover, 1971) allows them to rapidly recognize and take advantage of potential criminal opportunities. Their unique perspective toward the world results from learning experiences that have sensitized them to events that are ignored by most. Just as a carpenter looking at a house notes the quality of workmanship and other characteristics that are salient to him because of his profession, burglars assess the probability of gain versus the potential risk involved in burglarizing the site. They do not simply see an open window, rather the potential for covert entry and a "fast buck." These processes are almost automatic and are as much a part of the tools of the burglar as a pry bar or a window jimmy.

Some criminologists (Bennett & Wright, 1984; Brantingham & Brantingham, 1978, 1981; Brown & Altman, 1981; Cromwell et al., 1991; Rengert & Wasilchick, 1985, 1989) have focused on the burglar's use of distinctive environmental stimuli that function as signals or cues to provide salient information about the environment's temporal, spatial, sociocultural, psychological, and legal characteristics. An individual who is motivated to commit a crime uses these discriminative cues to locate and identify target sites. With practice the individual gains experience and learns which discriminative cues and which combination or sequence of cues are associated with "good" targets. These cues are "a template which is used in victim or target selection. Potential victims or targets are compared to the template and either rejected or accepted, depending on the congruence" (Brantingham & Brantingham, 1978, p. 108). In effect, these are decisions that do not require conscious analysis each time they are employed. Regardless of whether the individual is consciously aware of the construction and implementation of the template, each time it is successfully employed, it is reinforced and becomes relatively automatic. He or she may accept or reject a potential crime site based upon its fit with a mental template constructed and applied often without conscious awareness. One purpose of the present study is to evaluate this approach to understanding offender decision making.

Method

Sample

Thirty active burglars in an urban area of 250,000 population in a southwestern state were recruited as research subjects (hereinafter referred to as informants) using a snowball sampling procedure. They were promised complete anonymity and a "referral fee" of $50.00 for each active burglar referred by them and accepted for the study. They were also paid a stipend of $50.00 for each interview session. The initial three informants were introduced to the researchers by police burglary detectives who were asked to recommend "burglars who would be candid and cooperate with the study."

The final sample was made up of 27 men and 3 women; 10 were white, 9 Hispanic, and 11 African American. The mean age of the informants was 25 years; the range was 16 to 43 years.

Procedure

The procedure consisted of extensive interviews and "ride alongs," during which informants were asked to reconstruct burglaries they had previously committed and to evaluate sites that had been burglarized by other informants in the study. During the sessions, previously burglarized residences were visited, evaluated, and rated on their attractiveness as burglary targets. The informants were also asked to select sites in the same neighborhood of the previously burglarized sites that they considered too risky as burglary targets and to explain why these sites were considered less vulnerable than those previously burglarized. At each site informants were asked to rate the "hypothetical" vulnerability of the site to burglary on a scale of 0 to 10. A rating of 0 meant, "Under the circumstances that are present now, I would not burglarize this residence." A rating of 10 meant, "This is a very attractive and vulnerable target and I would definitely take steps to burglarize it right now." Informants were told that a rating of 5 was an "average" score. Sessions were conducted under all conditions in which burglars might conceivably commit their crimes: in the daytime or at night; when the informants were alone or grouped with their usual co-offenders; when the informants were using drugs, stable, or needing a drug administration. Before each session informants were asked to rate their own drug state at the time of the session and to recall their drug state at the time of the actual burglary being reenacted.

At the conclusion of the study, informants had participated in as many as nine sessions and had evaluated up to 30 previously burglarized and high risk sites. Four hundred and sixty previously burglarized and high risk sites were evaluated. Each session was tape recorded and verbatim transcripts were made.

Findings

Motivation

The motivation that drives the burglary event is a factor that has received much attention from researchers. Bennett and Wright (1984) found that burglars' motivations fell into six major categories, listed here in order of importance: (a) instrumental needs, (b) influence of others, (c) influence of presented opportunities, (d) none, the individual is constantly motivated, (e) expressive needs, and (f) alcohol.

Scarr (1973) found that burglars in his study cited, in order of importance: (a) need for money to buy drugs, (b) need for money to lead "fast expensive life," (c) social motives (gangs, delinquent subcultures, peer approval, status), and (d) idiosyncratic motives (kicks, thrills, pathological behavior, rebellion).

Reppetto's (1974) subjects reported satisfaction of their need for money as the primary motivation for their robberies and burglaries. Subsidiary satisfactions such as excitement, revenge, and curiosity were cited by a significant but smaller percentage of the subjects. Excitement as a motive was mentioned most often by the younger burglars and less often by the older. Only 10% of Reppetto's subjects stated that they would continue to commit burglary if their need for money, including money for drugs, were satisfied (p. 22).

Rengert and Wasilchick (1985) concluded, "The primary reason stated by burglars we interviewed for deciding to commit a burglary was simply to obtain money. . . . The need for money arose out of psychologically defined needs, not subsistence needs" (p. 54).

Our findings were consistent with those of Rengert and Wasilchick (1985), Scarr (1973), and to a lesser extent Reppetto (1974). Informants stressed need for money to fulfill expressive needs as the primary motivation for their criminal behavior. Only one informant reported a primary need for money for something other than purchasing alcohol or drugs or "partying." He used burglary proceeds primarily to support his gambling habit. Though virtually every burglar used some of his proceeds to pay for food, clothing, shelter, transportation, and other licit needs, the greatest percentage of the proceeds from burglary went toward the purchase of drugs and alcohol and for the activity the informants loosely labeled as "partying."

Second in importance was the need for money to maintain a "fast, expensive life." Keeping up appearances was stressed by many as a critical concern. One young burglar reported, "The ladies, they like a dude that's got good clothes. You gotta look good and you gotta have bread. Me, I'm always looking good."

Excitement and thrills were mentioned by almost every informant; however, only a few would commit a burglary for that purpose only. Like Reppetto (1974), we concluded that the younger, less experienced burglars were more prone to commit crimes for the thrill and excitement. However, many burglars reported that they had in the past committed a burglary for the excitement only.

About one third of the informants reported committing at least one burglary for revenge. They seldom obtained much material reward in revenge burglaries, reporting instead that they "trashed" the victim's house. This tendency was more pronounced among burglars under 25 years of age. One burglar told the interviewer that he had burglarized the home of a former friend that had "snitched" on him. He said, "I didn't take nothing except some food. Mainly I just trashed his place. I was really pissed off."

Time of Burglary

Rengert and Wasilchick (1985, 1989), in the definitive studies of use of time by residential burglars, found that the time patterns of burglars are determined by the time patterns of their victims. Burglars work during periods when residences are left unguarded. Our informants stated they preferred to work between 9:00 and 11:00 a.m. and in mid-afternoon. Most organized their working hours around school hours, particularly during the times when parents (usually mothers) took children to school and picked them up after school. Several told us that they waited "until the wife left to take the kids to school or to shopping." Most stated that they did not do burglaries on Saturday because most people were home then. Only a small number ($n = 3$) of burglars in our study committed burglaries at night. Most preferred to commit their crimes during hours when they expected people to be at work and out of the home. Those who did commit nighttime burglary usually knew the victims and their schedules or took advantage of people being away from home in the evening.

Inside Information

Burglars often work with "inside men" who have access to potential targets and advise the burglar about things to steal. They may also provide such critical information as times when the owner is away and of weaknesses in security. One female burglar reported that she maintained close contact with several women who worked as maids in affluent sections of the community. She would gain the necessary information from these women and later come back and break into the house, often entering by a door or window left open for her by the accomplice. Others gained information from friends and acquaintances who unwittingly revealed information about potential burglary targets. One told us, "I have friends who mow yards for people and work as maids and stuff. When they talk about the people they work for, I keep my ears open. They give me information without knowing it."

Information about potential targets was frequently gained from "fences." Because many fences have legitimate occupations, they may have knowledge of the existence of valuable property from social or business relationships. They can often provide the burglar with information about the owners' schedules and the security arrangements at the target site.

People involved in a variety of service jobs (repair, carpet cleaning, pizza delivery, lawn maintenance, plumbing, carpentry) enter many homes each day and have the opportunity to assess the quality of potential stolen merchandise and security measures taken by the residents. Burglars will often establish contact with employees of these businesses for purposes of obtaining this "inside" information. One informant said, "I know this guy who works for [carpet cleaning business]. He sometimes gives me information on a good place to hit and I split with him."

Occupancy Probes

Almost all burglars avoid selecting as targets houses that are occupied. Only two of our informants stated that they would enter a residence that they knew was occupied. Therefore, it is important that the burglar develop techniques to probe the potential target site to determine if anyone is at home. The most common probe used by our informants was to send one of the burglars to the door to knock or ring the doorbell. If someone answered, the prober would ask directions to a nearby address or for a nonexistent person—for example, "Is Ray home?" The prospective burglar would apologize and leave when told that he or she had the wrong address. Burglars also occasionally ring the doorbell and ask the resident to use the phone: "My car broke down across the street. May I use your phone to call a garage?" This is a good strategy. If the resident refuses, the prober can leave without arousing suspicion. If, however, the resident agrees, the prober has the additional opportunity to assess the quality and quantity of the potential take and to learn more about the security, location of windows and doors, dogs, alarms, and so forth.

Another informant, a female, carried her 2-year-old child to the target residence door, asking for directions to a nearby address. She reported, "I ask them for a drink [of water] for the baby. Even when they seem suspicious they almost always let me in to get the baby a drink."

Several informants reported obtaining the resident's name from the mailbox or from a sign over the door. They would then look up the telephone number and call the residence, leaving the phone ringing while they returned to the target home. If they could still hear the phone ringing when they arrived back at the house, they were sure that the house was unoccupied.

Burglar Alarms

Although several informants boasted about disarming alarms, when pressed for details, almost all admitted that they did not know how to accomplish that task. However, two informants had disarmed alarm systems and were not particularly deterred by them. Both stated that the presence of an alarm system gave them an additional cue as to the affluence of the residents, telling them that there was something worth protecting inside. One of them had purposely taken a job installing alarm systems in order to learn to disarm them. Another informant stated that although she could not disarm a burglar alarm, she was not deterred by an alarm. She stated that once the alarm was tripped, she still had time to complete the burglary and escape before police or private security arrived. She explained that she never took more than 10 minutes to enter, search and exit a house. She advised, "Police take 15 to 20 minutes to respond to an alarm. Security [private security] sometimes gets there a little faster. I'm gone before any of them gets there."

In general, however, burglars agreed that alarms were a definite deterrent to their activities. Other factors being equal, they preferred to locate a target that did not have an alarm rather than to take the additional risk involved in attempting to burglarize a house with an alarm system. Over 90% of the informants reported that they would not choose a target with an alarm system. Most (about 75%) were deterred merely by a sign or window sticker that stated that the house was protected by an alarm system. As Richard, an experienced burglar, stated, "Why take a chance? There's lots of places without alarms. Maybe they're bluffing, maybe they ain't."

Locks on Doors and Windows

Past research has been inconsistent regarding the deterrent value of locks on windows and doors. A few studies have reported that burglars consider the type of lock installed at a prospective target site in their target selection decision. Others have not found locks to be a significant factor in the target selection process.

The majority of informants in the present study initially stated that they were not deterred by locks, just as in the case of alarm systems. However, during burglary reconstructions, we discovered that given two potential target sites, all other factors being equal, burglars preferred not to deal with a deadbolt lock. Several told us that they allowed themselves only 1 or 2 minutes to effect entry and that a good deadbolt lock slowed them down too much.

The variation in findings regarding security hardware appears to be related to the level of expertise and experience of the burglar. To the extent to which burglars are primarily opportunistic and inexperienced, locks appear to have deterrent value. The opportunistic burglar chooses targets based upon their perceived vulnerability to burglary at a given time. Given a large number of potential targets, the burglar tends to select the most vulnerable of the target pool. A target with a good lock and fitted with other security hardware will usually not be perceived to be as vulnerable as one without those items. The professional or "good burglar" chooses his targets on the basis of other factors than situational vulnerability and conceives ways in which he or she can overcome impediments to the burglary (such as the target site being fitted with a high quality deadbolt lock). Thus to the extent that burglars are skilled and experienced, deadbolt locks have limited utility for crime prevention. However, our findings support the deterrent value of deadbolt locks. Seventy-five percent of the burglaries reconstructed during our research were opportunistic offenses. Many of those burglaries would have been prevented (or displaced) by the presence of a quality deadbolt lock. *It is important to note that nearly one half of the burglary sites in the present study were entered through open or unlocked windows and doors.*

Dogs

Almost all studies agree that dogs are an effective deterrent to burglary. Although there is some individual variation among burglars, the general rule is to bypass a house with a dog—any dog. Large dogs represent a physical threat to the burglar, and small ones are often noisy, attracting attention to his or her activities. We found that although many burglars have developed contingency plans to deal with dogs (petting them, feeding them, or even killing them), most burglars prefer to avoid them. When asked what were considered absolute "no go" factors, most burglars responded that dogs were second only to occupancy. However, approximately 30% of the informants *initially* discounted the presence of dogs as a deterrent. Yet during "ride alongs" the sight or sound of a dog at a potential target site almost invariably resulted in a "no go" decision. As

Richard said, "I don't mess with no dogs. If they got dogs I go someplace else." Debbie reported that she was concerned primarily with small dogs: "Little dogs yap too much. They [neighbors] look to see what they are so excited about. I don't like little yapping dogs."

Some of the more professional burglars were less concerned with dogs and had developed techniques for dealing with them. In general, however, the presence of a dog was considered an effective deterrent.

Drug Effects on Burglars' Decision Making

Research has consistently shown that a large proportion of property offenders are addicted to drugs or have used illegal drugs in the recent past (Bureau of Justice Statistics, 1988; Johnson et al., 1985; National Institute of Justice, 1989). If drug usage (and associated arousal and disequilibrium) affects the rational, sequential decision model of target selection by residential burglars, and if a substantial proportion of burglars are drug abusers, decision-making models that assume a rational cognitive state are limited in what they can explain, how well they predict behavior, and how generally they apply. One of the purposes of the present study is to determine how drug use affects burglary target selection and other decision-making processes of residential burglars, with particular emphasis on the influence of drugs on the rational decision model.

Interdependence of Drugs and Burglary

Our findings reveal an interdependence between drug abuse and residential burglary. This does not, however, imply that drug use is implicated in the etiology of burglary. In fact, most of our informants committed their first burglary before they began regular drug use. However, once they began to use drugs regularly, they usually began to rely, at least partially, on criminal activity to maintain the habit. As their drug use intensified, the users (particularly heroin addicts) found regular employment increasingly difficult to maintain, and they often dropped out of legitimate society and into a drug using, criminal subculture. Thereafter, most maintained their drug habit through full-time criminal activity. Because drug users must establish and maintain illicit contacts in order to buy drugs, they are drawn further into a network of criminal associates, and thus more deeply into a deviant life style.

One interesting finding regarding drugs was unexpected and, though reported previously (Bennett & Wright, 1984; Shover, 1971), has not been adequately discussed and analyzed. We had expected to find that burglars committed burglaries to buy drugs. We had not expected to find that burglars also used drugs to initiate and facilitate the commission of their burglaries. Twenty-eight informants stated that, when possible, they "fixed" or "got high" before entering a target site. They referred to the need to "be steady" or to "keep up my nerve." Although perhaps a placebo effect, most concluded that they were "better burglars" when under the moderate influence of drugs or alcohol. Some reported enhanced vision and more acute hearing while under the influence of marijuana. Others perceived themselves to be more efficient and to act faster and more decisively while using cocaine. A larger group, over one half of the informants, reported that they drank alcohol, "fixed," or smoked marijuana to overcome the fear brought on by the act of entering the target site. The drugs used to deal with fear were primarily central nervous system depressants. With only two exceptions, even the informants whose regular drug of choice was a stimulant, such as cocaine or "speed," used depressant drugs immediately before a burglary to lower anxiety and reduce fear, thus facilitating the criminal event. Many stated that without drugs or alcohol they would not have the courage to initiate the act or to stay in the residence long enough to search for and locate the items to steal. Further, they believed that without a calming drug, they tended to overlook important environmental cues related to risk and to overlook items hidden in the house that they otherwise would find. Wayne, an experienced burglar, stated that he always smoked marijuana before entering a target site "to reduce the paranoia" and to increase his awareness. He stated:

> I'm scared to death when I go in a house. If I didn't smoke a joint or have a few drinks I couldn't do it. If you get inside and you're not cool, I mean if you're not aware of what's going on around you, you're gonna get caught.

Another very experienced and skilled burglar stated that she "fixed," when possible, before doing a burglary:

> I'm so scared that I can't think straight without some junk or at least some weed. Once I've got straight, then I'm OK. I'm not afraid and I can think good enough to get the job done and get away safe.

Jamie, a heavy cocaine user, stated he would never use cocaine before doing a burglary:

> Coke makes you paranoid, man. If you're scared, then you don't need to get paranoid too. You get to running around on the inside of the house and you can't think right and you miss a lot of stuff.

By using depressant drugs or alcohol at an appropriate dose and time before entering a target site, the burglar may reduce the level of arousal brought on by fear and thereby possibly increase the range of cues utilized. To this extent, he or she may actually become a "better burglar." There is, however, an optimal level of arousal for a task, and reducing or increasing the level of arousal below or above an optimal point may impair rather than increase performance. The burglar who reduces arousal to the point of "nodding off," or the cocaine or methamphetamine user who attempts to ward off fear by using a stimulant such as cocaine or "speed," impairs rather than facilitates performance. Billy, a burglar who used marijuana and alcohol heavily, reported:

> One time, man, I smoked some dope before I went in this place. I was already about half drunk. I found this comic book inside one of the kid's bedroom and started reading it. I must have gone to sleep, man, cause the next thing I remember this cop was standing there shaking me and telling me to wake up.

Drug Effects on Burglary Attractiveness Ratings

During the burglary reconstructions we attempted to determine whether the type of drug used (stimulant vs. depressant) affected target selection decisions. The informants were asked to rate their drug state and to specify the type of drug being used at the time of the session. The burglary attractiveness ratings obtained during these sessions demonstrated significant differences between burglars using cocaine and those using heroin and marijuana, and between those using drugs and those who were not under the influence of drugs at the time of the session. As shown in Figure 2.1, heroin users gave significantly lower attractiveness ratings in the conditions that prevailed during the staged activity.

Cocaine users generally rated sites higher (more attractive) than did those who were not under the influence of drugs at the time of the staged activity and those who were using depressant drugs such as marijuana and heroin. Marijuana and heroin users rated sites less attractive as burglary sites than those who were not using drugs at the time of the staged activity. The trend was toward more cautious decisions on the part of those using depressant drugs and toward more risky decisions when using cocaine, a stimulant. Both depressant and stimulant drug users were differentiated from those who were not using drugs at the time of the staged activity—in the expected direction.

Opportunity and Burglary

Although the "professional burglars" among our informants tended to select targets in a purposive manner, analyzing the physical and social

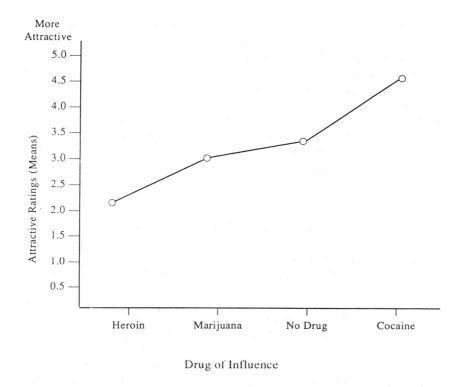

Figure 2.1 The individual burglary attractiveness ratings (means) of burglars alone under the circumstances that actually prevailed at the time of the site inspection (now) as a function of the drug of influence.

characteristics of the environment and choosing targets congruent with the "template" developed from experience, by far the greater proportion of the informants were opportunistic. The targets they chose appeared particularly vulnerable *at the time*. Thus most burglaries in the jurisdiction studied appear to result from the propitious juxtaposition of target, offender, and situation.

Our findings suggest that a burglar's decision to "hit" a target is based primarily on environmental cues that are perceived to have immediate consequences. Most burglars appear to attend only to the present; future events or consequences do not appear to weigh heavily in their risk versus gain calculation. Drug-using burglars and juveniles are particularly oriented to this immediate gain and immediate risk decision process. Non-drug-using experienced burglars are probably less likely to attend only to immediate risks and gains. Our informants, though experienced burglars, were all drug users and tended to have a "here and now" orientation toward the rewards and costs associated with burglary.

Exploiting opportunity characterized the target selection processes in over 75% of the burglaries reconstructed during our research. Even professional burglars among our informants often took advantage of presented opportunities when they arose. Chance opportunities occasionally presented themselves while the professional was "casing" and "probing" potential burglary targets chosen by more rational means. When these opportunities arose, the professional burglar was as likely as other burglars to take advantage of the situation.

Implications for Crime Prevention

This study suggests burglars may be much more opportunistic than previously believed. The opportunistic burglar chooses targets based upon their perceived vulnerability to burglary at a given time. Given a large number of potential targets, the burglar tends to select the most vulnerable of the target pool. The rational planning burglar chooses his targets on the basis of other factors than situational vulnerability alone and conceives ways in which he or she can overcome impediments to the burglary.

Programs designed to prevent burglary must be based upon valid assumptions about burglars and burglary. Measures designed to combat the relatively small population of high-incidence "professional" burglars tend to overemphasize the skill and determination of most burglars. They are expensive, complex, and require long-term commitment at many levels. The typical burglar is not a calculating professional against whom complex prevention tactics must be employed. In fact, most burglars are young, unskilled, and opportunistic. This suggests that emphasis should be directed at modifying situational cues relating to surveillability, occupancy, and accessibility. Dogs, good locks, and alarm systems deter most burglars. Methods that give a residence the "illusion of occupancy" (Cromwell, Olson, & Avary, 1991) deter almost all burglars and are maintained with little effort or cost. Our study suggests that these simple steps may be the most cost-efficient and effective means by which residents may insulate themselves from victimization by burglars.

Moreover, a crime prevention strategy that does not take into account the large percentage of burglars who use drugs and how drug use affects decision making will be ineffective. A cognitive-behavioral analysis of subroutines, which take into account drug effects within the larger template model, may serve as the most fertile paradigm with which to examine the burglar's decision-making process and to design and implement crime prevention strategies.

Discussion Questions

1. What is meant by "opportunity theory" as applied to the crime of burglary? Do you agree or disagree with this approach to understanding the offense of burglary? Why or why not?
2. How might a "field study" such as the one discussed in this chapter provide more valid and reliable data about burglary than one conducted using incarcerated offenders as subjects? Can you suggest some negative factors that might be associated with such a research methodology?
3. List and briefly discuss the primary "motives" for committing burglary. If burglars were provided adequate money to pay their legitimate living expenses (rent, food, utilities, transportation, clothing, etc.) do you think that most burglars would desist from committing burglaries? Why or why not?
4. What did this study learn about the burglars' use of time? What are the implications of this finding for burglary prevention and control?
5. What did the study report regarding the use of "inside information" in burglary? In this regard, what might you do to reduce the possibility of your home being burglarized?
6. What were the major finding(s) of the study with regard to "target hardening"?
7. How do drugs affect burglars' decision-making process? Which come first, drugs or crime? How are these two variables related in the burglar's activities?
8. Are burglars primarily opportunistic or rational planners? How might this knowledge affect burglary prevention strategies?

Note

1. Several factors may account for the low reporting rate. When the stolen property is minimal, some do not contact police believing that "nothing will be done." Others do not realize they have been burglarized for days or even weeks after the event and then do not call the police because they are unable to pinpoint the time of the burglary or cannot be sure the property taken was not lost. Burglars report that they sometimes find drugs and other contraband in houses and "know" that these victims will not call the police. Some victims simply do not trust the authorities and prefer to accept the loss to bringing in the police. Others know the burglar (a neighbor or acquaintance) and do not wish to have him or her arrested.

References

Bennett, T., & Wright, R. (1984). *Burglars on burglary: Prevention and the offender.* Aldershot: Gower.

Brantingham, P. J., & Brantingham, P. L. (1978). A theoretical model of crime site selection. In M. D. Krohn & R. L. Akers (Eds.), *Crime, law and sanctions* (pp. 105-118). Beverly Hills: Sage.

Brantingham, P. J., & Brantingham, P. L. (1981). *Environmental criminology.* Beverly Hills: Sage.

Brown, B. B., & Altman, I. (1981). Territoriality and residential crime: A conceptual framework. In P. J. Brantingham & P. L. Brantingham (Eds.), *Environmental criminology* (pp. 55-76). Beverly Hills: Sage. Reissued by Waveland, 1991.

Bureau of Justice Statistics. (1988). *BJS data report, 1988.* Washington, DC: Department of Justice.

Bureau of Justice Statistics [BJS]. (1991, October). *Criminal victimization 1990.* (Bureau of Justice Statistics Bulletin). Washington, DC: Department of Justice.

Cromwell, P., Olson, J. N., & Avary, D. (1991). *Breaking and entering: An ethnographic analysis of burglary.* Newbury Park, CA: Sage.

Johnson, B. D., Goldstein, P. J., Preble, E., Schneider, J., Lipton, D. S., Spunt, B., & Miller, T. (1985). *Taking care of business: The economics of crime by heroin abusers.* Lexington, MA: Lexington.

Lynch, J. P. (1990, November). Modeling target selection in burglary: Differentiating substance from method. Paper presented at the 1990 Annual Meeting of the American Society of Criminology in Baltimore, MD.

National Institute of Justice. (1989, August). *NIJ research in action.* Washington, DC: Author.

Rengert, G., & Wasilchick, J. (1985). *Suburban burglary: A time and a place for everything.* Springfield: Charles C Thomas.

Rengert, G., & Wasilchick, J. (1989). *Space, time and crime: Ethnographic insights into residential burglary.* A report prepared for the National Institute of Justice. (Mimeo).

Reppetto, T. G. (1974). *Residential crime.* Cambridge, MA: Ballinger.

Scarr, H. A. (1973). *Patterns of burglary.* Washington, DC: Government Printing Office.

Sessions, W. S. *Crime in the United States, 1990.* Washington, DC: Federal Bureau of Investigation.

Shover, N. (1971). *Burglary as an occupation.* (Doctoral dissertation, University of Illinois, 1975). *Dissertation Abstracts International, 2,* 598A.

3

Sex Offenders

Prevalence, Trends, Model Programs, and Costs

LORI KOESTER SCOTT

Jack was a 53-year-old businessman whose 13-year-old stepdaughter accused him of molesting her. She told her best friend that he had been grabbing her since she was 8 years old, forcing her to lie on top of him, and most recently, coming in to stare at her while she was bathing. When the police showed up at his house to interview him, he denied everything and threatened to kill himself.

By the time of his court date, Jack admitted that he had touched his stepdaughter, but only "because she was an overly affectionate child, and she was such a pest that he had to pinch her breasts to get rid of her." He was allowed to plead to a charge of attempted child molestation, ordered to have no contact with children, and sentenced to 5 years probation with a 6-month jail term. After a year of treatment with a traditional therapist, he was still minimizing his participation and blaming the victim for being seductive.

He was placed on a specialized caseload and sent to a cognitive-behavioral therapist. Once he began working specifically on his sexual deviancy, he began taking total responsibility for his actions, having explained to the victim in detail how he had fantasized every touch and set up every situation in which she was molested. His periodic polygraphs show no additional contact or sexual fantasies of children. All other family members have been in counseling, and the victim is now in college.

Richard, on the other hand, was arrested at age 25 on suspicion of rape. He was charged with breaking into 23 homes or apartments over the course of 2 years, threatening his victims, all in their 20s, with a knife, tying them up, and raping them repeatedly. Evidence found in his apartment, cheap jewelry or half-used bottles of perfume that he had taken from the victims and brought home to his wife, linked him conclusively to the crimes. He was convicted of eight of the charges and sentenced to 75 years in prison.

The decade of the 1980s saw a new focus on this growing segment of the criminal justice population: sex offenders. This was an issue that had been rumbling beneath the surface for generations, but the women's movement and a new courage to speak out on the part of victims brought more offenders into the court system. Flareups here and there gradually led to an eruption of cases, educational programs, expanded media attention, increased treatment for victims, and the inception of experimental treatment programs for offenders. However, as this review will reflect, sexual abuse in all its manifestations is a crime that is still not well understood and, for the most part, is inadequately managed by the majority of criminal justice systems.

Reported cases of child sex abuse increased by 2100% from 1976 to 1986, from 6,000 to 132,000. In 1991 reports totaled 432,000, an increase of another 227% (U.S. Dept of Health and Human Services, 1992). Over 85,000 sex offenders are now incarcerated in state and federal prisons, an increase of 48% in the 2 years from 1988 to 1990 (*Corrections Compendium*, July 1991). In Maricopa County, Arizona, reported and investigated sex crimes submitted to prosecutors by police doubled in the 2 years from 1989 to 1991.

Adult rape and sexual assault cases have been "legitimized" by the courts for some time, although the struggle to reduce sexual aggression in what many label our "rape-prone" society has not yet been successful (Herman, 1988; Koss, Didycz, & Wisniewski, 1987; Scully, 1990). Incest and child molest cases, however, had been rarely acknowledged and not aggressively prosecuted. As recently as 1953 Kinsey and his associates stated that there was no logical reason why children should be disturbed about sexual abuse (Salter, 1988). Not until 1963 did the state of Minnesota criminalize incest, a behavior that was thought to be extremely rare (Patton, 1991). Freud's attempt to explain the tormented sexual memories of his female patients as unconscious desires for their fathers was generally discredited in the 1980s; yet as recently as 1991 a Phoenix psychiatrist evaluated an incest case by stating that his 13-year-old female patient had unconsciously manipulated her father and that the offender's problems had evolved in part from "unresolved Oedipal feelings for his mother." He went on to describe the offense as "immature hysterical sexual behavior on both parts" (author's personal files).

The commitment to prosecute sex crimes of all types has greatly impacted the makeup of police, courts, prisons, and community corrections. Efforts are underway to expand the psychological knowledge and effective treatment and supervision of this most difficult, highly secretive, and consistently manipulative offender. However, in spite of the increased national consciousness paid to this issue in the past decade, there remains an abysmal amount of ignorance and denial on the part of the general public. At a distance they know it exists, but they would prefer that the offender remain the anonymous and horrible creature of headlines, books, and movies. When the reality of incest was ultimately acknowledged and discussed in the literature, a careful analysis shows that first the victim was blamed, and then the spouse; today, with reluctance by some professionals, there is finally a commitment to holding the adult perpetrator responsible for his actions, and the realization that the riskiest place for a child may, sadly, be his or her own home. At present, laws vary widely from state to state, with wide discrepancies in the very definition of forms of sexual abuse and the sentencing guidelines worked out by legislators.

Etiology

Several attempts have been made in the past decade to define and classify sex offenders in order to (a) assess risk for sentencing purposes; (b) determine amenability for treatment; (c) understand the etiology of such disorders in order that prevention and/or early intervention may reduce the frequency of victimization. A major contribution and impetus for further study was the work of Groth (1979) and Burgess, Groth, Holstrom, and Sgroi (1982). Dr. Groth, who had worked for many years with convicted sex offenders in Connecticut and Massachusetts, attempted to categorize different types of rapists and child molesters. He classified rapists as motivated by either "power" or "anger," and child molesters as "fixated" or "regressed," with the fixated molesters more commonly identified as true pedophiles, or those adult individuals who are interested exclusively in children for satisfying their sexual needs. The "regressed" molester was considered to be primarily attracted to adult partners, but had temporarily forsaken his normal adult desires for sex with an age-appropriate partner.

During the same time period, Dr. Gene Abel, a behavioral psychiatrist, and his associates, including Dr. Judith Becker, were conducting a landmark study of sex offenders at the New York State Psychiatric Institute. Four hundred and eleven offenders who were guaranteed confidentiality admitted that they had attempted 238,711 offenses and had completed 218,900 of them, for an average of 533 acts and 336 victims each. Offenders who had been identified with only one paraphilia, such as rapists, were found to have engaged in an average of 3.5 additional paraphilias, such as exhibitionism, voyeurism, obscene phone calls, child molestation, and bestiality. Many so-called incest offenders were in reality pedophiles; a large number who had avowed no attraction to same-sex children disclosed a history of victimization of children of both sexes; 44% of incest offenders revealed an astonishing number of nonrelated child victims in addition to numerous other paraphilias (Abel, Mittelman, & Becker, 1985).

Clinicians and corrections personnel who have used physiological testing in recent years to counteract the inadequate self-reporting of sex offenders have validated such findings. For example, in a recent sample of 41 exhibitionists referred by probation officers to a Phoenix treatment program, 38 admitted to additional "hands-on" behaviors involving minors. These are men who have long been considered by the courts to be relatively "harmless."

In a recent comprehensive study of 118 incestuous fathers, 26% of the men were classified as "sexually preoccupied," possessing a "clear and conscious (often obsessive) sexual interest in their daughters." Some of the men in this category were further classified as "early sexualizers," who admitted that they regarded their daughters as sex objects from birth. "One father reported that he had been stimulated by the sight of his daughter nursing and that he could never remember when he did not have sexual feelings for her. He began sexually abusing her when she was four weeks old" (Williams & Finkelhor, 1992).

Based on increasing information and extensive clinical experience, it has become more and more apparent to professionals that trying to fit sex offenders neatly into categories is not always possible. What appears to be a continuum of behaviors seems to be more accurate. Some offenders do not progress beyond certain stages; others left unchecked and unnoticed by the system may go on to cause irreparable damage to countless lives: the pedophile who grooms, violates, and then discards child after child, or the rapist who may at some point find ultimate satisfaction only in torturing and possibly murdering his victims.

Psychological Theories

Not all aberrant sexual behavior involves victims. A continuum of sexual behavior or addiction was explored by Patrick Carnes in the 1980s as he attempted to identify and treat sex offenders using the 12-step model. Carnes had been working with addicts and their families in Minnesota and had become increasingly aware that sometimes the patient who came in addicted to alcohol or drugs revealed an addiction to sexual behavior. These individuals gradually developed a pattern of needing to perform certain sex acts in a compulsive manner in an attempt to satisfy other needs. The definition of addiction also includes a person's willingness to sacrifice to the point of self-destructiveness for the taking of a drug or a specific experience, a phenomenon he noted in many sex offenders (Carnes, 1983).

However, the majority of the practitioners and researchers in the field follow what can best be described as a cognitive-behavioral model based on social learning theory: that sexually deviant behavior is the result of gradual conditioning to a powerful reinforcer (Knopp, 1984; Knopp, Freeman-Longo, & Stevenson, 1992). Offenders frequently present with a significantly disturbed developmental history; early feelings of emotional and social isolation, often combined with physical or sexual abuse, have led to cognitive distortions or mistaken belief systems about themselves, others, and the way in which the world operates. They often present in a state of "victim posture." Their belief systems form the beginning components of the "offense cycle" or chain of behaviors, as the offender develops a habit of using fantasies in order to manage emotional needs not met through healthy connectedness with others, sometimes along the lines of wealth, power, control, or revenge. At some point, deviant sexual fantasies become part of this repertoire.

The offender also begins to incorporate into his fantasy a pattern of rationalization and justification that further disinhibits him and desensitizes him to the taboo nature of the behavior (Wolf, 1984). Escaping to his fantasies places him in control.

This phase of the cycle objectifies sexual partners, increases the frequency of thoughts related to sex, reduces discrimination or selectivity of sex partners, rehearses sexual misbehavior and reinforces the individual's belief that the primary goal of sexual relations is to feel better about oneself. Behaviorally, the individual is likely to engage in compulsive masturbation, experience deficits with respect to touch discrimination, and make sexual decisions based upon opportunity. (Emerick, 1991, p. 8)

At some point, the offender begins cruising and grooming behavior around victims who match his deviant sexual interest.

Once the offender acts out at least part of his deviant interest, he feels very guilty and develops ineffective strategies to discontinue his deviant behavior. These strategies are partially contained in the final step, reconstitution, which is the use of socially appropriate behavior to an extreme to disguise the offender's deviant behavior and interest and to manage his guilt associated with his sexual misconduct. Because nothing has truly changed in the offender's life, he is again at step one, which is victim posture thinking, and begins the whole process anew. (Gray, 1991, p. 54)

The "relapse prevention" model of sex offender treatment, developed by Gordon Marlatt, demonstrates that there are a number of common factors or behaviors preceding a relapse into the offense cycle. Offenders often make apparently irrelevant decisions that bring them closer and closer to high-risk situations, lapse, and possible relapse, also supported by rationalization and denial (Laws, 1989). The primary emotion reported by child molesters preceding their offenses was depression; the primary emotion reported by rapists was anger.

Many offenders also present with a profile consistent with a diagnosis of character disorder, which includes qualities of narcissism and distorted perceptions of the world about them; they tend to be ruminative, chronically depressed, and sexually preoccupied (Wolf, 1984). Only a small percentage are diagnosed as psychotic or suffering from a chronic mental illness. A recent study of prisoners at a federal institution showed that offenders diagnosed as psychopaths were not likely to complete the treatment and could be screened out before using valuable time and space (Norris, 1991).

Assessing Risk

In order to make appropriate judgments about the disposition of sex offenders, many facets of the system usually look at the severity of the offense together with perceived risk to the community. This begins with the child protective services worker or police officer who initially investigate the case. Prosecuting attorneys often use criteria consisting of degrees of intrusion, force, or frequency to determine a basis for prosecution leading to trial or acceptable plea bargains. Probation officers include the impact on the victim in summarizing the case for the sentencing judge. All these individuals bring to the case their own personal beliefs and biases regarding such an emotional and still controversial crime. At this time there appears to be no uniformity in any of these assessment processes, which vary widely from state to state. For example, prosecutors or presentence investigators may decide that if there is actual intercourse in a case involving a child victim, they will accept no less than prison. Yet Hindman (1989), a nationally respected authority on the effects of sexual abuse on victims, suggests that many other factors might make the offense more traumatic and long lasting, such as the reaction of family and others to disclosure of the crime.

Little definitive data exists, unfortunately, on empirical studies that analyze the true recidivism rates of sex offenders and their risk to the community. Most risk assessments that have traditionally been used on the general prison population, for example, do not apply to many sex offenders, who, except for their hidden deviance, have often led much more stable and prosocial lifestyles than the average inmate.

James Breiling, the Director of the Antisocial and Violent Behavioral Branch of the National Institute of Mental Health (1991), suggests that criminal justice professionals need to ask:

1. Who is at high risk?
2. What conditions put the defendant at risk?
3. How can risk be lowered during probation/incarceration/treatment?

Risk analysis can focus on several different areas, including offender characteristics and history, together with elements of the crime. In a review of sex offender risk studies available through 1990, McGrath found that untreated exhibitionists have the highest reoffense rates. Recidivism rates of rapists vary widely (8-36%). Among untreated child molesters, non-familial molesters of boys were found to reoffend at twice the rate of nonfamilial molesters of girls (13% vs. 27%). Offenders with multiple paraphilias (more than one deviant method of acting out) were found to reoffend 5 times as often in Maletzky's Oregon study of 4,000 sex offenders. Abel found that 75% of the recidivists studied by him and his colleagues crossed both age and gender in their choice of victims (McGrath, 1991).

The criminal justice professional must examine these earlier studies carefully, however. At this time most studies of recidivism are almost meaningless because of methodological variability and ambiguity (Furby, Weinrott, & Blackshaw, 1989). Do the criteria include arrests or convictions? Are actual reoffense rates the only criteria? Only a small percentage of sex offenses are reported, and a smaller number result in conviction. Probation or parole violators sometimes admit to technical violations instead of the new offense. Many systems still allow sex offenders to plead to nonsex crimes, such as aggravated assault or criminal trespass. Are exhibitionists, supposedly the highest recidivists, more easily caught because of their visibility? There have been no long-term follow-up studies on sex offenders, partly because many of them disappear when they are released from prison or probation, moving to another state or even another country.

Max was a music school teacher who taught in several areas of the United States, Mexico, Africa, and the Middle East. When arrested at the age of 51 for soliciting the sexual favors of two 12-year-old boys, he disclosed a long history of pedophilia. He moved frequently because even though parents would find out what had happened and force him to leave, no one wanted to prosecute. He kept a diary of "well over 1,000 partners," which was found by the police upon his arrest.

Max related a childhood of being raised in an orphanage, in which he claimed that sexual experimentation was common. He defended his subsequent sexual behavior, stating that wherever he went, "young men flocked to him and wanted to have sex with him." Unfortunately, even in this arrest, the charge was pled to a minor felony because the children's parents did not want them to testify. He was originally placed on probation and ordered into intensive treatment, but refused to attend. His probation was revoked and he was sent to prison. After a short term of incarceration, unfortunately, he will be free at age 53 to go wherever he wishes.

Even though many states have enacted sex offender registration laws, there have been no studies conducted to examine their effectiveness in apprehending or deterring offenders.

At this time, a well-designed 15-year study is underway in California, examining the factors involved in the recidivism of treated versus non-treated sex offenders (Marques, Day, Nelson, & West, 1993; Marques, Day, Nelson, & Miner, 1989). Preliminary data from that study and from other treatment studies have begun to show that recidivism for treated offenders, with varying significance, is usually lower. One recommendation suggests that additional supervision and treatment provided to treatment subjects after their release from prison may be delaying reoffense. Marshall, Jones, Ward, Johnston, and Barbaree (1991) suggest that, at the very least, treatment and supervision can delay recidivism in some and prevent it in others.

Maletzky's (1991) 17-year analysis of Oregon sex offenders found that offenders who targeted out-of-home victims were 8 times more likely to reoffend, with rapists having the lowest success rate. Molesters with multiple victims were 5 times more likely to recidivate. He found no relationship between success in treatment and duration of offense or frequency of offending behaviors. Most studies show that offenders with any type of prior record, like the general population, are much more likely to offend again. McGrath (1991) concludes that the "true re-offense rates in these studies are likely to be much higher" (p. 335).

From clinical experience, therapists and corrections personnel see the rapist and the pedophile who victimizes young boys as most high risk and most unlikely to respond to treatment.

A respected member of the clergy had built a cabin outside of town that he used as a "retreat" for some of the boys in his ministry. Many of the parents were delighted to turn their children over to him for such outings. However, he was subsequently charged and convicted of molesting at least two of the boys who had been entrusted to him, in this case boys who had previously been abused by their stepfather. An evaluation and psychosexual history revealed a 20-year history of sexually exploiting young males, beginning with volunteer work as a Scout leader. After being on probation for a few months, he disappeared. Detectives found him in Florida, preparing to leave for an obscure ministry in South America.

Abel and colleagues found that 75% of recidivists crossed both age and gender in their choice of victims (Abel et al., 1985). The incest offender, on the other hand, shows up as a low recidivist in many studies, but that may be because his probation officer can fairly easily restrict his access to children, and he may not be as likely to look for victims outside the family unit. The therapist treated the following case as an incest offense, but probation officers kept the age difference in mind.

Don, age 35, had been placed on probation after a year in jail for the molestation of his 5-year-old stepdaughter. As part of the plea bargain, charges had been dropped involving his 13-year-old niece. He immediately became involved in therapy, working hard on all assignments. Three months after meeting a much younger woman at his church, he married her. The probation officer suspected that it was a way to obtain supervised contact with his two sons, but he was doing so well in therapy that he was allowed to go through with the marriage.

Before his therapist discharged Don from treatment, his probation officer ordered a polygraph. Don admitted that he was still occasionally fantasizing about young girls he saw in public places, such as the grocery store. Communication with police was increased as a precaution. Two months later Don approached a 12-year-old girl at a convenience market and tried to get her into his car to the point of offering her money. Even though he had not committed a new offense by touching her, she called police, who alerted the probation officer. Don was jailed for 30 days, placed on formal intensive probation, and moved up to high risk status.

If the results of the Williams and Finkelhor (1992) study are to be considered, then the younger the victim of incest, the higher the risk for reoffense.

Alcohol use or abuse appears to be a factor in half of all sex offenses. Although the use of alcohol does not cause such behavior (even though many offenders tend to use it as an excuse), it and other drugs can serve as disinhibitors to deviant activities.

After sniffing $100 worth of cocaine, 19-year-old Glenn had waited until two 17-year-old females working at a fast-food outlet left their jobs late one night, forced himself in their car, made them drive him to a deserted area, and then raped them both repeatedly for the next several hours. The judge requested that the presentence writer conduct as thorough an investigation as possible because he did not want to send the young man to prison for 20 years if he were "a drug addict and not a rapist." It was revealed that Glenn's childhood and adolescence were similar to that of many rapists: he had been physically abused by an alcoholic father during his entire childhood; in despair over her marriage, his mother had shot herself in the head in front of her son when he was 16 years old; his father had not allowed any of the children at the time to receive much-needed therapy.

Pornography is also often found to be a precursor to offending, even though by itself it does not cause the offense to occur. Sex offenders are frequently discovered to have large collections of pornography, which can include hard-core or child pornography. In treatment, they admit to using their pornography collections to fantasize and masturbate, although some may use innocent photographs or pictures from magazines or catalogs of attractive children. Child molesters sometimes force their young victims to watch and then imitate pornographic photos or videos. Hard-core pedophiles who are only attracted to children often have secret networks linking them to sources of illegal child pornography, the production of which escalated rapidly in the late 1970s (Finkelhor, 1984). The FBI and U.S. Postal Inspector's office try to maintain surveillance over such connections and arrest when possible. Offenders have gone to great lengths to place surveillance cameras and wireless microphones in public restrooms, for example, or have videotaped themselves having sex with their victims. A Phoenix rapist who broke into his victim's home and used her video camera to record the assault in all its brutalizing detail provided police and prosecutors with undeniable evidence and is now serving a lengthy aggravated sentence.

The offender's age is significant to some extent in predicting future behavior and assessing risk. McGrath (1991) reports that 88.2% of rapists are under 40 years of age, whereas there is little age distinction among molesters. Use of force or weapons is predictive of recidivism, as is a history of impulsivity. Such offenders have sometimes been diagnosed as hyperactive children, and have a history of instability in regard to employment, relationships, and general living skills. Several studies have found stable employment to be a significant factor in low recidivism, although this is also true for other types of offenders.

A diagnosis of antisocial personality disorder was found to be a significant predictor of recidivism among rapists in a Canadian study of 54 incarcerated rapists (McGrath, 1991). Two studies by Abel and his colleagues found that 29.1% of rapists were diagnosed as antisocial personalities versus 11.6% of child molesters; those molesters diagnosed as such tended to drop out of treatment (Abel, Becker, Blanchard, & Djenderedjian, 1978).

Disposition: Probation or Prison?

Because the determination of risk and/or offender typology is not definitive, and because many difficulties are involved in prosecuting and sentencing these offenders, it is not surprising that some type of community corrections is the final outcome of the majority of cases. The proportion of offenders sentenced to probation rather than prison can vary widely: for example, 88% in Minnesota compared to 66% in Arizona. Some states use a combination of prison, jail, or mental hospital confinement followed by community release. An informed risk assessment is invaluable to probation officers, who must assume the responsibility of monitoring the offender's freedom to move about the community. Arizona routinely sentences certain sex offenders convicted of "dangerous crimes against children" to lifetime probation, with the rationale that such offenders cannot ever be cured but can learn to control their behavior.

One such community program is based in Maricopa County (Phoenix), Arizona. Offenders placed on probation tend to be considered less dangerous and somewhat less risk to the community. Although a large percentage are incest offenders with female victims, the remainder are male-targeted pedophiles, rapists, and high-risk exhibitionists who need surveillance.

Operating on the principle that such offenders need external controls while they are learning to develop internal control, the program utilizes the services of surveillance officers as part of a probation team to monitor the evening and weekend activities of offenders. A list of 17 specialized terms for sex offenders is added to regular terms of probation, calling attention to the known behavior patterns of offenders and imposing prohibitions against situations that might lead to a reoffense. Utilizing the concepts of relapse prevention, cognitive-behavioral therapists work closely with probation officers to break through the offenders' entrenched denial, rationalizations, minimizations, and manipulations. The 17 terms of the Maricopa County program are as follows:

Maricopa County Probation Conditions
for Sex Offenders' Contact With Children

1. You shall not initiate, establish, or maintain contact with any male or female child under the age of 18 nor attempt to do so except under circumstances approved in advance and in writing by your probation officer.

2. You shall not reside with any child under the age of 18 or contact your children in any manner unless approved in advance and in writing by your probation officer.

3. You shall not enter onto the premises, travel past, or loiter near where the victim resides except under the circumstances approved in advance and in writing by your probation officer. You shall have no correspondence, telephone contact, or communication through a third party.

4. You shall not go to or loiter near school yards, parks, playgrounds, arcades, or other places primarily used by children under the age of 18.

5. You shall not date or socialize with anybody who has children under the age of 18 without permission of the probation officer.

Treatment

6. You shall actively participate in sex offender treatment and remain in such treatment at the direction of the supervising officer.
7. You shall submit to any program of psychological or physiological assessment at the direction of the probation officer, including the penile plethysmograph and/or the polygraph, to assist in treatment, planning, and case monitoring.
8. You shall allow the therapist to disclose to the court information about your attendance and participation in treatment.

Other Behavior

9. Register at the Maricopa County Sheriff's Office as a sex offender within 30 days of sentencing per A.R.S. 13-3821.
10. You shall reside at a place approved by your probation officer.
11. You shall abide by any curfew imposed by your probation officer.
12. You shall not possess any sexually stimulating or sexually oriented material as deemed inappropriate by treatment staff, nor patronize any place where such material or entertainment is available.
13. You shall be responsible for your appearance at all times. This includes the wearing of undergarments and clothing in places where another person may be expected to view you.
14. You shall not hitchhike or pick up hitchhikers.
15. You shall not utilize "900" telephone numbers without the permission of the supervising probation officer.
16. You shall not operate a motor vehicle alone without specific written permission of the probation officer or unless accompanied by an adult approved by the probation officer.
17. Abide by all terms and restrictions of the family reunification procedure as mandated in writing by the supervising probation officer.

All sex offenders are initially required to attend 45 hours of classes on human sexuality, the development of sexual deviancy, understanding the offense cycle, societal attitudes on male-female roles and stereotypes, and the impact of victimization. After that, the offender is placed into group treatment for as long as all involved believe that intense treatment is necessary. Groups have specific homework assignments that may include some form of behavioral conditioning designed to extinguish deviant arousal and encourage arousal to age-appropriate partners. Because sexual deviance is often ingrained, with lifelong habits of fantasizing and/or acting-out behaviors in total secrecy, offenders find that the group works as a supportive network of people who share the same problems that could never be discussed previously. At the same time, group members are not hesitant to confront each other about rationalizing, minimizing, and other thinking errors. Once the offender learns his offense cycle, he and the other group members share ways to "unlearn" it and interfere with the beginning stages of the cycle, following the concepts of relapse prevention.

One of the most difficult aspects of community supervision of sex offenders is the incest offender whose spouse desires reunification. In some states, probation departments such as Washington County, Oregon, and Sheboygan, Wisconsin, have developed a closely knit group of professionals who, as a team, supervise the family. Whether or not other agencies are involved, probation personnel should impose strict guidelines on any family contacts, and reunification should not take place for 2 years. (O'Connell, Leberg, & Donaldson, 1990).

Physiological Testing

Invaluable to the above-mentioned agencies and to any supervising body and treatment personnel is a complete assessment of the offender's sexual history and accurate information concerning the presenting offense. Physiological measurements of sex offenders are increasingly utilized as components of a full-scale evaluation in order to more accurately assess and treat all underlying paraphilias. Such programs are not without controversy, especially from those who are ignorant of the depth and extent of sexual abuse.

As previously noted, sex offenders are notoriously poor self-reporters and, as illustrated by Abel et al.'s 1978 study, very reluctant to divulge the extent of their paraphilias. In Salter's (1988) words, "Offenders, like icebergs, typically expose only a fraction of the problem initially." Many prior evaluations have relied on the offender's self-report. In fact, many of the earlier beliefs and perceptions about the role of the child in incest cases, for example, were taken from interviews with men who were involved in one-on-one therapist-patient relationships, and whose recall and rationalizations or denial of such behavior were accepted as true. Since the introduction of the penile plethysmograph as a measure of deviant arousal, and the polygraph as an assessment of a defendant's sexual history, offenders have begun to reveal information about themselves that was often suppressed and therefore unknown to their therapists.

As of 1991, penile plethysmography was reportedly used in 30% of the 745 treatment programs in the United States, both outpatient and institutional (Knopp, Freeman-Longo, & Stevenson, 1992). Previously used in the treatment of impotence, the penile plethysmograph is a small band or "strain gauge" that the patient places around the penis and that measures sexual arousal in much the same way as an electrocardiogram measures the workings of the heart. This is done in privacy and with the patient's consent. He is then shown a series of slides, audio, or videotapes that illustrate both deviant and nondeviant stimuli. Research indicates that a significant number of sex offenders are more highly aroused to thoughts or fantasies of sex with children or acts of sexual violence. For example, in a study by Pithers and Laws (1988) of 200 sex offenders, 60% of the rapists and 57% of the child molesters exhibited deviant sexual preferences during plethysmography. Pithers and Laws see the plethysmograph as a window to the offender's "sexual playground," wherein he explores and rehearses his deviant fantasies.

The plethysmograph can be extremely useful in breaking through denial and minimization but should never be used to determine guilt or innocence. Some offenders "flat line," never showing arousal to any stimuli, even appropriate partners. Others are able to consciously suppress their response. Arousal testing is useful in measuring progress in treatment, where it can be used as a type of biofeedback, for it is hoped that the offender will begin to substitute patterns of appropriate arousal for deviant ones. Therapists routinely report that many offenders are incapable of imagining themselves in a normal sexual encounter with an age-appropriate partner:

> Matt, age 18, was placed on probation for following a 13-year-old girl and forcing her off her bike and attempting to rape her. One of his homework assignments in therapy was to make a cassette tape of how he would fantasize himself and another 18-year-old female in a loving and consensual sexual activity. He could not do so. All of his tapes contained elements of forceful and violent behavior, with females highly objectified. This was validated by his plethysmograph evaluation.

The plethysmograph can also be helpful in determining the risk level for supervision purposes. Maletzky's (1991) studies revealed that offenders who showed the highest deviant arousal before they began treatment were 3 times more likely to reoffend. In most traditional clinical assessments, aberrant sexual arousal patterns and deviant sexual fantasies are not adequately evaluated; in reports by clinicians who do not specialize in the treatment of sex offenders, adequate confrontation may not occur. Numerous U.S. and Canadian specialists who regularly utilize the plethysmograph report that many offenders have a distorted view of their own arousal patterns and are in no way accurately perceiving their own environments (Abel et al., 1978; Laws, 1989; Maletzky, 1991; Marshall & Barbaree, 1988).

Training and information disseminated by the National Institute of Corrections regularly endorse plethysmography as a viable component of sex offender evaluation and treatment (Schwartz, 1988). According to

McGrath's comprehensive 1991 review of risk assessments, six out of seven studies showed positive correlations between deviant sexual arousal and reoffense. Yet the device is viewed with skepticism and even incredulity by some judges, legislators, the press, and other individuals who have not been educated to the specifics of the instrument, its limitations, and the overall dynamics of sexual deviance. As an increasing number of institutions and outpatient programs adopt it as part of a comprehensive treatment strategy, it should become more acceptable; this would also depend, of course, on present and future research, which will continue to be extensively reported.

Critics often express concern about the "invasiveness" of the instrument, possibly forgetting the invasiveness of the offender's prior behaviors; nevertheless, care must be taken to protect individual rights while attempting to lower the risk to others. The Association for the Treatment of Sexual Abusers, a nonprofit association comprised of therapists and criminal justice professionals, has formulated a series of guidelines for its members to follow in regulating the ethical use of the plethysmograph (Pithers & Laws, 1988).

The Phoenix program, along with 25% of all adult service providers, also relies on another somewhat controversial physiological device, the polygraph, although it is certainly more accepted as reliable (Abrams, 1989). Use of the polygraph serves two purposes. Initially, soon after sentencing or release from jail, the offender participates in a disclosure polygraph, designed to cover the defendant's sexual history, including first sexual experiences, any sexual relations with relatives, masturbation practices, exhibitionism, voyeurism, bestiality, other paraphilias, use of force, and sexual fantasies. In this examination, the offender is given an opportunity to discuss these issues before the test, often resulting in significant disclosure. He or she is also given a chance to discuss and perhaps clarify any questions on the actual polygraph test that may have indicated deception. The results are staffed with the therapist, probation officer, and the offender's therapy group. The goal is to begin treatment with a "clean" sexual history, so that the offender can learn to control all components of his deviant behavior, not just those he has chosen to disclose of his own accord.

Dr. H., a local chiropractor, had been accused of molesting a 6-year-old neighbor girl by placing his mouth on her vagina. The original and lengthy court proceedings resulted in a mistrial. He had already lost his license for allegedly fondling a female patient inappropriately. After numerous legal delays, during which Dr. H. continued to deny his guilt, he signed a "no contest" plea to sexual contact with a minor and was sentenced to 15 years probation.

A local psychologist had stated that there was nothing in Dr. H's testing to suggest that he was "anything but a conscientious individual who wants to be helpful—particularly through his own specific fields of expertise," and that he "does not have to go outside of his own marital relationship to have his [sexual] needs satisfied."

While on a general probation caseload, Dr. H. saw a therapist for individual sessions, who reported that the client was cooperative, was "doing well," and, after 15 sessions, did not need any more therapy. (He also was continuing to deny any deviancy.) He was placed on a specialized sex offender caseload because of his continuing denial and manipulative and domineering behavior. When the female officer attempted her first field visit, he hid behind the door, stating that he was nude. He highly objected to her subsequent decision to place him in a therapy group for sex offenders, and resisted for months when he was asked to be evaluated using the penile plethysmograph and the polygraph. He continually demanded hearings before the judge, who continued to order him to take the tests. Dr. H. also began writing or calling legislators and public officials to complain about the probation department's "harassment."

In the plethysmograph evaluation, he showed highest arousal to young pre-pubescent females. His veracity as a self-reporter was questioned. Finally, after submitting to the polygraph, after years of fighting the "system," he not only admitted to molesting the victim in the present case, but stated that he had engaged in sexual relations with at least 30 other children. He also disclosed that he had become involved in a wide range of sexual activities with female patients, sexually fondling an "unquantifiable" number of these patients.

He reported possessing a large variety of pornographic materials, including child pornography. He related that his current marriage was struggling due to his impotency and herpes. Finally he revealed that he was still fantasizing about sexual relations with children while masturbating four or more times a week. He was continued on probation, and is now progressing well in weekly group therapy.

A maintenance polygraph is utilized as the offender progresses through treatment, and is a useful tool for long-term supervision. Corrections personnel find both disclosure and maintenance polygraphs invaluable for planning, for family reunification procedures, and for help in determining risk. In a recidivism study conducted by the Jackson County, Oregon, probation department involving 173 offenders, only 5% were convicted of committing new sex crimes while under supervision, although 16% absconded and 13% of the total number were revoked to prison for various reasons, including noncompliance with treatment or prohibited contact with children (Association for the Treatment of Sexual Abusers, 1991). Legal challenges to the use of the polygraph as a term of probation have been upheld in Oregon (Abrams, 1993).

An important component of the Phoenix program is the intensity of offender surveillance. In 1989, in an effort to curtail the crowding of the state's prisons, extra community funding allowed the utilization of sex offender surveillance officers, who act as assistant probation officers, monitoring the offenders' activities on weekends and evenings. In line with the assumption that most sex offenders can only learn to control their behavior and cannot ever be considered "cured," and because Arizona law also provides for lifetime probation, some judges are currently sentencing offenders to prison for several years on one count and to lifetime probation on another. Although this allows strict community supervision, it also means that offenders will populate the department far longer than other probationers, and long-term planning is essential.

Cost

Treatment and surveillance as described in the above programs certainly increase the cost of supervising high-risk sex offenders, yet a study by Prentky and Burgess (1990) of Massachusetts reveals that the cost of prosecuting and incarcerating one sex offender who offends against a new victim greatly exceeds the relatively low cost to the state of appropriate supervision. Using Marshall and Barbaree's (1990) well-documented and conservative study of recidivism in treated (25%) versus untreated (40%) sex offenders, Prentky examined the costs of investigating, arresting, prosecuting, and incarcerating for 7 years a sex offender who had one victim, estimated at $183,333. In examining the costs of recidivism in untreated offenders, he devised a rather complicated formula using the above information to show a differential of $68,000 per case, concluding hypothetically that releasing 1,000 untreated sex offenders from prison would cost society about $68 million.

If we look at the estimated cost per case ($183,333) compared to the costs incurred with community-based treatment and supervision, the difference is dramatic. Maricopa County, Arizona, estimates the cost per day of their sex offender program to be $6.02, or about $2,200 per year. The offender is ordered to assume all costs of weekly group therapy ($25) and polygraph testing. Other costs of treatment, including the physiological evaluations, psychosexual education, and victim and family treatment, may be subsidized by the state, but are paid for by the defendant when possible. Even if the state assumed all costs, including those of the surveillance officer and equipment, the yearly cost would be much less than that of prison: $25,000 per year in many eastern states.

In Arizona, prosecuting and incarcerating a defendant for 7 years and providing victim assistance and treatment would cost $122,000, compared to a 7-year treatment and community supervision plan of $15,400 (see Table 3.1). If that offender can then be maintained for life on regular

TABLE 3.1 Comparative Costs of Prison Versus Probation and Treatment for
Sex Offenders in Arizona

	Probation and Treatment	Prison	Cost Saving per Year for One Offender	Cost Saving per Year for 100 Offenders
Cost per Day	$6.02	$44.00		
Cost per Year	$2,200	$16,000	$13,800	$1,380,000

probation, the cost drops to $720 per year. These costs, along with periodic polygraph testing, could be fully or partially paid by the offender.

Juvenile Offenders

The sex offender issue cannot be examined fully without a discussion of the juvenile offender population. Historically, juveniles were, for the most part, not held accountable for their actions, which were often considered "adolescent experimentation" or met with a "boys will be boys" attitude. Only in the late 1970s and 1980s was the extent and significance of the problem finally acknowledged. Programs specializing in the treatment of juvenile offenders grew from 50 in a 1982 survey to 520 by 1988 (Knopp et al., 1992).

Groth reported that 60 to 80% of adult offenders admitted that they had begun their deviant sexual behaviors as adolescents (Sgroi, 1982). Fifty-seven percent of Abel's group described their deviant arousal beginning in adolescence, many when they were 12 years old or younger. Treatment centers for victims of sexual abuse report that up to 56% of the assailants were under age 18. Groth described molesters and rapists as young as 9, cases which are not uncommon today. A third progressed from compulsive masturbatory activity, repetitive exhibitionism, and/or persistent voyeurism to more serious "hands-on" offenses, every bit as violent and traumatic to their victims as crimes committed by adults.

Why does a child act out sexually? Most experts agree that aggressive social behaviors are learned primarily through observation and by direct experience. The offense cycle as previously described often begins in childhood or early adolescence. "Cultural influences, the socialization process, chaotic, enmeshed or rigid families, imbalances of power and status, or early childhood experiences, particularly those involving sexual trauma, may be important factors in this learning process" (Knopp, 1985, p. 10). Becker describes children who at a very early age do not bond with other people, either their parents or their peers, and have difficulty forming attachments with people. . . . [T]hey have no respect for the rights of other people and are abusive toward other children and take advantage of other children, and have no feeling of remorse or empathy. (Meinig, 1990)

Knopp (1984) reported that sex offenders do not acknowledge a close, nurturing relationship with their fathers, who seem to be either abusive or physically or emotionally absent from the child's life.

Another commonality is the "great confusion about sexuality in general and positive sexuality in particular." There is a perception in our culture that sex is degrading and dirty; "if sex is devalued, then it can be used to degrade or humiliate another person, and sexuality becomes the means of expression of nonsexual needs" (Knopp, 1985, p. 24). The 1988 report from the Task Force on Juvenile Sex Offending echoes the need to be aware of the "inappropriate messages we convey as a society which support the development of exploitation, deviance, violence, aggression, and lack of empathy . . . violence and deviance in entertainment . . . the pairing of sex, degradation and violence" (Knopp, 1985). Good treatment needs to teach young offenders how to redirect their sexual feelings toward appropriate, consensual, and mutually satisfying sexuality.

Tommy was placed on adult probation at age 17, remanded from the justice system after he committed his second offense for sexually abusing 6-year-old and 10-year-old boys. His first sex offense, at age 14, had involved sodomy and threats with a weapon on a 10-year-old. His record also included arson, theft, and illegal drug use.

His family history was chaotic. Both he and his sister had been sexually abused for several years by their alcoholic father; twice during their early years the children had been removed from the home by the state because of neglect and physical abuse. Tommy's mother periodically deserted the children when she could not cope with their father, leaving them to grow up more or less on their own. Tommy spent most of his teen years in some form of juvenile institution, where he also claimed to have engaged in male sexual abuse.

He began his adult probation by causing all the toilets on his jail floor to flood the night before his release. After being penalized an extra month, he appeared to try to straighten out. He was intelligent and a hard worker if motivated. He tried living with his mother, who had become grossly overweight and constantly ill. She kept Tommy bonded to her through her own dysfunctional needs, using him as a meal ticket. He began reverting to old patterns of shoplifting and using illegal drugs, and was eventually revoked to prison when he refused to stay in treatment and was once again arrested for soliciting children for sex.

Becker (1988) reported that the average juvenile offender seen in her clinical studies had listed a total of seven victims, as compared to the average adult offender's total number of 380 victims. That statistic alone, even if it were one fourth as dramatic, should emphasize the importance of juvenile sex offender treatment as a preventive measure.

Prison Programs

Because most early legislation regarding sex offenders centered around the concept of the "sexual psychopath," the uncontrollable rapist who was psychologically sick or criminally insane, many attempts at treating sex offenders took place in state mental institutions. In some states, programs were operated under both jurisdictions, under dual and sometimes conflicting goals of treatment versus supervision and custody. In Alabama, offenders are treated in a comprehensive program located in a maximum security prison, but little community supervision is available. In Arizona, extensive community treatment and surveillance in Phoenix and Tucson contrasts with a part-time prison program that treats only 55 incarcerated offenders out of an estimated population of 2,200. In Salem, Oregon, the state has supported a major correctional treatment program at the Oregon State Hospital since 1978, offering the widest range of treatment modalities available in any single residential setting, including a separate unit serving low-functioning offenders. Oregon's program was the cooperative result of statewide planning, an effort seldom seen in other states.

The Adult Diagnostic and Treatment Center at Avenel, New Jersey, is a semiautonomous, medium security prison exclusively for the evaluation and treatment of adult sex offenders, offering a wide range of programs, and incorporating a prerelease component. In spite of the growth and success of the program, budget cutbacks have forced a reduction in staff that will keep many offenders from getting the treatment they need.

Most experts agree that if a program is located within a prison, it should at least be in a separate facility or wing of the institution. All staff should be dedicated only to that facility and the treatment of sex offenders, and all administrative and security decisions should be made by the director of the unit. Programs that are integrated into the general prison population constitute the majority, and least worthwhile, of any treatment model. "The great rolling momentum of the imprisonment experience overwhelms and overshadows the relatively brief therapeutic contact and nullifies their emotional impact" (Knopp, 1984, p. 123). Groth (Knopp, 1984, pp. 119-121) lists three defects in prison-based treatment programs:

1. The effects of prison labeling can reinforce the sex offender's minimization and denial of his sex-offense problem and encourage avoidance of therapy.

2 The sex offender's exposure to the prison's value system is at cross-purposes with treatment.

3. Prison structure and supervision create dependency and an unreal environment for the sex offender.

Those programs that are well managed and effective are usually run by committed staff who operate with the support of an enlightened administration. These are not necessarily in the most populated or "cutting edge" states. Alabama effectively treats 84 offenders in its Bullock County Correctional Facility, utilizing separate dormitory facilities, extensive evaluation procedures, the penile plethysmograph, group and behavioral therapy, and, most recently, polygraphy. The offender must be within 2 to 3 years of release, must admit guilt, and must give a detailed account of offense history. With space and dollars at a premium, most systems will not waste time on offenders who don't want to work on their issues. At present 109 adult prisons in 42 states offer some type of sex offender treatment (Knopp et al., 1992).

For many offenders, a 2- or 3-year residential program followed by gradual release into the community under specialized supervision would be practical. The state of Vermont appears to be most effective at assessing risk and combining incarceration with treatment. Unfortunately, only a small percentage of the 85,000 sex offender inmates nationwide will receive such treatment, yet 90% of them, having spent 4 or 6 or 10 years working on their fantasies, will eventually be back on the streets.

Pharmacologic Treatment

Use of antiandrogenic drugs in working with sex offenders has been practiced for many years, but it remains controversial and relatively expensive. Sapp and Vaughn (1991) report that of the 73 prison programs they studied, 9 use organic treatment to some degree; however, 45 of the program directors stated that they would use biological techniques if they could. Knopp et al. (1992) report that Depo-Provera is used in 11% of community-based programs.

Depo-Provera, or medroxyprogesterone acetate (MPA) is a hormone that reduces testosterone levels and thus the sex drive. Most notable for their work in this area are Dr. John Money and Dr. Fred Berlin of Johns Hopkins Medical School in Baltimore. At the Hopkins clinic, patients are evaluated to determine their degree of "compulsivity," such as highly compulsive exhibitionists who request help in controlling their urges. Offenders must come to the clinic every week for an injection that costs them approximately $50. Marshall cautions that therapists who use these procedures do not expect these medications to eliminate sex offending.

> Rather they are principally used as a way of reducing sexual activity to controllable levels in those offenders whose sex drive seems so excessively high as to put them at serious immediate risk to reoffend and to render then unresponsive to psychological interventions. (Marshall et al., 1991, p. 471)

Berlin and Meinecke (1981) reported that only 3 of 20 patients in one study showed recurrence of sexually deviant behavior while taking medication. However, 11 patients discontinued taking MPA against medical advice, and 10 of those 11 reoffended. Five were homosexual pedophiles. The authors concluded that the men seemed to do well in response to MPA as long as they continued taking it. Bradford (1988) reported success in reducing deviant arousal in 12 offenders given the androgen inhibitor CPA (cyproterone acetate). Becker (1992) in her review of the studies to date agrees with Marshall and his colleagues that controlled outcome studies with sufficient sample sizes should be conducted. Limited results thus far do not always distinguish between the effectiveness of the drug and the cognitive-behavioral therapy that may also be a component of treatment. Even though MPA and CPA do appear to be effective in some offenders, the side effects, cost, and high drop-out rates have so far resulted in limited use in most treatment programs.

Female Offenders

The number of convicted female offenders is increasing, although official reports can be misleading if crimes of prostitution are included. Finkelhor (1984) reports that approximately 34% of sexually abused males and 13% of sexually abused females had been victimized by females. In approximately half the cases, the female offender was acting in the company of others. Viewing females as perpetrators of sexual abuse, perhaps parallel to viewing males as victims, challenges society's stereotypes.

Although there is a paucity of research and data on female offenders, some clinicians have attempted to focus on specialized groups and compare them to male offenders. In a study of 25 female offenders in a Minnesota program, the women expressed many of the same needs and emotions as males in events leading up to their offenses. Two factors seem to differ: half the women offended in collusion with male partners and all but one related a history of sexual abuse as children, either in or out of the family or both. (The number of male offenders sexually abused as children appears to be about 30%.) Many women carry their childhood baggage with them:

> Gwen, age 24, was placed on probation after she orally raped her 6-year-old son. She was originally uncooperative and resistant to therapy, even though she took responsibility for her actions. She spent much of her time defending her relationship with her abusive boyfriend, who had watched her molest her child. After he was gone, she was placed in a women offenders' group and began examining her behavior in depth.
>
> She had been sexually used as a child by her father and uncle, as had her sisters. By the time she was 14, she had left the house and spent a year as a prostitute. When she came home, her father began having sex with her again. She and the father of her child were heavy drug users. Her next relationship was equally dysfunctional. However, after 2 years in therapy, and after meeting a man totally different from the others in her life, she was recovered enough to again gain custody of her son from the state and try to live a normal life.

Male and female offenders in therapy frequently describe instances of childhood sexual exploitation by mothers, baby-sitters, older sisters, and other caretakers, suggesting that instances of female abuse have long gone unreported and unresolved.

Future Directions

While theoretical debates and research continues, courts are faced with sentencing sex offenders in record numbers. Already three states, Washington, Minnesota, and Maine, list sex offenders as half their prison census (Morris & Tonry, 1990). The treatment/incarceration dilemma persists, as the pendulum swings from state to state. We must take stock of the fact that we have gained much knowledge in the past 15 years about a major issue that had rarely been discussed by the public, the media, or the professional literature. Abel and Osborn (1992, p. 301) state that "no public health problem has ever been reduced significantly by treating individuals after the fact. Instead, the cause of the problem must be addressed." Both the criminal justice and the treatment communities are beginning to realize that the combined efforts of both will be necessary to manage the problem. Few offenders remain in treatment on their own.

Courts must demand thorough risk evaluations from professionals who have developed the special skills and knowledge to effectively treat the sex offender. Prosecutors and defense attorneys alike should demand that legislatures implement rational and enlightened sentencing and punishment policies, taking a close look at the monetary implications of those policies. We can reduce sexual violence cost-effectively in community corrections by utilizing the services of treatment experts, physiological checkups, specialized officers, and a continuum of supervision. Most important, greater focus should be placed in the area which will have the greatest impact on victims—the juvenile offender. If we can intervene early and effectively with a teenage pedophile, we may save 300 or 400 child victims from harm.

The survivors of sexual trauma impact our society in a hundred ways: teenage girls who become self-destructive drug abusers, premature mothers, prostitutes, school dropouts, wives of abusive men, mothers of another generation of abused children. Conflicted young boys can grow up to repeat their own victimization, some as prostitutes, some as offenders, exponentially and predictably. It is an issue we cannot, in any sense, afford to ignore.

Discussion Questions

1. How did the Abel-Becker study of sex offenders contribute to our knowledge of these offenders and their paraphilias?
2. Based on data accumulated up to this time, what appear to be the highest risk factors involved in sex offender recidivism?
3. How has physiological testing contributed to the treatment and supervision of sex offenders? How is it controversial?
4. Discuss the cost savings in supervising certain sex offenders in the community and how accepting you think society is of the increasing use of this alternative to incarceration.
5. What are the disadvantages to intensive sex offender treatment in the prison system? How might these disadvantages be resolved?
6. Why is it important to impact the juvenile offender? Discuss the development of sexual violence in juveniles and its implications on the future of the criminal justice system.

References

Abel, G. G., Becker, J. V., Blanchard, E., & Djenderedjian, A. (1978). Differentiating sexual aggressives with penile measures. *Criminal Justice and Behavior, 5*(4), 315-332.

Abel, G. G., Mittelman, M. S., & Becker, J. V. (1985). Sexual offenders: Results of assessment and recommendations for treatment. In M. H. Ben-Aron, S. J. Hucker, & C. D. Webster (Eds.), *Clinical criminology: The assessment and treatment of criminal behavior* (pp. 191-205). Toronto: University of Toronto.

Abel, G. G., & Osborn, C. (1992). Stopping sexual violence. *Psychiatric Annals, 22*(6), 301-306.

Abrams, S., & Abrams, J. B. (1993). *Polygraph testing of the pedophile.* Portland, OR: Ryan Gwinner Press.

Association for the Treatment of Sexual Abusers. (1991). History of the Jackson County Sexual Offender Treatment Program. *ATSA Professional Forum, 5*(2), 3-10.

Barbaree, H. E., & Marshall, W. L. (1988). Deviant sexual arousal, offense history, and demographic variables as predictors of reoffense among child molesters. *Behavioral Science and the Law, 6,* 267-280.

Becker, J. V. (1988). Adolescent sex offenders. *Behavior Therapist, 11*(9), 185-187.

Becker, J. V. (1992). Evaluation of treatment outcome for adult perpetrators of child sexual abuse. *Criminal Justice and Behavior, 19*(1), 74-92.

Berlin, F. S., & Meinecke, C. F. (1981). Treatment of sex offenders with antiandrogenic medication: Conceptualization, review of treatment modalities, and preliminary findings. *American Journal of Psychiatry, 138,* 601-607.

Breiling, J. (1991, November). A Washington perspective: Major developments and new issues. Paper presented at the Tenth Annual Research Conference of the Association for the Treatment of Sexual Abusers, Fort Worth, TX.

Burgess, A. W., Groth, A. N., Holmstrom, L. L., & Sgroi, S. M. (1982). *Sexual assault of children and adolescents.* Lexington, MA: Lexington.

Carnes, P. (1983). *Out of the shadows.* Minneapolis: CompCare.

Contact Center, Inc. (1992). *Corrections compendium.* Lincoln, NE: Author.

Emerick, R. L. (1991). *Continuing education manual for providers of management and treatment of convicted sexual abusers and their victims.* Phoenix, AZ: Western Correctional Association Working Edition.

Finkelhor, D. (1984). *Child sexual abuse: New theory and research.* New York: Free Press.

Furby, L., Weinrott, M. R., & Blackshaw, L. (1989). Sex offender recidivism: A review. *Psychological Bulletin, 105*(1), 3-30.

Gray, S. (1991). Therapeutic models for the treatment of sex offenders. In R. Emerick (Ed.), *Continuing education manual for providers of management and treatment of convicted sexual abusers and their victims.* Phoenix, AZ: Western Correctional Association Working Edition.

Groth, N. (1979). *Men who rape: The psychology of the offender.* New York: Plenum.

Herman, J. (1988). Considering sex offenders. *Signs, 13,* 695-724.

Hindman, J. (1989). *Just before dawn.* Ontario, OR: Alexandria.

Kinsey, A. C., Pomeroy, W. B., Martin, C. E., & Gebhard, P. H. (1953). *Sexual behavior in the human female.* Philadelphia: W. B. Saunders.

Knopp, F. H. (1984). *Retraining adult sex offenders: Methods and models.* Orwell, VT: Safer Society.

Knopp, F. H. (1985). *The youthful sex offender: The rationale and goals of early intervention and treatment.* Orwell, VT: Safer Society.

Knopp, F. H., Freeman-Longo, R., & Stevenson, W. (1992). *Nationwide survey of juvenile & adult sex-offender treatment programs and models.* Orwell, VT: Safer Society.

Koss, M. P., Gidycz, C. A., & Wisniewski, N. (1987). The scope of rape: Incidence and prevalence of sexual aggression and victimization in a national sample of students in higher education. *Journal of Consulting and Clinical Psychology, 55,* 162-170.

Laws, D. R. (1989). *Relapse prevention with sex offenders.* New York: Guilford.

Maletsky, B. M. (1991). *Treating the sexual offender.* Newbury Park, CA: Sage.

Marques, J., & Day, D. M., Nelson, C., & West, M. (1993). Findings and recommendations from California's Experimental Treatment Program. In J. Graham, G. Hall, R. Hirshman, & M. Zaragoza (Eds.), *Sexual aggressors: Issues in assessment and treatment* (pp. 197-214). Bristol, PA: Taylor and Francis.

Marques, J., Day, D. M., Nelson, C., & Miner, M. H. (1989). The Sex Offender Treatment and Evaluation Project: California's relapse prevention program. In R. Laws (Ed.), *Relapse prevention with sex offenders* (pp. 247-267). New York: Guilford.

Marshall, W. L., & Barbaree, H. E. (1990). Outcome of comprehensive cognitive-behavioral treatment programs. In W. L. Marshall, D. R. Laws, & H. E. Barbaree (Eds.), *Handbook of sexual assault: Issues, theories and treatment of the offender* (pp. 363-385). New York: Plenum.

Marshall, W. L., Jones, R., Ward, T., Johnston, P., & Barbaree, H. E. (1991). Treatment outcome with sex offenders. *Clinical Psychology Review, 11,* 465-485.

McGrath, R. (1991). Sex offender risk assessment and disposition planning: A review of empirical and clinical findings. *International Journal of Offender Therapy and Comparative Criminology, 35,* 329-351.

Meinig, M. B. (1992, February). Profile: Judith Becker. *Violence Update, 2,* 4-10.

Morris, N., & Tonry, M. (1990). *Between prison and probation.* New York: Oxford University Press.

Norris, C. (1991, November). The feasibility of treating the psychopath in a residential sex offender program. Paper presented at the National Conference of the Association for the Treatment of Sexual Abusers, Fort Worth, TX.

O'Connell, M., Leberg, E., & Donaldson, C. (1990). *Working with sex offenders: Guidelines for therapist selection.* Newbury Park, CA: Sage.

Patton, M. Q. (1991). *Family sexual abuse: Frontline research and evaluation.* Newbury Park, CA: Sage.

Pithers, W. D., & Laws, D. R. (1988). The penile plethysmograph. In B. K. Schwartz (Ed.), *A practitioner's guide to treating the incarcerated male sex offender* (pp. 85-94). Washington, DC: Author.

Prentky, R., & Burgess, A. (1990). Rehabilitation of child molesters: A cost-benefit analysis. *American Journal of Orthopsychiatry, 60,* 108-117.

Salter, A. (1988). *Treating child sex offenders and victims: A practical guide.* Newbury Park, CA: Sage.

Sapp, A. D., & Vaughn, M. S. (1991). Sex offender rehabilitation programs in state prisons: A nationwide survey. *Journal of Offender Rehabilitation, 17,* 55-75.

Schwartz, B. K. (Ed.). (1988). *A practitioner's guide to treating the incarcerated male sex offender.* Washington, DC: U.S. Department of Justice.

Scully, D. (1990). *Understanding sexual violence.* Cambridge, MA: Unwin Hyman.

Sgroi, S. (1982). *Handbook of clinical intervention in child sexual abuse.* Lexington, MA: D. C. Heath.

U.S. Department of Health & Human Services. (1992). Working Paper #1 of the National Center on Child Abuse and Neglect Clearing House. Washington, DC: Author.

Williams, L., & Finkelhor, D. (1992). The characteristics of incestuous fathers. Unpublished manuscript, University of New Hampshire Research Lab.

Wolf, S. C. (1984, November). A multi-factor model of deviant Sexuality. Presented at the Third International Conference on Victimology, Lisbon, Portugal.

4

White-Collar Crime

Prevalence, Trends, and Costs

CHARLES F. WELLFORD

BARTON L. INGRAHAM

In recent years, the observation that "more money has been stolen at the point of a fountain pen than at the point of a gun" (Schmalleger, 1991) has been forcefully brought to our attention. The names of Ivan Boesky and Michael Milken have become symbols for the rampant abuse of financial markets in the 1980s. Boesky is estimated to have earned more than $200 million from insider trading, and Milken's fine of $600 million left him with an estimated $400 million in net worth. Our federal government continues to struggle to fund the bailout of failed savings and loans. Charles Keating's alleged criminal mismanagement of the Lincoln Savings and Loan will cost taxpayers an estimated $2.5 billion, and the rescue of Silverado Savings and Loan (the financial base for President Bush's son) will cost approximately $1 billion. In total, the savings and loan scandal will cost taxpayers 400 to 500 billion dollars. Chambliss (1988) has concluded that crime is an integral part of business in contemporary American society.[1]

As we have become more aware of the cost and impact of crimes committed with "the pen" rather than the gun (for examples, see Bequai, 1979; Ermann & Lundman, 1987; Hagan & Parker, 1985; Hill, 1987; and Pizzo, Fricker, & Muolo, 1989), we have begun to focus more attention on defining, counting, and estimating the cost of what criminologists have called white-collar crime. To date there are no acceptable estimates of the total cost of this type of crime. The U.S. Chamber of Commerce has estimated that employee theft alone accounts for 20% of the cost of all manufactured goods. However, this estimate is poorly constructed and obviously ignores other forms of business crimes. The essential secret nature of this type of crime (i.e., the "victims" are not aware of the fact that they have been victimized) makes counting this type of crime very difficult (Reiss, 1987; Wheeler & Rothman, 1982).

In this chapter we explore this problem by considering how white-collar crime should be defined and how it can be better counted. Until these issues are resolved we will continue to be ignorant of the extent and impact of this type of crime.

Toward a National Assessment of White-Collar Crime

Over 50 years ago Edwin Sutherland introduced the concept of white-collar crime to criminal justice officials, criminologists, and the public. Since that time, the concept has become an integral part of criminological research and in recent years has frequently been a type of crime of intense interest to policy makers and to the public. This interest has reached its peak most recently with increased understanding of the savings and loan crisis and the allegations of significant insider fraud. Increasingly, public opinion polls have demonstrated that the general public has come to recognize the importance of white-collar crime and to demand government action to prevent and control it. During this 50-year period much research has been done, primarily of a case study nature, to better understand the occurrence of white-collar crime. A smaller number of larger scale studies have analyzed the criminal prosecution of white-collar crimes.

Throughout this period, there has been a recognition that the absence of a national uniform white-collar crime reporting system has hampered our ability to understand the phenomenon and to develop appropriate strategies for its prevention and control. The Bureau of Justice Statistics has indicated an interest in determining whether such a system is feasible at this time. Prior research conducted by Reiss and Biderman (1980) suggested that the difficulties of the measurement of white-collar crime were almost insurmountable. This was because the concept was poorly defined, poorly understood, and therefore difficult to measure in any consistent way across various units of the government and geographical areas. The position taken in this chapter is that it is now time to begin the construction of a national uniform white-collar crime reporting system. Although such a system cannot possibly capture all instances of white-collar crime, it can focus on instances of white-collar crime on which there is a clear agreement. With it we can attempt to move beyond the obvious limitations of understanding white-collar crime only through the instances when it results in criminal prosecution.

In order to develop the rationale for a national uniform white-collar crime reporting system, this chapter will first consider the obvious difficulties in defining white-collar crime, will review current efforts to provide data on white-collar crime, and will propose the steps that could be taken to begin the collection, analysis, and routine distribution of white-collar crime data.

Definitions of White-Collar Crime

A consensus exists among scholars today that the term "white-collar crime" lacks precision and covers an extremely broad spectrum of illegal behaviors committed by both individuals and organizations (Block & Geis, 1970, p. 299; Clinard & Quinney, 1967, pp. 130-132; Coleman, 1987, p. 406; Geis & Stotland, 1980, p. 11). This has led many scholars to break down the concept into smaller, more homogeneous categories of behavior, such as occupational crime (Clinard & Quinney, 1967; Quinney, 1964); business crime (Conklin, 1977); organizational crime (Reasons, 1982; Schrager & Short, 1977), corporate crime (Clinard & Yeager, 1980), elite deviance (Simon & Eitzen, 1986), corporate and governmental deviance (Ermann & Lundman, 1982), and organizational deviance (Douglas & Johnson, 1977). Some of these subcategories of white-collar crime will be discussed in greater detail later in this chapter. For the moment it needs to be emphasized that there is also substantial agreement, in academic circles at least, that what is being described is recognizable and distinct in many ways from ordinary, or "street," crime.

Sutherland's Definition

According to Sutherland (1983), "White-collar crime may be defined approximately as a crime committed by a person of respectability and high social status in the course of his occupation" (p. 7). As originally formulated, this definition requires a considerable amount of interpretation. It has only two identifying criteria: (a) that the "crime" be committed by a person who occupies a position that entitles him to respect and high social status; and (b) that the "crime" be committed by that person "in the course of his occupation."

Sutherland (1983) went on to say that the definition "excludes many crimes of the upper class such as most cases of murder, intoxication, or adultery, since these are not part of occupational procedures. Also, it excludes the confidence games of wealthy members of the underworld, since they are not persons of respectability and high social status" (p. 7). Although he added in a footnote (p. 7, n. 7) that the term was meant to apply "principally" to the business managers and executives of corporations, it is clear from later comments that he also intended to include high-status politicians (p. 8) and professionals (p. 9). Nevertheless, almost the entirety of his book is taken up with the discussion of the violation by major U.S. corporations of federal regulatory laws (antitrust laws, patent-trademark-copyright infringement, misleading advertising, unfair labor practices under the National Labor Relations Act, violations of securities and banking regulations, wartime price regulation, and health and safety laws). In a later chapter (Chapter 14) he describes white-collar crime as "organized crime," not in the sense that we use the term today, but meaning crime committed in the context of an organization, with organizational norms and values favoring the evasion or violation of laws and regulations.

Sutherland has been criticized for his vague and expansive definition of "crime." In his seminal writings on white-collar crime (1945; 1983, chap. 4), he expanded the concept of "crime" (for the purposes of studying the phenomenon) to include civil prosecutions for injunctions or private actions for civil damages whenever the statute provided both civil *and* *criminal* sanctions for the same acts and whenever the sanction requested or imposed could be characterized as "punitive." Without going into the fine points of the debate as to how many law violations of civil/criminal statutes one should count as "crimes," we merely wish to observe here two facts that emerge not only from research that has already been done (e.g., Clinard & Yeager, 1980, pp. 149-150; Shapiro, 1984; Sutherland, 1983) but also from our own preliminary research.

1. In situations where the law offers the option of proceeding either civilly (in court or in administrative proceedings) or criminally, the usual choice is civil prosecution; criminal prosecutions are brought in only a small percentage of the cases reported to the enforcement agency.

2. It is possible, with white-collar crimes, to pick a point in the process, between initial report of the offense to the enforcement agency and referral to the

prosecutor, where a determination is made that a probably prosecutable offense exists, whether or not the decision is made later to prosecute.

Thus, in light of these two facts, a statistical analysis of white-collar crime, in order not to underestimate the amount of such crime, must follow Sutherland to the extent of including within the count acts that have not yet received the label of crime by being the subject of a criminal prosecution.

In sum, this academic/criminological conception of white-collar crime, derived from the seminal work of Edwin Sutherland (1983) and greatly elaborated since then by his successors, seems to have as its core the commission of a nonviolent illegal act within an organizational context by an individual who does not normally regard himself as a criminal because most of his or her time is spent in legitimate activities. Nevertheless, there is a continuing ambiguity about the extent to which the crime must necessarily be committed within the context of an organization, and, if it is, whether the offense must be committed *for* the organization or can also be committed *against* it (e.g., embezzlement). Thus the concept has expanded to include many economic crimes that were not originally within the scope of what Sutherland considered "white-collar crime."

Practitioner Definitions

In the course of our analysis of white-collar crime we mailed a questionnaire to the attorneys general of all 50 states in order to determine the nature and extent of their white-collar crime enforcement activities. We received returns from 38 of the states. Respondents were asked to describe their understandings of the concept or definition of white-collar crime, and further to list the kinds of crime each would include within its definition. An interesting finding is that most of our respondents do not have a definition. Indeed, one stated that although he could not define it, he knew white-collar crime when he saw it. Several respondents had as an operating definition either the Edelhertz definition (see below) or one approximating that found in *Black's Law Dictionary.*[2] Perhaps the most common "definition" given was one that merely pointed to a list of representative crimes.

As for the second part of the question, we received a variety of answers. From these responses we have compiled a list of 29 crimes. A perusal of this list reveals very broad coverage of nonviolent economic crimes.

We have not conducted a similar survey of federal prosecutors (94 U.S. attorneys), but there is impressionistic evidence that they share the views and perspectives of their state counterparts. In general, they both look more to the *way* the crime is committed (by violation of trust, fraud, or concealment; nonphysical, nonviolent means) than to the nature or social status of the offender or the social context in which the crime is committed. For example, in a Report of the U.S. Attorney-General entitled *National Priorities for the Investigation and Prosecution of White Collar Crime* (U.S. Department of Justice, Office of the Attorney General, 1980, p. 5), white-collar crimes are identified as "those classes of non-violent illegal activities which principally involve traditional notions of deceit, deception, concealment, manipulation, breach of trust, subterfuge, or illegal circumvention." The Federal Bureau of Investigation's operating definition is similar (U.S. Department of Justice, Office of the Attorney General, 1980, p. 5):

> Those illegal acts characterized by deceit, concealment, violation of trust, and not dependent upon the application or threat of physical force or violence. They are committed to obtain money, property, or services; or to avoid the payment or loss of money, property, or services; or to secure personal or business advantage.

The most scholarly exposition of the kind of definition favored by practitioners is that of Herbert Edelhertz (1970). Edelhertz was chief of the Fraud Section, Criminal Division of the U.S. Department of Justice, at the time he wrote his monograph *The Nature, Impact and Prosecution of White-Collar Crime* for the National Institute of Law Enforcement and Criminal Justice, and his approach reflects the practical concerns of prosecutors in identifying crimes by their act attributes rather than by their perpetrator attributes. His definition, which greatly resembles the FBI's working definition (see above) and probably influenced it, is as follows: "an illegal act or series of illegal acts committed by non-physical means and by concealment or guile to obtain money or property to avoid the payment or loss of money or property, or to obtain business or personal advantage" (1970, p. 3). Edelhertz lays great stress on intentional fraud or concealment as a necessary aspect of all white-collar offenses (1970, pp. 12-18), but his list of white-collar crimes (1970, pp. 73-75, Appendix A) includes crimes that do not necessarily involve acts of fraud, concealment, or even violations or abuses of trust (e.g., some antitrust violations, some housing code violations, some security law violations, etc.). Therefore, in some respects, Edelhertz's definition is too restrictive and would omit crimes that everyone would regard as "white-collar."

Edelhertz also suggests that for the purposes of distinguishing crimes according to the motivations of the perpetrators and hence assisting in programs of deterrence and prevention, and of identifying the particular environments that breed certain forms of white-collar crime, it would be useful to divide the phenomenon into subcategories (1970, pp. 19-20). He suggests the following:

1. Crimes committed by persons operating on an individual, *ad hoc* basis, for personal gain in a nonbusiness context (hereinafter referred to as *"personal crimes"*).
2. Crimes committed in the course of their occupations by those operating inside businesses, Government, or other establishments, or in a professional capacity, in violation of their duty of loyalty and fidelity to employer or client (hereinafter referred to as *"abuses of trust"*).
3. Crimes incidental to and committed in furtherance of business operations, but not the central purpose of such business operations (herein after referred to as *"business crimes"*).
4. White collar crime as a business, or as the central activity of the business (hereinafter referred to as *"con games"*).

In sum, the major challenge to the definition of academic white-collar crime of scholars has been posed by the law enforcement community. The latter has greatly expanded the category beyond the core concept first formulated by Sutherland. It now includes virtually any nonviolent crime committed for financial gain or personal advancement by persons whose occupational status is entrepreneurial, professional, or semiprofessional and sometimes by persons of no legitimate occupation or profession. Indeed, the category is now so broad as to demand a breakdown of the concept into subcategories so that data regarding these subclassifications can be studied separately.

Because of the complexity of this white-collar crime, the need to differentiate it has become apparent. Coleman (1989) and Green (1990) have begun to focus our attention on different types of white-collar crime. Coleman notes a distinction based on crimes affecting property and those affecting persons. He argues that at least these two types need to be distinguished because of their different social impacts and costs.

Green deals only with crimes committed during the course of a legitimate occupation. He describes four types: (a) crimes to benefit the employee's organization; (b) crimes of abuse of state authority; (c) crimes by professionals (directors, lawyers, etc.) in the course of their profession; and (d) individual employee crimes (e.g., employee theft). We build upon Green's approach below to elaborate a more comprehensive typology to cover all white-collar crimes, including occupational crimes.

Proposed Working Definitions
of Three Classes of White-Collar Crime

Drawing on our analysis and critique of existing definitions of white-collar crime, we propose a tripartite division of the concept into the following categories:

1. **BUSINESS AND PROFESSIONAL CRIMES:** nonviolent crimes committed by or on behalf of businesses, professional organizations, and political organizations for profit or enhancement.[3]
2. **OCCUPATIONAL CRIMES:** business-, profession-, party-related crimes of fraud,[4] misappropriation,[5] and corruption,[6] committed by persons in a business, professional, or political setting for purely personal gain and to the detriment of the business, professional group, or political organization for which the perpetrators are working. (Unlike the crimes in category 1, these could be referred to as "*anti*-business" crimes, inasmuch as they benefit the perpetrator without conferring any benefit on the group for which he works.)
3. **INDIVIDUAL FRAUDS:** nonbusiness, nonoccupational crimes of fraud, misappropriation, and corruption committed by individuals alone or in concert with others. Examples are tax fraud and evasion; forgery and counterfeiting; individual bribery of a public official; confidence games and other scams; consumer frauds committed neither by nor against businesses; and self-enrichment frauds committed by individual investors and buyers.

This tripartite division has several advantages. It is useful for government to make a distinction between how much crime is being committed every year by businesses, the professions (as organizations), and political groups and how much is being committed *against* them (and also against the general public) by persons within their ranks.

This information will be of interest not only to the public and to criminologists analyzing different kinds of economic crimes, but also to businessmen and professionals. Two questions may be posed: (a) *Where to point the accusing finger.* If the public is being defrauded, is it really businesses and the professions as organizations that are doing so, or is it the work of dishonest and corrupt employees and officials for whose wrongs the organizations cannot be blamed? (b) *Where remedial measures should be taken.* Does the ethical climate of the business promote probusiness but anticonsumer crime, or is management failing to screen out corrupt employees or to supervise their activities?

Counting White-Collar Crime

Fundamentally, the problem of counting white-collar crime involves two issues: first, selection of the types of statutory or regulatory violations that will be included within the categories of white-collar crimes that we have designated, and second, the determination of how an act of the type included within one of our categories is to be operationalized. The first problem involves operationalizing the concept; the second, operationalizing indicators of the concept.

A first step in developing a national white-collar crime reporting system focusing on federal agencies would be to operationalize the definitions that we have proposed for white-collar crime. To that end we have considered all of the federal laws we could identify that grant to agencies the ability to control various behaviors that could be considered white-collar crime, and we have categorized those statutes under the three types of white-collar crime noted above (available from authors upon request). As one might expect, there are some statutes where there would be, because of the general nature of the statute, overlap between the various categories. These statutes must be given further consideration so that it can be decided either that those particular statutes not be included, or that those more familiar with the operation of those statutes determine which agencies have primary responsibility and what types of cases actually fall under them. With that information, one should be able, in the vast majority of cases, to assign statutes to particular categories of white-collar crime.

That step completed, the next step would be to decide what indicators will be used to count violations of the particular statutes chosen as white-collar crimes. After reviewing the information available in the federal agencies and considering the wide range of statutes, we recommend that the national white-collar crime reporting system proceed in the following manner. Four agencies have substantial amounts of information on the various indicators that we have suggested. These are: (a) the Securities and Exchange Commission, (b) the Internal Revenue Service, (c) the Office of the Comptroller General, and (d) the Federal Bureau of Investigation. Each of these agencies has developed sophisticated management information systems to track matters that are referred to them, and each of these agencies has a primary involvement in the white-collar crime area. We estimate, based on a review of the statutes falling within our three categories, that these agencies, together, handle (civilly, criminally, or administratively) over 60% of all white-collar crimes and civil violations that are investigated by the federal agencies.

These agencies provide us with an opportunity to move beyond arrests or prosecutions in estimating the extent of white-collar crime. Using the classic funnel model that has been used to describe more conventional crimes, we suggest moving back from the arrest information to the white-collar equivalent of "crimes known to police."

The concept of "crimes known to police" has been an important one in the development of data for a national counting of ordinary crimes. The *Uniform Crime Reports* rely upon crimes known to police as their primary measure of the extent of crime, and although they recognize that this is not a measure of the true extent of crime, it has proved to be important particularly in identifying crime trends and in helping us understand the

activities and crimes in which police are involved. With the cooperation
of the above-mentioned agencies, a similar system could be initiated for
white-collar crime. In each of these agencies, there is a threshold that must
be reached before the agency will log in the event as something they are
investigating. It is at this point that a trained, competent professional
makes a determination that an allegation or information provided is of
sufficient merit to warrant further investigation by the agency. This triggers a system of record keeping that provides detailed information on the
nature of the case, processing of the case, and its eventual outcome. By
collecting this information, the federal government could initiate a national uniform white-collar crime-reporting system that would tell us the
numbers of white-collar crimes known to the agencies that are directly
responsible for their prevention and control and would allow us to track
those matters through to their eventual disposition, whether administratively, civilly, criminally, or otherwise.

These systems, particularly those at the Securities and Exchange Commission, the IRS, and the Office of the Comptroller General, contain
substantial amounts of information about the matters under their consideration and provide detailed information on the processing of the cases.

Other agencies are moving in the direction of establishing systems that
could also participate in this proposed national uniform white-collar crime
reporting system. The Environmental Protection Agency, the various in-
spectors general offices, and all regulatory agencies that have undertaken
similar automation that could be included in the proposed system.

The fundamental point, however, is that this system would provide
information on cases prior to the time of arrest and/or prosecution. That
would considerably extend our knowledge of white-collar crimes (particularly their number and prevalence) to a degree comparable to crimes
reported to police in the case of street crimes. At the same time it would
provide us with information about victims and offenders as both are
identified in these systems.

It is therefore our recommendation that the federal government undertake the following plan. First, the Attorney General should bring together
the heads of the federal agencies just mentioned to discuss the beginnings
of the national uniform white-collar crime reporting system. These discussions would be to describe the proposed system and to gain their assur-
ances that information maintained in each agency's information system
would be provided. Second, all other regulatory agencies with responsibilities for other white-collar crime activities would be contacted to secure
their participation. Third, the primary agencies would agree to provide
data from their information systems on all activities for each year specified. This would include matters opened, cases closed, and all the infor-

mation describing activities about the nature of cases and their processing between those two points. These data would then be assembled by agency and aggregated for totals on the matters opened and the matters closed, with descriptions of the activities for each category. Fourth, as time progresses, the system would be expanded by adding other federal agencies, particularly focusing on the agencies that have primary responsibility for the statutes noted in our analysis of the white-collar crime concept. In addition, in order to provide total coverage, a sample of all statutes not routinely included in the report would be collected by contacting the specific agencies with responsibility for those statutes and securing similar information from their records system. Once this system was operating, we could develop estimates of white-collar crime for the entire federal system, although the routine collection would only be for those primary agencies that can easily supply that information due to their current levels of automation. Fifth, the federal government should at the same time undertake an effort to encourage states to develop state uniform white-collar crime-reporting systems. It should establish guidelines for these systems and should provide funding to states where the development of such systems would materially increase our ability to assess the extent of white-collar crime. Finally, there will be the need for a series of reliability and validity studies, or audits, of those federal agencies' management information systems that are reporting to the national program. These audits should be directed primarily toward understanding the degree to which the systems are accurately capturing and fully reporting information on white-collar crime.

We think this program of a national white-collar crime-reporting system, limited though it would be, would be of significant benefit for understanding white-collar crime and would open up a vast area for further research on trends and developments in white-collar crime activities. We recognize that this system would not be the perfect measure of white-collar crime, that it would be subject to the vagaries of administrative decisions within agencies, and that it would obviously undercount the true extent of white-collar crime. The same can be said, of course, for almost any government statistical system, and particularly those that deal with agency-based measures of criminal activity, but we think this is a reasonable approach for moving toward a comprehensive national white-collar crime-reporting system. If the federal government and Bureau of Justice Statistics wait until the perfect system can be launched, we will continue to have very limited data to help us understand and through that understanding control white-collar crime.

The model we have proposed would not be excessively expensive. Fundamentally, the systems for data collection are in place, and the data are being collected in various agencies. What needs to be done is to capture those collections and to develop the formats for organizing those disparate data systems into a common reporting system. We think this could be done at a very reasonable cost, perhaps on the order of $250,000 to $300,000 per year. The costs of the other aspects of the program, such as the development of state systems and the development of audits for federal agencies, are more difficult to estimate, but these estimates could easily be made during the next stage of the development of the national uniform white-collar crime-reporting system.

Discussion Questions

1. What is white-collar crime? How do the different approaches to defining it affect how we respond to it?
2. Why has law enforcement not responded to white-collar crime as aggressively as it has to street crime?
3. White-collar crime victims do not usually know they are victims. What can we do to change this situation?
4. The largest set of white-collar crimes in recent years was the savings and loan crisis. How was this crisis discovered? Select one such bank failure and analyze it using the theories and classifications of white-collar crime discussed in this chapter.
5. Why do we need to find a better way to estimate the number and costs of white-collar crime? Who would use this information? How?
6. Select one kind of white-collar crime and develop a plan to reduce its occurrence. What could citizens do to prevent and control the extent and costs of white-collar crime? What could police and courts do?

Notes

1. For a careful analysis of white-collar crime and its role in corporate activities, see Simpson (1992).

2. *Black's Law Dictionary* (5th ed., 1979, pp. 1431-1432) describes white-collar crimes as "law violations by corporations or individuals including theft or fraud and other violations of trust committed in the course of the offender's occupation (e.g., embezzlement, price fixing, antitrust violations, and the like)."

3. A more precise definition of this category of white-collar crime is: a regulatory offense committed by a legal organization, an owner, manager, or agent of a legitimate business, a professional, or a public official or public employee for the purpose of enhancing the value of that person's business or his or her professional, political, or occupational well-being.

"For the purpose of enhancing the value of that person's business or his or her professional, political, or occupational well-being." The motivation for white-collar crime is often mixed. A white-collar offender may recognize his act as being illegal, and perhaps even as harmful to his organization in the short term, but he or she may also see it as enhancing his or her position within the organization and as justified in the long-term interests of that organization and its goals. Embezzlements and similar transactions, designed merely to bleed an organization of its funds and assets for personal enrichment, however, cannot be regarded in this light and are excluded.

4. "Fraud" may be more particularly defined as the intentional misleading of a person through information known or believed to be false, inaccurate, or misleading or by concealment of information that there is a legal duty to impart.

5. "Misappropriation" is defined as the nonviolent acquisition of possession/title, use, or disposition of anything of value with the intent of fraudulently terminating or abridging the legal interest of another, whether that intent exists at the time of the wrongful act or is formed later. Misappropriation includes the physical destruction of property or its abandonment if the intent and effect of the act is to terminate or abridge the true owner/possessor's interest in the thing. It also includes the sale or resale of such interest. It does not include the forcible taking of such property (robbery or extortion) or physical invasions of property in order to effect such takings (e.g., trespass or burglary).

6. "Corruption" may be defined as the doing of any act or promising to do any act that lies within one's official discretionary function in return for an illegal consideration; also the paying or promising of such illegal consideration to an official for the doing of a discretionary official act; also, the utilizing of one's official position for personal, unauthorized enrichment. Examples are self-dealing by an employee or officer of a business, by a professional, or by a politician; embezzlement or employee theft; offering a bribe on the part of businessman or professional to an officeholder; soliciting a bribe or accepting one by an officeholder; insider trading; and self-interested stock manipulations by corporate officers, stockbrokers, etc.

References

Bequai, A. (1979). *White collar crime: A 20th century crisis.* Lexington, MA: Lexington.

Black's law dictionary. (5th ed.) (1979). St. Paul, MN: West.

Block, H. A., & Geis, G. (1970). *Man, crime, and society* (2nd ed.). New York: Random House.

Bureau of Justice Statistics. (1981). *Dictionary of criminal justice data terminology* (2nd ed.). Washington, DC: Department of Justice.

Chambliss, W. (1988). *Exploring criminology.* New York: Macmillan.

Clinard, M. B., & Quinney, R. (1967). *Criminal behavior systems: A typology.* New York: Holt, Rinehart & Winston.

Clinard, M. B. & Yeager, P. C. (1980). *Corporate crime.* New York: Free Press.

Coleman, J. W. (1987). Toward an integrated theory of white collar crime. *American Journal of Sociology, 93,* 406-439.

Coleman, J. W. (1989). *The criminal elite.* New York: St. Martin's.

Conklin, J. E. (1977). *Illegal but not criminal: Business crime in the United States.* Englewood Cliffs, NJ: Prentice Hall.

Douglas, J. D., & Johnson, J. M. (Eds.). (1977). *Official deviance: Readings in malfeasance, misfeasance, and other forms of corruption.* New York: J. B. Lippincott.

Edelhertz, H. (1970). *The nature, impact, and prosecution of white collar crime.* Washington, DC: Government Printing Office.

Ermann, M. D., & Lundman, R. J. (Eds.) (1982). *Corporate and governmental deviance: Problems of organizational behavior in contemporary society* (2nd ed.). New York: Oxford University Press.

Ermann, M. D., & Lundman, R. J. (Eds.). (1987). *Corporate and governmental deviance.* New York: Oxford University Press.

Geis, G., & Stotland, E. (Eds.). (1980). *White collar crime: Theory and research.* Beverly Hills, CA: Sage.

Green, G. S. (1990). *Occupational crime.* Chicago: Nelson-Hall.

Hagan, J., & Parker, P. (1985). White collar crime and punishment: The class structure and legal sanctions of securities violations. *American Sociological Review, 50,* pp. 302-316.

Hill, S. (Ed.). (1987). *Corporate violence.* Totowa, NJ: Rowan & Littlefield.

Pizzo, S., Fricker, M., & Muolo, P. (1989). *Inside job: The lootings of America's savings and loans.* New York: McGraw-Hill.

Quinney, R. (1964). The study of white collar crime: Toward a reorientation in theory and research. *Journal of Criminal Law, Criminology, and Police Science, 55,* 208-314.

Reasons, C. E. (1982). Crime and abuse of power: Offenses and offenders beyond the reach of the law. In P. Wickman & T. Dailey (Eds.), *White collar and economic crime: Multidisciplinary and cross-national perspectives* (pp. 59-72). Lexington, MA: Lexington Books.

Reiss, A. J. (1987, September). Measuring white collar law-breaking. Paper presented at *Symposium 87: White Collar/Institutional Crime—Its Measurement and Analysis.* Cosponsored by the Office of the California Attorney General, Bureau of Criminal Statistics and the University of California, Berkeley.

Reiss, A. J., & Biderman, A. D. (1980). *Data sources on white collar law-breaking.* Washington, DC: Department of Justice, National Institute of Justice.

Schmalleger, F. (1991). *Criminal justice today.* Englewood Cliffs, NJ: Prentice Hall.

Schrager, L. S., & Short, J. F., Jr. (1977). Toward a sociology of organizational crime. *Social Problems, 25,* 407-419.

Shapiro, S. P. (1984). *Wayward capitalists: Target of the Securities and Exchange Commission.* New Haven: Yale University Press.

Simon, D. R., & Eitzen, D. S. (1986). *Elite deviance* (2nd ed.). Boston: Allyn & Bacon.

Simpson, S. S. (1992). Corporate crime deterrence and corporate crime-control policies. In K. Schlegel & D. Weisburd (Eds.), *White collar crime reconsidered* (pp. 32-58). Boston: Northeastern University Press.

Sutherland, E. H. (1983). *White collar crime: The uncut version.* New Haven: Yale University Press.

Sutherland, E. H. (1945). Is "white collar crime" crime? *American Sociological Review, 10,* 132-139.

U.S. Department of Justice, Office of the Attorney General. (1980, August). *National priorities for the investigation and prosecution of white collar crime: Report of the Attorney General.* Washington, DC: Author.

Wheeler, S., & Rothman, M. L. (1982). The organization as weapon in white collar crime. *Michigan Law Review, 80,* 1403-1426.

PART II

LAW ENFORCEMENT

5

Education Versus Training

The Debate Continues

BRUCE L. BERG

Higher Education and Police Officers

You're seated at a desk in a classroom. Around you sit 20 other young women and men wearing khaki-colored uniforms and polished black shoes, and sporting short-cropped hair. You think to yourself how people had tried to talk you out of coming this morning—even your own parents thought your choice was a mistake. But you had scored a 92 on the entrance exam and were among the first applicants interviewed for the position. You reaffirm to yourself that you do not care if others think this an unladylike career choice, you have always wanted to be a police officer.

You imagine back to watching *Cagney and Lacey* on television and thinking how neat it would actually be to become a police detective. All that action! Car chases, shoot-outs, courtroom drama—wow! Now you've made it. You're on your way to fulfilling your childhood dream. You wonder when you would get your gun and night stick and when you'll practice driving in high-speed pursuits. So far, all you've received is a notebook, a copy of the state penal and vehicle codes, and a lot of hostile shouts and scoldings from various academy staff. Suddenly, your daydreaming is interrupted by someone shouting "Attention!" You spring to your feet, along with the other recruits.

A tall well-built officer walks in. He is wearing a neatly pressed blue uniform and has short-cropped hair. The badge on his shirt is gleaming, and he looks every bit like the kind of officer you imagined should be your instructor. He introduces himself and passes out a sheet of paper. At the top of the paper is the heading "Academy Modular Schedule." It looks like a kind of calendar, but in each day's box is the description of a different training segment or module. Let's see, the first 2 weeks are filled with the words "Penal Code." The next couple of boxes say, "Constitutional Law." Weeks 5 and 6 are labeled "Vehicle Code," and week 7 is "Trucking and Transportation Regulations." Wait a minute, where does it say shooting? There's a module on "Communications" and one on "Spanish for Police." There's even one on "First Response First Aid." What's going on? Okay, okay, here it is in week 14, "Service Weapons and Range Qualification," one week? "Defensive Driving," one week. Defensive driving, defensive driving, what the heck is that? You want to know how to chase down bad guys or to shoot their eyes out. What gives?

Modern police academies are often surprises for new recruits. As the old Bob Dylan song lyrics go, "The times they are a changin'." No longer do most police academies place major emphasis on weapons, driving, and physical skills. More frequently they are placing a growing emphasis on academic areas. Naturally, this is not to suggest that traditional police skill training has been abolished. What does appear to be happening, however, is that many entry level police officers are starting their careers with higher levels of education. In turn, academies are able to offer higher levels of training. This chapter will explore this phenomenon and some possible explanations for the growing need by policing as an institution to encourage college educations for their entry level officers.

Training Versus Education

For the uninitiated, the differentiation between training and education may appear at first to be only semantic. But it is much more. Although one could reasonably contend that at times training and education overlap, they are not synonymous. When one thinks of training, one should envision learning the ropes to some process or procedure: learning through example or explicit instruction how something operates, proceeds, or should be undertaken.

Education, on the other hand, should be conceived as somewhat more tacit and cerebral. It involves understanding how, why, and with what alternatives a process operates. It includes abstract thoughts and symbolic representations about relationships and outcomes from actions.

On a more mundane level, training tends to direct attention toward the mechanics of various skill acquisitions, whereas education aims to develop mental capacities. For example, skills such as defensive driving, first aid, firearms, or traffic accident investigations all require development of competencies not restricted to the mind. On the other hand, applying communications theory in an effort to calm a domestic dispute or using one's psychological knowledge about how parents might feel when they learn about their child falling victim to an assault reflect competence gained from education.

Only a fool would attempt to argue that training was not important in policing today. But it seems just as foolish to argue that officers do not require college educations. Training and education offer excellent means of improving the relationships between police and various ethnic and cultural groups in the communities they serve.

One essential purpose of training is to keep police personnel apprised of innovations in policing. In another sense, however, training's orientation and impact depend largely on the way society chooses to define the role of police. Throughout the 1950s and early 1960s the suppression of civil disturbances was a primary activity of police, and their role became that of political social worker. In the late 1960s and 1970s, the emphasis shifted toward crime fighting, and their role as law enforcers was emphasized (Broderick, 1987; Staufenberger, 1980). In the 1980s and 1990s, with the official "war on drugs" declared, the crime-fighting role persists and expands to include one of "noble sentinel." Also in the 1990s, police have renewed their social worker role and learned that they had to improve police community relations, especially in communities composed of various ethnic minorities.

Training in the 1990s, then, must include emphasis on various negotiating techniques and information about how to handle a growing number of non-law-enforcement problems that arise in communities. Communications theory, greater knowledge of ethnic and cultural ways, psychology, sociology, and even counseling seem important if not essential tools for police officers of the 1990s. The question remains, however, concerning where these pieces of necessary knowledge should be learned.

To be sure, police academies' training requirements and training methods have obtained greater respect and status during the past decade (Marsh & Grosskopf, 1991). Yet an assortment of conditions affect what training should be undertaken and for how long a period.

The question of police training requisites is itself seen by many trainers as problematic. For example, how many hours in the academy are necessary or sufficient to place officers safely in the field? Which areas should be emphasized in the training program, and what proportion of hours should each area be given? At what levels should passing and failing be established? Should physical training be given equal, more, or less time than more academic areas of study? Should rookie officers be permitted simply to begin police work after completing a classroom training program, or should they be required to have a structured field training experience first? And finally, exactly what is the purpose or goal of police training? Unfortunately, an unending debate is likely to arise regardless of how one attempts to answer any of these questions. At least partially as a result of this circumstance, training is typically given a fairly low priority in most police departments nationally (Samaha, 1988, p. 275).

Perhaps owing to the size of a department and the policing environment, many police chiefs would prefer to do on the job training rather than send their recruits to an academy. One reason for this certainly is financial. During the time the recruit is attending the academy, the chief must pay the officer's salary without receiving the benefit of the officer's service. One partial remedy for this has sprung up in many communities across the country. This remedy is usually called "self-sponsorship" at the academy. The idea here is that individuals interested in becoming police officers must first obtain certification before applying for a position. In short, they must attend a certified academy at their own expense.

A Brief History of Police Education

The interest in upgrading the entry level educational requirements for police officers has a long history. August Vollmer was among the earliest proponents of higher education for police officers. As early as 1917, Vollmer (Vollmer & Schneider, 1917) urged adoption of a college education as a basic employment requirement. Yet little progress was made until the late 1960s. In 1967, the President's Commission on Law Enforcement and the Administration of Justice suggested that "the ultimate aim of all police departments should be that all personnel with enforcement powers have baccalaureate degrees" (President's Commission on Law Enforcement, 1967, p. 107).

The impact of the President's Commission could be felt by the influx of federal monies through programs such as the Law Enforcement Educational Program (LEEP). As a result of the availability of money, police departments and American colleges and universities began directing attention toward improving the educational opportunities available for police officers. Money was suddenly accessible both for officers who desired to pursue college educations and for colleges and universities interested in developing police-oriented courses and programs. Prior to 1967, only 184 institutions of higher education had established police-oriented programs; by 1974, over 1,030 institutions had developed law-enforcement-related courses and programs (Staufenberger, 1980).

The reason behind this early reformist movement toward improved educations for police officers was simple: College-educated officers were believed to be more highly motivated and more capable of using innovations (Bell, 1979; Hayeslip, 1989). Ironically, much of this early supposition was based on common sense or intuitive hunches; so few officers actually held college degrees in the early 1960s that empirical evidence could not have been adequately undertaken (Worden, 1990). Research during the 1970s often appeared to support the notion that police performance and attitudes could be improved with a college degree. Locke and Smith (1976), for example, claimed that higher education reduced the tendency toward authoritarianism commonly associated with police officers' personalities during the late 1960s and 1970s.

In 1973, The National Advisory Commission on Criminal Justice Standards and Goals urged that police agencies begin gradually to require some college education among new recruits (Berg, 1992). They recommended beginning with a requirement of 1 year of college during 1973 and increasing this to 2 years of college by 1975, 3 years by 1978, and a 4-year degree by 1982 (National Advisory Commission, 1973, p. 369).

The push for college-educated police officers, however, was and is not uniformly supported. Today, as during the past three decades, controversial issues regarding educational reform among police continue to persist. In large part the question becomes one of utility and relevance of academic preparation for police, given their daily work expectations. This may be related to society's inability or reluctance to identify exactly what our expectations of police work are. This is true even among those who support college educations for police. For example, some people believe that it is the whole college experience that positively impacts potential police officers.

From this holistic stance, one might argue that the undergraduate experience expands one's thinking and one's general knowledge base. Consequently, undergraduate students begin to see the world around them as a complex matrix of grays and intricate patterns rather than black and white and straight lines. Because police officers usually operate rather independently in the field, they exercise considerable discretion. Many proponents of college for police argue that the collegiate experience will allow officers to better empathize with members of the community they police and that their college experience will broaden their tolerance of people different from themselves. Finally, proponents suggest that many of the academic areas usually included as requirements for a baccalaureate (courses in sociology, psychology, anthropology, and criminology) improve potential officers' awareness about themselves and others.

Others in policing believe that it is particular courses or sets of curricula that are most important (Cox, 1990). For example, Broderick (1987) writes:

> As late as 1985 data were still being gathered which indicated that many in academia, for example advisors of undergraduate pre-law students, still perceived criminal justice to be too heavily weighted toward technical and vocational training and too often taught by faculty which did not have the proper credentials. (p. 218)

Following this line, undergraduates may be understood to attend college in order to master a particular area of curriculum, or for a singular purpose. In our pragmatic society, many young people now attend college only because they believe that it will enhance their employment opportunities. Try a quick experiment and do a poll in your class. Be honest in your own response to the question, Why are you in college? It is very likely the overwhelming response will be related to getting or keeping a good-paying job. Why, one may ask, is a college education perceived as being so helpful toward obtaining a job? A simplistic answer might be that the college degree requirement of today has simply replaced the high school diploma requirement common 30 or 40 years ago. This academic inflation may also be seen as reflecting the advances of technology, computers, and the sciences in society today.

Many people involved in policing during the 1970s believed that college education could offer very little for the average police officer (see Erickson & Neary, 1975; Hayeslip, 1989). The invariable mundane activities typically associated with patrol officers, especially entry level ones, were suggested as reasons why higher education for officers might be useless (Sherman & Bennis, 1977).

The slow response to various research studies and commission recommendations for baccalaureate-prepared officers continued into the 1980s. Geoffrey Alpert and Roger Dunham (1988, p. 186) suggest that at least one reason for not following the recommendations may be administrative concern about accusations of discrimination. The Urban League has argued, for example, that any education requirements for entry level positions should be relevant to the job. In the case of law enforcement, the Urban League maintains that a high school diploma or its equivalent should be the maximum requirement for entry level positions (Reynolds, 1980).

The liability concern expressed by police administrators does not genuinely reflect concern over equal opportunities for minorities. And the claim that minority group members have a disproportionate access to higher education compared to whites may well reflect a kind of lazy racism. In other words, this claim suggests that there are very few or no qualified minorities possessing higher educational levels—a subtle but racist attitude that is untrue.

In a recent study, Carter, Sapp, and Stephens (1988) examined 104,000 geographically distributed police officers. Among other questions examined was the number of years of education officers had. Carter et al. found that

> in 1967 the average educational level for police was 12.4 years—barely more than a high school diploma. In 1988, the mean educational level for officers was well into the sophomore year of college with 13.6 years. Importantly, the increased educational levels are not limited to white males. . . . [A]verage educational levels of the various racial and ethnic groups have no significant variance. Furthermore, the average education of women officers is a full year higher than that of men. (p. 19)

Police executives, however, are faced with a dilemma. If the desire to upgrade educational requirements arbitrarily excludes certain ethnic or racial minorities (regardless of intentions) it is illegal. If, on the other hand, the requirement of a baccalaureate as a condition for employment can be shown to be necessary to carry out the job effectively, it may be permissible—even if some persons in society continue to be excluded.

The issues of public safety and responsibility are commonly used to demonstrate when a job requirement is not discriminatory. Stated differently, it is recognized that certain job requirements may appear to discriminate against federally protected groups. However, as Carter et al. (1988) suggest, "discrimination may be justified when balanced against the broader more compelling need of public safety" (p. 11).

Do Police Need College at Entry Level?

The obvious question to be asked now is, "Do entry level police officers actually need college educations?" A fair number of you are sitting in your classroom reading this and thinking, "I sure hope so, because I'm here in college and want to become a police officer!" In fact, most people agree that some amount of college education is very beneficial for policing.

Several questions—none of which, unfortunately, have completely convincing answers—continue to plague those who argue for higher education for police officers. First, do police really need a degree or just some college experience? Is it sufficient for an entry level officer to have 1 year or less of college? How about an associate degree, usually entailing 60 credits taken over approximately 2 years? Or should entry level officers possess a baccalaureate degree, typically representing 124 credits taken over approximately 4 years of full-time study?

Second, at what level should policing require a college education? Is it necessary for entry level police officers or officers at some other level of the police hierarchy (Patterson, 1991)?

Third, might one sort of degree be better than another (Fischer, 1981)? Stated differently, is a degree in criminal justice better for a potential officer than one in sociology, psychology, or history?

In 1983, Fyfe reported on a study he conducted for the International City Management Association, surveying police administrators to assess their views on education. Fyfe found that among the 1,087 responding administrators, only 4 indicated that their agency required a 4-year college degree as a condition of employment. Nearly 8% stated they required a high school diploma or equivalency.

In 1988 a survey of police departments servicing cities with populations of 50,000 or more found that just about half of the police administrators responding indicated a preference for hiring recruits who majored in criminal justice (Sapp & Carter, 1988). However, an almost identical number of administrators indicated no particular preference in the recruit's major. This same study suggested that most police administrators see colleges and universities as having inadequate curricula for *training* potential police officers (Sapp & Carter, 1988; Sapp, Carter, & Stephens, 1989). The recommendation from the police administrators who responded was for colleges and universities to concentrate in the academic areas and leave training to the police academies (Sapp, Carter, & Stephens, 1989)!

Bracey (1990) similarly argues that it seems fairly reasonable to suggest that during our lifetimes a substantial portion of the police's clientele will become better educated and more sophisticated in their criminal behavior. Scientific medical advances made during the past decade such as organ transplants well may lead to innovative crimes such as organ piracy during the next decade. Growing dependence upon computer technology by large corporations and financial institutions invites parallel advances in technology among criminals. Increasing complexity in criminal activities will require advances in methods of detecting, apprehending criminals, and perhaps drawing inferences from evidence. It does not require a college education to see that these police activities will require highly educated personnel.

It is true that college educations for police officers are likely to become a necessity. It remains arguable, however, whether a 4-year degree is absolutely necessary for entry level policing. It is likely that a growing number of police agencies will support in-service officers obtaining educational credentials. In either event, it appears that the overall educational levels for American police officers will continue to increase in the future.

There is, however, considerable evidence of an increasing desire for college-educated police in entry level positions. As previously mentioned, a recent study (Sapp et al., 1989) sponsored by the Police Executive Research Forum found a preference among police administrators to hire recruits who possessed college degrees. This same study found that 62% of the surveyed agencies did have some form of educational incentive program but only 13.8% required a college degree as a prerequisite for employment (Mahan, 1991, p. 282).

There have also been several congressional efforts to fund undergraduates as an incentive for them to join police agencies. In 1989 and 1990 Congress failed to pass the Police Corps Act. This bill enabled participating college students to secure federally guaranteed loans for their college educations. After graduating, the students would repay up to $40,000 by serving in either the state police or a local police department in the sponsoring state (American Press, 1989; Berg, 1992). The duration of "pay-back service" would amount to about 4 years.

The Police Corps was the brain child of Adam Walinsky, a former aide to Robert Kennedy. The Police Corps promised three major benefits. Many urban police departments have difficulty attracting qualified minority recruits. A Justice Department survey has concluded that many inner city minority youths would find the corps' "service-for-college" trade attractive. Second, the increase in college-educated, entry level officers would improve the overall educational level of local police forces nationally. Finally, in time, a sizable number of civilians would gain a new appreciation for police officers and police work because they would have served as police officers—even if only for 4 years to pay back the loan (Kramer, 1990).

However, not everyone in policing is in favor of a Police Corps Bill. The International Association of Chiefs of Police (IACP) has consistently lobbied in opposition to this piece of legislation (Constantine, 1992). The central argument offered by the IACP Executive Committee is that the proposed bills simply have not been realistic. The basis of the most recent version of the Police Corps Bill is the expectation that police agency strength will be increased by 100,000 officers during a 5-year period (Constantine, 1992). Yet many, and perhaps most, agencies nationally lack budgets to support even their current authorized strengths. How then, one might ask, will agencies manage filling their current complements as well as increasing their personnel size under the proposed bill?

Other problems with the proposed Bill, according to the IACP Executive Committee, include the potential costs for training and administrating of officers who potentially offer an agency only a 4-year career. Cost estimates are as high as $40,000 for each recruit (Constantine, 1992). Also, there are no federal reimbursements for agencies that expend money on candidates for the program during their educational phase (for screening tests and summer training). Should candidates default, choose to pay back, or qualify for the alternative pay-back in community service, agencies would be out considerable sums of money (Constantine, 1992).

In 1990, the U.S. Department of Education altered their Perkins Loan policy to create a forgivable loan to potential law enforcement officers (U.S. Department of Education, 1992). A Perkins Loan is a low-interest loan offered to undergraduate and graduate students who meet certain financial requirements. Traditionally, Perkins Loans were forgiven if one became a teacher or full-time staff member in a Head Start program or if one became a Peace Corps or Vista volunteer (U.S. Department of Education, 1992, p. 30). Beginning on November 29, 1990, cancellation of the Perkins Loans was offered to students who became full-time police officers after completing their education (U.S. Department of Education, 1992, p. 30).

Interestingly, few in-service or potential police officer students have taken advantage of this financial opportunity. Although one can only speculate, it is likely that the underuse of Perkins Loans reflects a lack in awareness of its availability by college-bound in-service or future officers.

Experience Is an Officer's Best Instructor

While the debate between training and education rages on, a third position is periodically stated: that regardless of one's education or training there is no substitute for street experience. If one follows this argument to its logical conclusion, neither the skills learned at the academy nor the knowledge gained from a college education is sufficient. One still needs to experience working through confrontations in the real world. If one accepts this view as correct, it follows that the best police officers should be the oldest, most seasoned field veterans, regardless of their educational levels. Also, the only people competent to make comments and judgments in a supervisory capacity should be those still actively working the streets. In effect, the argument is analogous to the absurd claim that in order to study drug addiction, one must first be a drug addict. Few officers would argue, as stated here, that only actively working police officers are competent to assess, supervise, or educate recruits.

As implied above, and as Bayley and Bittner (1984) state, "what police say about how policing is learned [experientially] is not incompatible with attempts to make instruction in the skills of policing more self-critical and systematic." Bayley and Bittner even recommend a kind of blending of theoretically based material with more practical experiential learning strategies. In this regard, frank discussion of actual case studies and the kinds of decisions that went into each would be instructive. Bayley and Bittner warn, however, that there is an important distinction to be made between having instructors excite recruits with war stories and offering authentic case examples for illustrative purposes. Related to this, then, it seems necessary that instructors themselves be well educated in both law enforcement issues and material and educational procedures and techniques (Berg, 1990).

Are College-Educated Police Valuable?

Given the foregoing discussion on college-educated police officers, a natural question becomes, "Are college-educated police valuable?" The answer to this question remains controversial. There is some research to suggest that college-prepared officers tend to perform their function as police officers better than their non-college-prepared counterparts (see Sanderson, 1977; Trojanowicz & Nicholson, 1976).

For instance, Trojanowicz and Nicholson (1976) write that the college-prepared officer is

> willing to experiment and try new things as opposed to preferring the established and conventional way of doing things; assumes a leadership role and likes to direct and supervise the work of others; uses a step-by-step method for processing information and reaching decisions; likes to engage in work providing a lot of excitement and a great deal of variety as opposed to work providing a stable and secure future; and he values himself by his achievement of status symbols established by his culture. (p. 58)

These notions indicate that both implicitly and explicitly, college-educated officers are thought to improve the quality of policing. At least partially this involves possessing certain values and attitudes as police officers shaped by the college experience. Accordingly, the college educated officer should better appreciate his or her social role(s) and be more tolerant of differences in others than a non-college-educated counterpart (Worden, 1990).

Critics of college educational requirements for police argue that most police functions require little more than common sense and street smarts. As such, these tasks are not performed any better when an officer possesses a college education. These critics are also quick to point out that merely having a college education does not immediately translate into better police work. Often improvements in training and enforcement of training standards can provide as effective or more effective paths to increased quality policing. As Burbeck and Furnham (1985) state, "Intelligence and education do not guarantee success in the police office, although they are of predictive use at the training school. Higher levels of education may paradoxically give rise to more dissatisfaction and higher wastage" (p. 62).

Other research indicates that there is little difference in performance between college- and high-school-prepared officers (see, for example, Miller & Fry, 1978; Weirman, 1978). For example, Witte (1969) compared two groups of police officers in the field. One group contained officers with college degrees, and the other was composed of high school graduates. Witte found that after 6 months, the crime rates in each group's area had remained relatively constant. Witte did report, however, that citizen complaints were fewer among the college-educated officers, and that their response time in answering calls was faster than that of the high-school-prepared officers.

Cascio (1977) and Sanderson (1977) found similar indirect evidence of a benefit from college-prepared officers. In Cascio's (1977) case, the higher level of education among Dade County, Florida, officers was associated with increased communication abilities resulting in fewer on the job injuries during officer/citizen interactions; fewer sick days taken each year; and fewer allegations of unnecessary use of force. Sanderson (1977) found that educational levels among officers in the Los Angeles Police department could be positively correlated with performance during an officer's academy training period, and later with the likelihood of promotions.

After an exhaustive review of the extant literature on higher education and policing, Bowker (1980) concluded that college educations had a number of benefits for police officers. These benefits included higher morale, a decreased amount of dogmatism and authoritarianism, more liberal social attitudes, fewer disciplinary problems, and fewer citizen complaints (see also Finckenauer, 1975; Parker, Donnelly, Gerwitz, Marcus, & Kowalewski, 1976; and Roberg, 1978).

Regardless of the debate and controversy that surrounds the issue of college-educated police officers, there is a fairly strong tendency for officers interested in rapid advancement through the ranks to secure college degrees. It is perhaps ironic that because so many officers have sought college and graduate school educations, the mere possession of a college or graduate school credential no longer assures rapid advancement.

For example, one study by Fischer, Golden, and Heininger (1985) found that promotional chances are not enhanced by officers' possessing college degrees. Although most officers in the study who did obtain promotions possessed college degrees, it was not the degree that made "a unique or essential contribution to the chances for promotion" (p. 335). Stated slightly differently, so many officers have now begun to accumulate college degrees that such credentials no longer set them apart from other applicants for promotion. This finding about the plenitude of college-prepared officers may provide at least a partial explanation for the dissatisfaction to which Burbeck and Furnham (1985) refer. Because college-educated police officers are becoming more prevalent, their job dissatisfaction may be attributed to the effects of the mundane and routine patrol work typical in policing. In other words, college-prepared officers may have gained social tolerance and a greater depth of knowledge in college, but they may have also accepted the idea that college preparation is the ticket to advancement—and in policing, experience continues to be a necessary requisite for command positions, regardless of one's educational achievements.

What is particularly interesting about the Fischer et al. (1985) finding is that it suggests that there are substantial numbers of college-prepared officers at all levels and ranks of law enforcement. In other words, policing is not administrated disproportionately by overeducated ranking officers, nor is it commanded by undereducated streetwise officials. Instead, there is apparently a far more heterogeneous mix of educational backgrounds.

From High School Diploma to Baccalaureate

The standard of a high school diploma as a basic requirement for entry level police positions (and other occupations) has prevailed for many years. It can easily be argued that at one time this standard served a functional purpose, namely, the identification of people possessing superior levels of formal education. But today, when academic credential inflation has evolved enormously, the high school diploma no longer signifies as it may have prior to World War II, above average mental ability or a significant level of educational accomplishment.

More (1985, p. 306) reports that in 1946, the Department of Health, Education and Welfare claimed that less than one half of the 17-year-old population had completed high school. By 1969, this figure had risen to over 78%. By 1985, just over 93% of American youths between the ages of 14 and 17 were enrolled in high school programs, and the majority of them were expected to obtain their diploma (Bogue, 1985; Molotsky, 1984). Certainly, the criterion of a high school diploma has become a taken-for-granted minimum expectation rather than an important factor in hiring personnel.

Many in our society, however, claim that although the general population has attained high levels of academic credentials and education, these laurels are unnecessary for basic police functions. As More (1985) indicates, this attitude persists among many critics of police officers even today. The assumption is that issuing tickets, directing snarled traffic, and conducting permit inspections simply do not require high levels of education. But these are not the sole responsibilities of most contemporary police officers. In fact, in many modern police agencies these more mundane tasks have been delegated to civilian employees or private subcontractors. Thus contemporary police officers are charged with more essential and pressing tasks such as reducing fear and anxiety about crime among community members, resolving major crimes, preserving constitutional rights, and assuring public safety in general. The need for police officers who are educated, articulate, tolerant of others, politically aware, and knowledgeable about the various social and cultural influences operating in the community they serve should be obvious.

A Futuristic Look at Police Education

Debate about the value of college educations for police officers continues today, but with somewhat less intensity than during previous decades. Some of the previous problems involved confusion among both academics and police officials concerning whether college educations for police officers should be vocational training programs. Indeed, many of the early junior college programs as well as a good many baccalaureate programs that arose during the LEEP years (the late 1960s and early 1970s) may have been more vocational than academic. Today, although some vocationally oriented programs persist, many of the early vocational programs have evolved into scholarly academically oriented educational programs. Many of these programs are no longer designed exclusively for police officer types. Rather, serious students of police studies have begun to fill the seats in many criminal justice programs.

The debate over where training ends and education begins and whether more than merely high school preparation should be a national standard for entry level police officers may not be settled soon. Yet there is growing appreciation among ranking police officials of the value of a wide range and depth of knowledge in police and academic subjects. Recently police researchers and police officials have begun to come together in many of their understandings on contemporary police issues. In keeping with this, one can expect the future for police education to hold high academic, training, and performance standards. Police work is fast becoming recognized as a skilled occupation of competitively educated, technically sophisticated, empathic, and humane people.

Discussion Questions

1. How can one distinguish between police training and police education?
2. What are some of the advantages of having college-educated police? Are there any disadvantages?
3. Why do some people maintain that requirements of college education among entry level officers may lead to institutionalized discrimination?
4. How were police officers of the past able to function effectively without college educations?
5. How do you suppose field training programs stack up against college programs?
6. Are college educations more beneficial for administrators or line officers? How might you defend your answer?
7. What courses in a college program might be good ones for prospective police officers to take? Why?

References

Alpert, G., & Dunham, R. G. (1988). *Policing urban America.* Prospect Heights, IL: Waveland.

Bayley, D. H., & Bittner, E. (1984). Learning the skills of policing. *Law and Contemporary Problems, 47*(4), 35-59.

Bell, D. J. (1979). The police role and higher education. *Journal of Police Science and Administration, 7*(4), 467-475.

Berg, B. L. (1990). Who should teach police: A typology and assessment of police academy instructors. *American Journal of Police, 9*(2), 79-100.

Berg, B. L. (1992). *Law enforcement: An introduction to police in society.* Boston: Allyn & Bacon.

Bogue, D. J. (1985). *The population of the United States: Historical trends and future predictions.* New York: Free Press.

Bowker, L. H. (1980). A theory of educational needs of law enforcement officers. *Journal of Contemporary Criminal Justice, 1,* 17-24.

Bracey, D. H. (1990). Preparing police leaders for the future. *Police Studies, 13*(3), 178-189.

Broderick, J. J. (1987). *Police in a time of change.* Prospect Heights, IL: Waveland.

Burbeck, E., & Furnham, A. (1985). Police officer selection: A critical review of the literature. *Journal of Police Science and Administration, 13*(1), 58-69.

Carter, D. L., Sapp, A., & Stephens, D. W. (1988). Higher education as a bona fide occupational qualification (BFOQ) for police: A blueprint. *American Journal of Police, 17,* 1-27.

Cascio, W. (1977). Formal education and police officer performance. *Journal of Police Science and Administration, 5,* 89.

Constantine, T. (1992, February). The Police Corps Bill: Law enforcement concerns. *Police Chief,* pp. 12-13.

Cox, S. M. (1990). Policing in the twenty-first century. *Police Studies, 13*(4), 168-177.

Erickson, J., & Neary, M. (1975). Criminal justice education: Is it criminal? *Police Chief, 42,* 38.

Finckenauer, J. O. (1975). Higher education and police discretion. *Journal of Police Science and Administration, 3,* 450-457.

Fischer, R. J. (1981). Is education really an alternative? The end of a long controversy. *Journal of Police Science and Administration, 9*(3), 313-316.

Fischer, R. J., Golden, K. M., & Heininger, B. L. (1985). Issues in higher education for law enforcement officers: An Illinois study. *Journal of Criminal Justice, 13,* 329-338.

Fyfe, J. F. (1983). *Police personnel practices: Baseline data reports.* Washington, DC: International City Management Association.

Hayeslip, D. W. (1989). Higher education and police performance revisited: The evidence examined through meta-analysis. *American Journal of Police, 8*(2), 49-59.

Kramer, M. (1990, March 15). From college to cops. *Time,* p. 19.

Locke, B., & Smith, A. B. (1976). Police who go to college. In A. Niederhoffer & A. S. Blumberg (Eds.), *The ambivalent force* (2nd ed.) (pp. 144-147). New York: Holt, Rinehart & Winston.

Mahan, R. (1991, January). Personnel selection in police agencies: Educational requirements for entry level. *Law and Order,* pp. 282-286.

Marsh, H. L., & Grosskopf, E. (1991). The key factor in law enforcement training: Requirements, assessments and methods. *The Police Chief, 53*(11), 64-66.

Miller, J., & Fry, L. (1978, August). Some evidence on the impact of higher education for law enforcement personnel. *Police Chief,* pp. 30-33.

Molotsky, I. (1984, December 19). 31 states gain in college test scores. *New York Times,* p. B6.

More, H. W., Jr. (1985). *Critical issues in law enforcement.* Cincinnati: Anderson.

National Advisory Commission on Criminal Justice Standards and Goals. (1973). *Police.* Washington, DC: U.S. Government Printing Office.

Parker, L. C., Donnelly, M., Gerwitz, D., Marcus, J. M., & Kowalewski, V. (1976, July). Higher education: Its impact on police attitudes. *Police Chief,* pp. 33-35.

Patterson, D. (1991). College educated police officers: Some impact on the internal organization. *Law and Order, 39*(11), 68-71.

Plan would boost nation's police force by 100,000. (1989, July 12). *Indiana Gazette,* pp. 1, 6.

President's Commission on Law Enforcement and Administration of Justice. (1967). *Task force report: The police.* Washington, DC: Government Printing Office.

Reynolds, L. H. (1980). *Eliminators of obstacles: Irrelevant selection criteria.* New York: National Urban League, Inc.

Roberg, R. (1978). An analysis of the relationship among higher education belief systems and job performance of patrol officers. *Journal of Police Science and Administration, 6,* 344-366.

Samaha, J. (1988). *Criminal justice.* St. Paul, MN: West.

Sanderson, B. E. (1977). Police officers: The relationship of a college education to job performance. *Police Chief, 44,* 62.

Sapp, A. D., & Carter, D. (1988). Educational institution and police executive college degree preferences. *ACJS Today, 7*(2), 1.

Sapp, A. D., Carter, D., & Stephens, D. (1989). Police chiefs: CJ curricula inconsistent with contemporary police needs. *ACJS Today, 7*(4), 1, 5.

Sherman, L., & Bennis, W. (1977). Higher education for police officers: The central issues. *Police Chief, 44,* 32.

Staufenberger, R. A. (1980). *Progress in policing: Essays on change.* Cambridge, MA: Ballinger.

Trojanowicz, R., & Nicholson, T. (1976). A comparison of behavioral styles of college graduate police officers vs. non-college going police officers. *Police Chief, 43,* 57.

U.S. Department of Education. (1972). *The student guide: Financial aid from the U.S. Department of Education 1992-93.* Washington, DC: Author.

Vollmer, A., & Schneider, S. (1917, March). The school for police as planned at Berkeley. *Journal of the American Institute of Criminal Law in Criminology,* pp. 875-883.

Weirman, C. L. (1978). The educated policeman. *Journal of Police Science and Administration, 4,* 450-457.

Witte, R. P. (1969). The dumb cop. *Police Chief, 36,* 38.

Worden, R. E. (1990). A badge and a baccalaureate: Policies, hypotheses, and further evidence. *Justice Quarterly, 7,* 566-590.

6

Police Use of Excessive Force

Exploring Various Control Mechanisms

MARK BLUMBERG

The recent riot in Los Angeles has done much to sensitize Americans to the problem of police brutality. Thanks to the media, millions of citizens were able to witness the videotaped beating of Rodney King. One year later, television viewers saw the violence that developed after a suburban Los Angeles jury acquitted the officers of state criminal charges that had been filed as a result of their participation in this incident.[1] Although this was the worst riot in recent American history, it was by no means the first time that civil unrest was precipitated by an overzealous police action. As the Kerner Commission noted way back in the 1960s, the catalyst behind most of the riots in that decade was a police shooting or beating that was perceived as unjust by a substantial portion of the minority community.

Police violence does not inevitably result in civil unrest. Likewise, it would be unfair to lay the blame on the police for the horrendous social and economic problems that exist in many of our inner cities. In these communities, factors such as extensive unemployment, a high rate of poverty, poor schools, a declining industrial economy, limited opportunities for unskilled workers, racial discrimination, and hopelessness combine to create conditions that are conducive to the development of riots.

Too often, though, an incident involving the use of excessive force by the police serves as the spark that triggers a violent reaction.

Policy makers must take the necessary steps to prevent this unfortunate chain of events from occurring. This chapter explores the various institutional mechanisms that are available to accomplish this goal. The discussion begins by defining what is meant by excessive police force and attempting to outline the scope of the problem. This is followed by an examination of the limitations inherent in a number of proposed external controls (i.e., those that originate outside the department) that seek to achieve this goal. Next, the potential for controlling excessive force through internal means is explored. Finally, the chapter contrasts two police agencies that have responded to this concern in very different ways.

Police Use of Excessive Force

Society has given police officers the authority to utilize force in those situations where it is necessary for self-defense, to lawfully arrest a suspect, or to prevent criminal activity. Excessive force is defined as that which exceeds the minimum amount needed to achieve the objective. As Flanagan and Vaughn (1993, p. 6) note, this term "denotes a *continuum* of activities and interactions rather than a specific behavior on the part of the police." At one end of the spectrum, it can refer to the behavior of an officer who intentionally handcuffs a suspect in a manner meant to cause discomfort. On the other hand, it can be as severe as the beating administered to Rodney King.

There are no national data on the incidence of excessive force by police officers. Although a number of researchers have relied on citizen interviews (Campbell & Schuman, 1969) or observational research (Reiss, 1971) to assess the extent of this problem in various communities, most of these studies are quite dated. The best recent estimate of police misuse of force is a Gallup Poll taken in March 1991, where a sample of Americans were asked, "Have you ever been physically mistreated or abused by the police?" (Flanagan & Vaughn, 1993). Five percent of the respondents and 9% of nonwhites reported that they had. In addition, the respondents were also asked whether someone in their own household had been physically mistreated or abused. Eight percent answered in the affirmative. This proportion rose to 20% when the question was asked with respect to someone they knew (Flanagan & Vaughn, in press).

Despite the lack of a national reporting system, there is good reason to believe that this is a problem that varies greatly from department to department. Previous research studies have found large variations in the rate of police shootings between various jurisdictions (Sherman & Cohn, 1986) that cannot be explained as a result of differences in the crime rate or the arrest rate (Milton, Halleck, Lardner, & Abrecht, 1977). There is no reason to believe that the pattern would be different for reports of excessive force.

The circumstances surrounding such incidents are another issue that has received attention in the literature. In general, researchers have found that this type of misconduct is less common than other forms of police misbehavior such as verbal abuse or utilizing illegal methods of gathering evidence (Reiss, 1971). Nonetheless, allegations of excessive force account for the largest proportion of complaints filed against police officers in most cities (Walker, 1992, p. 237). In addition, studies indicate that targets of abuse are almost always lower class males and that the most common factor associated with this practice is citizen disrespect for the police (Reiss, 1971). Finally, it should be noted that the overwhelming majority of encounters between officers and offenders do not involve the use of any, let alone excessive, force (Friedrich, 1980).

External Controls

Several institutional mechanisms have been proposed as means of curbing the problem of excessive police force. Because these originate from outside the department, they are often termed "external" methods of controls. Included in this category are such potential remedies as: (a) relying on the U.S. Supreme Court, (b) criminal prosecution of violent police officers, (c) civil litigation, (d) appealing for redress to municipal officials, and (e) establishing civilian oversight over the police department. In this section, each of these methods is examined, with a particular focus on the shortcomings of the various approaches.

The Supreme Court

In the 1960s, the U.S. Supreme Court handed down a number of important decisions that were designed to curb various forms of police misconduct. The most far-reaching rulings were the cases of *Mapp v. Ohio* (1961) and *Miranda v. Arizona* (1966). In *Mapp,* the court ruled that evidence seized illegally by the police could no longer be used at trial in any state criminal procedure. In effect, the exclusionary rule was applied to state courts as well as the federal judiciary. The *Miranda* decision dealt with the issue of police interrogations. The Supreme Court held that statements by suspects would no longer be admissible in a court of law unless certain procedural requirements had been followed. Part of the rationale for these decisions was to eliminate police abuses of important constitutional rights.

These rulings by the U.S. Supreme Court, although extremely controversial, have little effect on the use of excessive force by the police. The greatest impact of the *Mapp* decision was on police practices with respect to search and seizure. *Miranda* was intended to change the manner in which police conducted interrogations of suspects. Other decisions dealt with such law enforcement practices as wiretaps, lineups, and the right to consult with counsel when in police custody. If the police violated any of these rights, the evidence could not be used against the defendant. Presumably, this would serve to deter officers from acting in a manner inconsistent with the Constitution.

There are several explanations for the extremely limited impact of these decisions on police use of excessive force. For one thing, many of these rulings relate to legal and constitutional issues that are peripheral to the question of unjustified police force (e.g., search and seizure). Second, these decisions only apply in situations where the police have made an arrest. Many encounters between citizens and law enforcement officers do not result in an arrest, and a substantial number of complaints are filed by citizens who have not been arrested. Finally, in order for these constitutional provisions to serve as a deterrent to misconduct, the police must be interested in convicting the suspect. In many cases where "street justice" is administered, this objective takes a backseat to teaching the complainant a lesson about "respect" for the law.

Obviously, these U.S. Supreme Court decisions have had an impact on many aspects of police behavior. It would be implausible to argue that police practices with respect to search and seizure have not improved significantly in the last three decades as a result of the *Mapp* decision. There is also merit in the argument that these rulings stimulated efforts to upgrade the quality of policing in America. However, it is incorrect to suggest that the oversight exerted by the U.S. Supreme Court has had a major impact on police use of excessive force, except perhaps in the area of interrogation practices.

Criminal Prosecution

Police officers who use unnecessary force against citizens may face criminal prosecution either under state laws that prohibit assaultive behavior or in federal court under the U.S. civil rights statute. Although such prosecutions are possible, the reality is that criminal charges are rarely filed in these situations. For a variety of reasons, prosecutors are reluctant to initiate a criminal case against a police officer who has used excessive force against a citizen.

For one thing, the prosecutor must maintain a close working relationship with the police department. Without the cooperation of the police, the prosecutor is unable to perform his or her job. Prosecutors are dependent on the police to undertake an adequate investigation of criminal activity. If the police become reluctant to assist in this effort, it becomes much more difficult for the prosecutor to obtain convictions. As a consequence, the prosecutor must be careful not to antagonize the police by becoming overzealous in his or her pursuit of police misconduct.

Another problem that prosecutors must confront is the fact that obtaining a conviction against a police officer is very difficult. As the first Rodney King trial demonstrated, juries are extremely reluctant to convict police officers who have been charged with assaulting citizens.

A variety of factors make these cases difficult to win. For one thing, persons who are targets of police violence are not sympathetic figures to many jurors. As a general rule, police officers do not abuse corporate executives or doctors. Mostly these victims are poor and/or members of minority groups. In many cases, the individual has been involved in criminal activity. On the other hand, jurors do empathize with police officers. To the average citizen who sits on a jury, the police officer is a person who is risking his or her life in the defense of life and property. Because jurors see police as the "good guys," they are quite reluctant to convict even in situations where an officer may have stepped over the line of what is lawful conduct.

Adding to the prosecutor's burden is the fact that from an evidentiary standpoint, these are very difficult cases to win. Most allegations of police misconduct are ambiguous fact situations. Generally, it is the officer's word versus that of the complainant. In most cases, there are no impartial observers who have witnessed the encounter. If there are any observers, these are likely to be other police officers or friends of the complainant. As a consequence, there is no way for the jury to determine who is telling the truth. Not surprisingly, they often take the word of the police officer over that of the complainant.

Ambiguous fact situations are not the only evidentiary problem in these cases. Achieving a successful prosecution is also made more difficult by the "blue curtain" of silence that is common among police officers. This term refers to the extreme reluctance of law enforcement personnel to testify against fellow officers. The Independent Commission established in the aftermath of the Rodney King incident noted that this is perhaps the greatest barrier to an effective investigation of police misconduct directed against citizens (Christopher, 1991, p. 14). Unfortunately, the unwritten code of silence is not limited to Los Angeles.

Goldstein (1977) has advanced five reasons that account for the pervasive nature of this phenomena among police officers. These include: (a) the police see themselves as members of a group aligned against common enemies, (b) police officers are generally dependent upon one another for help in difficult situations, (c) the police see themselves as quite vulnerable to false accusations by citizens, (d) police officers understand that there is quite a disparity between formal departmental policies and actual police practices on the street, and (e) police officers have no occupational mobility (pp. 165-166).

There are other difficulties for prosecutors as well when they bring criminal charges against police officers. In order to gain a conviction, it is not enough to show that the officer in fact did the act in question. They must also prove beyond a reasonable doubt that the officer acted with criminal intent. If the case has been filed under the federal civil rights statute, the government must prove that the officer intended to deny the citizen his or her constitutional or federally protected rights. This is not generally an easy task. Juries must be persuaded that the alleged behavior is so serious that the officer should not only lose his or her job, but be subjected to criminal penalties as well.

Finally, the prosecutor must be concerned about appearing too overzealous in the battle against police misconduct. There is a great deal of public anxiety regarding violent crime in our society. As a general rule, most citizens are far less worried about police brutality than about street crime. As a consequence, a prosecutor who spends what is perceived as an inordinate amount of time prosecuting errant police officers is likely to open him- or herself up to the charge that he or she is handcuffing the police. A local prosecutor who alienates the rank and file may also be inviting police retaliation at the ballot box. Although federal prosecutors do not have this concern because they are appointed, they still face all the other hurdles in cases of this nature.

Given these factors, it is not surprising that criminal prosecutions of police officers for excessive use of force are relatively infrequent. This is not to say that they do not occur. Prosecutors do sometimes file charges, especially in situations that involve serious misconduct and where there is some likelihood of obtaining a conviction. However, the difficulties inherent in pursuing this course of action lead many prosecutors to believe that administrative sanctions by police agencies are a more effective remedy against police violence than criminal prosecution.

Civil Litigation

In recent years, the number of lawsuits filed against the police has increased substantially. To a large extent, this has resulted from court decisions that have made it much easier for citizens to file lawsuits both against individual officers and police agencies. Del Carmen (1987, p. 398) reports that not only has the number of lawsuits increased in recent years, but there is some evidence that the average size of jury awards has risen as well.

Citizens who have been the victims of police misconduct may either file a tort action in state court or initiate a lawsuit in federal court under Title 42, Section 1983 of the U.S. Civil Rights Code. Torts are defined "as a civil wrong in which the action of one person causes injury to the person or property of another, in violation of a legal duty imposed by law" (del Carmen, 1987, p. 400). Officers who employ excessive force may be liable under these statutes for assault and battery. In situations where the action results in a fatality, a wrongful death suit may be filed.

Despite the availability of state tort remedies, the majority of cases against public officials are filed in federal court under Section 1983 (del Carmen, 1991, p. 409). There are a number of reasons for this phenomenon, including more liberal discovery rules in the federal courts and the fact that since 1976, courts have been able to award attorney's fees to successful plaintiffs (Kappeler, 1993, p. 36). In addition, the U.S. Supreme Court ruled in 1978 that local municipalities are not protected by sovereign immunity and may under certain situations be held liable for the actions of their employees (*Monell v. Department of Social Services,* 1978). One recent analysis of published federal district court decisions indicates that almost half the cases involved an allegation of either excessive force or assault and battery (Kappeler & Kappeler, 1992, p. 71).

The evidentiary standard in a civil case is much lower (i.e., preponderance of the evidence) than in a criminal prosecution, where the state or federal government must prove guilt beyond a reasonable doubt. Nonetheless, citizens who sue the police face a number of very serious hurdles. For one thing, as already noted, juries tend to be quite sympathetic toward police officers and are not favorably disposed toward many of the individuals who file claims, especially members of minority groups or persons with a prior criminal record (Project, 1979). If the case comes down to the word of a citizen versus that of the officer, the jury will generally be inclined to believe the latter. Second, there are a number of defenses available to police officers, such as the claim that they were acting in "good faith." These tend to make it more difficult for citizens to prevail. Third, many police officers are what lawyers would term "judgment-proof." In other words, they do not earn a large salary and are unlikely to have much in the way of resources that could be attached even if the lawsuit was successful. As a consequence, any sizeable judgment that is awarded may ultimately be uncollectible.

Persons who file lawsuits under Section 1983 are not limited to seeking compensation from the individual. These cases may result in damage awards against the municipality as well. The rationale for holding the jurisdiction liable is that cities and counties are in a far better position to reimburse plaintiffs than are individual officers. After all, local government can always raise taxes if necessary to pay the judgment. In addition, it has been asserted that holding the municipality liable will create a financial incentive for the agency to correct the problem. The hope is that taxpayers and insurance carriers will not be anxious to pay repeated claims that result from misconduct on the part of their employees.

Despite the advantages of a Section 1983 lawsuit, there are a number of serious obstacles. For one thing, the plaintiff must prove that a serious violation of a constitutional or federally protected right occurred. Minor acts of police misconduct such as "mere words, threats, a push, a shove, a temporary inconvenience, or even a single punch in the face" (del Carmen, 1991, p. 412) may not be grounds for recovery. In addition, in order to hold the municipality liable, the plaintiff must demonstrate that the officer's action was the product of an official policy or organizational custom that was either created or condoned by a high-level municipal policy maker (Kappeler, 1993, p. 41). This requires the plaintiff to establish not only a pattern of constitutional violations but an awareness of these violations by top administrators within the agency (Kappeler, 1993, p. 43). From an evidentiary standard, this may be a difficult burden to meet.

Despite the increased volume of litigation, the data indicate that most of the lawsuits filed against public officials do not succeed and that a great majority of cases do not even get to the trial stage (del Carmen, 1987, p. 398). Although a recent study suggests that plaintiffs may be prevailing in a greater number of cases (Kappeler & Kappeler, 1992), it is unclear what impact these judgments are having on law enforcement agencies. For example, it has been reported that a substantial increase in damage awards against the city of Detroit had no impact on police operations (Walker, 1992, p. 288). Likewise, the Independent Commission on the Los Angeles Police Department (Christopher, 1991) noted that discipline against officers was frequently light or nonexistent even in cases that involved a settlement or judgment in excess of $15,000. This was so even though "a majority of cases involved clear and often egregious officer misconduct resulting in serious injury or death to the victim" (Christopher, 1991, p. 5). Finally, the New York City Comptroller has asserted that the police department does not even regularly monitor lawsuits alleging police misconduct ("Claims Up, Says Report," 1992).

Municipal Officials

Municipal executives (i.e., mayors and city managers) and members of the city council are responsible for exercising leadership with respect to issues that impact on their community. Unfortunately, they have few mechanisms at their disposal to deal with the problem of controlling police use of excessive force. Several factors account for their inability to discipline rogue officers.

For one thing, a tradition has developed in the United States that politicians should not become involved in police matters. During the 19th century and the early part of the 20th century, there was a great deal of collusion between corrupt public officials and the police. In many cities, the police protected the interests of entrenched political machines at the expense of the citizenry. One of the reforms enacted to deal with this situation was the establishment of mechanisms that insulated the police from political influence. As a result, it became taboo for local municipal officials to become involved in the internal affairs of the police department. Any politician who violates this norm is likely to be the recipient of considerable negative publicity.

Second, there is generally little motivation for the municipal executive or city councilperson to take action in situations involving questionable police behavior. Although various Los Angeles municipal officials spoke out quite vigorously in the aftermath of the Rodney King incident, this response is the exception. Most allegations of police brutality are not videotaped, and the alleged conduct is rarely so offensive. As a general rule, community sympathy does not lie with the complainant. Because most citizens are much more concerned about crime than about the occasional use of excessive force by the police, public officials have little to gain and much to lose by becoming involved. Politicians must be concerned about winning the next election; charges that they are picking on the police can easily become the "kiss of death."

There is a final reason why municipal officials do not take action against officers who may have used excessive force or abused the rights of citizens. Basically, it is that they have no power to do so even if they were so inclined. As a result of civil service reforms enacted during the reform era in American policing, municipal executives lost the right to hire and fire police officers. Personnel decisions must now be made in accordance with civil service provisions, and municipal officials are not part of the discipline process. The goal is to insure that departments are protected from political pressures and that positions are not filled through patronage appointments. However, it also has meant that municipal officials cannot discipline or terminate officers who engage in brutality or other forms of misconduct.

Although municipal officials cannot take action against individual police officers, they can have an indirect impact on police policy. As a general rule, the top municipal official (e.g., the mayor or city manager) or his or her appointees select the police chief. The chief not only sets the tone for the department with respect to such matters as policy, supervision, and training, but is often a significant player in the disciplinary process as well. The appointment process therefore gives municipal officials some leverage over the police department over the long term.

Civilian Oversight of the Police

Police use of excessive force became an emotionally charged issue during the turbulent decade of the 1960s. This was a period marked by widespread political protests, numerous urban riots, a dramatic increase in violent crime, and general social and political upheaval. Because part of the task of the police is to maintain order, frequent confrontations developed between law enforcement officers and those who sought to challenge the status quo. Often there were complaints from protestors that the police were not impartial and that they used excessive force in dealing with demonstrators. In addition, there were allegations from civil libertarians and civil rights groups that the police frequently engaged in brutality, especially against members of minority groups. To deal with these concerns, critics demanded the establishment of civilian review boards.

Allegations of police brutality and other complaints filed against police officers generally are investigated within the department. However, it is often asserted that the agency either cannot or will not adequately discipline officers who abuse the rights of citizens. For this reason, there have been frequent suggestions dating back to the 1960s that a review panel of persons outside the department be established to hear complaints. Although the civilian review board would hear evidence and make recommendations, it would not have the power to discipline officers. Nonetheless, the police were initially quite adamant in their opposition to the creation of review boards.

There were many reasons that the police were vigorously opposed to this concept. For one thing, they greatly distrusted its proponents who they feared would gain control of the board. Second, spokespersons for police organizations and unions asserted that only individuals with a law enforcement background could properly evaluate the propriety of police actions in various situations. Citizens could not perform this function because they lacked the necessary expertise and training. Third, the police felt that they were being singled out for criticism. After all, there is no citizen body to hear complaints directed against teachers, social workers, or other municipal employees. Why should things be different when it comes to the police? Finally, it was argued that the civilian review board would handcuff the police in the battle against violent crime. It was suggested that officers might not be as aggressive if they had to worry that their actions would be second-guessed by civilians.

The opposition of the police was so intense during the decade of the 1960s that not only did very few cities implement civilian review boards, they were also disbanded in several jurisdictions that had initially established this oversight mechanism. The most acrimonious battle took place in New York City, where the issue was put to a public referendum in November 1966 at the behest of the Patrolmen's Benevolent Association. Despite the support of the mayor and other prominent politicians, it was defeated by a margin of 2 to 1. Furthermore, New York City was not alone. Police opposition also led to the abolition of the citizen complaint review board in Philadelphia, the other large city that had implemented this panel.

Although most of the early boards met with failure, recent years have seen a renewal of interest in this concept and the emergence of a second generation of civilian oversight boards (Alpert & Dunham, 1992, p. 118). According to a recent study, civilian review procedures now exist in 30 of the nation's 50 largest cities (Walker & Bumpus, 1991, p. 1). These researchers report that procedures vary considerably among communities: "some have subpoena power, while others do not. Some conduct public hearings, while others do not. Some have the power to make recommendations about general police policies, while most do not" (p. 5).

Second generation civilian oversight boards have not encountered the intense level of opposition that earlier proposals faced. To a large extent, this is the result of a less turbulent social and political climate than existed in the 1960s. In addition, many of the recent complaint mechanisms have been more carefully introduced than was the case of earlier efforts (West, 1991). Finally, police opposition in some communities has been diminished by oversight procedures that apply not just to law enforcement but to other municipal employees as well.

It is ironic that despite the acrimonious debate that has raged over this issue, there is evidence from a number of cities that civilian oversight boards are actually less likely to find police officers guilty of misconduct than internal investigators from within the department. In addition, civilian reviewers are generally more lenient in their disciplinary recommendations when they do find that officers have misbehaved (Kerstetter, 1985). This has been attributed to several factors, including problems that reviewers have in obtaining access to information, the substantial procedural safeguards that are provided for officers accused of misconduct, and the civilian investigators' poor understanding of both the police subculture and various police practices (Kerstetter, 1985, pp. 162-163).

Despite public demands for civilian oversight of law enforcement agencies, it is clear that this approach is not a remedy to the problem of excessive police force. Not only are such boards less aggressive in disciplining officers, they are generally reactive instruments. In other words, the concern in most cases is to determine whether punishment is justified for past misconduct and not on implementing the types of policies and training that can prevent future abuses from occurring in the first place.

Internal Control

None of the external controls reviewed offers a satisfactory remedy to the question of excessive police force. Clearly, this is a problem whose solution does not lie outside the department. Instead, what is required is a firm commitment at the highest level of the organization that misconduct will not be tolerated. To achieve this goal, the chief must be determined to curb brutality. Because the chief sets the tone for the entire agency, it is imperative that clear signals be sent to both supervisory personnel and rank and file members that excessive force will be punished.

In addition, "police administrators can do much of a positive nature to achieve conformity with desired standards of conduct" (Goldstein, 1977, p. 167). Departmental standards regarding selection, training, supervision, and policy are all relevant to this goal. Each of these should be reviewed with an eye toward preventing needless incidents from ever occurring in the first place.

Selection practices determine who can become a police officer. Many departments not only undertake an extensive background investigation to weed out unsuitable candidates but utilize some form of psychological screening as well. If properly performed, these tests can eliminate persons who have traits that are undesirable in a law enforcement officer. It is estimated that between 2% and 5% of applicants are rejected due to an emotional or mental dysfunction (Benner, 1989, p. 80).

Recruitment is only part of the process. Not only must good candidates be selected, they must also be properly trained. Specifically, officers must be taught how to deal with incidents in a manner that defuses the potential for violence instead of escalating potential conflicts to the point that force is required. In addition, departments must enhance the communications skills of officers. This training should focus on the difference between words and actions that are likely to lessen the likelihood for violence and those which are likely to anger citizens.

Supervision is another important means of preventing physical abuse. If the administration is really determined to eliminate the use of excessive force, supervisors must be held accountable for the actions of their subordinates. As Goldstein (1977) has noted, an overly aggressive officer who constantly offends citizens should be viewed as a serious administrative problem, not as a valuable employee who sometimes gets into trouble. Sergeants must be informed in no uncertain terms that they will be subject to discipline if they fail to take action against officers under their command who use unnecessary force against citizens. This is critical because if supervisors tolerate this type of conduct, patrol officers are likely to believe that the department condones their actions.

The chief police executive must also pay close attention to departmental policies. These guidelines should explicitly state the circumstances under which officers are authorized to use force. In addition, it must be stressed that anything beyond the minimum amount necessary is a serious violation of departmental rules that will result in swift punishment. Previous studies have demonstrated that a restrictive departmental policy can reduce the number of police shootings (Fyfe, 1979; Sherman, 1983). There is no reason to believe that policy cannot be an equally effective tool in curbing other types of police violence.

Finally, there is the issue of discipline. If officers are not penalized for abusing the rights of citizens, improvements in other areas will make little difference. Therefore, it is imperative that agencies not only welcome citizen complaints, but investigate these cases in a fair and impartial manner. To achieve this goal, the overwhelming majority of large police departments have established an Internal Affairs or similar unit (West, 1988). There is much reason to believe that if the commitment is present, these investigators can be far more effective in dealing with allegations of excessive force than other proposed control mechanisms such as civilian oversight boards.

Internal control is more likely to be successful for a number of reasons (Kerstetter, 1985). For one thing, personnel from within the department do not have to establish their credibility with the police. Second, being trained law enforcement investigators, these individuals are in a much better position to gather the necessary information required to resolve complaints. Third, both supervisors and line personnel are much more likely to cooperate in a police investigation than in one commanded by outsiders. In the latter situation, an "us versus them" mentality is likely to develop.

Finally, departmental personnel are likely to have greater procedural latitude in conducting investigations than a civilian oversight board would possess.

Despite the evidence that internal control is more effective, the public is often skeptical that departments can be trusted to police themselves. Internal Affairs investigators basically do not have the credibility that outsiders possess. For this reason, police administrators must work diligently to convince the community that the agency does not cover up wrongdoing and that abusive officers receive swift punishment. Nonetheless, it is inevitable that some citizens will mistrust the findings of any investigation conducted within the department. To overcome this problem, Kerstetter (1985) has suggested that the police be given primary responsibility for investigating misconduct but that an outside review procedure also be established. This external review would focus "on the adequacy and integrity of the police department's response to complaints" (Kerstetter, 1985, p. 181). Citizens who were dissatisfied with the internal investigation would thus have an avenue of redress.

A Tale of Two Cities

This section examines the experience of two cities that have taken different paths with respect to internal control of excessive police force. The first case is Los Angeles. Recent events involving the police in that community are well known. The story of the videotaped beating of Rodney King has been told and retold many times. Although it received far less attention, a similar incident occurred in Kansas City (Missouri) during 1990, when a cameraman for a local television station videotaped the beating of a suspect by officers with a blackjack-like weapon after a high-speed chase. Despite the similarity of these incidents, the response of the two departments was quite different.

After the beating of Rodney King, an independent commission was convened to examine the issue of excessive force by members of the Los Angeles Police Department (LAPD). Their report outlined a number of factors that contributed to brutality. Among other things, the commission found that

> there is a significant number of LAPD officers who repetitively misuse force and persistently ignore the written policies and guidelines of the Department regarding force.... Senior and rank-and-file officers generally stated that a significant number of officers tended to use force excessively, that these problem officers were well known in their divisions, that the Department's efforts to control or discipline those officers were inadequate, and that their supervisors were not held

accountable for excessive use of force by officers in their command. (Christopher, 1991, p. 3)

The problems in Los Angeles were compounded by the unique situation of the police chief. Unlike any other municipal official in the United States, the police chief in this department was protected by a civil service status that in effect provided him with lifetime job tenure. For this reason, neither the Police Commission nor the city council had the power to remove Daryl Gates despite a history of inflammatory statements that angered various minority groups and the widely held perception that his department condoned the use of excessive force. Despite the Rodney King incident and the ensuing controversy, the chief was able to resist repeated calls for his resignation. In 1992, he finally agreed to voluntarily step down and retired from the department.

The Kansas City (Missouri) Police Department also had its share of problems when Steve Bishop was appointed chief in 1990. In addition to the videotaped beating already noted, there was a string of other incidents involving the use of excessive force, including a case in which a black clergyman was struck with the butt of a shotgun during a robbery investigation. Unlike the situation in Los Angeles, the chief responded to this situation in an aggressive manner. Within 14 months of taking office, he forced out 24 officers for misconduct (Terry, 1991). In addition, the department compiled a list of 25 officers who together accounted for more than half the citizen complaints filed against the agency. These so-called "bad boys" were given special training in an attempt to improve their communications skills in dealing with the public. The administration was seeking to convey the message that brutality would not be tolerated and that officers who used excessive force could expect to receive punishment. So far, this approach seems to be effective. The number of complaints filed against officers has dropped by 22%, the first time that these have decreased in 10 years (Terry, 1991).

Conclusion

This chapter has examined the issue of excessive police force. Various external methods of controlling this problem were examined. Each of these was found to be lacking in important ways that diminish their effectiveness. Internal control of unjustified police force was also explored. It was noted that departments have the capacity to insure officer compliance with legal requirements if the administration is inclined to exercise this authority. Two examples were cited: Los Angeles, where this important supervisory function has been neglected according to the report of the Independent Commission (Christopher, 1991), and Kansas City (Missouri), where meaningful steps have been taken to prevent abuses of citizens.

Discussion Questions

1. What constitutes the use of excessive force by police officers?
2. Explain the difference between internal and external controls on police misconduct.
3. Why is it difficult for a citizen to successfully sue the police?
4. Why are prosecutors often reluctant to file criminal charges against police officers who have used excessive force against citizens?
5. What is a civilian review board? Is this an effective means of controlling police misconduct? What factors lead you to this conclusion?
6. Discuss the factors that limit the ability of municipal officials to discipline police officers who have used excessive force.

Note

1. Two of the officers were later convicted in federal court for violating Rodney King's civil rights.

References

Alpert, G. P., & Dunham, R. C. (1992). *Policing urban America* (2nd ed.). Prospect Heights, IL: Waveland.

Benner, A. W. (1989). Psychological screening of police applicants. In R. C. Dunham & G. P. Alpert (Eds.), *Critical issues in policing: Contemporary readings* (pp. 72-86). Prospect Heights, IL: Waveland.

Campbell, A., & Schuman, H. (1969). Racial attitudes in fifteen American cities. (Supplemental study for the National Advisory Commission on Civil Disorders). Washington, DC: Government Printing Office.

Christopher, W. (1991). Report of the Independent Commission on the Los Angeles Police Department: Summary. Unpublished paper.

Claims up, says report: NYPD fails to monitor police misconduct suits. (1992, March 6). *Chief-Leader.*

del Carmen, R. V. (1987). *Criminal procedure for law enforcement personnel.* Monterey, CA: Brooks/Cole.

del Carmen, R. V. (1991). Civil and criminal liabilities of police officers. In T. Barker & D. L. Carter (Eds.), *Police deviance* (2nd ed.) (pp. 405-426). Cincinnati: Anderson.

Flanagan, T. J., & Vaughn, M. S. (in press). Public opinion about police abuse of force. In W. A. Geller & H. Toch (Eds.), *Police use of excessive force and its control: Key issues facing the nation.* Washington, DC: Police Executive Research Forum/National Institute of Justice.

Friedrich, R. J. (1980). Police use of force: Individuals, situations and organizations. *Annals of the American Academy of Political and Social Science, 452,* 82-97.

Fyfe, J. J. (1979). Administrative interventions on police shooting discretion: An empirical examination. *Journal of Criminal Justice, 7*(4), 309-323.

Goldstein, H. (1977). *Policing a free society.* Cambridge, MA: Ballinger.

Kappeler, V. E. (1993). *Critical issues in police civil liability.* Prospect Heights, IL: Waveland.

Kappeler, S. F., & Kappeler, V. E. (1992). A research note on Section 1983 claims against the police: Cases before the federal district courts in 1990. *American Journal of Police, 11*(a), 65-73.

Kerstetter, W. A. (1985). Who disciplines the police? Who should? In W. A. Geller (Ed.), Police leadership in America (pp. 149-182). New York: Praeger.

Mapp v. Ohio, 367 U.S. 643 (1961).

Milton, C. H., Halleck, J. W., Lardner, J., & Abrecht, G. L. (1977). *Police use of deadly force.* Washington, DC: Police Foundation.

Miranda v. Arizona, 384 U.S. 436 (1966).

Monell v. Department of Social Services, 436 U.S. 658 (1978).

Project (1979). Suing the police in federal court. *Yale Law Journal, 88*(4), 781-824.

Reiss, A. J. (1971). *The police and the public.* New Haven: Yale University Press.

Sherman, L. W. (1983). Reducing police gun use: Critical events, administrative policy, and organizational change. In M. Punch (Ed.), *Control in the police organization* (pp. 88-125). Cambridge: M.I.T. Press.

Sherman, L. W., & Cohn, E. G. (with Gartin, P., Hamilton, E. E., & Rogan, D. P.). (1986). *Citizens killed by big city police, 1970-84.* Washington, DC: Crime Control Institute.

Terry, D. (1991, September 10). Kansas City police go after their "bad boys." *New York Times,* p. A1.

Walker, S. (1992). *The police in America: An introduction.* New York: McGraw Hill.

Walker, S., & Bumpus, V. W. (1991). Civilian review of the police: A national survey of the 50 largest cities, 1991. Unpublished paper.

West, P. (1988). Investigation of complaints against the police: Summary report of a national survey. *American Journal of Police, 7,* 101-121.

West, P. (1991) Investigation and review of complaints against police officers: An overview of issues and philosophies. In T. Barker & D. L. Carter (eds.) *Police Deviance* (2nd ed.) (pp. 373-404). Cincinnati, OH: Anderson.

7

Community Policing

Trends, Policies, Programs, and Definitions

JOSEPH F. RYAN

Police in Action

The next time you observe a police officer performing a particular task, such as directing traffic, stop and think of how that officer might respond to the question, "What is your goal as a police officer?" If you proceed with this fantasy and decide to ask that question, hopefully the officer will not think you are trying to be a wise guy.

Under a research grant from the National Institute of Justice to define community policing, the above question was asked of approximately 60 officers, of various ranks, in six police agencies around the country (Ryan, 1993). The responses were quite astonishing. Of the three traditionally recognized goals of law enforcement, that is, (a) to protect life and property, (b) prevent crime, and (c) to apprehend offenders, only one—that

AUTHOR'S NOTE: This chapter draws on the author's *Community Policing: Breaking the Thin Blue Line,* a final report submitted to the National Institute of Justice in 1993. This research was supported under award #91-IJ-CX-0025 from the National Institute of Justice, Office of Justice Programs. Points of view in this document are those of the author and do not necessarily represent the official position of the U.S. Department of Justice.

of protecting life and property—was mentioned, and that by only one officer. Most officers could not state any goal.

In view of these nonresponses, a contingency question of "What do you do every day?" was presented. At this point these officers gave a gamut of responses, the most common being, "We do everything," or "We answer radio calls." From these statements, one could conclude that the goal of policing is elusive. If our officers are unsure of their goals, even though some police agencies display the logo "To Protect and Serve" on the side of their police vehicles, who then will know what our police are supposed to give us?

Community Policing

Amidst this confusion arises (or, as some cynics believe, re-arises under a different name) the current push to implement a new strategy and philosophy of policing throughout the country. This latest innovation in policing is called community policing, and everyone is scrambling to define it (National Institute of Justice, 1992). The process of searching for a definition has generated a focus on the central question of policing—"What do we want from our police?" In essence, it is an acknowledgment that no one knows with certainty the best police strategy to deal with crime and violence.

Adding to the confusion concerning what the police can and cannot do is the new emphasis on "quality of life" issues, which seems to have become part and parcel of community policing. Dirty streets, noisy radios, and other urban annoyances are now being considered part of the crime problem. Like the directing of traffic, the task of a traffic department in many locations, these duties have no clearly explained effect on crime rates (e.g., what do dirty streets have to do with crime?) and obscure the role of the police as "crime fighters."

The inability to define "quality of life" illustrates another difficulty in understanding the focus of community policing. In this context, it is important to appreciate the ramifications of the meaning of "quality of life." In one sense this can be an easily attained goal of community policing. There seems to be some consensus among citizens that whatever conflict exists in a neighborhood, it would be nice if the streets were clean, the toilets in tenements operated, and so forth. Would this consensus extend to improving "quality of life" in a neighborhood by obtaining a Philharmonic Concert Hall or other notable socially uplifting institutions?

If the community is going to have an input in deciding what quality of life issues the police will address, who will draw the line on what is law enforcement related? Unless such uncertainties are clarified, community policing will be merely another new police program, and it will meet the fate of all its predecessors. In order to understand why some believe it is just another new police program, it is necessary to examine what is meant by *community policing* in contrast to traditional policing.

Traditional Policing
Versus Community Policing

Discussions of community policing suggest it differs from traditional policing in that traditional policing is primarily *reactive,* with activities like responding to emergency calls, whereas community policing takes a more *proactive* stance toward crime. Another form of policing that at times is juxtaposed with community policing is "problem-oriented policing." This style of policing focuses on police as problem solvers, but it is not the focus of this chapter.

Are there genuine differences among community policing, problem-solving policing, and traditional policing? In essence, one could strongly argue that all of them are the underlying strategies and tactics (tools) of a philosophy held by a "good" police officer, who uses different ones for different conditions. One could further argue, therefore, that if traditional police officers were equipped with all of these tools, there would be no need to invent new programs called community policing or problem-solving policing.

What Are the Benefits
of a New Style of Policing?

The purported benefits that neighborhoods would realize if their local police agency were to employ a community policing strategy would lead one to believe that the answer to society's crime problem has been found. As with most simplistic beliefs, this is open to challenge on several fronts:

1. Impact on taxpayers—foot patrols, individual problem solving, attending meetings, and other community policing strategies require both police time and significant resources.
2. Securing funding—law enforcement officers are not yet highly skilled in justifying demands for more monies and/or more personnel or in being accountable to the taxpayers beyond conducting follow-up interviews to crime victims or knocking on doors.

3. Evaluation—Experts in policing have yet to develop a method to assess the benefits of community versus traditional policing in terms of reducing crime and improving the quality of life.

Most citizens do not realize the amount of taxes they pay to support their police departments. New York City has at least three separate police departments: the New York City Police, employing approximately 28,000 uniformed officers; the Transit Police; and the Housing Police. (There are other police units that provide coverage to selected locations in New York, such as Parks, Amtrak Trains, Port Authority, and so on.)

In 1993, the cost for the regular New York City police alone is over $1.7 billion dollars annually. That amount equals the cost for all of the different human resource service agencies in New York City, such as child and adult welfare. This cost factor is just one component of the dilemma society faces. The important question one needs to answer is, "What are the goal(s) society is seeking to achieve with this significant investment?"

Historical Perspective
on the Goals of Policing

Concern about community policing centers on society's expectations of its police. A definition of these expectations would have to rest upon the goals described in dictionaries and texts on police, which are: (a) protecting life and property, (b) preventing crime, and (c) apprehending offenders.

The fullest definition of the goals of policing is found in the nine tenets set forth by Sir Robert Peel in 1829. They include not only a basic restatement of the above three goals, but also two crucial ones that modern law enforcement officers seem to have forgotten. These are:

1. To maintain at all times a relationship with the public that gives reality to the historic tradition that the police are the public and that the public are the police; the police being only members of the public who are paid to give full-time attention to duties which are incumbent on every citizen, in the interests of community welfare and existence . . . [and]
2. To recognize always that the test of police efficiency is the absence of crime and disorder, and not the visible evidence of police action in dealing with them. (Reith, 1948, p. 18)

When one juxtaposes the three issues of community policing noted earlier—impact on taxpayers, securing funding, and evaluation—a quandary emerges. Obviously, the goals of policing have been with us since Peel's directions. The failure to achieve them seems clear if we listen to citizen concerns. Therefore we need to ask not only "What is community policing," but "What is policing?" Confusion on this issue becomes obvious when police keep reinventing police strategies over and over again.

In one sense, it is easy to start with the definition of community policing offered by its supporters. The best means of understanding community policing is the analogy of an inverted pyramid. At the bottom of the pyramid are the small rural police departments, where the police and community exist on an intimate basis, where everyone *knows* each other. Proceeding up this inverted diagram, you encounter suburban communities. Here, some community residents know the police and some do not. At the top of the pyramid are the large urban centers. At this level, community intimacy is difficult to envision. How likely is it that citizens residing in multiple highrises will know who their community patrol officer is—unless we take the absurd measure of deploying one officer to each highrise?

Peel's tenets seem originally intended for a community more reflective of our present-day rural neighborhoods than our large modern urban centers—thus underscoring our quandary. As his tenets were originally dictated, they may not be completely adaptable to present-day police strategies. Obviously, we have an emerging redefinition of the role of the police, or, as the noted police researcher George Kelling suggested, we are heading toward a new concept of policing (Kelling, 1991).

What Is Policing?

There are a number of attempts to explain what policing can be about. Herman Goldstein's most recent book, entitled *Problem-Oriented Policing* (1990), is a valuable contribution to policing. It focuses on what a police officer can or could do, assuming agreement with his view of officers as problem solvers. The difficulty with this approach is our inability to assess its effectiveness: that is, how can you measure anecdotal reports of problem-solving scenarios?

This author's contacts with community police officers in New York City's Model Precinct offer another perspective on policing that has implications within the context of crime and quality of life concerns. Officers there point out, "Yes, the neighborhood looks cleaner; the peddlers and loiterers who hang around are gone; yet Mr. and Mrs. Jones still tell me there is crime in their neighborhood. Now what do we do?" Their question is particularly appropriate to the ninth tenet of Peel's policing: that is, community policing may be just another high-visibility strategy that does not substantially reduce crime and disorder, unless we redefine disorder.

Policing experts readily support this perspective. The pessimistic outlook is that no police-related tasks, in any type of policing, "appear" (the use of these quotes reflects the recognition of existing measures of policing's effect) to have any significant long-term impact upon reducing crime and disorder.

A visual tour of an area with community policing strategies in use may reveal some of the short-term benefits of community policing: cleaner streets, clean and fenced-in empty lots, murals painted on walls, and so on. On the surface, the neighborhood appears to have been reborn. But to the Model Precinct community police officers, this success has also brought a sense of disillusionment. Repeated contacts by this researcher with these officers revealed that although they believed they were crime fighters, they felt they had not reduced crime or disorder. The failure of community policing to deal with this perception raises questions concerning the merits of the "broken windows" theory—the theory that broken windows, dirty streets, and other signs of deterioration set the stage for crime to enter a neighborhood—and the role of police in stemming such deterioration (Wilson & Kelling, 1982). As one officer stated, "Why are we the ones attempting to lead communities to clean the litter in streets and empty lots? We are crime fighters, not supervisors for the sanitation department."

Part of this disillusionment centered on these officers' inability to exceed the boundaries of what they perceived to be the limits of policing. Although the neighborhood was clean, residents still expressed fear about crime. Community police officers would visit apartments and listen to tenants express fears about known criminals, drug dealers, violence next door, the inability of the families to provide children with adequate care, and many other social ills.

The experiences of one pioneer and "model" community patrol officer in New York City illustrates another aspect of the dilemma faced by these officers. This individual was a white officer who worked off duty as a karate instructor and received numerous awards from the community for his professional efforts. The neighborhood he worked in was a high-crime area in New York City, and according to the 1980 census approximately 90% of the residents were black.

The officer was successful in moving drugs out of his beat area while he was working. However, residents informed him that while he was on lunch, drug dealers would return to a local store and sell contraband. To correct this condition, he asked for a table and chair, which he placed in front of the store and proceeded to eat his lunch there daily. The problem moved away, or as experts would state, was more than likely displaced.

The response from police hierarchy was to label him as a "psycho" (although they would never publicly acknowledge this). This label was applied partly because they felt he was developing too high a profile: The community knew this officer and not the precinct commander. From a management liability perspective, there was a possible justification in the argument, "Why doesn't he take a lunch like everyone else? If he keeps this up he is going to step on someone's toes and get hurt." Management was correct. His aggressiveness did not go unnoticed in the community. One day while he was walking under an elevated train, an unknown person dropped a cinder block, hitting him on the shoulder. Because of this injury, he subsequently had to retire on disability.

In reaction to what they perceived as their inability to deal with crime and go beyond the known boundaries of policing, officers assigned to New York's Model Precinct began to request transfers back to traditional patrol. The problem became so severe that by the end of the first year and a half, approximately 70% of the officers in the Model Precinct had returned to traditional patrol or other duties, without a sense of accomplishment.

This constant expansion and redefinition of the role of the police only contribute to the growing confusion faced by the officers. As noted earlier, no one is clear on how the police should best attempt to deal with the crime problem. And yet it is necessary to return to the simplest of questions: What are taxpayers getting from using their police, let alone community police officers, as their agents of social control?

Recognizing this confusion on what community policing is, as well as what police should do in general, the National Institute of Justice supported a research effort to define community policing (Ryan, 1993). This author took the approach that in order to define community policing one also needed to first grasp what police do. The most logical way envisioned to accomplish this task was simply to ask police to state their goals, on the assumption that one's daily activities should have some overall connection to a goal(s), whether from a personal or an organizational perspective.

Method

From a good management perspective, measuring or evaluating the effectiveness of any endeavor requires that one first define the goal(s) that describe what one intends to achieve. If we are to achieve the recognized goals of policing, we need to know not only the goals but the concomitant objectives. For example, if the goal is crime prevention, how do we achieve that goal? Once we know this elementary component, we can (hopefully) proceed to measure it and then say whether we are succeeding or failing, and where we need to direct (or redirect) our efforts.

The goal of this research was an attempt to develop a perspective on how to define policing (and community policing) by determining its goals and objectives. The objective entailed interviewing two groups of police: those who chose or were given labels as either traditional or community policing officers. It is important to note that in view of the lack of a definition of community policing, no police agencies currently use a pure concept (if such exists) of community policing.

Departments were selected on the basis of their proclaimed statements about community policing efforts. (There is no official estimate of the number of law enforcement agencies engaged in this style of policing.) Because this research was purely exploratory, there was no attempt to make the selection process random. Personal contacts with the police chiefs/commissioners concerning their willingness to permit their officers to be interviewed were the major determining selection factor. The sites chosen were Philadelphia, New Haven, Portland (Oregon), San Diego, Harrison (New York), and a pretest location.

Although the selection process sought officers who in the assessment of their chief were best able to articulate what they did, the primary consideration was to ensure that the officers were not selected simply because they supported their chief's administration. The selection proved accurate, as evidenced in some critical comments offered against the chief. Before conducting the interview, the officers were informed of the nature of the survey: that is, to develop a framework for what the police can provide society.

Fixed format questions were not used because they would give officers key words and phrases, such as "crime prevention," that might bias their response. Open-ended questions were used to provide them with the opportunity to develop their own personalized definitions of policing. To facilitate this inquiry, an analogy to the medical profession was offered to the officers. The analogy went as follows:

> Officer, assume there were a doctor in this room. If you were to ask that person what is her goal as a doctor, she might respond that her goal is to save lives. If you asked how she achieves that goal (her objectives), the doctor might respond that she is an open heart surgeon and performs open heart surgery. If you then ask the doctor to assess her effectiveness, she might respond that last year she saved many lives. Using that framework, officer, what is your goal as a police person?

Findings

Before discussing the findings of this study, it is important to note that this was exploratory research, not aimed at providing definitive answers. It was an attempt to begin to define community policing. In the context of exploratory research, open-ended questions were used to elicit the perspectives of officers engaged in traditional and community policing activities. In responding to such questions, some officers used similar phrases to describe certain activities, but few have been repeated verbatim beyond a few key words. For example, in responding to the questions of whether the police and other government agencies could work together, one officer would respond, "I guess so," another, "Why not," and another, "Sure." In reporting such findings, we used broad statements that imply that most officers believe police and other government workers can work together, unless a significantly different response was offered.

In preparing to conduct research on determining a definition of community policing, one could argue that it would be pointless to go beyond what had already been offered by authors such as Trojanowicz and Bucqueroux (1990), Goldstein (1990), or Greene and Mastrofski (1991). But the debate of these researchers over whether community policing is rhetoric or reality suggests that there is no consensus among police practitioners and researchers that a definition exists.

Although a significant amount of attention has been given to defining the authority and legitimacy of policing, scant, if any, attention has been given to clearly defining, as a first step, what we want our police to do. Our study was set up to provide that answer by asking officers what their goals as police officers were.

The answer that emerged practically from the onset was that no definition of community policing would be obtained from this study, let alone one for policing itself. However, what did emerge was an understanding of why police are trying to latch onto community policing.

The findings of the study (Ryan, 1993) were originally presented in two sections. Part I contained a general discussion of the community policing efforts at the sites that were visited. Part II contained the results of the interviews with the officers to determine their goals. This chapter will discuss the latter part of the research.

The number of officers interviewed was based on the size of the agency. Fifteen officers were interviewed in Philadelphia, 10 in New Haven, San Diego, Portland and the pretest site, and 5 in Harrison, for a total of 60 officers. These interviews do not include those conducted with the chiefs and or designated individuals who assisted in articulating that agencies' depiction of community policing.

The decision process to determine who was involved in community or traditional policing was based on the officers' statements that they were engaged in said activities. Excluding the 10 officers in San Diego who are in involved in POP and the 5 from Harrison who did not avow any particular police strategy leaves 45 officers. Of this 45, only 16 claimed that they were specifically engaged in community policing.

The responses to the questionnaire were clearly consistent. This consistency existed not only among the various ranks, but across the six sites. After about 20 to 30 interviews, a temptation to cease this process arose. However, logic dictated that more interviews would strengthen the findings in this study. In view of the consistency, this report does not discuss whether the responses in San Diego were different from those in Philadelphia, or whether a chief's response was different from that of a patrol officer.

The only difference was noted in the response to the question of whether the officers could provide documentation of their purported claims of success. That sole difference occurred between officers who did traditional policing and officers who claimed they had a "community policing" background. That finding will be discussed shortly.

It was during the early stages of the research that it became clear that a precise definition of community policing would not emerge. As previously noted, during the pretesting of the questionnaire, the 10 officers were asked, in the context of an analogy to the medical profession, "What is your goal as a police officer?" None of these officers, nor those from the five research sites (with the exception of one supervisor indicating a goal of "protecting the people"), were able to state a goal. One officer did state that his goal was to go home at the end of the day.

When officers were asked the contingency question of "What do you do every day?" the responses immediately began to flow. Responses such as "We do everything" or "We do whatever the politicians or the chief wants" were in the majority.

Those officers engaged in community policing were more likely to say they were engaged in community policing activities. Some indicated the stereotyped tactics such as foot patrol or knocking on doors. Others broadened their tasks to include getting the homeless off the streets, getting drug users into treatment centers, or securing abandoned buildings.

In response to the contingency question of "What do you do every day?" 15 officers stated, "We do everything." This was the most common response, followed by "We respond to calls for service (or radio runs or the dispatcher)," stated by 12 officers. Other responses included "I help people" and "The boss tells me what to do." The remaining responses were singular and continued to reflect some of the piecemeal perceptions of what the police do (e.g., get a cat out of a tree).

The most significant finding to emerge from these interviews was in response to the question of whether the officers believed they were successful and if they had evidence to support this belief. The 16 officers in this study who stated that they engaged in community policing differed significantly from traditional officers in their response to the latter question.

When self-avowed traditional officers were asked whether they perceived they were successful, the response was "Yes" or "Absolutely." But when asked if there was supporting evidence, they were unable to provide such information. At least 10 officers stated "If you look at the crime statistics, I guess you could say we are not." However, most if not all of the 16 community police officers immediately stated in one fashion or another that they were successful and that they had proof.

When asked the nature of the proof, one officer stated, "I have a trophy from the community." Others acknowledged letters received back from the community thanking them for their efforts, or said that crime victims that they had revisited said the information they gave was helpful and thanked them for coming back and asked how they were doing. These perceptions are the most significant in the context of defining a difference between community and traditional policing.

In those instances when Portland officers indicated they were engaged in community policing activities, they were able to provide documentation of their anecdotal stories. Evidence of their success was found in Portland's "Community Policing Problem Solving Action Plan and Partnership Agreements." These forms were nonbinding community agreements made by communities and police for the purpose of working together to resolve a problem.

One could argue from a mental health perspective that the community police officers seemed to be happier, and in this study this did appear to be the case. Their outlook was generally optimistic about what they were doing, and they were able to offer proof of their success immediately when asked. However, that is a subjective statement, and the matter will be left to those experts who know how to measure "happiness."

If happiness results from the perception of one's success, one could argue that police unions and their membership would support community policing more if management included them in developing the strategies for it. One interview in particular illustrates this argument. An officer who was asked to define his goal as a police officer and how that was achieved stated,

> I am told it is community policing, but I don't know what that is. For example, I am directed to get out of my car each morning at a set time, turn on the roof light, and stay there for a half hour. One day when I was approached by a citizen as to what I was doing, I responded I don't know. The citizen walked away confused. So was I.

At this time I offered a possible explanation for the officer's assignment. A police vehicle could have been sitting on that corner for months, and after a while no one would have noticed—it would have become part of the landscape. Community policing includes attempts to increase the visibility of the police, and the turning on of the lights, like the use of roadblocks in the Newark community policing experiment, accomplishes that task. The officer was astonished at the simplicity of the explanation and responded, "If someone had told me that, I could have appreciated what I was doing."

The next major question asked of the officers was, "If data reveal that it is questionable whether the police are winning the war on crime/drugs, what should the goals of the police be?" At this point, five officers offered the goal of "crime prevention," and three stated that we needed "to arrest offenders."

The questionnaire was designed so that if the officers did not articulate specific goals at this point, they would be offered the three traditional goals (i.e., preventing crime, protecting life and property, and apprehending offenders) and asked whether those goals should be retained. The overwhelming response was, "Oh, those—absolutely." Several officers believed that the "drug dilemma" would make it next to impossible to deal with crime. Ten of the community policing officers said that a goal of policing should be community policing, but they could not articulate what they meant by that.

When asked to define their concept of community, most officers gave one or more of the acknowledged components, such as residents or churches. However, a number of officers recognized that there were barriers of individual personalities (on both sides, police and community) or race that would make it difficult, but not impossible, for the police and community to work together.

In response to the veiled question, "In the context of this relationship (i.e., working with the community) is there a time when it could come 'too close'?", 10 officers immediately recognized a corruption potential. The potential, they believed, lay in the vague guidelines on what are acceptable police-community relationships, such as when it is appropriate to accept a free cup of coffee. Forty-two officers (consistently across the ranks) acknowledged that although their departments officially prohibited free cups of coffee, they did not see any harm if these were offered in the context of a community meeting or in a store where officers began to engage in community policing activities.

When officers were asked whether they believe they could work with other government agencies in dealing with related issues, most gave simplistic responses, such as "I guess so," "Why not?" or "Sure." However, at least 20 officers basically stated that they believed it would be difficult for the police to work with other government agencies. The basis for this belief was that they would be "stepping on [other agencies'] turf," or that other agencies (e.g., child protective agencies) might raise confidentiality as a barrier.

The last significant issue raised during these interviews was to have the officers focus on a particular police activity or incident in which they had participated and attempt to see if their previously stated beliefs matched up with what had actually occurred. They were also asked whether they were aware of the enlightened strategies suggested by advocates of community policing.

In this series of questions the officers were asked to select a recent police activity or incident. In the case of the seven ride-alongs, officers were asked about the last assignment they handled. All were asked to respond whether they were satisfied with what they were able to give to the citizen, what barriers (e.g., lack of management support) might have inhibited their response, and whether they, the community, or any other government agency could have prevented the incident from occurring.

With 60 officers, there were almost 60 different incidents. In the context of police activities, supervisors and managers offered their insights on their respective roles. Rather than discuss each as an anecdotal story, this report highlights only a few incidents. These were chosen because they reveal the depth of police knowledge, or lack of it, on how these incidents should have been handled or whether they could have been prevented, or, more important, the role the community or other government agencies could have played—an important dilemma for community policing.

A captain in one city spoke with enthusiasm for community policing. Community policing, as this captain perceived it, permitted supervisors to confront community problems directly. At community meetings police management and community now had the ability to confront the front line officer. In a recent meeting, when citizens had complained of abandoned autos, the captain turned and said to the officer in the audience, "That is the officer you need to see." This captain was extremely pleased with community policing because he no longer had to return to work the next day to tell the lieutenant to tell the sergeant to tell the officer to do something about the particular community concerns raised at last evening's meeting.

Some officers had to go back a couple of days to find an activity that they handled. The officers in Philadelphia were quick to criticize their required task of transporting sick persons, arguing that it was a waste of their talents. In Harrison, an officer spoke of handling a motor vehicle accident that occurred during a rain storm. It was hard to affix blame on the driver because the weather was really bad, or on the manufacturer of the car because nothing was wrong with the vehicle. The only person injured was a child who was not wearing a seat belt. The officer felt that if there had been stricter enforcement of seat belt requirements for children under a certain age (the child was under 6 years), the child would have escaped injury.

Most of the community police officers who were interviewed were better able to express an understanding of the role of other government agencies. One of these officers discussed his role in preventing individuals from committing crimes. He gave the example of someone who was snatching purses in a local mall and who used a local abandoned building as a place to flee and hide. This officer was proud that he was able, by using the resources of another government agency, to locate the landlord of the building and "force" (he did not reveal what force meant) the owner to seal the building off. In the context of prevention, he felt that if corrections agencies were to do their job, such as at least holding criminals for as long as possible, or if the local government passed stricter laws on securing abandoned buildings, the problem would not disappear, but it would have certainly been "lessened."

Other community police officers also highlighted the role of a housing agency or knowledge of where to find landlord information as crucial in being able to secure abandoned buildings frequented by drug users. Some officers recognized the need to work with child protective agencies, or the need for referral sources for victims of crime, or for anyone else who erroneously calls the police for services that they cannot provide (e.g., potholes in front of their house or garbage that was not picked up).

The inability of police to articulate a more detailed role for other government agencies, as shown above, represents a major concern for community policing. Although most of the community police officers recognized the value of knowing available resources, only the officers in Portland were quickly able to point out that they could call their "Community Policing Support Division," a unit that served as a resource for the officers looking for referrals or other information that could lead to solving a problem.

Harrison was selected because it is a small community where the police and community are more likely to know each other, and this could be considered a self-fulfilling definition of where community policing begins. Harrison Police Department has 58 uniformed and 7 civilian members. The approximately 23,000 residents are 98% white and are in the upper and affluent income brackets. Most homes have a real estate value starting around $400,000. There were 45,541 calls for service, 18 violent crimes, and 492 property offenses.

The interviews with Harrison police personnel were very illuminating. In reality, it would appear that everyone does know his or her neighbor in Harrison. When citizens leave for vacation, many of them come to the police and fill out a form indicating that they will be out of town for a while. This does not require the police to visit these locations, but it permits them to be able to notify the owner if something happens.

It was interesting to note that these officers had a difficult time in selecting a police activity they could use as a reference point during the interview. Three of the five officers cited one vehicle accident they all responded to.

More important, a gap between what the public expects of their police did emerge from these interviews. The community complains about seeing their officers sitting in the cars doing nothing (or "goofing off"). However, as one officer honestly noted, it is obvious that in the absence of a significant police workload, "what else do they want us to do?"

As a side note to this site visit, a larger policing question deals with residents notifying the police that they are away on vacation. From the interviews there is no clearcut reason why the police no longer respond to these homes to conduct house checks. However, each of these houses is connected to an alarm company, and it appears that this activity has been unofficially taken away from this local police department.

Could these officers make use of their time in visiting these houses? According to Harrison Police Department statistics, burglaries are not a problem. The major concern is criminal mischief, youth activity, and minor larcenies, which make up the bulk of the 492 offenses noted above. The question then becomes, "What should be the goal of these officers?"

Conclusion

From the differences in policing strategies in the sites visited, and with the present stage of community policing development in this country, it was not possible to arrive at a concise definition of community policing. That is, the research could not provide a concrete depiction that would assist a locality in developing a community policing strategy. It might be possible for a given department to cull ideas from different efforts and further develop its own model of community policing. What did surface from this research is a philosophy and strategy for community policing that may be viewed as different from that of traditional policing.

If there is a historical perspective for the philosophy of traditional policing, it is one that involves "fighting crime reactively." In this study, it appears that community policing involves a different philosophy and strategies. It is characterized by the police "recognizing the need to be accountable to those they serve" or, as some officers believed, "bridging the gap between the community and the police," and then taking efforts through the various community policing strategies to reach these goals. This belief is supported by the fact that in three of the sites a search for a new strategy was spurred by a conflict in the community where the police were unable to address the problem through traditional policing efforts. In one sense adoption of community policing is saying to the community that we (the police) are letting them in on our secret, that is, that we do not yet know how to control crime and that we need their help.

From the interviews, one might suggest that community policing is a style of policing that can improve relations between the police and those they serve by attempting to hold police accountable for their actions (or failure to act). This was evident in Philadelphia's efforts to have their community police officers attend community meetings where residents could give those officers their specific complaints. The efforts in Portland argue strongly for police accountability. Portland's Community Policing Problem Solving Action Plan and Partnership Agreements better enable the police to solve problems and reveal who is responsible for not correcting the condition, whether the police, other government agencies, or the community itself. Additionally, Philadelphia's designating a title for a community police officer as an "abandoned auto" officer, like Portland's partnership agreements, illustrates a concern for improving the quality of life by including issues beyond those directly related to crime. It should be noted that efforts to increase police accountability have not yet included efforts to clarify police goals (e.g., protect life and property) and means of accomplishing them.

Although no clear definition is in sight for community policing in the near future, this study does reveal the potential value of community policing as a strategy for dealing with crime. Portland's Community Policing Problem Solving Action Plan and Partnership Agreements provide a qualitative strategy that offers a beginning point for dealing with disorder and crime. The obvious difficulty lies in our ability to nurture it in a timely fashion so that it may be considered a viable strategy in society's war on crime.

More important, Portland's Community Policing Problem Solving Action Plan and Partnership Agreements and the responses from community police officers that they had evidence of their success are significant contributions that have emerged from the experiences with community policing. In one sense, they give the police a perception that they can start to make changes by first focusing on "small wins." This feature of community policing might also provide insight on how administrators can reinvigorate the morale of their officers by at least giving them a sense of accomplishment for what they are doing.

This study also raises the issue of the responsibility of other government and criminal justice agencies for police success or failure in meeting their goals. As some officers noted, police are effective at tasks within their traditional competencies, such as making arrests. They believe their arrests would be more effective if the people they arrested were sentenced to jail and kept there rather than becoming repeat offenders. Similarly, if other government agencies were to more effectively deal with conditions that were referred to them, such as family violence, then maybe these conditions would not keep coming back to the attention of the police.

In summation, the simple starting point required for police goal and objective setting is a consensus on what we want from our police. They cannot be an agency that believes they are responsible for "everything."

There is no concise definition of community policing in terms of strategy—the six sites visited deployed different strategies. But there has been a significant push toward the development of new police strategies. In the absence of a model community policing effort, is this trend largely a matter of rhetoric or do the new strategies really differ substantially from those of traditional policing? The answer lies in the term *community policing* itself—that is, community. Police are now realizing that they do not exist in a vacuum. The actions they take, the strategies they employ to deal with crime, suggest that the community needs to be part of their efforts. In essence, community policing can be defined in terms of having the police be accountable to those they serve. Maybe another term should be substituted so we can call community policing what it really is: accountable policing.

Discussion Questions

1. If you were to ask a police officer who was transporting a patient to a hospital in a police vehicle, "What are your goals as a police officer in relation to this task?" what type of response would you expect?

2. Why does the author suggest that community policing be redefined as "accountable policing"?

3. When advocates of community policing are asked if community policing is working, their most common response is to offer anecdotal stories. How do you measure the success or failure of such singular events in the larger context of policing?

4. Why are the two selected tenets of Roberts Peel's original understanding of policing important to community policing? Translate the two tenets into their actual meaning for police strategies.

5. If community policing is difficult to assess in terms of traditional measures of policing, that is complaints and arrests, how might society assess its effectiveness?

6. Do you believe community policing is a viable policing strategy?

References

Goldstein, H. (1990). *Problem-oriented policing.* Philadelphia: Temple University Press.

Greene, J., & Mastrofski, S. (1991). *Community policing: Rhetoric or reality.* New York: Praeger.

Kelling, G. (1991, Autumn). Crime and metaphor: Toward a new concept of policing. *(New York) City Journal,* pp. 65-72.

National Institute of Justice. (1992, August). Community policing. *National Institute of Justice Journal.*

Reith, C. (1948). *A short history of the British police.* London: Oxford University Press.

Ryan, J. F. (1993). Community policing: Breaking the thin blue line. Final Report submitted to the National Institute of Justice.

Trojanowicz, R., & Bucqueroux, B. (1990). *Community policing: A contemporary perspective.* Cincinnati: Anderson.

Wilson, J., & Kelling, G. L. (1982, March). The police and neighborhood safety. *Atlantic Monthly,* pp. 29-38.

8

Auto Theft

Countering Violent Trends for the 90s

MARY ELLEN BEEKMAN

According to the most recent Uniform Crime Reporting (UCR) statistics, over 1,661,700 vehicle thefts occurred in 1991 (Federal Bureau of Investigation, August 1992). This record-high number continues an alarming trend that began in the mid-1980s. Between 1984 and 1991, the number of vehicle thefts increased by 61%. In 1991, direct losses to the American public traceable to this crime totaled nearly $8.3 million (Federal Bureau of Investigation, October 1992).

As disturbing as the rising rate of vehicle theft is an even more ominous trend recently began to dominate the nation's headlines. Armed vehicle theft, led by its most infamous and widespread variety—carjacking—represents a violent escalation in an already-booming area of criminal activity.

AUTHOR'S NOTE: From "Auto Theft" by M. E. Beekman, 1993 (October), *F.B.I. Law Enforcement Bulletin, 62,* pp. 17-22. Adapted with the permission of the Federal Bureau of Investigation.

Armed Vehicle Theft

Carjacking

An informal survey of FBI field divisions determined that just over 19,000 carjackings occurred throughout the United States in 1991; over 25,000 were estimated to have occurred in 1992 (Federal Bureau of Investigation, October 1992). Although these figures actually represent a small proportion of the overall number of vehicle thefts (less than 1%), the random nature, acute sense of violation, and threat of violence inherent in carjacking provoke intense community fear of this crime.

Although a limited number of armed vehicle thefts appear to be sponsored by theft rings or criminal gangs, carjacking, in general, continues to be a crime of opportunity committed by individuals or small groups. Analysis of FBI cases and discussion with supervisors in more than 30 field offices who maintain regular contact with local and state police agencies reinforce the position that very few armed vehicle thefts are actually the work of organized theft rings or criminal gangs.

Methods used by carjackers vary. For the most part, more organized groups tend to commit the highly publicized "bump and run" and "rolling road block" thefts. However, analysis indicates that the majority of carjackings occur in parking lots, residential streets or driveways, service stations, and intersections.

Theft From Parking Garages

Although the now-familiar carjacking method is the most notorious strain of armed vehicle theft, it is not the only type. Car thieves in metropolitan areas have also been known to "case" parking garages looking for vehicles, which they then steal after incapacitating garage attendants.

In a scheme investigated by the FBI's New York City field office during "Operation Fleetwheels," several armed individuals would enter 24-hour public parking garages that were "inventoried" earlier in the day by a member of the theft ring to ensure a sufficient number of targeted vehicles. The subjects forced the garage attendant(s) at gunpoint into the trunk of a nearby vehicle as a member of the theft ring located the keys to selected automobiles. Within minutes, each ring member drove out of the garage with a luxury vehicle.

To evade the police, the perpetrators parked the stolen vehicles in another 24-hour garage. The thieves left with a parking stub, while the police searched nearby roadways for the recently stolen vehicles.

Later, ring members removed the license plates and placed temporary tags on the vehicles. After a day or so, the perpetrators retrieved the stolen vehicles and drove them to a new location, usually during rush hour. The perpetrators then stored the vehicles in a garage in another part of the city until they were resold.

The Key Is the Key

These types of crimes stem from a basic rule of today's car thieves: Obtain the keys, as well as the vehicle. Stealing cars, especially expensive automobiles, without keys invariably results in considerable damage to the vehicles and thus lowers their price in the illegal markets.

The situation exists largely because manufacturers of luxury automobiles are taking steps to ensure that only individuals possessing the original keys can operate vehicles. Some manufacturers now make keys that cannot be easily duplicated commercially: The manufacturer is the only source of the key. Other auto makers embed computer chips into ignition keys. Removing the key from the ignition immobilizes the vehicle, and only a key with a matching computer chip can start the motor.

In addition to the growing sophistication of factory precautions and the need to safeguard the value of stolen automobiles, the prevalence of vehicle security systems also underscores the need for thieves to steal the keys along with the vehicles. All of these factors seem to lead to a shift from traditional vehicle-theft techniques to more confrontational and violent methods.

Backlash

A reformed car thief recently told investigators that "for every pro there is a con." The individual elaborated that whenever confronted by an obstacle, thieves find a way around it. Applying this to the automobile theft trade, he stated that the more sophisticated antitheft devices become, the more cunning thieves must be to overcome them.

This reasoning may help to explain the dramatic rise in armed vehicle thefts. In many cases, carjacking represents a reckless, but effective, backlash against the use of sophisticated antitheft devices. From a thief's perspective, putting a gun to a victim's head overcomes any antitheft device.

At the same time, the use of sophisticated antitheft devices leads some drivers to assume a false sense of security. This sometimes causes them to abandon normal precautions. Investigators concur that thieves will find a way to steal a vehicle, regardless of any antitheft system in place. Recently, thieves stole a stretch limousine from a driveway at the owner's business. They left behind only one item: the antitheft device that the owner had attached to the steering wheel.

The Thieves and the Market

The majority of vehicles stolen by carjackers are taken for joy rides or to use in committing other crimes. Analysis suggests that nationally as many as 90% of the vehicles taken in carjackings are eventually recovered.

However, some vehicles taken through carjacking and the majority of vehicles stolen by conventional means, especially luxury automobiles, find their way to enterprises known as "chop shops," which deal in stolen car parts. The market for stolen vehicles also includes local drug dealers or other wealthy criminals who "order" specific luxury automobiles as status symbols.

Like most people, criminals enjoy a bargain and will seek to purchase "previously owned" vehicles at drastically discounted prices. Criminals order luxury automobiles through intermediaries who purchase these stolen vehicles from street thieves.

Disposal of Stolen Vehicles

When carjackers or other thieves steal vehicles for profit, they generally attempt to dispose of them quickly through intermediaries. Once the intermediaries have the vehicles in their possession, they determine the next step for them: either dismantling or alteration.

Although some vehicles are entirely dismantled, or "chopped," for parts, in most cases either the front or rear end of a stolen vehicle will be attached to a legitimate vehicle of the same type that has been damaged. In this way, the entire vehicle now becomes "legitimate." Chop shop operators then dismantle the rest of the stolen vehicle or discard the remaining parts completely.

If operators decide to make the entire stolen vehicle legitimate, they take it to an individual who specializes in altering vehicle identification numbers (VINs). This task became more complex in recent years as manufacturers began imprinting the VIN in several different locations within vehicles. Intermediaries rely on skilled alterers because quality workmanship ensures a higher resale price. Generally, these specialists earn between $1,500 and $3,000 per vehicle.

In addition to the VIN, however, alterers must also legitimize the plastic MYLAR stickers that federal law now requires manufacturers to place on certain major automobile parts. Because altering this sticker is more difficult than changing the VIN, some alterers purchase counterfeit MYLAR plates. In many jurisdictions, it appears that this type of counterfeiting is on the rise, aided by new computer technology that makes MYLAR counterfeiting easier.

Documentation and Insurance

Although altering the VIN and MYLAR plates effectively creates a "new" vehicle to sell, intermediaries must still obtain documentation so that the vehicle may be registered or exported (Beekman & Daly, 1990). Accordingly, these intermediaries generally know where and how to obtain counterfeit paperwork. Other times, they may attempt to legitimize vehicles by obtaining valid state titles.

Investigators also believe that some of these vehicles carry legitimate automobile insurance obtained through assigned risk pools by brokers who are aware of the vehicles' true status. Intermediaries who wish to bypass the expense of securing legitimate insurance can purchase less expensive fraudulent insurance identification cards.

To prove the "reauthentication" of a luxury vehicle, intermediaries may take prospective buyers for a test drive. During the drive, the intermediaries may try to intentionally seek out a police patrol car and deliberately make a maneuver for which the vehicle will be stopped. The intermediary then allows officers to inspect the vehicle and even produces registration and insurance paperwork. This, of course, is to prove to the potential buyer that the true origin of the altered vehicle is undetectable, even by the police. Accordingly, vehicles that pass this test sell for a higher price.

Shipping Vehicles Across State Lines

Theft rings also transport a number of altered vehicles to other states, where they are purchased by drug dealers or other criminals. Because state police agencies stop many of these stolen vehicles while en route via interstate highways, one ring of clever thieves recently began using car carriers to transport multiple vehicles. The perpetrators determined that the police rarely stop car carriers to examine the vehicles being transported.

Countering the Problem

Because aspects of motor vehicle theft come under both federal and state laws, successful enforcement often requires the cooperation of various federal, state, and local agencies. This is especially true in cases that involve organized crime groups, gang-sponsored theft rings, and the more violent groups of carjackers.

Cooperative Efforts

Cooperation in the form of multiagency task forces can be a successful strategy that impacts significantly on armed motor vehicle thefts. Agencies in areas with high rates of violent vehicle theft should also consider establishing carjacking units and regional auto theft teams.

In some areas, previously existing task forces now place a new emphasis on violent vehicle thefts. In Atlanta, Georgia, the Metro Armed Robbery Task Force, which combines the resources of the FBI and several other agencies, arrested a subject for carjacking in connection with surveillance being conducted regarding bank robberies. In Dallas, Texas, the multiagency Interstate Theft Squad now places a priority on investigations of automobile theft with suspected gang connections.

A rash of carjackings in the summer of 1991 led the Detroit, Michigan, Police Department to create a special task force to combat the problem. According to Lt. Madelyn Williams of the Armed Robbery Unit of the Detroit Police Department,

> This departmental task force operates in addition to the multiagency Fugitive Task Force that focuses on the interstate aspects of violent vehicle theft. The Detroit Police Departmental task force serves as a central repository for reports, as a processing center for individuals arrested for carjacking, and as a source of information regarding manpower deployment.
>
> Officers from the patrol force, the commercial auto theft unit, and the armed robbery unit make up the task force. The use of patrol officers on the task force prevents the depletion of personnel from one command and provides a source of information regarding the activities of individuals in their respective patrol areas. Personnel from the other two units give the task force the expertise needed to investigate and prosecute carjackings from all aspects, as well as to provide investigative training to less experienced members.
>
> In addition, crime scene technicians, latent print experts, and crime analysts support the investigative efforts of the task force. Combining the efforts of the task force and support units allows criminal investigations to be consolidated, which ultimately increases the number of cases resolved.
>
> The task force concentrates its efforts on a comprehensive crime prevention program, an intensified patrol force, the identification of habitual offenders, and the assurance of arrest and prosecution. With these methods, the task force works to minimize the impact of carjackings on the citizens of Detroit.
>
> By educating and reminding the public of basic crime prevention techniques, the task force hopes to reduce the probability of a citizen becoming a victim.

Augmenting the police force with roving uniform patrols and surveillance units enables the department to concentrate its crime reduction efforts in areas experiencing high rates of criminal activity and allows for high police visibility. This high visibility also enhances community relations, increases the rate of apprehension, and serves as a deterrent to would-be carjackers.

The identification and apprehension of habitual offenders significantly reduces the number of carjackings because this random crime depends on opportunity. The department determined that a minority of the criminal element committed the majority of the crimes. Therefore linking an individual to more than one crime proves to be a valuable tool in decreasing the number of future incidents. Also, obtaining multiple warrants enables prosecutors to employ habitual offenders status, which provides the court system with the means to give offenders longer sentences.

Because lack of prosecution and uncertainty of punishment caused the criminal element in Detroit to become more brazen in their acts against society, special prosecutors from the Wayne County Prosecutor's Office work with the task force to prevent these felons from slipping through the system. The prosecutors' involvement begins with the warrant and continues through sentencing. The use of special prosecutors aids victims who usually feel abandoned or confused with the criminal justice process, ensures that the suspects are properly charged, and sends a message that such serious offenses will be prosecuted to the fullest extent of the law.

While forming a task force did not provide an instant solution to the carjacking problem, it did help to reduce and control this criminal enterprise. Carjacking may be the wave of the 1990's. However, by combining crime prevention with intensified patrol and investigation and successful prosecution, this crime may soon be considered a relic of the past. (Beekman, 1993, p. 20)

Since the establishment of the task force, investigators in the area have been successful in reducing overall carjacking rates, as well as recovering the majority of vehicles stolen by carjackers.

Federal Legislation

Congress responded to the carjacking problem by passing the Anti-Car Theft Act of 1992, which makes carjacking a federal offense (House of Representatives, 1992). Motor vehicle theft is covered by this federal legislation when an individual (or group of individuals) possessing a firearm takes, or attempts to take, a vehicle from another person by force, violence, or intimidation. The act also imposes severe penalties for convicted carjackers, to include fines and sentences up to life in prison.

The criminal justice system also needs to rethink the prosecution of armed motor vehicle thefts. Many of these crimes can be prosecuted under already existing federal statutes. In New York State, for example, prosecutors succeeded in winning convictions against several carjackers under the Racketeer Influenced Corrupt Organizations (RICO) statute. In this respect, agencies should work with U.S. attorneys offices to develop aggressive enforcement and prosecutorial strategies.

Involving the Community

As with other crimes, public awareness concerning the techniques and motivations of carjackers and vehicle theft rings in general may represent the most effective countermeasure. Working with community groups to develop prevention programs helps to combat the problem. Accordingly, law enforcement agencies should publicize and encourage citizens to adopt effective precautionary strategies.

According to Inspector Charles DeRienzo of the New York City Police Department's Auto Crime Unit and the FBI's Criminal Investigative Division, drivers should be encouraged to follow these safeguards against carjacking:

- Lock all doors, even when driving.
- When stopped at a traffic light, leave enough space between your car and the car ahead for quick departure.
- If another driver bumps your vehicle, do not stop. Either drive to a well-traveled area to inspect the damage or attempt to get the vehicle's license plate number and report it immediately to the police.
- If parked in a shopping mall or supermarket parking lot, look around for anyone or anything suspicious before approaching the car. If you feel you are being watched, go back to the store and ask someone to escort you or call the police.
- Because many carjackings occur at gas stations, avoid filling up at stations in high-crime areas or at night. To avoid being placed in vulnerable situations, keep the vehicle's gas tank as full as possible.
- If available, take freeways rather than streets through high-crime areas.
- While driving, stay in the center lane; avoid being blocked into the curb lane.
- Above all, if there is no escape, do not resist. (Beekman, 1993, p. 22)

Conclusion

Motor vehicle theft has plagued society since the first Model Ts drove off assembly lines. However, this crime, often viewed as "victimless," recently assumed a much more serious and violent tone. Armed vehicle theft, in all its forms, threatens the public's sense of safety and security.

Some observers note that by allowing car thieves to go largely unpunished for so many years, the criminal justice system paved the way for more violent forms of vehicle theft. Others claim that the growing sophistication of automobile security systems drove thieves to more confrontational and brutal means.

Although the root causes of armed vehicle theft may be debated for some time, the current task of law enforcement is to identify and employ effective measures to counter this crime. Experienced auto theft investigators understand that carjackings represent, in part, a natural and desperate reaction by car thieves to overcome obstacles placed before them. However, through cooperation, legislation, crime-fighting initiatives, and aggressive prosecution, the criminal justice system can meet the challenges presented by this ever-growing crime problem.

Discussion Questions

1. To what extent have motor vehicle thefts and carjackings increased during the past decade?
2. Why do some authorities view carjacking as the crime wave of the 1990s?
3. On a personal level, what can you do to prevent your car from being a target of carjackers?
4. What countermeasures and prevention strategies can your local county or city police department initiate in order to lessen the number of carjackings in your town or city?
5. What types of enforcement and prosecutorial strategies should U.S. attorneys use to obtain convictions of the perpetrators of armed vehicle thefts?

References

Federal Bureau of Investigation. (1992, August). *Crime in the United States, 1991: Uniform crime reports.* Washington, DC: Author.

Federal Bureau of Investigation. (1992, October). An analysis of carjacking in the United States. Washington, DC: Federal Bureau of Investigation, Violent Crimes and Major Offender Section.

Beekman, M. E. (1992, October). Auto theft. *FBI Law Enforcement Bulletin, 62,* 17-22.

Beekman, M. E., & Daly, M. R. (1990, September). Motor vehicle theft investigations: Emerging international trends. *FBI Law Enforcement Bulletin, 14.*

H.R. 4542 (1992). 102nd Congress, Pub. L. 102-519, 106 Stat. 3384.

PART III

JUVENILE JUSTICE

9

National Trends in Offenses and Case Dispositions

C. AARON McNEECE

In April of 1991 a 15-year-old boy in Tallahassee, Florida, walked up to a car parked at a convenience store and shot and killed his cousin's former girlfriend. Cries of outrage appeared on the front page of the newspaper over the next few days, generally echoing the sentiment, "How could this have happened?"

The chief of police released some startling information to the press a few days after this murder. The alleged killer had been arrested on approximately 30 other occasions. He had been arrested for several felonies and for crimes of violence against other persons, yet he had never spent a single night in detention. The local detention facility was operating under a court order to prevent overcrowding, and there just wasn't enough room for him.

Aside from the fact that it was a homicide, this was not a unique case. The police estimated that the "average" juvenile offender was arrested about 10 times before being detained. That same month another 15-year-old boy was arrested after a 26-minute high-speed chase. Before that he had been arrested an average of nearly once every four days between

AUTHOR'S NOTE: The primary data files utilized in this chapter were developed by the National Center for Juvenile Justice (NCJJ) and originally analyzed for the *Juvenile Court Statistics* series.

January 1 and April 13, 18 times for felonies. A 14-year-old boy with 33 arrests was on a waiting list for a juvenile program when he was rearrested for beating up a girl on a street corner who refused to have sex with him (Salmon, 1992).

In the following discussion of trends in juvenile offenses and case dispositions, the reader must bear in mind that we are dealing only with estimates that are based on officially reported offenses. The official cases are those that proceed beyond police encounters with juveniles. In cities such as Tallahassee, where police estimate that they spend 90% of their time dealing with juvenile crime, there is a tendency to ignore misdemeanors and concentrate only on the more serious felony offenses. When there are inadequate personnel and resources to deal with serious juvenile felony offenses, juvenile misdemeanors are ignored. The majority of police encounters with juveniles and the overwhelming bulk of juvenile crimes are never recorded in any official statistics. In most cases it is only after a juvenile has established a history of relatively serious delinquent behavior that he or she will be referred to the court.

Official Statistics

Since 1929 the primary source of information on the activities of the nation's juvenile courts has been the series *Juvenile Court Statistics*. The first report described cases handled by 42 courts during 1927. This was (and still is) a voluntary reporting system, and few courts maintained and reported case-level data on juvenile clients. By 1937 case-level reporting was dropped for dependency cases, and a few years later the decision was made to switch the reporting system for both dependency and delinquency cases to aggregate counts only.

In 1957 the Children's Bureau initiated a new data collection program that enabled the production of national estimates of juvenile court actions through a stratified probability sample of over 500 courts. Although this early effort was aborted, the National Center for Juvenile Justice (NCJJ) was awarded a grant by the Office of Juvenile Justice and Delinquency prevention (OJJDP) in 1975. By this time many more courts were keeping automated records on juvenile cases to meet their own needs, so that estimating national trends became somewhat easier.

The primary NCJJ data files used in this chapter provide estimates of the delinquency cases disposed by juvenile courts in the United States for the years 1985-1989. These estimates are based on (a) minimum samples of at least 525,854 individual case records from over 1,000 jurisdictions in 23 states with jurisdiction over 44% (1989) to 60% (1985) of the nation's youth population at risk and (b) a sample of compatible court-level aggregate statistics on more than 100,000 additional delinquency cases from other states. Estimates based on these data are presented in the reports *Juvenile Court Statistics,* 1985-1989, which are published by the U.S. Department of Justice (National Center for Juvenile Justice, 1991).

The official statistics indicate that roughly 1.8 to 2.2 million juvenile arrests are made each year (Federal Bureau of Investigation, 1987), but that only about half of those arrested are referred to juvenile court. The others are not charged, or the charges against them are dropped. Another 250,000 juveniles are referred to court without an arrest by parents, schools, human service agencies, and other citizens. Of the total number of cases referred to juvenile court (approximately 1,189,200 in 1989), about half subsequently involve a delinquency hearing. Of those youths, three fourths will be adjudicated as "delinquent" and placed on probation, made to pay fines or restitution, ordered to undergo counseling, or placed in an institution (U.S. Department of Justice, 1983).

The number of juvenile offenders processed by the courts has remained relatively constant over the past few years (Table 9.1). We must keep in mind, however, that while the total number of juvenile cases processed increased only 7% between 1985 and 1989, there was also a 0.89% *decrease* in the age 12-18 child population during this same time (U.S. Department of Commerce, 1991).

Major Policy Shifts

Three major shifts in federal juvenile policy have occurred since the 1960s (Ohlin, 1983). In the early 1960s federal policy makers used community organization models to foster local responsibility for juvenile misbehavior. Unfortunately, these programs were generally not successful. The second shift in policy came from a number of presidential commissions studying the problems of crime and violence. In 1967 the first of these commissions recommended sweeping changes such as the decriminalization of status offenses, the diversion of juvenile offenders from official court processing, and the deinstitutionalization of juvenile offenders. The Juvenile Justice and Delinquency Prevention Act of 1974 was the culmination of this policy shift (McNeece, 1980). Although the bill was opposed by both the Nixon and Ford administrations, it passed in the House of Representatives by a vote of 329 to 20, and it received only one negative vote in the Senate. The intent of this bill was to deinstitutionalize status offenders, provide additional funds to communities to improve delinquency prevention programs, establish new mechanisms for dealing

TABLE 9.1 National Estimates of Referrals to Juvenile Court (1,000s),
            1985-1989

1985	1986	1987	1988	1989
1,112	1,150	1,146	1,151	1,189

with runaway youth, and remove juveniles from adult jails and lock-up facilities (Bartol & Bartol, 1989).

The third major shift began in the mid-1970s along with a federal shift toward a "law and order" commitment. Although basically preventive in its philosophy, the result of the JJDPA legislation soon became more *controlling.* The act was amended in 1977, partly as a response to alleged increases in school violence and vandalism, to allow more flexibility in the deinstitutionalization process. Throughout the late 1970s an "iron-fisted" punitive approach to nonstatus offenders emerged (Hellum, 1979), and a growing fear of crime pushed the juvenile justice system toward more repressive action (Ohlin, 1983).

In 1981 the Reagan administration, in targeting serious or repetitive juvenile offenders for special attention, once more shifted the system in the direction of control. In 1984 the National Advisory Committee for juvenile justice and Delinquency Prevention recommended that grants to states for the continued deinstitutionalization of status offenders not be renewed. The Reagan administration believed that for too long the juvenile justice system had been overly concerned with the protection of juvenile offenders at the expense of society and its victims (Bartol & Bartol, 1989). This new "get-tough" approach was evident in the Comprehensive Crime Control Act of 1984.

Meanwhile, the courts had dramatically changed other important aspects of the juvenile justice system through a number of decisions that were issued beginning in the 1960s. Since the beginning of the juvenile court movement at the turn of the century, disparities in the legal rights accorded to children and adults were tolerated. The less rigorous standards applied to juveniles were justified as being in the child's best interest. Children were also believed to have substantially different constitutional rights than adults. Beginning in the mid-1960s, however, a number of Supreme Court decisions strengthened some of the rights of children. *Kent* (1966) extended limited due process guarantees to juveniles. *In re Gault* (1967) provided juveniles with the right to notice of the charges, the right to counsel, the privilege against self-incrimination, and the right to confront and examine witnesses. *In re Winship* (1970) applied the "reasonable doubt" standard to juvenile cases.

Nevertheless, in *McKeiver v. Pennsylvania* (1970), the Supreme Court maintained some different standards for juveniles in rejecting the argument that children were entitled to a jury trial. Proof that the *parens patriae* concept was still alive came in the *Schall v. Martin* (1984) decision, when the court said that "juveniles, unlike adults, are always in some form of custody." Thus, although children still do not have exactly the same constitutional guarantees as adults, the legal system has moved in that direction. Juveniles accused of criminal offenses may not be treated as arbitrarily or capriciously as they were in the first half of this century.

In recent years reforms at the state level have been suggested in at least three different areas. Several states have lowered the age at which youths may be tried as adult offenders for serious offenses, and others have made it much easier to allow juveniles of any age to be waived to adult courts. Some have called for the abolition of the juvenile court altogether, arguing that the U.S. Supreme Court has made the juvenile and adult systems so similar that it no longer makes sense to have two separate systems (Schichor, 1983). Others have suggested that we abandon therapy or rehabilitation in favor of protecting the public and *punishing* and *confining* dangerous young offenders.

It seems only reasonable that the courts may have responded to the current conservative backlash regarding juvenile offenders by taking somewhat more punitive actions in processing at least a portion of these clients. We will be looking for those trends in the data described in the following pages.

Offenses

The distribution of offenses in four broad categories from 1985 through 1989 is provided in Table 9.2. These offense categories are defined as:

- Crimes Against Persons—This category includes criminal homicide, forcible rape, robbery, aggravated assault, simple assault, and other person offenses.
- Crimes Against Property—This category includes burglary, larceny, motor vehicle theft, arson, vandalism, stolen property offenses, trespassing, and other property offenses.
- Drug Law Violations—Unlawful sale, purchase, distribution, manufacture, cultivation, transport, possession, or use of a controlled or prohibited substance or drug, or drug paraphernalia, or attempt to commit these acts. Sniffing of glue, paint, gasoline and other inhalants are also included; hence the term is broader than the UCR category drug abuse violations.

TABLE 9.2 National Estimates of Juvenile Delinquency Cases: Offenses,
1985-1989

	Persons	Property	Drugs	Pub. Ord.	Total
1985	175,300	662,600	76,200	197,600	1,111,800
	15.8%	59.6%	6.9%	17.8%	100.0%
1986	184,700	667,800	73,400	214,400	1,150,300
	16.1%	58.9%	6.4%	18.6%	100.0%
1987	183,600	680,600	72,900	208,300	1,145,500
	16.0%	59.4%	6.4%	18.2%	100.0%
1988	189,200	678,400	80,300	203,200	1,151,000
	16.4%	58.9%	7.0%	17.7%	100.0%
1989	206,300	689,100	77,300	216,500	1,189,200
	17.3%	57.9%	6.5%	18.2%	100.0%

- Offenses Against Public Order—This category includes weapons offenses;
  nonviolent sex offenses; liquor law violations, not status; disorderly conduct;
  obstruction of justice; and other offenses against public order.

The overall increase of 7.0% in juvenile delinquency cases between
1985 and 1989 masks some important changes in the specific offense
categories. For example, although drug offenses increased by only 1.4%,
crimes against persons increased by 17.7%. Of course these broad categories almost certainly hide some equally important variations within more
specific offenses. Where records are available, there are indications that there
has been a much greater increase in drug *trafficking* by juveniles (Florida
Department of Health and Rehabilitative Services [DSHRS], 1992) compared
to drug *possession*. In fact, misdemeanor drug offenses in Florida actually
decreased between 1985 and 1989, while felony drug charges increased
by almost 4 times. There is also considerable speculation that much of the
increase in serious crimes against persons is drug related. Unfortunately,
there is no national data base available that provides the degree of speci-
ficity one would need to examine the exact nature of juvenile offenses.

Although the proportion of crimes against persons attributed to nonwhite juveniles has remained relatively constant (between 42.1% and
44.3%), the proportion of drug cases attributed to minority youth has risen
dramatically—from 20.0% in 1985 to 29.8% in 1989. According to a recent
study of 696 local jurisdictions white youth were 3 times more likely than
nonwhite youth to be referred to court for alcohol offenses, whereas
nonwhite males were referred for drug offenses at a 16% higher rate than
white males (National Institute of Justice [NIJ], 1989).

Although the vast majority of all juvenile delinquency referrals are male (81.4% in 1989), there are some important differences in offense patterns related to gender. Females account for 20.5% of all public order offenses but only 13.9% of all drug offenses. However, although nonwhite males are 7 times more likely than nonwhite females to be referred to court for drug offenses, white females were referred for drug offenses at a 66% higher rate than nonwhite females (NIJ, 1989).

Detention

Detention refers to the placement of a youth in a restrictive facility between referral to court intake and case disposition. Table 9.3 provides the national estimates for detention decisions from 1985 through 1989.

The increase in juveniles detained (13.0%) was more than twice the increase in those not detained (5.4%). Though the increase in detention for females was only 4.3%, the detention of nonwhite juveniles increased by 37.9%. During this same period, Florida's detention of African-American youth increased by 70.0% (FDHRS, 1992).

Manner of Handling

The manner of handling is a general classification of case processing within the court system. Petitioned (formally handled) cases are those that appear on the official court calendar in response to the filing of a petition or other legal instrument requesting the court to adjudicate the youth a delinquent, a status offender, or a dependent child, or to waive the youth to criminal court for processing as an adult. Nonpetitioned (informally handled) cases are those cases that duly authorized court personnel screen for adjustment prior to the filing of a formal petition. Such personnel include judges, referees, probation officers, other officers of the court, and/or an agency statutorily designated to conduct petition screening for the juvenile court.

Table 9.4 shows national estimates for petitioned versus nonpetitioned juvenile delinquency cases for the years 1985-1989. While the growth in nonpetitioned cases (0.3%) lagged far behind the overall increase in juvenile cases, petitioned cases grew by 14.7%. The number of female juveniles who were petitioned increased by 13.5%, and nonwhite petitions grew by 30.7%. Other recent studies have indicated that juvenile courts did not handle alcohol and drug cases with a formal petition as often as they did other delinquency cases, but that drug cases (47%) were more

TABLE 9.3 National Estimates of Juvenile Delinquency Cases: Detention
Decisions, 1985-1989

	Detained	Not Detained	Total
1985	229,600	882,100	1,111,800
	20.7%	79.3%	100.0%
1986	239,500	910,800	1,150,300
	20.8%	79.2%	100.0%
1987	226,800	918,700	1,145,500
	19.8%	80.2%	100.0%
1988	235,400	915,600	1,151,000
	20.4%	79.6%	100.0%
1989	259,400	929,800	1,189,200
	21.8%	78.2%	100.0%

likely than alcohol cases (38%) to be formally petitioned (Office of
Juvenile Justice and Delinquency Prevention [OJJDP], 1991).

In Florida the rate of growth in petitioned cases involving white juveniles was only slightly higher (15.9%) than the national increase, but there
was a 63.9% increase in formal petitions for African-American youth
(FDHRS, 1992).

Adjudication Decisions

A juvenile who is adjudicated is judicially determined (judged) to be a
delinquent or status offender. Table 9.5 provides the national estimates of
both adjudicated and juvenile cases from 1985 through 1989.

Adjudicated cases grew more slowly (4.4%) than the overall case rate,
whereas nonadjudicated cases increased by a modest 8.1%. The rate of
growth in female adjudications was also quite small (1.7%), but once again
nonwhite juveniles experienced a substantial increase in more severe
handling at this stage, with a 23.2% increase in adjudications.

Dispositions

Dispositions are categorized below as the most severe action taken or
treatment plan decided upon or initiated in a particular case (see Table 9.6).
Case dispositions are coded into the following categories:

TABLE 9.4 National Estimates of Juvenile Delinquency Cases: Manner of Handling, 1985-1989

	Petitioned	*Nonpetitioned*	*Total*
1985	515,300	596,500	1,111,800
	46.3%	53.7%	100.0%
1986	540,200	610,200	1,150,300
	47.0%	53.0%	100.0%
1987	539,000	606,500	1,145,500
	47.1%	52.9%	100.0%
1988	557,100	593,900	1,151,000
	48.4%	51.6%	100.0%
1989	591,300	598,000	1,189,200
	49.7%	50.3%	100.0%

- Waived—Cases that were waived or transferred to a criminal court as the result of a waiver or transfer hearing.
- Placement—Cases in which youth were placed out of the home in a residential facility housing delinquents or status offenders or were otherwise removed from their home.
- Probation—Cases in which youth were placed on informal/voluntary or formal/court-ordered probation or supervision.
- Dismissed—Cases that were dismissed (including those warned, counseled, and released) with no further disposition anticipated.
- Other—A variety of miscellaneous dispositions not included above. This category includes such dispositions as fines, restitution, and community service, referrals outside the court for services with minimal or no further court involvement anticipated.

Two categories of dispositions merit our attention. Though dismissals and "other" increased only slightly more than the total case increase, and probation decreased slightly, placements went up by 17.2%, and waivers to adult court increased by a dramatic 77.7%.

Though still a relatively small proportion of the total waivers (800 in 1989), female waivers did increase by 60% since 1985. Female out-of-home placements (13,900 in 1989) were up by 8.6%, and male placements increased by 18.3% during the same period.

The most dramatic increases in dispositions are noted in examining white and nonwhite youth who were waived or placed. The increase in waivers of white juveniles was 47.1%, whereas nonwhite waivers increased by 117.9%. The increase in white placements was only 4.1%,

TABLE 9.5 National Estimate of Juvenile Delinquency Cases: Adjudication
Decisions, 1985-1989

	Adjudicated	Nonadjudicated	Total
1985	335,200	776,500	1,111,800
	30.2%	69.8%	100.0%
1986	345,200	804,900	1,150,300
	30.0%	70.0%	100.0%
1987	326,900	818,600	1,145,500
	28.5%	71.5%	100.0%
1988	322,000	829,100	1,151,000
	28.0%	72.0%	100.0%
1989	350,000	839,200	1,189,200
	29.4%	70.6%	100.0%

while nonwhite placements grew by 42.3%. In Florida, African-American
juveniles experienced an increase of 76.4% in commitments to secure
programs and an increase in waiver to adult courts of 133.2%. There was
a 700% increase in the waiver of African-American juveniles charged with
felony drug offenses (FDHRS, 1992). Nonwhite males are clearly receiving more severe dispositions than other juvenile offenders.

Disturbing Trends in Offenses
and Case Processing

On the surface it appears that little has changed in case processing
decisions in the juvenile courts during the past few years. The number of
cases has held at about the same level, and there has been little movement
in the proportion of cases detained, formally petitioned, or adjudicated.
These data, when partitioned by race and offense, lend support to the
contention noted earlier that we are currently operating under a "get-
tough" philosophy regarding delinquent behavior by minority youth. In
fact, when it comes to minority youth who are charged with drug offenses,
we are headed rapidly toward treating them as adult criminals (Table 9.7).
It is obvious that the change in offense patterns noted in the data is due at
least as much to law enforcement practices as to actual change in delinquent behavior. In the space of 1 year (1986-1987) in Florida, felony drug
offenses increased by 72%, and felony drug offenses charged to black
youth increased from 696 cases to 1,687 cases! (McNeece, 1994). It is

TABLE 9.6 National Estimates of Juvenile Delinquency Cases: Dispositions, 1985-1989

	Waived	Placed	Probation	Dismissed	Other	Total
1985	9,000	99,100	411,000	430,700	161,900	1,111,800
	0.8%	8.9%	37.0%	38.7%	14.6%	100.0%
1986	10,200	106,700	419,300	438,300	175,800	1,150,300
	0.9%	9.3%	36.5%	38.1%	15.3%	100.0%
1987	10,900	103,900	423,600	433,900	173,200	1,145,500
	1.0%	9.1%	37.0%	37.9%	15.1%	100.0%
1988	12,400	101,700	422,700	438,700	175,500	1,151,000
	1.1%	8.8%	36.7%	38.1%	15.2%	100.0%
1989	16,000	116,100	409,300	472,800	175,000	1,189,200
	1.3%	9.8%	34.4%	39.8%	14.7%	100.0%

highly improbable that such a dramatic increase in arrests for this particular offense is due to a corresponding increase in actual behavior.

Nationally, the total waivers of male, nonwhite juveniles to adult courts more than doubled from 1985 to 1989, but waivers of nonwhite males charged with drug offenses increased by *8½ times!* In addition, the out-of-home placement of nonwhite males charged with drug offenses and kept within the juvenile justice system increased almost threefold, and the placement of all nonwhite male juveniles increased by 43.9%.

To further illustrate the risk of more severe handling experienced by nonwhite youth, we have compared dispositions for white and nonwhite 17-year-old male drug offenders in Table 9.8. The nonwhite juveniles in this group are much more likely to be waived or placed, whereas white juveniles tend to have their charges dismissed or to be placed on probation more often.

Conclusions and Recommendations

Young black men are more likely to be in prison or under some type of justice system supervision than they are to be enrolled in a college or university, and since 1990 minorities have accounted for more than half of all juveniles in public and private facilities. The proportion of minority youth in public custody grew 13% between 1985 and 1989, while the proportion of white juveniles declined by 13% (OJJDP, 1991).

A decade ago, an article on juvenile justice policy recommended that until we know how to provide effective treatment for juvenile offenders,

TABLE 9.7   National Estimates of Juvenile Delinquency Cases: Nonwhite
Males Waived to Adult Court by Offense, 1985-1989

	Person	Property	Drugs	Pub Order	Total
1985	1700	1600	200	300	3800
1986	1700	1700	300	300	4000
1987	1900	1900	600	300	4700
1988	2200	2300	1000	400	5800
1989	3000	2700	1900	500	8100
% increase,					
1985-1989	76.5%	68.8%	850.0%	66.7%	113.2%

we should concentrate on making the juvenile justice system as equitable,
just, and humane as possible (McNeece, 1983). Though we have not
addressed the issue of humaneness in this chapter, it is obvious that we still
have problems in achieving equity, and it is doubtful that justice is being done.
We should *immediately* take action to address the differential processing of
minority and nonminority juvenile offenders. Even if a disproportionate
number of older, black youth are involved in felony drug cases, rather than
continuing to commit them to adult prisons, we should take whatever action
is necessary to prevent these tragedies from occurring in the first place.

To allow the present situation to continue is no more justifiable than
allowing a disproportionate number of minority adults to be sentenced to
death. Until our legal system seriously addresses the issue of equal justice
for both juveniles and adults, we will remain a nation divided.

Discussion Questions

1. Why do you think that a juvenile must establish a history of relatively serious
   offenses before he or she will be referred to juvenile court?
2. What have been the major changes in federal juvenile justice policy since
   1960?
3. What impact have the courts had in the last few decades on changing juvenile
   justice policy?
4. Compare the changes in juvenile offenses for white and nonwhite youth: for
   female and male offenders.
5. How do you explain the different rates of increase in petitioned versus
   nonpetitioned cases? What role do race, gender, and drugs play in explaining
   these differences?

TABLE 9.8 National Estimates of Juvenile Delinquency Cases, 1989: Race by Disposition for 17-Year-Old Males Charged With Drug Offenses

	Waived	Placed	Probtn	Dismiss	Other	Total
White						
Counts	200	1100	4000	4400	1700	11400
Row %	2.2%	9.7%	35.0%	38.4%	14.8%	100.0%
Col %	19.1%	43.5%	62.1%	64.4%	66.0%	58.1%
Nonwhite						
Counts	1000	1400	2400	2400	900	8200
Row %	12.8%	17.5%	29.7%	29.4%	10.6%	100.0%
Col %	80.9%	56.5%	37.9%	35.6%	34.0%	41.9%
Totals						
Counts	1300	2500	6400	6800	2600	19600
Row %	6.6%	13.0%	32.8%	34.6%	3.0%	100.0%
Col %	100.0%	100.0%	100.0%	100.0%	100.0%	100.0%

6. How can the dramatic increase in the more severe dispositions for nonwhite youth, especially males, be explained?

7. What are the implications of these trends in juvenile court case processing for American society in the 21st century?

References

Bartol, C., & Bartol, A. (1989). *Juvenile delinquency: A systems approach.* Englewood Cliffs, NJ: Prentice Hall.

Federal Bureau of Investigation. (1987). *Uniform crime reports.* Washington, DC: Government Printing Office.

Florida Department of Health and Rehabilitative Services [FDHRS]. (1992). *Profile of delinquency cases at various stages of the Florida juvenile justice system.* Tallahassee, FL: Author.

Hellum, F. (1979). Juvenile justice: The second revolution. *Crime and Delinquency, 25,* 299-317.

In re Gault, 387 U.S. 1 (1967).

In re Winship, 397 U.S. 358 (1970).

Juvenile Justice and Delinquency Prevention Act of 1974, 42 U.S.C. sec. 5633 (1974).

Kent v. United States, 383 U.S. 541 (1966).

McKeiver v. Pennsylvania, 403 U.S. 528 (1971).

McNeece, C. A. (1980). The deinstitutionalization of juvenile status offenders: New myths and old realities. *Journal of Sociology and Social Welfare, 7,* 236-245.

McNeece, C. (1983). Juvenile justice policy. In A. Roberts (Ed.), *Social work in justice settings* (pp. 19-44). Springfield, IL: Charles C Thomas.

McNeece, C. (1994). Comparative state of the child: Juvenile justice in Florida. In A. Imershein, M. Mathis, & C. A. McNeece (Eds.), *Who cares for the children?* New York: General Hall.

National Institute of Justice. (1989). Juvenile courts vary greatly in how they handle drug and alcohol cases. *OJJDP Update on Statistics.* Washington, DC: Government Printing Office.

National Center for Juvenile Justice. National Juvenile Court Data Archive. (1991). National estimates of juvenile court delinquency cases: 1985-89 (machine-readable data file). Prepared through grants from the Office of Juvenile Justice and Delinquency Prevention, Department of Justice. Pittsburgh, PA.

Office of Juvenile Justice and Delinquency Prevention [OJJDP]. U.S. Department of Justice. (1991). *Juveniles taken into custody: Fiscal year 1990 report.* Washington, DC: Government Printing Office.

Ohlin, L. (1983). Interview with Lloyd E. Ohlin, June 22, 1979. In J. Laub (Ed.), *Criminology in the making: An oral history.* Boston: Northeastern University Press.

Salmon, B. (1992, May 7). Florida targeting juvenile crime. *Tallahassee Democrat,* pp. B1, B3.

Schall v. Martin, 104 S. Ct. 2403 (1984).

Schichor, D. (1983). Historical and current trends in American juvenile justice. *Juvenile and Family Court Journal, 34,* 61-75.

U.S. Department of Commerce. (1991). *Statistical abstract of the United States* (11th ed.). Washington, DC: Government Printing Office.

U.S. Department of Justice. (1983). *Report to the nation on crime and justice: The data.* Washington, DC: Government Printing Office.

10

Inner City Adolescents and Drug Abuse

JOHN G. ROBERTSON

JUDITH E. WATERS

A young man, Rashid, 16 years old, appears for an assessment interview at a service agency. He is African-American. He has been ordered to the agency because he was arrested selling drugs on a street corner. He denies his drug involvement. He says he was just going to the corner store when the cops pulled him over, made him stand with his hands above his head, and searched him. He says they put five vials of cocaine (crack) on him. The police found $150.00 when they searched him. He says his mother had given the money to him to go shopping for a winter coat.

In talking with him, the intake worker finds that his father has been in prison for 5 years for an armed robbery he committed to get drugs to support his heroin habit. The young man's aunt died of AIDS 6 months before his appointment with the agency. His aunt acquired the virus because her common-law husband was a drug addict. The young man has not attended school for a year. He was placed in a special education class in the ninth grade. In the seventh grade, however, his marks had been "As" and "Bs". Now he no longer wants to go to school. He worked for a month at a fast food restaurant but was fired because he was late too often. He says he doesn't want to work there anyway. He felt ashamed in front of his friends when they found out he was working at "Mickee Dees."

The youth's mother accompanies him to the appointment. She is in her early thirties. She works full time in a hospital in the housekeeping department. She also has a weekend job at a nursing home. She has an older son who is in and out of her home. He too sells drugs. He spent 6 months in an adolescent detention center the previous year because of his drug selling. She has three younger children: a daughter who is 14 years old, another daughter who is 10, and a son who is 8. She is very angry at Rashid for hanging out on the street, getting involved with the wrong crowd, and refusing to go to school. She is at the end of her resources. Though she does not want to see her son go to prison or to throw

him out of her home, she feels she has no control over him. His father is an
alcoholic and an addict; she hates addiction, drugs, and alcohol. She has tried
hard to teach her children not to involve themselves with drugs or to drink. She
can't understand what has gone wrong.

This story is repeated often in all the inner-city neighborhoods in America.
It will continue to be repeated unless effective interventions are developed
and implemented.

Introduction

Drug use became a very serious problem in the United States in the late
1970s. From college campuses to Wall Street, the rates of illegal drug use,
especially cocaine, rose at a dramatic rate. The whole country became
concerned about the problem. The death of the entertainer John Belushi
and the athlete Len Bias from cocaine overdoses made national headlines.
The First Lady, Nancy Reagan, and other national figures became involved
in the war against drugs. In many states, schools were required to develop
curriculum plans about drug use. Legislatures passed tougher laws against
drug selling, including mandatory sentences for those arrested. By the late
1980s, however, it appeared that the total amount of drug use had begun
to recede. The National Household Survey on Drug Abuse (NHSDA)
(1990) and the National Survey of High School Seniors (NSHSS) (1990)
both recorded lower rates of casual drug use beginning in 1988. Some
people started to talk about winning the war on drugs.

However, there were serious problems with these predictions of victory.
Eric Wish (1991) examined the data from the National Household Survey
and the High School Senior Survey and compared the results to the National
Institute of Justice's Drug Use Forecasting (DUF) program. DUF measures
the self-reported use of drug and the urinalysis results of arrestees in the
country's 22 largest cities. Wish found that there were more weekly, regular
drug users among those who were arrested in the country's 22 largest cities
than the National Household Survey found in the entire country.

The discrepancy can be explained by examining the samples used by the
NHSDA and NSHSS. The National Household Survey does not gather data
on people living in group homes, the military, dormitories, hotels, hospi-

tals, or jails, or on transients, including the homeless—all populations at high risk for drug abuse. The National Survey of High School Seniors only counts students in school, not dropouts, who are more likely to be substance abusers. Drug use is increasingly becoming a phenomenon that exists mainly in poor inner city communities, among the so-called "underclass" of America. The incidence of drug abuse is not decreasing in urban areas as it is in middle-class neighborhoods, but is in fact increasing. Consequently, there are more regular drug users in the criminal justice system than can be found in the entire mainstream culture.

Drug prevention policy in the 1980s focused on programs in middle-class communities and interdiction of the drugs where they are grown and imported. With the threat to the middle class lessened, there is legitimate concern that the country will lose its interest in prevention and treatment of drug abuse and see the problem completely in terms of law enforcement. Wish (1991) recommends that drug prevention programs be directed toward juvenile detainees, with the funding of demonstration projects to reduce drug use among adult and juvenile populations in detention. As we will discuss, there is a pressing need to focus these programs on the neighborhoods and communities from which the offenders come.

Violence

In attempting to understand the relationship between drug abuse and crime, researchers and policy makers encounter several problems. One difficulty in drawing an accurate picture of the impact of drug abuse on the crime rates in major urban areas is the definition of drug abuse violations. Violations related to illicit drugs are defined as the unlawful sale/manufacture or the possession/use of such narcotics and drugs as opium and cocaine and their derivatives, marijuana and hashish, synthetic narcotics (e.g., Demerol and methadone), and other dangerous non-narcotic drugs (e.g., barbiturates, amphetamines, and hallucinogens) (Attorney of the State of New Jersey, 1991). Robberies, burglaries, and aggravated assaults that are committed in order to support a drug habit are not counted. This error can be illustrated by examining the data on homicide. In the state of New Jersey, 151 murders occurred within Essex County, the highest incidence for the state. It is known that 18 of these murders clearly related to drugs and/or alcohol. One hundred and thirty murders were described as "circumstance undetermined." Upon closer examination, many of these cases can be linked to substance abuse in one way or another. Another reason that the connection between drug abuse and crime is underestimated is that many crimes go unreported because the victims fear the criminal justice system more than the criminal.

Even with these limitations, a superficial examination of the drug abuse violations for youth in 1990 demonstrates the extent of the problem. In New Jersey in 1990, there were 52,566 drug-related arrests, down 24% from an all-time high of 63,163 in 1989 (see Tables 10.1 and 10.2).

Drug-related crime is predominantly an occupation for young people (i.e., those under 30) in New Jersey. There were 12,705 youth (under 18) taken into custody for all types of crime in Essex County in 1990 alone. The predominant number, 9,095 (71.6%), were referred to juvenile court; 3,518 (27.7%) were handled within the police department and released.

Whether drug involvement causes crime, crime causes drug involvement, some underlying factor causes both, or a combination of all three, there is no doubt that violence is associated with drugs and drug distribution. There were 90,009 drug arrests of individuals under the age of 18 and 256,541 drug arrests of individuals under the age of 21 in 1989. This was a 12.5% increase since 1985 and a 10.4% increase since 1988. Approximately 50% of these arrests were of African Americans (Federal Bureau of Investigation, 1990). Juvenile narcotic arrests in California increased 559% from 1983 to 1988 to a total of 8,008 arrests. In the same period, victims of homicide between the ages of 15 and 19 increased 37% to 336 individuals. There were 369 adolescents aged 15 and 19 arrested for homicide. Gangs, drugs, and arguments were the cause of 76.4% of these homicides. It is likely that all of these events were drug related (Bureau of Crime Statistics and Special Services, 1989a, 1989b). In fact, homicide is the leading cause of death in drug users (Goldstein, 1985).

Drug dealing leads to violence. There are few alternatives to violence that resolve conflicts among those in the drug-dealing business. In many cases, violence is the preferred method of conflict resolution. Of all illegal drugs, crack has the highest level of violence associated with its distribution (Fagan & Chin, 1990). Goldstein (1985) describes three reasons for violence in drug related activities: psychopharmacological, economic compulsion, and systemic. For example, certain drugs are associated with violence when the person is under the influence. The use of alcohol can make people violent; amphetamines and cocaine can lead to violence. Crack intoxication is associated with violence (Brody, 1990). Other drugs can cause violence to erupt if an individual is in "withdrawal." Heroin addicts can become violent in the search to "get high." According to Goldstein, a second reason for violence among those involved with drugs is economic compulsion. In other words, the need to get money to buy drugs can lead to aggressive behavior. The third reason for drug-related

TABLE 10.1 All Drug Abuse Violations for New Jersey in 1990 by 5-Year Age Groupings

Age	Number Arrested	Age	Number Arrested
Under 10	17	40-44	2,147
10-14	559	45-49	879
15-19	11,576	50-54	369
20-24	13,755	55-59	163
25-29	11,040	60-64	83
30-34	7,593	65+	55
35-39	4,273	Total	52,566

SOURCE: Adapted from *Uniform crime reports, state of New Jersey–1990* by the Attorney of the State of New Jersey, 1991, West Trenton, NJ: Division of State Police, Uniform Crime Reporting Unit.

TABLE 10.2 Drug Abuse Violations for New Jersey in 1990 by Year for Those Between Ages 15 and 24

Age	Number Arrested	Age	Number Arrested
15	869	20	3,166
16	1,570	21	2,752
17	2,496	22	2,636
18	3,306	23	2,623
19	3,335	24	2,578

SOURCE: Adapted from *Uniform crime reports, state of New Jersey–1990* by the Attorney of the State of New Jersey, 1991, West Trenton, NJ: Division of State Police, Uniform Crime Reporting Unit.

violence is systemic. The drug business has territorial disputes, disputes over who's in charge, and disputes over who works for whom. Informers are punished, bad drugs are sold, customers are "ripped off," and others do not pay debts. Dealers are afraid that if they do not act, they will be acted upon. In the "streets," as the way of life is often called, all of these reasons can lead to violence and murder. In a situation where a dealer suspects that an outsider or even a partner in crime might have learned something potentially damaging about his operation, violence and death become almost inevitable.

Many people in the drug treatment center where we work had dealings with the principals in the following story. The *Newark Star Ledger* (November 5, 1991) reported the case of Bilal Pretlow, a 21-year-old resident of Elizabeth, New Jersey, and a drug kingpin who was brought to trial in the first federal death penalty case to be tried in New Jersey. The prosecution claimed that Pretlow's organization "not only executed and dismembered its victims, but kept an entire community in fear." The organization, known as the "E-Port Posse," recruited teenagers to sell drugs, rewarding them with shopping sprees. The E-Port Posse was supposed to have "abducted, beaten, decapitated and dismembered" a potential government witness and killed a 15 year-old girl who "inadvertently stumbled on one of the ring's stash houses." According to authorities, Pretlow started on his career of "drug related terrors" when he was just out of high school. Being jailed did not deter him. He is said to have continued his operations from prison using a telephone conferencing system to contact his subordinates. In 1989, Pretlow's brother Robert was murdered by a rival gang member. His brother, Thomas, is presently serving a ten year prison sentence for shooting and killing Bobby Ray Davis, a drug dealer from Elizabeth who was believed to have killed Robert. Later, Bilal Pretlow was found hanged in his cell, an apparent victim of suicide. In our work, every week brings stories of violent death and maiming like this one.

Violence and drug dealing are serious problems in the inner cities where economic opportunities are limited. The Sentencing Project in Washington, DC, found that 25% of all African-American males between the ages of 18 and 29 are in some form of supervision by the criminal justice system. Also, the highest rate of homicide in America is between African-American male perpetrators and African-American male victims. In New York State, 60% of all 16- to 19-year-olds arrested for homicide are black as compared to 36% who are white. Of the victims of homicide between the ages of 16 and 19, 62% are black and 37% are white (New York Division of Criminal Justice Services, 1990). Of the 10,518 murders committed in the United States in 1989, 45% were black on black (i.e., a black person killing a black person). White on white murder accounted for 42% of the victims. Black on white murder accounted for 6% and white on black murder for 3%. Blacks make up 17% of the American population; whites make up 74%. Black on black murder is a major epidemic in the United States. Between 60% and 70% of these homicides are drug-related crimes. The problem exists in other minority communities but to a lesser degree.

Racism is very much related to the problems of the inner city. When entire sections of a city have no inhabitants of the majority culture, the quality of life in that part of the city declines. Cities are shaped by those with money and power. Neglect of the inner cities leads to poor housing, lack of medical care, lack of recreational facilities, lack of employment opportunities, poor schools, and an environment of extreme danger. Each of these factors contributes to the problem of substance abuse. All of these factors are associated with racism in American culture.

Teens, Drugs, and the System

In neighborhood centers, schools, businesses, the courts, and hospitals in the city, there are teenagers facing serious choices about how to handle the drug culture and the drug economy. Many of them experiment with the alternatives. For some, dealing is similar to having a paper route, a way to make some extra money or buy a fast car that will attract girls. For others, it is so much a part of their own life experiences and that of their families and neighborhoods that passing into active drug involvement may start simply by being sent to the corner to buy drugs for mom or for dad. For still others, it is a way to prove that they are men, tough enough to take risks. Dealing drugs becomes a part of being a member of the "in crowd."

Whatever the original motive, these adolescents usually become involved by first selling drugs on the street. Selling drugs is not a particularly attractive occupation. The youthful dealers are out on street corners in the rain and snow, during the day and in the middle of the night. Selling drugs is a very dangerous activity. Many youth get caught in territorial disputes; others get hurt by addicts without money who need and want their drugs. Still others get robbed for their money. There is the constant threat of the police, undercover or in uniform. Getting arrested means losing the money they made, losing the remaining drugs, and spending time in jail.

"Clocking"

Many teenage dealers say that they can make a great deal of money "clocking" (selling drugs) in only a few hours. Yet it has been demonstrated that most adolescents who sell drugs on the corner do not actually earn the minimum wage when their incomes are averaged over 3 years, including "down time" for being injured or incarcerated (Kolata, 1989). Still, adolescent (or adult, for that matter) drug dealers are seduced by the display of wealth exhibited by other dealers. Experience tells even the novice that he can gross $1,000 in a short period of time depending on the location he works by selling 10 vials for $50 every few minutes. Sixty percent of that income goes to the supplier; the dealer keeps 40%. Acquiring a good location first necessitates working as a lookout or runner for a while and/or employing violence. From their remaining income, adolescent drug dealers feel responsible for maintaining visibly affluent lifestyles to impress the community. They feel compelled to spend money on friends and buy expensive clothes and jewelry.

Most of these adolescents have been told that they can make at least as much money working in fast food restaurants with far fewer risks and fewer hassles of daily living. Working in fast food outlets or any job in the secondary labor market (dead-end jobs) lacks status. It is clear that no one gets in with the "in crowd" by working at Burger King. Moreover, everyone can see the fancy cars and other expensive trappings of the few successful dealers; adolescents want these things.

Although they may begin by being drug free, as time goes on, the young dealers begin to drink regularly as part of their drug selling lifestyle. Beer or wine cooler is the same price as soda and delivers a "buzz." The teenage seller may begin to smoke marijuana as well. Most of these teens, however, pride themselves on being sellers and not users. They even look down on their own customers. Despite negative attitudes toward addicts, after 2 to 4 years of selling, the dealers begin to "taste" their own product. There is external pressure to do so. Tasting is one of the major quality control methods for drug sellers. Selling bad drugs can be very dangerous because the cheated customer will want retribution. Finally, if the adolescent keeps selling drugs, he will probably be his own best customer. Thus selling turns to addiction. Users can no longer be trusted by the distributors to handle drugs for sale. Using drugs ends a successful career as a seller. The National Institute of Drug Abuse reports that the normal age of onset for cocaine and heroin addiction is 19 to 21 years. The first addiction in the sequence, however, is to the money and the status that comes from drug selling.

Not everyone passes from selling to addiction. The drug abuse sequence parallels the pattern with alcohol. The question of why some people can drink heavily and not become alcoholics while others can't has plagued researchers, treatment professionals, and the general public. Some drug sellers remain just that, drug sellers. A very few sellers become distributors, move up in the system, and begin to share in the large profits of the drug trade. A small percentage continue selling in a small way, often in conjunction with an ordinary job. But most drug sellers end up addicted, in jail, injured, or dead (or some combination of the above).

The Role of Women

Up to this point in the chapter, the discussion has focused on males who are dealers. In reality, the occupation of drug seller is a "macho" job; females are not usually dealers. Young men stand on the street corner selling drugs, engage in turf wars, and use sophisticated weapons to kill each other. Females, on the other hand, either "hold" or store drugs for their boy friends or male family members. Normally, females are not searched by the police, and even when they are discovered with drugs, they are frequently able to avoid criminal penalties by blaming their boyfriends, fathers, brothers, and other male relatives.

Some young women become involved with drugs through romantic attachments. The young men they find attractive are the ones with money who host the parties, have expensive cars, and are most frequently the local drug dealers. These young men use their drugs or their drug money to get what they want from the women in the neighborhood. Many females are first introduced to drugs by their boyfriends. Not only do these young women acquire expensive drug habits, but more often than not, they become pregnant. Their boyfriends like the idea of having a child. Having a baby proves their manhood and gives them status among their friends. The young women also like the idea of having a child. Having a baby makes them feel grown up; a child gives them someone to care for, and they think it will bind the young men to them. In no time at all, the young dealer and his girlfriend have become teen parents, sometimes with a baby born addicted to drugs and perhaps even HIV positive. It would be inaccurate to imply that all inner city neighborhood teenagers are involved in drugs. It would be equally inaccurate to suggest that most teen parents are involved in drugs. But it is true that those teens who involve themselves in drugs are often teen parents.

Family Systems

Addiction runs in families. Addiction treatment professionals frequently state that if one parent is addicted, the child has a 50% chance of becoming addicted; if both parents are addicted, there is a 90% chance that the child will become addicted (Wegschieder, 1981). Some theorists think addiction is a genetic disorder. Others think of it as a socially learned behavior where the child mimics the parents' coping mechanisms and turns to mood-altering substances to handle life's problems. When the development of addiction patterns in family systems is studied, it does not appear to matter whether the primary substance is heroin, some other opiate, cocaine, barbiturates, or alcohol. All of these substances can be abused by different members of the family or by the same members at different times or even simultaneously. Therefore the primary drug of choice is more closely related to personal preference and availability than it is to any other variable. In fact, many treatment programs address all addictions in a generic way, making only some concessions to the factors associated with specific drugs. Dealing as part of the addiction syndrome also runs in families.

Families with addiction problems tend to turn inward. They become distrustful of outsiders, try to solve their problems themselves, and impose internal rules of silence (i.e., they do not talk about their problems outside of the family). They are certainly not prone to asking for help. Thus it is widely accepted that growing up in an addicted family will affect many

aspects of a child's life, most especially self-esteem and school performance. Children and adolescents who are having difficulties in school are
unlikely to discuss their family problems with even the most sympathetic
of counselors or teachers. Just to make matters worse, some children
become orphans due to their parents' substance abuse problems and AIDS,
thereby losing what little support they once had (Gross, 1992).

Addicts typically suffer from denial. They deny their addiction and will
say that they can stop any time they want to stop. Addicted families, who
as a unit behave similarly to the individual addict, deny their addictive
problems to outsiders and to themselves. They say, "Mom doesn't drink
any more than anyone else; she just likes to party." The drug sellers
previously described very often have addiction problems in their own
families. They were involved with the cycle of addiction even before they
started selling drugs themselves and were at high risk for addiction without
the added problems of being dealers.

Addiction in a family increases or even causes poverty. A high percentage of available income is spent to acquire the illegal and costly substance,
and addictive behavior leads to absenteeism, lack of concentration, and
wide mood swings, which interfere with job performance and continued
employment. Families whose principal breadwinners are addicts often end
up poor even if they once were middle class. Many adolescents who live
in the inner city may be there because of addicted family systems. The
interaction between addiction and poverty has not been studied sufficiently. Frequently when it is studied the basic assumption is that the
poverty causes the addiction. An alternative view is that the family cycle
of addiction leads to poverty. As with many overdetermined phenomena,
both sides have a point. The evidence is not clear.

The Police

The police become involved with adolescent drug dealers in their efforts
to enforce the laws. Street sellers are the most visible and easily accessed
element of the drug business; they are the local retailers on the street
corner. The police have discretionary power as to when to arrest them and
which group of sellers to arrest. The phenomenon of neighborhood drug
dealers has generated considerable criticism of police within urban neighborhoods. Many residents feel that police and other public authorities turn
a blind eye to drug-dealing activity in the inner cities when such activities
would not be tolerated at all in middle-class areas. Of course, many urban
adolescents are actually arrested by police for their drug-related offenses.
The charges can vary from the possession of alcohol to distribution of very
large quantities of illegal drugs.

Police also become involved with inner city adolescents due to the violence that occurs in the drug business. They not only investigate drug-related shootings, assaults, and murders, but they also respond to the domestic violence that stems from addicted families. More police officers are injured in these domestic disputes than in any other part of their law enforcement role.

Drugs in the inner city create a very ambivalent relationship between police and the community. On the one hand, responsible people in the neighborhood want drug-related activity controlled and stopped. On the other hand, many of these same residents find it difficult to watch a whole generation of local young men get arrested and eventually incarcerated. Police frequently develop negative attitudes about the neighborhood because they feel as if they are fighting a war on foreign soil without the support of the local population. This is particularly true when a large part of the police force is of European descent and the neighborhood is composed of people of color.

Police officers pick up a large number of adolescents, more than they arrest. They release some to their families without filing a complaint, hoping that the mere act of "taking the kid in" will deter further criminal involvement. They file complaints against others and then release them to adult guardians; still others are made to spend time in juvenile detention.

Drugs and Schools

As we have described earlier, the NIDA National Household Survey on Drug Abuse is the single most important measure of drug abuse in our general population. However, the homeless, college students, and people incarcerated in the prison system are not represented in the sample. The High School Senior Survey also suffers from serious limitations in that "dropouts" are not studied. The drug use rate is higher in the dropout population than it is for students who complete their secondary education. It is very interesting to note that African American students who stay in school are less prone to use illegal drugs than white students (High School Senior Survey, 1988). Though a full discussion of the school system and drugs is beyond the scope of this chapter, we recognize that schools constitute such an important factor in the life of adolescents that there should be at least some mention made of the role they play. Along with families and the court system, the schools face the problem of drug selling. In some inner city neighborhoods, up to 75% of high school students leave school before graduating. There is also a significant connection between delinquency and learning disabilities (Brier, 1989; Hengeller, 1989), but no connection has yet been traced between involvement with substances and learning disabilities. It seems likely that there would be such a connection, so the issue needs further research. Many of these dropouts either fall into the drug lifestyle or are already involved with drugs. Because teenagers have a tendency to want to "belong," to be where other teenagers are, and to do what their peers do, those who have left school still congregate around the building at lunch time and when school lets out. Although school authorities attempt to keep drugs out of school with educational programs and individual counseling sessions, the schools can become a battleground for the drug wars.

The Courts

The courts are overburdened with alcohol and drug-related cases. In 1989-1990, in Essex County, New Jersey, alone, there were 12,705 juvenile delinquency complaints filed. Of these, two thirds were for drug and alcohol related crimes. The vast majority of these cases were for drug selling.

The court handles drug cases in several ways. Some of them are diverted to community-based programs prior to the assessment of guilt or innocence, thus protecting the juvenile from having a permanent record. Others are decided by the court, and then the adolescent is sentenced either to a treatment or prevention program and/or probation. The adolescent court has a system of plea bargaining where the prosecuting attorney and the defense attorney (often a public defender) negotiate a sentence. In these cases, the juvenile does not see the judge. This gives him or her the impression that the court system functions in the same way that the drug world does; the system is a market and everything is for sale. Moreover, adolescents typically tend to see life in "black and white." Even the most streetwise can have a very simplistic view of the world. The plea bargaining pattern within the court system leads to a further misunderstanding of law. For many, it is not until they encounter the adult court with its much stiffer sentences that they come to comprehend the real consequences of selling drugs. The court needs to understand the importance of using visible power the same way that the Wizard of Oz used smoke and staging to elicit and maintain respect for his power. For adolescents, power needs to be seen. In order for them to accept the judgments, there must be a show of strength and fairness.

Judges frequently feel powerless to know how to respond to teenage drug sellers. These juveniles do not appear to need drug treatment because they have not yet developed an addiction. There are not enough facilities to incarcerate them all, and even if there were enough detention beds, there is the viable argument that youth detention centers only prove to be schools for criminal behavior rather than rehabilitation programs. For those on probation, case loads are very large. Consequently, there is very little supervision. At the present time, the only real option is a program designed to prevent future criminal activity and addiction. Many juveniles are sentenced to such a program. Roberts and Camasso (1991), in a review of the literature, have found that programs for juvenile offenders are cost effective: The programs are cheaper than not having a program in what they save in future law enforcement costs.

Programs for Juveniles Involved With Drugs

Assessment

The judge can ask the intake unit of the court, the investigations unit, probation, or a private program to provide an assessment of the adolescent and make a recommendation as to which program would be most effective for the individual. During the typical assessment interview, the adolescent's level of drinking and drug use is evaluated. Because there is a normal tendency to minimize or deny use of substances, the agency representative doing the assessment will often seek collateral information from the family, school, or other sources. Assessments require a skilled counselor who has experience with the particular population being evaluated. Because of the denial, minimization, and defensiveness of substance abusers, it is important that the counselor be able to both establish rapport with the client and probe the client's experience for signs of substance abuse. These signs include changes in friendship patterns, repeated negative interactions with authority, health problems (especially trips to the emergency room), conflict with family members, and sleeplessness, combined, of course, with a pattern of drug and/or alcohol use.

If regular use is established, the adolescent will normally be ordered to residential treatment program for a period of time. Studies have shown that even court-mandated treatment is as effective as voluntary treatment. The client spends time in treatment and, though resistant at first, receives the benefit of it (DeLeon, 1988a). If the client does not show signs of addiction, but is involved with selling drugs and is out of school, he or she may be ordered to a day treatment program that includes education, group therapy, and work or recreation. If the client has manifested some distress or if the parents exhibit sufficient distress, the adolescent may be referred to a mental health clinic. If the client is still in school, he or she may be mandated to participate in a neighborhood recreational program.

Treatment Modalities for Adolescents

Programs that address teenage drug involvement range from long-term residential to short minimal interventions. For an adolescent who is not in control of his or her use of drugs and alcohol, residential treatment is usually required. There are two common types, the medical model and the therapeutic community (Breschner & Friedman, 1985).

Medical Model or Short-Term Treatment

The first is called the medical model, 28-day treatment, or short-term treatment. This type of treatment usually takes place in a hospital-related facility. However, free-standing treatment centers do exist. Such programs are based on the 12 Steps of Alcoholics Anonymous. They attempt to enable the client to overcome his or her denial and to understand the various forces that have kept him or her bound to the addiction. The goal is to have the client participate in outpatient therapy after the residential stay. It is during the outpatient phase, usually lasting from 18 to 36 months, that many of the objectives of treatment are accomplished. The residential phase is intended to motivate the client for continued treatment. Outpatient treatment is useful for a client with a stable support system at home, in the community, and at school. The therapy is conducted on a outpatient basis and not in the artificial environment of an institution so that it blends naturally into the client's real life.

Therapeutic Community

Clients who do not have a stable home, have dropped out of school, have had multiple involvements with the police because of delinquent behavior, and are out of control need long-term residential treatment (DeLeon, 1988b; Schiff, 1984). The therapeutic community (TC) is highly structured. Clients live for 6 to 24 months in a community of recovering people. The treatment process occurs in the interaction between the recovering clients, who help one another handle their emotions and see one another struggle to remain in the program and stay drug and alcohol free. Most staff members, the role models, are also recovering addicts who have come through the TC and are rebuilding their lives after addiction. Clients are held accountable for negative behavior, are required to do routine and mundane activities such as cleaning the facilities and manual work, and are required to monitor their own behavior in order to control their impulses and cope with the boredom of life. Both boredom and lack of impulse control often lead to relapse. By the time a client has completed the TC program, he or she will have concrete plans for the future (e.g., returning to school, acquiring a skill, or going to work). Clients normally live in a halfway house before they begin these new activities and prior to returning to their families or establishing independent living arrangements.

Both treatment methods use the group as a primary therapeutic tool. Addicts respond to group therapy and group interactions much more consistently than they do to one-on-one activities. In addition, both these modalities agree that recovery from compulsive use of drugs or alcohol requires lifelong work, an ongoing involvement in a support group such as AA or NA, and a change in the choice of friends, recreation, and other productive activities.

Many adolescents, as discussed above, are not yet addicted to drugs but are deeply involved in drug selling. Because some of these young dealers lack supportive homes and are out of school, they might respond very well to the TC environment.

Day Treatment

If there is a stable home, it is often better to have the adolescent in a day treatment program. These programs provide education, recreation, vocational activities, and group therapy, often in conjunction with a residential treatment facility or as part of a recreational or vocational program. The program can be held 5 to 7 days a week, may range from 6 to 16 hours per day, and may last from 3 months to 1 year. The strength of day treatment, if there is a stable home environment, is that the change that occurs in the treatment center is immediately incorporated into the client's way of life. At the end of the day treatment program, an aftercare plan is developed that includes education and/or vocational training, employment, and recreation.

Issues in Treatment

The need for good employment opportunities cannot be stressed too strongly. Young dealers have grown accustomed to having money from drug sales. They must develop alternative ways to earn an income legally, or the fear of poverty and the seduction of drug money will draw them back to selling. Often, as a treatment provider, one hears that a certain young person is "doing fine," not on the street corner, not selling drugs, and staying in the house all the time. In fact, upon exploration, one finds that is *all* that is happening. The adolescent is *not* going to school, is *not* working, and has *not* developed positive recreational activities. The young person is simply "on hold"; he or she has not made a choice of lifestyles. Eventually, if positive goals are not defined, these former dealers will undoubtedly return to the "street" and drug involvement. In order to succeed, youths need a program that will confront their irrational thinking and help them to establish a productive way of life.

Youth at risk need adequate time to explore feelings and experiences that occurred within the family environment earlier in their lives. It is common for them to have an addicted parent or family member and a family member who is incarcerated. The groups help to provide an understanding of the family cycle of addiction. They help these youth to see that their experiences were not unique but common to others who grew up in similar homes. Young people often blame themselves for their parents' drug use and their parents' anger related to the drug and alcohol use. In addicted families, there are strong patterns of guilt, anger, blaming, and denial. All these patterns are common defenses used by addicts and then by their families (Bry, 1988; Wegschieder, 1981). Because addiction runs in families, family involvement in treatment is necessary. Family groups and individual family counseling sessions are needed to help the parent(s) and the adolescents change their ways of relating and solve family conflicts and problems.

Males involved in "street activities" are in part seeking male companionship, status in the male world, and role modeling as to how to behave as a male. Effective treatment programs hire staff who can fulfill the need for good role models. Moreover, some of the staff need to be the same social class and race as the client group. If the agency services different client groups, the staff need to reflect that fact. Recovering addicts and alcoholics also have a very important role in the staff mix, for they have a unique understanding of the drug-using culture and the dynamics in the addicted family.

Recreation is also a major need for these young people. Primarily, their friends have been peers involved with drugs. Their time has been spent in drug- or "street"-related activities. They are used to excitement, thrills, and tension. In order to redirect their interest and energies, high action and competitive sports can often be very appealing to these youth. Skiing, wind surfing, rock climbing are activities that can provide the clients with new ways to fulfill natural needs. Intermural leagues of baseball, hockey, and basketball also allow these teenagers to work out tensions and aggression in appropriate ways.

Conclusion

Despite the recent reported downturn in general drug use, addiction and dealing are still very serious problems in adolescent populations. In addition, poor, minority, inner city young people are heavily impacted. The incidence of violence is very high in drug-related activities, with juveniles who are involved with drugs being inexorably drawn into violent crime. Because the courts, the police, schools, families, and communities are all affected, they need to cooperate in the development of realistic, cost-effective prevention and intervention programs. All of the youth currently in the criminal justice system and in danger of further criminal activity, even the ones who are not addicted, would benefit from some form of drug-related intervention. Optimally, interventions should be delivered in a group setting. The programs should employ a staff that includes recovering addicts, a significant number of males, and counselors who represent the same racial mix and social class as the clients being treated. The programs can range from short-term, outpatient, minimal interventions to long-term residential treatment, depending on the needs of the particular clients to be served. Without the development of effective programs, we will essentially be forced to write off a whole generation of the youth of this country.

Discussion Questions

1. What parts of society are involved in adolescent drug use?
2. What are the institutions affected by the expansion of drug involvement?
3. What are the institutional goals with regard to drug involvement by adolescents?
4. Why are adolescents involved with drugs?
5. What role does race and social class play in drug involvement?
6. What can you do to address the issue of adolescents and drugs?

References

Attorney of the State of New Jersey. (1991). *Uniform Crime Reports, State of New Jersey–1990*. West Trenton, NJ: Division of State Police, Uniform Crime Reporting Unit.

Breschner, G. M., & Friedman, A. S. (1985). Treatment of adolescent drug abusers. *International Journal of the Addictions, 20*, 971-993.

Brier, N. (1989). The relationship between learning disability and delinquency: A review and reappraisal. *Journal of Learning Disabilities, 22*, 546-553.

Brody, S. (1990). Violence associated with acute cocaine use in patients admitted to a medical emergency department. In M. De La Rosa, E. Y. Lambert, & B. Gropper (Eds.), *Drugs and violence: Cause, correlates and consequences* (pp. 44-59). NIDA Monograph No. 103. Rockville, MD: National Institute of Drug Abuse.

Bry, B. H. (1988). Family based treatment approaches to reducing adolescent substance use: Theories, techniques and findings. In E. R. Rahdert & J. Grabowski (Eds.), *Adolescent drug abuse: Analysis of treatment research* (pp. 39-68). NIDA Research Monograph No. 77. Rockville, MD: Department of Health and Human Services.

Bureau of Crime Statistics and Special Services. (1989a). *Crime and delinquency in California 1988.* Sacramento, CA: Office of the Attorney General.

Bureau of Crime Statistics and Special Services. (1989b). *Homicide in California 1988.* Sacramento, CA: Office of the Attorney General.

De Leon, G. (1988a). Legal pressure in therapeutic communities. *Journal of Drug Issues, 18,* 625-640.

De Leon, G. (1988b). The therapeutic community perspective and approach for adolescent substance abusers. *Adolescent Psychiatry, 15,* 535-556.

Fagan, J., & Chin, K. (1990). Violence as regulation and social control in the distribution of crack. In M. De La Rosa, E. Y. Lambert, & B. Gropper (Eds.), *Drugs and violence: Cause, correlates and consequences.* NIDA Monograph No. 103 (pp. 8-43). Rockville, MD: National Institute of Drug Abuse.

Federal Bureau of Investigation. (1990). *Crime in the United States: The uniform crime report 1989.* Washington, DC: Government Printing Office.

Goldstein, P. J. (1985). The drug/violence nexus: A trip conceptual framework. *Journal of Drug Issues, 15,* 493-506.

Hengeller, S. W. (1989). *Delinquency in adolescents.* Newbury Park, CA: Sage.

Kolata, G. (1989, November 26). Despite its promise, the crack trade seldom pays. *New York Times,* p. 1.

New York Division of Criminal Justice Services. (1990). *Crime and justice annual report 1989.* Albany, NY: Office of the Attorney General, New York State.

Roberts, A. R., & Camasso, M. J. (1991). Juvenile offender treatment programs and cost-benefit analysis. *Juvenile and Family Court Journal, 42,* 37-45.

Robertson, J. G., Waters, J., & D'Amico, M. (1991). *PIE Program Evaluation.* Newark, NJ: Integrity.

Schiff, J. E. (1984). The legal rights of adolescents placed in "therapeutic communities." *Children's Legal Rights Journal, 5*(4), 8-19.

Wegschieder, S. (1981). *Another chance: Hope and health for the alcoholic family.* Palo Alto, CA: Science and Behavior Books.

Wish, E. D. (1991). U.S. drug policy in the 1990's: Insights from new data from arrestees. *International Journal of the Addictions, 25,* 377-409.

11

Recent Developments in Programming for High-Risk Juvenile Parolees

Assessment Findings and Program Prototype Development

TROY L. ARMSTRONG

DAVID M. ALTSCHULER

A dilemma currently faces criminal justice educators who hope to share information with students and colleagues about the nature and effectiveness of program innovations and intervention strategies that target high-risk juvenile offenders being released on parole from correctional facilities. Until quite recently little had been done for most of the past two decades either by way of research and evaluation or program development in this particular sector of the juvenile justice system. This has translated into an almost

AUTHORS' NOTE: This research is supported by Grant 87-JS-CX-K094 from the Office of Juvenile Justice and Delinquency Prevention, U.S. Department of Justice. Points of view are those of the authors and do not represent the opinion of the Department of Justice. An earlier version of the paper was presented at the Annual Meeting of the Academy of Criminal Justice Sciences, Pittsburgh, PA, in March 1992 (revised November 30, 1992).

total lack of published information about juvenile aftercare, especially with regard to high-risk offenders and intensive supervision techniques.

This chapter presents an overview of an ongoing research and development initiative funded by the Office of Juvenile Justice and Delinquency Prevention (OJJDP) in 1988 to achieve a set of linked goals: to conduct a comprehensive assessment nationwide of intensive juvenile aftercare, to develop a generic model/prototype appropriate for testing, and to provide training and technical assistance to aid the development of pilot projects in selected jurisdictions to test the model. This overview also examines those antecedents relevant to recent developments characterizing an earlier period of change and innovation in community corrections in the late 1960s and early 1970s as well as the impediments to community programming that followed in the 1980s during the ascendancy of the "get tough" movement in corrections. Finally, the chapter places current developments in juvenile aftercare within the context of the recently emerging intensive supervision movement.

Historical Context of the Reemerging Interest in Community-Based Corrections for Juvenile Offenders

During the 1960s, it increasingly became a policy position within the more progressive wing of the juvenile justice field that the correctional expectations of training schools and reformatories over the preceding several decades had simply not been met (Abadinsky, 1991). In fact, the legitimacy of the community corrections movement was derived in part from the critical findings of various research studies regarding the failure of the traditional correctional system to resolve the problems of offenders. In this regard, Dean-Myrda and Cullen (1985, p. 19) have observed:

> For one thing, research on recidivism rates revealed that prisons did little to diminish criminogenic predispositions. It was estimated that somewhere between fifty and eighty-five percent of all children committed to a reformatory eventually returned to crime after release (Jensen & Rojek, 1980, p. 50; Horwitz & Wasserman, 1977).

Culminating a period of professional discontent and insight about the level of continuing failure of the system to reform delinquents, major alterations in the way juvenile offenders were defined and processed—spurred largely by the emergence of important new ideas about human development and the negative effects of social isolation—began to occur in the late 1960s across the country. Underlying these changes were persistent criticisms of numerous principles and practices that had previously been highly regarded and viewed as virtually unassailable.

A significant development in this call for reform was the increasingly active role taken by the federal government in stimulating planned change in the juvenile justice arena. Particularly critical in these governmental efforts was the issuance of a major report by the President's Commission on Law Enforcement and Administration of Justice (Armstrong & Altschuler, 1982a). This policy initiative called for reform in four key areas of juvenile justice: decriminalization, due process, deinstitutionalization, and diversion (Blackmore, 1980). Within this mandate for change, the primary thrust of deinstitutionalization/diversion strategies to reverse the excesses of many years of overreliance upon secure, institutional placement was to promote the development of coherent systems of community-based alternatives for juvenile offenders at the state and local levels.

Although emphasis in this movement was initially placed on less severely delinquent youths, the community-based strategies eventually came to embrace youthful offenders exhibiting the entire gamut of criminal misconduct. Hence arose the idea for designing and implementing specialized programs and supervision modalities in the community for high-risk, chronic, and even violent delinquents. These experiments extended to serious juvenile offenders who had required commitment to secure correctional facilities and then needed to be successfully reintegrated in their home communities. Noteworthy in these efforts to normalize juvenile parolees in the community was a series of programs designed and implemented by the California Youth Authority during the 1960s and 1970s (Armstrong, 1991). In spite of some promising results with normalization and long-term behavioral change (Johnson, 1962; Palmer, 1971, 1973, 1974a; Pond, 1970; Roberts, 1970), funding for such aftercare programs began to disappear as interest in specialized treatment began to wane nationwide by the mid-1970s.

The national reaction to the apparent failure to achieve the goals initially envisioned for this community corrections movement has been succinctly summarized by Dean-Myrda and Cullen (1985, p. 22). They note:

> The policy of treating offenders in the community promised to be cost effective, fundamentally humane, and a therapeutic panacea for all but the most sociopathic among us. But, remarkably, the appeal of this policy agenda was not sustained for long. Conservatives, as might be anticipated, criticized such notions as diversion and deinstitutionalization as merely more attempts by liberals to coddle offenders and to rob the criminal sanction of its deterrent powers.

The redirection of resources, restatement of philosophy, and restructuring of programs that marked the decline of community corrections in the late 1970s was a direct reflection of the emerging "get tough" movement. In part predicated on the notion that juvenile crime had reached epidemic proportions, proponents of the "get tough" movement argued that delinquency could only be brought under control through the adoption of harsher policies. This decline in community corrections and ascendancy of a much more stringent, punitive sanctioning approach to correction intervention was characterized by a new set of objectives for the system. The agenda for change relied almost exclusively on the increased use of automatic waiver/transfer of youth to criminal court jurisdiction, a lowered age for criminal court jurisdiction, mandatory sentencing, and the return to a much wider utilization of long-term, secure confinement (Armstrong & Altschuler, 1982b).

Perhaps more than anything else, the "get tough" movement riveted the attention of the professional juvenile justice community and the general public alike on the serious, chronic and violent delinquent. Issues of offender accountability and community protection came to the fore as strategies were devised and programs restructured to guarantee the imposition of high levels of social control over this population, especially when such youngsters were being maintained in the community.

As with all correctional fads and movements, the "get tough" school has begun to show signs of weakening over the past several years (Palmer, 1992). The recent reemergence of community corrections programming for juvenile offenders has been driven by a variety of factors. For one, costs of confinement in and construction of secure correctional facilities have caused both elected officials and juvenile professionals to return to the drawing board to explore more cost-effective ways of sanctioning and supervising juvenile offenders. Another growing realization is the recognition that incapacitation has done little to stem rising crime rates, especially serious crimes being perpetrated by juveniles. The late 1980s and early 1990s are clearly showing a pattern of greatly increased violence among juvenile offenders at the same time that juvenile correctional facilities are again beginning to bulge at the seams. Third has been a grudging acknowledgment by many in the justice field, as well as by the public at large, that just maybe some things "do work" in the attempt to rehabilitate juvenile offenders and adjust them to normal community life. A new rehabilitative literature is beginning to emerge and is revealing that certain treatment modalities are demonstrating long-term positive effects with delinquents.

Interestingly, the renewed interest starting in the mid-1980s in community-based intervention strategies both as alternatives to incarceration and as reintegrative approaches has largely focused upon the problems posed by the most severely delinquent segment of this nation's larger juvenile offender population (Palmer, 1991). These developmental efforts and the particular nature of the reforms can readily be shown to follow both from the impact of the "get tough" school and from a number of research-based but widely disseminated insights about the relative role of serious juvenile offenders within the larger crime patterns of adolescent offenders in the United States. With regard to the influence of the get-tough school of the late 1970s and early 1980s, juvenile justice planners and practitioners were forced to take into consideration in designing and operating new programs the public demands that serious juvenile offenders be held much more accountable for their criminal behavior and that relatively high levels of social control be imposed upon them, especially while being managed in the community. In fact, much of the interest shown in juvenile restitution programs throughout the 1980s can be readily tied to their ability to satisfy the widespread call for more accountability.

The clearest result of targeting severely delinquent youth for intervention has been the system's response of launching experimental program initiatives under the rubric of intensive supervision. Intensive juvenile aftercare as a coherent programming approach can be traced to experiences during the past decade in adult intensive probation supervision and then subsequently to experiments with intensive supervision in juvenile probation (Armstrong, 1991). The recent spread of a nationwide juvenile intensive probation supervision movement (JIPS) has important implications for the design and operation of juvenile intensive aftercare programs (Clear, 1991; Steenson, 1986; Wiebush & Hamparian, 1991). Although grounded in some notion of enhanced surveillance and heightened social control, JIPS has assumed a number of forms, the majority of which include various combinations of intensified surveillance/monitoring and highly specialized treatment modalities along with supportive service provision.

Current insight about designing and implementing intensive aftercare has also drawn inspiration from the movement to expand and improve upon noncustodial correctional alternatives that were most prevalent during the 1960s and 1970s. Several of the approaches and techniques that proved useful in diverting offenders from secure confinement are, in fact, prime candidates for transferability to highly structured and programmatically rich aftercare settings (Altschuler & Armstrong, 1990). Key among such innovations were:

1. Involvement of private agencies and citizens as well as noncorrectional public agencies in the community corrections process through the use of both volunteer and paraprofessionals and through purchase of service agreements

2. Adoption of a new stance by the community corrections agency that stresses resource brokerage and advocacy rather than direct delivery of all services to offenders

3. A case management approach that stresses continuity of services and ongoing communications between all involved agencies

These techniques, which undergirded much of professional practice during the height of the community corrections movement, have quite recently been combined with newly formulated precepts for the supervision of high-risk delinquents. Central to these precepts are ideas concerning risk assessment and high-tech monitoring of behavior.

The Current OJJDP-Funded Research and Development Initiative in Intensive Juvenile Aftercare Programming

Growing concerns about institutional crowding, high rates of recidivism, and escalating costs of confinement have fueled renewed interest in bringing fresh ideas and innovative programming to juvenile aftercare/ parole philosophy and practice. A dismal record has been compiled by the correctional field in its efforts to reduce the recidivism rate for substantial numbers of juvenile offenders coming out of secure correctional confinement. This failure appears to occur disproportionately with a subgroup of institutionalized juvenile offenders who have established a long record of criminal misconduct that began at an early age and was usually quite serious in nature. Not only do they exhibit a persistent pattern of intense and severe delinquent activity, but also large numbers of this high-risk group are plagued by a multitude of other problems. Often they experience a variety of emotional and interpersonal problems, sometimes accompanied by physical health problems; most come out of family settings characterized by high levels of violence, chaos, and dysfunction; many are engaged in excessive alcohol and drug consumption and abuse; and a substantial proportion have become chronically truant or have dropped out of school altogether.

Responding to a growing awareness of this problem, the OJJDP issued a request for proposals entitled "Intensive Community-Based Aftercare Programs" in July 1987. This research and development initiative was designed to assess current knowledge and programs in this field, to develop a promising program model, to disseminate information about the proposed model, and to test this model in selected jurisdictions. The project is viewed by OJJDP as one means to assist public and private correction agencies in developing and implementing effective aftercare approaches for chronic serious juvenile offenders who initially require secure confinement. The Johns Hopkins University's Institute for Policy Studies, in collaboration with California State University at Sacramento's Division of Criminal Justice, was funded in the spring of 1988 to conduct this multistage project. The remainder of the chapter provides an account of results of this project to date in several key areas: the assessment process and the development of a proposed aftercare model for testing.

Assessment Efforts and Findings

Assessment efforts have focused on three key types of activities: (a) An update on the existing state of knowledge based on a thorough and comprehensive review of the literature regarding issues critical to the design and operation of intensive aftercare programs, (b) a description of innovative and promising programs identified through a national mail survey and follow-up telephone interviews, and (c) an analysis of intensive aftercare approaches and practices examined during a series of site visits.

As an initial comment, it is worth noting that several interesting findings from the assessment arose from collected data that were not technically part of the design for our fact finding and analysis. For example, characteristics of the total body of literature that was identified for review provide an insight into the varying status of research studies and descriptive accounts of programming in juvenile aftercare over the past several decades. In reviewing more than 3,500 citations on aftercare that extend over a period from the 1950s until the late mid-1980s (1986-1987), we found a distinct gap in the literature that covered a period from the mid-1970s until the early mid-1980s (1983-1985). This hiatus in research, writing, and program experimentation clearly reflects the major shift in juvenile justice priorities during this time, when community-based approaches and treatment were under a very dark cloud as a result of the continuing assault by proponents of the "get-tough" school of correction. In addition, studies that have again begun to appear addressing a variety of topics relevant to juvenile aftercare place far greater emphasis on problems of managing the serious chronic juvenile offender as compared to studies appearing during the 1950s, 1960s, and early 1970s, when much more attention was directed at less serious juvenile misconduct (e.g., deinstitutionalization of status offenders and diversion of misdemeanants prior to court contact). In contrast, many of the newer studies fall under the topical heading of intensive supervision.

Another interesting pattern identified as an aside during our assessment is that **major innovations in intensive juvenile aftercare have been**

largely concentrated across a small group of jurisdictions, where, for a number of reasons, the momentum for change in parole philosophy and practices has led to experimentation and reform. For the most part, juvenile aftercare across the nation continues to be a virtual wasteland for implementing progressive and promising policies. This reflects the historical indifference on the part of the larger system toward this one area of juvenile corrections. Further, to the extent that recent, substantial innovations have been introduced into juvenile aftercare, these changes are associated with techniques and strategies being devised and implemented as part of the intensive supervision movement.

More intentional and formal findings from the assessment stage of this R&D project regarding the nature of and trends in intensive juvenile aftercare included information related to the following issues: (a) the appropriate target population, (b) assessment of risk and need, and (c) the blend of social control and rehabilitative approaches.

Target Population

The population targeting efforts in those jurisdictions committed to the use of an intensive supervision model of aftercare were to focus on the subgrouping of institutionalized juvenile offenders who *tend* to exhibit the highest rate of failure after release. The implication of this procedure is that the accurate identification and appropriate management of those youths at highest risk for reoffending remain at the heart of any effort to stabilize serious juvenile offenders long term in the community. Prior research into the characteristics and behavior of this subgroup suggest, however, that it is largely composed of property offenders (Armstrong & Altschuler, 1982; Bleich, 1987; Strasburg, 1984; Zimring, 1978). Further, research on the effectiveness of programs working with chronic juvenile offenders has consistently shown that high-rate offenders often exhibit a qualitatively different response to traditional treatment and are uniquely resistant to conventional intervention strategies (Agee, 1979; Coates, 1984; Gadow & McKibbon, 1984).

In addition to identifying a target population on the basis of high risk of reoffending, these jurisdictions often defined youths as appropriate for participation in certain forms of intensive aftercare because they exhibited particular problems and needs requiring highly specialized forms of treatment. This categorization tends to include a number of emotional, cognitive, and other developmental problem areas. The central concern in these cases is that such youths usually have a very poor prognosis for successful community reintegration and adjustment unless their special problems are responded to through intensified programming and service provision as well as monitoring. Very often, these "special-needs" youths are multi-problem individuals who are plagued by the presence of numerous disabling factors. Further, these deficits may coincide with violent and chronic delinquent behaviors, thereby posing an even more difficult problem. The set of special-needs subpopulations currently receiving increased attention in the juvenile correctional system includes youngsters who are learning disabled, drug and alcohol dependent, emotionally disturbed/mentally disordered, neurophysiologically impaired, sex offenders, or otherwise developmentally disabled (e.g., mentally retarded).

Risk and Need Assessment

In the vast majority of jurisdictions identified in our assessment as experimenting with various forms of intensive aftercare, there were steps being taken to adopt procedures for risk and/or need assessment to guide decision making for surveillance/supervision and treatment/service provision. With regard to risk assessment, each jurisdiction had to develop and field test a risk screening device that effectively discriminated their own population according to the probability of rearrest or reconviction. These instruments are based on aggregate characteristics, indicating that they do not predict exactly which individuals within a particular subgroup will recidivate, but rather predict failure rates for each subgroup as a whole. When validated, quantitative risk assessment instruments have been shown reasonably successful in distinguishing among groups of offenders exhibiting different levels of risk of reoffending. But devising valid scales for predicting recidivism among juvenile offenders is more difficult than assessing adult offenders. Youths are often volatile and impulsive, often experience rapidly changing personal characteristics and needs, and are not likely to have developed longstanding patterns of behavior and habits on which to predict future misconduct. This suggests the need for frequent reassessment of individual juvenile parolees. A further cautionary note is that any net-widening tendency to extend the use of intensive supervision to lower risk juvenile offenders may prove to be extremely counterproductive. Not only does it appear inefficient and impractical, but also mounting evidence suggests that intensive supervision as opposed to traditional parole with lower risk offenders leads to increased technical violations and subsequent reincarceration of juvenile parolees who would in all likelihood remain on community supervision (Clear, 1988a, 1988b).

Closely linked to the determination of risk levels is need assessment and those procedures necessary to classify juvenile offenders in terms of their problems and deficits. Much of the burgeoning interest in developing schemes to classify need has centered on making a scientifically driven, correct match between the offender's underlying problems and the appropriate intervention strategy. Decision making for this purpose has been characterized by efforts (based largely on technical advances in diagnostic procedures) to subdivide juvenile offenders into carefully defined subpopulations that make sense in terms of providing more specialized and appropriate interventions.

Unlike risk assessment instruments, need assessment devices do *not* depend upon the use of predictive scales. They are usually developed from staff efforts to articulate and formalize case management procedures through a structured process of identification, definition, and prioritization of problems frequently encountered in clients. Need scales do not need to be complicated and in most cases are straightforward systems for rating the severity of common potential problem areas. Because these instruments address generic problem areas for juvenile offenders, they are generally considered transferable across jurisdictions, with minor modifications to reflect differences in the targeted populations.

Intensive Intervention Based on a Blend of Social Control and Treatment/Service Provision Strategies

Though more frequent monitoring and supervision of parolees is one important aspect of intensive aftercare programs (IAPs), so too are services and support. The various approaches to scaling risk that are being experimented with tend to identify and rely upon risk factors, including both offense- and need-related items. This finding of our assessment strongly supports the impression of the key role assigned to both risk and need. For example, risk assessment scales usually include factors such as age at first referral, the number and severity of prior offenses, and the number of previous commitments, as well as family problems, association with negative peer groups, school-related failure, and substance abuse. Given the inclusion of such "need-related" items, there can be little doubt that strictly surveillance-oriented IAP (e.g., frequent and random "eyeball" supervision, house arrest, electronic monitoring, drug and alcohol testing) is not addressing the programming or service side of the high-risk parolee problem. Clearly in these instances, the challenge facing IAP is that the need-related factors defining essential "core" services must be made available.

On the surveillance and supervision side of IAP, it is important to emphasize that this social control function is not designed merely as a means to deter misconduct. Here the various techniques that can be used to monitor the movement and behavior of high-risk parolees are meant to give IAP staff the means: (a) to recognize immediately when infractions, as well as progress, occur, (b) to know beforehand when circumstances may be prompting misconduct or leading to problems, and (c) to respond accordingly by relying on both rewards and graduated sanctions. It is because of these three objectives that the limits of electronic monitoring and drug testing are apparent. They are not an early warning signal; they do not address precipitating circumstances; and they do not detect positive accomplishment. Though special technology innovations do have a valuable role to perform in relation to surveillance, their limits should be noted. Swift and certain responses on both the reward and sanction sides of IAP are extremely important tools.

Close surveillance is one reliable way to be certain that the services are provided as planned and that the youth participates. If a program is not working properly, for whatever reasons, this situation needs to be detected and acted upon as quickly as possible. This is clearly one aspect of system accountability. Both the service provider and the youth need to know what the realistic expectations for both parties are and that both will be held accountable. It may be necessary to shift a youth into another program or adjust a program's service plan and staffing. Critical to the IAP is the primary aftercare case manager working in tandem with every member of the service provision team and serving as a backup to service provider and the youth.

Identification of Promising Programs and Systemwide Innovation

Mail Survey and Telephone Interviews

The mail survey and telephone interviews were designed to identify innovative, promising, or commendable IAPs and to gather policy and program information relevant to the testing of a recommended prototype. The mail survey generated a total of 36 recommended programs that were contacted and administered a detailed telephone interview. Based upon the information obtained from these interviews, a program typology was developed reflecting three possible models of supervision and service delivery: (a) institution-based (prerelease) programs, (b) integrated institutional/aftercare programs, and (c) community-based programs— residential and nonresidential—that largely commence operation once a youth is released from institutional confinement. (See Altschuler & Armstrong, 1990, for a detailed description of these programs.)

Three institution-based programs were identified in the survey, each operating out of state-run correctional facilities. All three programs stressed *independent living skills, education, and vocational training.* Especially interesting within this category was *Free Venture,* a training and work experience program intended to provide youth with requisite employment skills to compete effectively in the outside job market. **Operating under the auspices of the California Youth Authority (CYA), Free Venture is a partnership between various private sector corporations/industries and a public sector correctional agency in California.** Private sector vendors are contracted by CYA to provide program participants with work equipment, job training, employment experience, and supervision of performance, as well as salary. In addition, at the time these youths are paroled, steps are taken to locate skilled employment in the community for those who have performed well in the program. Payment of wages (ranging up to $5.67 per hour) to participants in the institution is divided according to the following formula: (a) 20% to CYA for costs incurred, (b) 15% to a restitution fund available to victims, (c) 25% to an institutional canteen fund accessible to wards throughout program participation, and (d) 40% to a personal savings account accessible at the time of parole.

Eligibility requirements imposed by CYA include wards being free of any disciplinary actions for the 60 to 90 day period preceding enrollment in the program. The private corporations also impose a set of criteria on enrollment; these include demonstrated signs of maturity and initiative to work, as well as signs of sufficient ability, intelligence, and resourcefulness to perform satisfactorily on the job. It is worth noting that a number of participants had been adjudicated for violent offenses. Since the program began in 1985, over 1900 CYA wards have participated.

The second type of identified program consisted of institutional prerelease programs in which aftercare components were more fully integrated with community-based programs. Four of these program were identified in the survey. Staff in these programs tended to be involved in both pre- and postinstitutional confinement activities. **An excellent example of how an integration of prerelease activities and aftercare services can be combined into one transitional program is represented by Special Vocational Services in Salt Lake City, Utah.** It is a privately operated, nonresidential program under contract with the Utah Division of Youth Corrections for high-risk/high-need juvenile parolees being released from secure confinement. The individual services and activities offered under this program's organizational umbrella are usually brokered from other community-based agencies. Most of the youth participating in the program are either 16 or 17 years old; at any point in time, as many as 175 youth may be enrolled in the program.

Based upon its networking strategy, this program is able to offer an extremely wide array of services. These include: foster/proctor care, tracking and monitoring, transitional/independent living assistance, psychological/psychiatric counseling services, and vocational assessment, training, and job placement. A key factor in the operation of this transitional program is that it is structured in a way allowing the delivery of selected services to begin while these youth are still in secure confinement. As part of this process, individual service plans addressing both institutions-based and community activities are developed jointly by the aftercare and institutional staffs. Special attention is directed toward continuity of management and service provision. Involvement with youth begins in the institutions and continues through their placement and supervision in the community.

Some services, primarily those tied to vocational assessment, training, and job placement, are handled much more directly by the staff of Special Vocational Services instead of being brokered to other agencies. In this situation, staff members are actively working with juvenile offenders both in the institutions and in the community after release. One innovation that has been adopted for achieving this goal of continuous case management is to shift program staff who have been working with youth in the institutions by moving these staff with the youth to the community. This allows the same staff members to follow a cadre of clients throughout the instructional and training process in the various placement settings. In this way, the staff can build upon their relationships that were already developed with clients while still inside the secure correctional facilities. This strategy is designed to avoid the abrupt shift to the community that so often generates confusion and uncertainty among parolees following release.

The third program type identified in the survey was community-based aftercare. Not surprisingly, the largest number—29 programs—were identified as appropriate for inclusion in this category. These programs included a wide array of services. Services from several of these programs in any jurisdiction are often combined into individualized constellations reflecting more comprehensive responses to the set of problems and needs being exhibited by severely delinquent youngsters, most of whom are high risk and multiproblem. A youth may at any point in time be involved in a number of different community-based programs including such functional areas as social skill development, vocational training, special education in an alternative school, family therapy, and monitoring by a tracker. The following program descriptions represent some of the more innovative, specialized approaches identified in the national survey. Collectively, they point to a central theme emphasized throughout this chapter, namely, that appropriate community-based interventions for this targeted population require a mix of surveillance/social control and treatment/service provision techniques in order to achieve the indicated level of structured supervision and also to offer hope of long-term behavioral change.

The Special Testing, Evaluation and Placement (STEP) program, which operates under the auspices of the Chicago Board of Education,

is geared toward the staged re-entry and mainstreaming of juvenile parolees in the public school system. Intake criteria state that those youth who will be considered for acceptance must have "reasonable" chance of succeeding upon their return to public schools. This translates into a population composed of "mid-range" delinquents who have spent time in secure facilities, are chronic offenders, and are perceived as having substantial adjustment problems but are felt to be amenable to intervention. The key goal is to achieve a satisfactory level of normalization in the classroom following extensive histories of unsatisfactory behavior and disruption in public schools.

Although all clients entering this program have been closely scrutinized and have repeatedly been the subject of social and psychological assessment, each referral is given a complete diagnostic workup in preparation both for immediate delivery of services and for preparation for eventual return to a regular classroom. The range of diagnostic areas to which this assessment is directed includes: (a) a behavioral profile, (b) a family and social history, (c) a complete psychological workup, and (d) a thorough medical checkup. Special emphasis is placed on issues directly connected to normalization of behavior in school. Eventually, the decision about the school setting in which to place the youth is reached through a multidisciplinary staffing procedure where all program staff—psychologist, social worker, teacher, and nurse—offer their recommendations.

The actual school experience that is undertaken while youths are participating in this program occurs onsite and continues for 6 to 8 weeks. Regular group and one-on-one counseling is provided throughout the time the youths are in the program and are preparing for readmission to the public school system. Approximately 90 students are enrolled at STEP at any time. They are assigned to classes of no more than 20 students each.

Once the decision is made about where to place the students, their parole officers are required to establish and maintain regular contact with the designated school. Communication and contact with school officials and teachers must be maintained as long as the youths remain on parole. In addition, a representative from STEP (the instructional intervention teacher) is also actively involved in this follow-up process, making regular contact with school administrators and teachers.

The Transitional Treatment Foster Care program, located in Kansas City, Kansas, is a residential placement resource operated by Associated Youth Services for Juvenile parolees returning from secure correctional confinement. The targeted population is intentionally quite young, averaging 15 years of age. These youth are selected primarily on the basis of not having natural home placements available to them upon release. The program combines a residential facility housing 18 juvenile parolees in a group home setting with a number of individual foster care homes in the surrounding community.

Foster families who are part of the treatment team and are defined as paraprofessionals receive a minimum of 40 hours of training each year. They are required to keep daily behavior logs that include positive as well as negative behavioral observations. As part of the treatment process, program staff maintain weekly contact with the foster family and the youth. Crisis intervention is available 24 hours per day. Eventually, all youth being housed in the group home are transitioned into foster home placements. The length of preliminary stay in the residential facility prior to foster care placement ranges from 4 to 6 months.

The underlying philosophy of the Transitional Treatment Foster Care program is that every possible step be taken to encourage the eventual return of these youth to their natural homes. As part of this strategy, program staff work with natural parents throughout a youth's participation in the program. Further, all youth, whether residing in the facility or in foster care placements, are required to participate regularly in activities at the group home. All youth are also involved with family therapists on a regular basis. These services are obtained on a contractual basis in the community. Although most of these youth are legally too young for independent living placement, the awareness that they may eventually need independent living arrangement leads the program to focus attention upon early planning and training for this necessity.

The Intensive Supervision Program (ISP) is a delinquency intervention concept that has been implemented by the Texas Youth Commission (TYC) in three urban sites in Texas (Brownville, Houston, and San Antonio) and is based upon a detached worker model. All clients enter the program upon parole and are referred on the basis of being among the most severely delinquent youth under TYC jurisdiction. Ages range from 14 to 17 years; the majority of participants are black and Hispanic, residing in the inner city areas of the three communities where the programs are based.

Operated by Texas Key, Inc., the ISP program does not utilize any formal facilities to which participants are drawn. Rather, extensive contact is made by program staff with each youth in his or her neighborhood. Overall, 50 youth are monitored at any time in the three metropolitan sites. The core activity in the program's design is the intensive monitoring and surveillance of these youth throughout each day. Usually, two or three face-to-face contacts per day occur between the youth and the detached worker. In addition to intensive supervision, clients participate in organized recreational activities each week, as well as attending 5 hours of counseling per week. Youth remain in the program for a minimum of 90 days, and some remain for as long as 6 months. Completion of the program is marked by graduation ceremonies that place great importance on the symbolic aspects of being successful. Following graduation, clients are returned to regular parole status.

In summary, the findings of this survey seem to suggest that the concept of "promising" and "innovative" as applied to individual programs differed greatly among the contacted jurisdictions and appeared to depend upon the level of attention and amount of resources being directed to juvenile aftercare in the jurisdiction. Innovation and promise are a function of what constitutes customary practice in the jurisdiction, and thus anything different will likely be conceived as innovative. Our overall impression of utilizing a self-report methodology to allow jurisdictions to provide information about what they felt was innovative and/or promising in their aftercare practices resulted in many instances in descriptive accounts of activities of minimal interest to the juvenile correctional field. Additionally, because few of the surveyed programs had been evaluated, it was impossible to say with any precision whether the programs were in fact successful. This dilemma poses considerable difficulty in deciding whether a program that "appears" to be working well is actually effective and should be considered for adoption elsewhere. By the same token, it underscores the importance of developing an overall program model for doing intensive aftercare and having a sound evaluation in place that can both determine program integrity and measure outcome in relation to a control or matched comparison group.

Anther observation arising from the survey was that the identified aftercare programs were diverse in the goals, methods, levels of resources, and populations served. In fact, there was a lack of uniformity on what constituted the primary components of "intensive" aftercare supervision. Few programs maintained any degree of meaningful staff continuity across the institutional-aftercare boundary, and even rudimentary continuity of care was not evident. This suggests that the move toward developing the design and implementation of intensive aftercare at present remains more a worthy goal than a reality.

Site Visit Fact Finding

Based upon the literature review, the mail survey and resulting telephone interviews, and information provided by policy makers, administrators, practitioners, researchers, and knowledgeable individuals active in youth corrections, a set of factors emerged that began to define the nature and structure of intensive juvenile aftercare. This process led to the designation of criteria critical to the selection of sites for more detailed, firsthand program observation. It was recognized early in the project that IAPs that embraced the key criteria in various forms and combinations, as well as to different degrees, would be identified as possible candidates for site visit fact finding. The kinds of approaches and strategies that were targeted for further inquiry included encouraging the development of new community resources through purchase-of-service arrangements with private sector providers; ensuring continuity of care and case management across the institution-aftercare continuum; initiating assessment and classifications systems; and devising a network of coordinated services and system of supervision suitable for inner city and rural environments, respectively.

When the final determination of sites was undertaken, project staff discovered that intensive aftercare innovation had been largely concentrated across a small group of jurisdictions where, for a number of reasons, the momentum for change in juvenile aftercare had led to experimentation and reform. For example, in Florida the *Bobby M. Consent Decree* had forced the state to restructure juvenile corrections in fundamental ways including the approach being taken in the provision of aftercare. In a somewhat different fashion, in Pennsylvania the *Juvenile Court Judges Commission's Aftercare Project* spurred the development of numerous aftercare programs operated through county probation. This effort included experimentation with intensive aftercare.

It also became clear during site screening that for aftercare to provide such things as continuity of care and reentry incorporating graduated sanctions and positive reinforcement, it was essential that a systemwide perspective cutting across separate and sometimes rival justice system components (i.e., courts, corrections, parole, and community resources) as well as human service system components (e.g., corrections, mental health, education) be in evidence. Consequently, the selection of sites was driven by the decision to focus more on programming and approaches that possessed some kind of systemwide orientation (i.e., entire states or regions, multicounty efforts, countywide initiatives) rather than a single aftercare program.

The Proposed IAP Model

The IAP model represents an effort to combine in a coherent fashion the most innovative strategies that have been identified nationally to facilitate effective transitioning of high-risk juvenile parolees back into the community and to offer a reasonable chance for long-term positive adjustment and reduced recidivism. Underpinning the proposed approach are several key ideas. It is eminently clear that if properly designed and implemented, the IAP model will address two of the most troubling deficiencies plaguing most juvenile correctional systems throughout the country: (a) that institutional confinement does not adequately prepare youths for return to the community, and (b) that the lessons learned and skills acquired while in secure confinement are not being sufficiently built upon and reinforced outside the institution following release.

The IAP model is grounded in a set of assumptions about the need to specify clearly the range of factors that generate and are highly correlated with chronic, serious delinquency. This identification process should logically suggest promising strategies of intervention that are theoretically linked with these factors. Consequently, the model is theory driven and provides a framework of differential responses designed to meet the problems and need of individual juvenile offenders. In turn, it is possible through a formal evaluation process to determine whether the proposed intervention techniques are in fact effective in achieving their stated goals and outcome. It is our impression—based on a number of year of examining the program planning process—that when the basic conceptual or theoretical principles of a program model either have not been stated or are ambiguously stated, it is difficult if not impossible for staff, program participants, or any other observers to understand with any degree of clarity what practices, services, and approaches should be pursued and why, how they should be accomplished and when, with what kinds of youths, and so forth.

At the most abstract level of conceptualization, that is, "grand" theory, the IAP model is driven by an integration of social control, strain, and social learning theories. In this sense, it is consistent with a number of previously applied research initiatives to develop an intervention framework for serious, chronic juvenile offenders (Elliott, Huizinga, & Agetone, 1985; Fagan & Jones, 1984; Greenwood & Zimring, 1985; Weis & Hawkins, 1981). Distinctive to the IAP model, however, is a present focus upon the numerous issues and concerns arising out of the largely disconnected and fragmented movement of offenders from court disposition to state correctional commitment/institutionalization, to parole/aftercare supervision, and finally to discharge from the juvenile correctional system.

In terms of targeting particular subgroups of high-risk offenders within the overall juvenile parole population for specialized, more intensive intervention (in terms of both supervision/surveillance and treatment/service provision), one of the principal findings of our assessment and model development process was that risk factors regularly associated with juvenile reoffending behavior broadly defined include both justice system factors (e.g., age of youth at first justice system contact, number of prior contacts, severity of previous offenses) and need-related factors (e.g., problems with family, peers, school, and substance abuse). In addition, they include a variety of other special-need and ancillary factors, which, though not necessarily predictive of recidivism, remain common among juvenile offenders (e.g., learning disabilities, low self-esteem, skill deficits, marginal socialization). Finally, a small minority of these offenders have other very serious problems such as emotional disturbance and developmental disabilities.

Given the range and nature of both offense and need-related risk factors as well as of other special need and ancillary factors, the challenge to correctional aftercare professionals becomes one of linking youths who manifest this array of factors in various combinations (i.e., youths will exhibit these factors in different constellations) with sufficiently broad-based, comprehensive strategies that ease the reintegrative process, reduce recidivism, and normalize behavior on a long-term basis in the community.

Based upon a careful assessment of the national juvenile correctional scene, our impression is that it is simply inadequate and irresponsible to approach the task of reintegrating high-risk juvenile offenders in less than a comprehensive, carefully coordinated, multifaceted fashion across institutional and professional boundaries. Given these cautions, five principles of programmatic action appear requisite to the IAP model and fully embody the theoretical assumptions and empirical evidence regarding both the multiple causes and correlates of, and behavior change associated with, reoffending behavior and recidivism. These principles are:

1. Preparing youths for progressively increased responsibility and freedom in the community
2. Facilitating youth-community interaction and involvement
3. Working with both the offender and targeted community support systems (e.g., families, peers, schools, employers) on qualities needed for constructive interaction and the youth's successful community adjustment
4. Developing new resources and support where needed
5. Monitoring and testing the youths and the community on their ability to deal with each other productively

These five principles, which derive directly from the integrated theoretical framework, collectively establish a set of fundamental operational goals upon which the IAP model rests. They are general in the sense that they allow for a reasonable degree of flexibility in how the goals will be achieved. But although it is essential to the nature of this generic model to give planners, administrators, and staff sufficient latitude to consider a range of components, features, and processes that best suit the needs and circumstances of any correctional system and its wider environment, three major elements and five subelements must be taken into account as planners and practitioners translate the IAP theory and principles into practice.

The three major elements of the model are:

1. Organizational and structural characteristics
2. Case management
3. Management information and program evaluation

Organizational and structural characteristics concern the fact that the administration and organization of juvenile parole varies substantially from jurisdiction to jurisdiction across the country. Differences in factors such as state laws; institutional arrangements involving the role of the judiciary, youth authorities, independent boards, and other agencies; level of resources available; number and geographical location of involved youths; degree of urbanization; reliance upon the private providers and purchase-of-service contracts; civil service; unionization; and community attitudes establish an organizational and environmental climate within which juvenile parole must function. Understanding the nature and status of juvenile parole as it functions within the juvenile justice system, the child welfare service delivery system and the private provider child-serving delivery system is a key first step in an IAP development process. Because IAPs can take a variety of forms, such as a collaborative, publicly run program, a jointly funded purchase-of-service approach, or some other venture based on interagency agreements, having the support of all potentially involved interests is a necessity.

In general terms, *case management* in the context of the secure care-intensive aftercare continuum for high-risk delinquents refers to the process by which coordinated and comprehensive planning, information exchange, continuity, consistency, service provision and referral, and monitoring can be achieved with juvenile offenders who have been committed to secure confinements and who will need to be transitioned to, and maintained on, an intensive aftercare status. Particular attention is focused on five discrete components or subelements that outline the specific areas being coordinated among, and jointly planned by, key staff who are involved with the designated high-risk cases from the point of commitment to secure confinement until discharge from parole status. The five case management components include:

1. Assessment, classification, and selection criteria
2. Individual case planning incorporating a family and community perspective
3. A mix of intensive surveillance and services

4. A balance of incentives and graduated consequences coupled with the imposition of realistic, enforceable conditions
5. Service brokerage with community resources and linkage with social networks

What the components require is the active involvement of the aftercare counselor in the case as soon as secure confinement commences, and the initiation of service provision by other involved aftercare service providers prior to discharge from secure confinement. Among some of the more serious problems that have confronted aftercare historically are the lack of meaningful full involvement of the aftercare worker until the final phase of confinement, if at all; little coordination, transitioning, continuity, or consistency between what occurs inside a secure facility and afterward while on parole status; negligible attention to family concerns during most of the confinement period and frequently afterward; and sporadic monitoring of parolees and aftercare service providers.

The final program element in the IAP model, *management information and program evaluation,* emerges from all other elements as well as from the underlying principles. It is imperative to maintain close oversight over implementation and quality control and to determine the overall effectiveness of the program. With regard to process evaluation, an ongoing management information system is required to insure the operational integrity of IAP. Assessing outcome can be quite complex and should be assigned to well-qualified individuals. Particular attention should be given in the research design to finding an appropriate comparison group, including multiple measures of recidivism as well as cognitive, behavioral, and emotional outcomes; following outcome for at least a year after discharge from IAP participation; and serving enough high-risk cases to provide IAP with a sufficiently large experimental sample to accommodate data analysis for rendering valid findings.

Conclusion

Continuing concerns about crowding in secure juvenile correctional facilities, high rates of recidivism, and escalating costs of confinement have fueled renewed interest in bringing change and innovative programming to juvenile aftercare/parole philosophy and practice. A dismal record has been compiled by the juvenile correctional field in its effort to reduce the reoffending rate for a substantial number of juveniles released from secure confinement. Research indicates that failure tends to occur disproportionately with a subgroup of released juvenile offenders who have established a long record of misconduct that began at an early age. Not only do such "high-risk" youth tend to exhibit a persistent pattern of *juvenile system contact* (e.g., arrests, adjudications, placements), but also they are plagued by a number of other *need-related* risk factors frequently involving a combination of problems associated with family, negative peer influence, school difficulties, and substance abuse. There are also various other ancillary needs and problems that although not generally "predictive" of reoffending are still problems that high-risk youngsters possess and that when present must be addressed.

Recent developments aimed at responding to this difficult population can be traced to experiences during the past decade in adult probation supervision and then subsequently to experiments with intensive supervision in juvenile probation. However, many of these prior intensive intervention strategies focusing almost solely upon social control have been shown to be approaches that too narrowly defined the set of requisite program components necessary for success with this population. Consequently, recent experiments in both juvenile intensive aftercare and probation have become much more sensitive to the need to direct increased attention to both close monitoring and the provision of services/specialized treatment, that is, a balanced approach to the community supervision of severely delinquent juvenile offenders. The Intensive Community-Based Aftercare Programs project funded by OJJDP in 1988 and upon which this chapter is based is an example of a research and development effort to produce a more balanced, highly structured, and comprehensive model of intervention for chronic, serious juvenile offenders being transitioned into the community.

The proposed IAP model has at its foundation the idea that any attempt to lower the rate of recidivism with high-risk juvenile offenders on aftercare/parole status must include a substantial intensification of intervention strategies in terms of *both* social control and service provision. Further, the model is theory driven and provides a framework of individual assessment and differential response designed to meet the problems and needs of specific juvenile offenders.

It is anticipated that this OJJDP-funded research and development project will generate nationwide a number of demonstration programs at the state level over the next decade. Hopefully, these activities will begin to alter markedly the way juvenile aftercare is conceptualized, implemented, and managed for high-risk parolees (Altschuler & Armstrong, 1992). As state juvenile correctional agencies test versions of the generic IAP model, it is only logical that these pilot programs will be incorporated as a standard part of the larger system, especially as mechanisms for reducing the unacceptable rates of failure experienced by severely delinquent youth being transitioned back into their home communities.

Discussion Questions

1. In what ways does the current IAP initiative build upon earlier community-based programs that were implemented during the 1960s and 1970s?
2. What have been the major factors that have driven the field of youth corrections to reexamine its philosophies and practices in the area of juvenile parole/aftercare?
3. Why was there a major hiatus in research and publications concerning juvenile parole/aftercare during the period from the mid-1970s until the early mid-1980s (1983-1985)?
4. Why is such special emphasis and great care being placed upon developing innovative interventions for high-risk juveniles at the point of reentry into the community?
5. Why is it important to balance the imposition of high levels of social control with equally high levels of resources and specialized services for serious juvenile offenders?
6. Why is it essential when developing the proposed IAP model to utilize an integrated theoretical framework for conceptualizing appropriate responses to high-risk delinquency?

References

Abadinsky, H. (1991). *Probation and parole: Theory and practice.* Englewood Cliffs, NJ: Prentice Hall.

Agee, V. D. (1979). *Treatment of the violent incorrigible adolescent.* Lexington, MA: D. C. Heath.

Altschuler, D. M., & Armstrong, T. L. (1992). Intensive aftercare for high-risk juvenile parolees: A model program design. Occasional Paper No. 11, Institute for Policy Studies. Baltimore: Johns Hopkins University.

Altschuler, D. M., & Armstrong, T. L. (1990). Intensive community-based aftercare programs: Assessment report. Report submitted to Office of Juvenile Justice and Delinquency Prevention, Department of Justice.

Armstrong, T. L. (Ed.). (1991). *Intensive interventions with high-risk youths: Promising approaches in juvenile probation and parole.* Monsey, NY: Criminal Justice Press.

Armstrong, T. L., & Altschuler, D. M. (1982a). Community-based program interventions for the serious juvenile offender: Targeting, strategies and issues. Report submitted to Office of Juvenile Justice and Delinquency Prevention, Department of Justice.

Armstrong, T. L., & Altschuler, D. M. (1982b). Conflicting trends in juvenile justice sanctioning: Divergent strategies in the handling of the serious juvenile offender. *Journal of Juvenile and Family Courts, 33*(d), 15-30.

Bleich, J. (1987). Toward an effective policy for handling dangerous juvenile offenders. In F. S. Hartman (Ed.), *From children to citizens: Vol. 2. The role of the juvenile court* (pp. 143-175). New York: Springer-Verlag.

Blackmore, J. (1980, October). Community corrections. *Corrections Magazine, 6*(5), 4-14.

Clear, T. R. (1988a). Statistical prediction in corrections. *Research in Corrections, 1,* 1-52. Washington, DC: National Institute of Corrections.

Clear, T. R. (1988b). A critical assessment of electronic monitoring in corrections. *Policy Studies Review, 1*(c), 671-681.

Clear, T. R. (1991). Juvenile intensive probation supervision: Theory and rationale. In T. L. Armstrong (Ed.), *Intensive interventions with high-risk youths: Promising approaches in juvenile probation and parole* (pp. 29-44). Monsey, NY: Criminal Justice Press.

Coates, R. B. (1984). Appropriate alternatives for the violent juvenile offender. In R. Mathias, P. DeMuro & R. Allinson (Eds.), *Violent juvenile offenders: An anthology* (pp. 181-186). San Francisco: National Council on Crime and Delinquency.

Dean-Myrda, M. C., & Cullen, F. T. (1985). The panacea pendulum: An account of community as a response to crime. In L. F. Travis (Ed.), *Probation, parole, and community corrections* (pp. 9-29). Prospect Heights, IL: Waveland.

Elliott, D. S., Huizinga, D., & Agetone, S. S. (1985). *Explaining delinquency and drug use.* Beverly Hills, CA: Sage.

Fagan, J. A., & Jones, S. J. (1984). Toward a theoretical model for intervention with violent juvenile offenders. In R. Mathias, P. DeMuro, & R. Allinson (Eds.), *Violent juvenile offenders: An anthology* (pp. 53-69). San Francisco: National Council on Crime and Delinquency.

Gadow, D., & McKibbon, J. (1984). Discipline and the institutionalized violent delinquent. In R. Mathias, P. DeMuro, & R. Allinson (Eds.), *Violent juvenile offenders: An anthology* (pp. 311-325). San Francisco: National Council on Crime and Delinquency.

Greenwood, P., & Zimring, F. (1985). *One more chance: The pursuit of promising intervention strategies for chronic juvenile offenders.* Santa Monica, CA: RAND.

Horwitz, A., & Wasserman, M. (1977, November). *A cross-sectional and longitudinal study of the labeling perspective.* Paper presented at the Annual Meeting of the American Society of Criminology.

Jensen, G. F., & Rojek, D. G. (1980). *Delinquency: A sociological view.* Lexington: D. C. Heath.

Johnson, B. M. (1962). Parole performance of the first year's releases—Parole Research Project: Evaluation of reduced caseloads. Research Report No. 27. Sacramento, CA: California Youth Authority.

Palmer, T. (1971). California's Community Treatment Program for Delinquent Adolescents. *Journal of Research in Crime and Delinquency, 8*(a), 74-92.

Palmer, T. (1973). The Community Treatment Project in perspective: 1961-1973. *Youth Authority Quarterly, 26*(c), 29-43.

Palmer, T. (1974). The Youth Authority's Community Treatment Project. *Federal Probation, 38*(a), 3-14.

Palmer, T. (1991). Intervention with juvenile offenders: Recent and long-term changes. In T. L. Armstrong (Ed.), *Intensive interventions with high-risk youths: Promising approaches in juvenile probations and parole.* Monsey, NY: Criminal Justice Press.

Palmer, T. (1992). *The re-emergence of correctional intervention.* Newbury Park, CA: Sage.

Pond, E. M. (1970). The Los Angeles Community Delinquency Control Project: An experiment in the rehabilitation of delinquents in an urban community. Research Report No. 60. Sacramento, CA: California Youth Authority.

Roberts, C. F. (1970). A final evaluation of the Narcotic Control Program. Research Report No. 58. Sacramento, CA: California Youth Authority.

Steenson, D. (1986). *A symposium on juvenile intensive probation supervision: The JIPS Proceedings*. Minneapolis: Hennepin County Bureau of Community Corrections, Juvenile Division.

Strasburg, P. A. (1984). Recent national trends in serious juvenile crime. In R. Mathias, P. DeMuro, & R. Allinson (Eds.), *Violent juvenile offenders: An anthology* (pp. 5-30). San Francisco: National Council on Crime and Delinquency.

Weis, J. G., & Hawkins, J. (1981). *Reports of the National Juvenile Justice Assessment Centers: Preventing delinquency*. Washington, DC: National Institute for Juvenile Justice and Delinquency Prevention.

Wiebush, R. G., & Hamparian, D. M. (1991). Variations in "doing" juvenile intensive supervision: Programmatic issues in four Ohio jurisdictions. In T. L. Armstrong (Ed.), *Intensive interventions with high-risk youths: Promising approaches in juvenile probation and parole* (pp. 153-188). Monsey, NY: Criminal Justice Press.

Zimring, F. E. (1978). *Confronting youth crime: Report of the Twentieth Century Fund on sentencing policy toward young offenders*. New York: Holmes & Meier.

PART IV

THE COURTS

12

Determinant Sentencing

The Experiment That Went Awry

N . GARY HOLTEN

ROGER HANDBERG

Rough Justice: Hard Time and No Time

Two defendants were seated next to each other in a sheriff's van speeding them back to jail from their sentencing hearings in the county superior court. One was 19 years of age. He had been in trouble with the law before (a shoplifting case) 3 years earlier as a juvenile and a grand theft a year and a half later that got him 6 months probation and an order for restitution. The other guy was 34, a grizzled veteran of the felony courts. He had already spent two 3-year terms in the state prison on assorted convictions for robbery, assault, and grand theft. Earlier convictions had led to probation and community service.

The older man, having nothing to do but kill time, demanded that the younger one tell what he had done and what his sentence was. The kid hesitated, wanting to say, "It's none of your damn business," but instead he blurted out, "Breaking and entering, and they're sending me upstate for 4 years!" The older man grinned slowly and with a smirk said, "Same as me and I've got priors that would choke a horse or a prosecutor. How 'bout you?" The younger man described his record; the older just laughed loudly.

"What it is," he said, "is luck of the draw. See, dummy, I got me a slick lawyer who saved my sorry ass from 20 years with no early release. Prosecutor hit me with a habitual offender charge, but my lawyer got her to back off when she threatened to go to trial. Look, man, the evidence they had on me wasn't real good. The only witness they had was scared shitless to testify, so they settled for one charge of grand theft worth 4 years with parole possible after one and a half. They even dropped the gun I used to scare the bitch because it carried a 3-year mandatory. My lawyer said, 'No way.' "

The younger was speechless and angry. He had pleaded guilty to breaking and entering and grand theft. After all, the cops had nailed him as soon as he walked out of the store he was stealing from. He had the damn stereos in the back of his pickup, caught red handed. But he hadn't threatened anyone, didn't even carry a gun or knife. He knew he had been had when his public defender urged him to plead straight up because a trial would result in a sure conviction and a minimum 5-year term. Damn if it didn't turn out that the judge he saw today wasn't taking much into consideration at sentencing. Though the prosecutor agreed to recommend a split sentence of 6 months in prison and then 5 years probation, the judge decided that people who broke into stores, even stores that were unoccupied at the time, were going to get some real prison time. Teach the punks a lesson. The young man muttered bitterly to himself, "luck of the draw."

From the viewpoint of the defendant, no decision made by officials of the criminal justice system is more important than that made by the judge (or, in a few states, the jury) at sentencing. So too, from the perspective of the lawmakers, provisions regarding what penalties ought to be imposed on convicted criminals are of paramount importance because those penalties embody the very purpose of the criminal code and are a definitive statement of social morality.

Despite or perhaps because of the crucial nature of sentencing, there is no step in the criminal justice process over which there is less agreement and in the practice of which there appears to be less consistency. Many observers speak or write of the "anarchy" of sentencing, every judge deciding for him or herself. Therefore society has attempted to control that judge discretion, but unfortunately no effort resolves all problems; rather, one picks and chooses one's desired goals.

Penal Codes:
Determinate Versus Indeterminate Sentencing

In a very general sense, state penal codes can be placed along a spectrum representing the extent to which prison terms are fixed or subject to being shortened by prison and parole authorities. On one end of this spectrum is the determinate, or fixed, sentence of a given period of months or years. A completely determinate sentence is pronounced by the judge and must be served to the exact day. This is also called flat-time sentencing. At the other end of the spectrum is the indeterminate sentence, under which the judge sets no definite term. The parole authority may release the offender at any time up to the completion of the legal maximum for the particular crime committed.

All existing schemes lie between the extremes of determinate and indeterminate sentencing. Most states permit the judge to set both a maximum and minimum sentence, with the parole authority permitted to grant parole only within that specified range. Some states require that the minimum sentence be a certain percentage (say, 30%) of the maximum and provide therefore that the minimum be set by whatever maximum the judge pronounces (Holten and Lamar, 1991, pp. 306-307).

Of course, other factors further complicate this picture. There is the matter of "good time," or reduction of sentence for good behavior. In some states inmates automatically earn a set amount of good time (say, 1 day per week), which is deducted from the sentence unless the inmate is subject to disciplinary action for specific violations of prison rules. In other states, good time must be earned, and the extent to which the inmate's sentence may be shortened depends on the exact policies and practices of the particular prison. From the inmate's perspective, the definiteness of the sentence depends heavily upon this factor: in other words, whether he or she can count on a specified reduction of sentence or whether release is subject to the will of prison officials.

Then there is the difference between states that provide parole, or release of inmates under supervision before completion of their sentence, and states that permit early release with no parole. In effect, the latter constitutes early termination of sentence, and neither parole board nor parole supervision exists. Maine now uses this approach. This is not to be confused with flat time, however, in which the alternative is no early release.

There are two essentially contradictory approaches to what justice demands in terms of processing cases and defendants. One calls for similar if not identical treatment for all those who commit similar crimes or crimes of equal seriousness—in other words, the "legal justice" approach. The other calls for distinctions to be made among and between defendants of varying backgrounds, criminal records, motivations, and propensities for rehabilitation—in other words, the "justice of dispensation." The argument over whether the punishment should fit the crime or the criminal is centuries old. We shall not resolve it here. It is central, however, to any attempt to define what is meant by "disparity." The proponents of legal justice view the individualization of treatment as automatically disparate, whereas those who believe in fitting the treatment to individual offenders are convinced that disparities result from identical punishments. It is important to note that disparities result when similar situations are treated very differently, but disparities also result when very different situations are treated similarly.

Such disparities can only be explained by reference to the operating penal philosophy; hence we should look for evidence of disparities only within states or within the federal system. Comparing states with one another or with the federal system is inappropriate because differing penal philosophies and statutory provisions are at work. We can study disparity, then, only by looking at how armed robbers are treated in various counties in a single state, such as Texas, or how corporate executives convicted of price fixing are treated in the federal district courts in different regions of the country. The fact that professional burglars may serve an average of 5 years in maximum security in one state and 18 months in community treatment centers in another does not indicate a disparity as we have defined it.

There is more than ample evidence of the existence, even the prevalence, of disparities in sentencing, almost no matter how one wishes to define the term. As Blumstein, Cohen, Martin, and Tonry put it, "the evidence for sentencing disparities is extensive but data on the sources of that disparity are scarce" (1983, pp. 118-119). In the 1970s, policy makers in many states decided that the problem was severe enough to require concerted action to combat it. Especially disturbing to many of them was the suggestion that minorities, especially African Americans, were being sentenced to prison more often, and for longer times, than their numbers and offenses would justify. There were also widespread indications of geographic disparities, that is, harsher sentencing in some counties or districts than others or substantially different sentencing patterns in rural areas or suburbs versus urban centers. Whether the concerns were primarily over geographic or social disparities, the motivation that emerged was to reduce such differences through some form of more determinate sentencing.

Understanding the Past

In order to understand why determinate sentencing is perceived by many as at least a partial answer to the disparity issue, one must have some understanding of the issue's history (Tonry, 1988). Crime and punishment are hotly debated issues within the context of American society. Generally, it is assumed that individuals who violate the law (society's norms) must be punished for their transgressions. Lack of punishment makes a society without law, one that is incapable of maintaining civil order and citizen safety. Because Americans have chosen to enact and enforce as effectively as possible laws punishing such transgressions, the issue has broadened to consider whether other values should be expressed in the criminal justice system besides mere punishment of the felon. Reformers earlier proposed and developed a punishment system whose focus, aside from just punishment, was upon rehabilitation of criminals.

Rehabilitation as a goal did not displace punishment, but in effect put a positive twist upon its continued use (Rackmill, 1991). Essentially, individuals were punished for their crimes to a certain point (i.e., were given a minimum sentence), but after that point their term of imprisonment depended upon their progress on the road to rehabilitation from a life of crime. Under such a penal system, prisoners served what were termed indeterminate sentences where minimum sentence length was generally set by the judge (or the relevant statute) but the total possible length was often fairly long (i.e., a minimum of 4 years and a maximum of 10). Thus the prisoner was left in an ambiguous situation, with no real knowledge as to how long a sentence had to be served.

A parole board usually determined the ultimate length of the final sentence served, based upon their evaluation of the prisoner's progress toward rehabilitation. That progress was measured by the prisoner's discipline record in the correctional institution, measurable individual accomplishments such as completion of formal and vocational education, positive attitudes or adjustment as identified through personal statements and evaluations by counselors and others, and, finally, personal interviews with the parole board. If convinced, the board released the individual on parole. If the individual was not granted release, he or she remained in prison for normally another year before being reconsidered. Under such a system, for example, Charles Manson recurringly appears before California authorities seeking release in his unique and bizarre manner.

Obviously, weird inmates aside, prisoners differ in their individual ability to convince parole boards as to their rehabilitation, so that two individuals could serve vastly different term lengths in prison for essentially the same offense. That disparity in and of itself would not have necessarily been distressing to policy makers if those released had been truly rehabilitated. The view was that the prisoner by his or her behavior held the keys to the cell door. But evidence accumulated that indicated that although rehabilitation did in fact occur in many cases, the failure rate as measured by recidivism was extraordinarily high (Palmer, 1992). The conclusion was that individuals served widely disparate sentence lengths for what proved to be no justifiable public purpose.

Determinate Sentencing as the Alternative

The failure of rehabilitation has been overexaggerated, but the new philosophy espoused in many states is that prisoners should serve a sentence commensurate with their crime and its seriousness (the notion of "just deserts"). The idea is that we make the punishment fit the crime rather than attempting to achieve other often desirable social goals through the corrections process. A prisoner entering such a determinate sentencing system knows almost to the day how long he or she will be incarcerated. Concomitant with this change, the individual once released is usually free from state control such as a parole board. The transgressor has paid the necessary price for his crime, and no more is required. Such a sentencing system, in theory, embodies a carefully calculated sense of what payment is demanded by society in terms of the criminal's life.

There are several ways states can attempt to reduce unwarranted disparities at sentencing. They include appellate review of sentences, the establishment of sentencing councils, and the adoption of mandatory minimums for selected offenses. The first two of these have not been widely adopted and, in the absence of clear standards as to what sentences ought to be, were doomed as effective limits on trial judges' discretion. The mandatory minimum approach, on the other hand, is a blunt instrument that is, by its nature, selective in terms of what crimes are isolated for such treatment, and that results in sentencing power being largely thrust into the hands of prosecutors, who decide when charges carrying such penalties should be filed and pursued.

More likely to have a broad impact on sentencing practices are presumptive sentencing schemes. Basically, these involve establishing a bench mark sentence for each class or type of offense and then providing for reductions from or additions to that presumed sentence if specific mitigating or aggravating circumstances are found to be present. Judges are required to use the presumed sentence or justify in writing their deviation by citing specific distinguishing circumstances. There are variations on this theme. In California, for example, in addition to reductions in sentence linked to mitigating circumstances and increases linked to aggravating circumstances, there are "enhancements" for such specific matters as use of a firearm, great pecuniary loss to victims, previous record of imprisonment, and multiple offenses.

There are two ways through which states have implemented sentencing schemes involving the above characteristics. One way is for the legislature to act as the body that develops the sentencing system. The other approach is for a commission to be established that prepares a set of sentencing guidelines that govern judicial decision making.

California led the way when in 1976 it scrapped one of the most indeterminate systems in the country for a Determinate Sentencing Law drafted by the legislature that took effect on July 1, 1977. Crimes were divided into five classes, with presumptive sentences attached to each class. The law stipulated that these presumptive sentences could be subtracted from upon a finding of mitigating circumstances or added to if aggravating circumstances were present. There are also "enhancements" as mentioned above, but the law does not require that imprisonment be used by judges except in certain situations covered by specific provisions. Nevertheless, prison (and, for that matter, jail) time has increased in proportion to nonincarcerative sentences, although this trend began before the new law went into effect. The California statute also takes one other step toward determinacy: elimination of the authority of the parole board to decide when convicts should be released. Terms are reduced only by good-time provisions, and there is 1 year of parole supervision for offenders once they are released.

The state of Indiana has a presumptive sentencing plan that carries longer presumptive terms than that of California and provides for more adjustment in the face of either aggravating or mitigating circumstances. The Indiana plan also has a longer list of offenses for which probation may not be selected and provides for mandatory additions of 30 years to the terms of those with two previous felony convictions. The Indiana parole board does not decide early releases—those are matters of earned good time as in California—but can decide whether to rerelease an offender whose parole it has revoked. Indiana clearly opted for a tough crime control approach.

Other Determinate Schemes

Illinois and Maine have sentencing schemes that do not involve presumptive sentences but do permit the judge to choose a specific length of time from a wide range of terms. The major difference between the two states is that Maine provides no minimums for crimes less than murder, whereas Illinois provides minimums for each crime listed. The determinate character of both plans rests on the fact that once the judge has pronounced the sentence, no other authority may alter it. Maine, in fact, abolished its parole board, and Illinois limited its board to cases dealing with revocation, release from prison, and early release from parole.

What all these legislatively dictated schemes have done is to introduce more determinacy into sentencing: that is, they enable inmates to predict more reliably their release dates. Some schemes reduce the discretion of judges; others actually increase judicial discretion in some regards while eliminating or severely limiting the discretion of parole boards to shorten terms of imprisonment.

Sentencing Guidelines as the Next Stage

A very different approach to achieving more determinacy and reducing disparity is found in the development of guidelines by the courts or their designated administrators or study teams. The guideline approach does not assume changes in the law regarding the terms or conditions of sentence or the authority of either courts or parole boards. It is essentially an attempt on the part of courts to clean up their own house and provide a scheme whereby laws do not necessarily become harsher.

Sentencing guideline reforms also began in the 1970s, originally as voluntary programs that proved ineffectual because judges had no reason to conform to the guidelines (Rich, Sutton, Clear, & Saks, 1982). Voluntary guidelines were effectively the same as no guidelines at all. Later sentencing guideline systems have been mandatory in nature, with appellate review to identify noncompliance (Tonry, 1991). That is, if a sentence fails to conform to the guidelines, it can be appealed and overturned by an appellate court. The trial court is admonished to resentence the offender within the applicable statutory provisions.

Essentially, what a guidelines system does is assign points to various aspects of the sentencing decision (von Hirsch, Knapp, & Tonry, 1987). Determining what exact points are assigned for a specific act or status is the critical issue in setting up a sentencing guidelines system. By raising or lowering those points, one can make the sentences harsher or more lenient. Such a process makes very obvious the punishment choices being made by those involved. For example, clear distinctions can be made between property and violent offenders. Certain sex offenses can be singled out for harsher punishment. By adopting certain point values, one can make the prior record of the offender carry as much weight as, or more weight than, the current offense.

Operationally, the system works to score items related both to the immediate offense and the record of the offender. For example, the Florida scheme permits scores for the offender's prior record, multiple charges in a single incident (if any), victim injury, and whether the offender was under some legal status at the time of the offense such as pretrial release, probation, or parole. In a sentencing guidelines system, all offenses (usually only felonies, but misdemeanors can be included) are assigned levels of seriousness to which point totals are associated. By ranking all included offenses, those deciding usually formulate some rule of thumb as to the relative weight assigned a particular offense in terms of harshness. These weights represent their collective judgment as to society's relative concern with certain types of offenses. For example, in Florida, due to the perceived psychological terror inflicted upon homeowners, household burglary was assigned a punitiveness score out of line with its status as a property offense. This reflects the view that the sense of violation of privacy and loss of a sense of security is more damaging than the physical crime itself. With middle-class fears of crime widely prevalent, such a view was readily acceptable to the Florida Sentencing Guidelines Commission, which recommended the change (Holten & Handberg, 1990).

The points from all these various factors are added together to create a total that is then referenced to a sentencing grid. The grid allows one to precisely identify the expected sentence length for that particular incident (Tonry, 1988; von Hirsch et al., 1987). Grids vary by state as to what exactly is on each axis, but in several the two variables are offense seriousness and the offender's prior criminal history. One identifies the charge (by seriousness or points assigned), then looks for the relevant offender history. Where the two lines intersect within the grid indicates the presumed sentence. In Florida, the grid uses one axis and resembles a thermometer. Because offender as well as offense characteristics are all scored, one derives a total of all points that places the case in a cell on the single vertical grid. The sentence length listed is usually a narrow range (in terms of years or months) within which the judge can sentence an individual. Sentences above or below the expected range are not prohibited, but their use is restricted. The restrictions are that before the judge can mitigate (lower) or aggravate (raise) the sentence, specific legal reasons must be offered justifying the exception, such exceptions being normally reviewable by appellate courts, with prosecutors appealing mitigations and defendants any aggravations. Appellate courts by their actions or inactions determine how stringently the guidelines are enforced.

From the guidelines' perspective, judge discretion is not abolished; rather, the explicit intention is to channel its exercise within acceptable boundaries. Sentencing guidelines, by establishing a set of enforceable expectations about acceptable sentences, provide a frame of reference by which to evaluate judge decisions. Practically speaking, judges do lose some of their power under this system due to the tightness of the limits.

As a result, judges often fight to loosen the limits, thus increasing their discretion, and in Maine have even successfully fought establishment of guidelines in the first place (Lein, Richards, & Fabelo, 1992; Tonry, 1991).

The goal, however, remains reduction of sentencing disparities by controlling the sentencing options held by the judge. For a sentencing guidelines system to be effective, it has been suggested that several features need to be present (Holten & Lamar, 1991, pp. 369-370):

1. The guidelines must provide an explicit general policy to guide decisions in individual cases.
2. They must employ explicit weights and criteria.
3. They must employ charts or a grid.
4. They must structure but not eliminate discretion.
5. Judges must provide reasons for any departures.
6. There must be a monitoring and feedback system.
7. Authorities must have the power to modify the guidelines whenever circumstances make modification desirable.
8. There must be some allowance for modifying the general policy "in response to experience, resultant learning and to social change."
9. The guidelines must be open to the public.

Guidelines are intended to reduce disparities, but they do not necessarily dictate that all sentences have a common purpose. Minnesota's guidelines have the dominant but not exclusive goal of retribution. Though Florida's guidelines state that retribution is the primary goal of the penal sanction, they allow for other goals to be utilized in determining sentences, especially in those cases in which the scores fall below the level indicating a prison term. Pennsylvania's system maintains the requirements of that state's statutory and case law that the diverse goals of rehabilitation, deterrence, incapacitation, and retribution all have their place in determining appropriate sentences.

The best known presumptive guidelines are those of Minnesota (the pioneer), Washington, and Pennsylvania. Minnesota uses the single two-axis grid. One feature that sets this state's approach apart from the others is the legislative mandate that requires correctional resources to be taken into "substantial consideration" and the commission's decision that guidelines provisions be geared to prevent the prison population from outgrowing existing capacity. Pennsylvania's system is looser than Minnesota's and provides three ranges—a normal range, a mitigated range, and an aggravated range—for every offense, including misdemeanors. These ranges are very broad (e.g. 9 to 36 months). Although the judge must give reasons for the range utilized, there are no specific rules governing the selection or even for departures from the ranges altogether. As Tonry points out, with this much leeway permitted the judges, "substantial disparities can occur even within the guidelines" (Tonry, 1988, p. 287). Washington state's system is closer to Minnesota both in form and substance, but is not as restrictive in its ranges. On the other hand, it governs all felony sentences, not just prison sentences.

Florida's less known system stands apart largely because of its very complexity. The current scheme (a totally revised one is under consideration at this writing) utilizes nine distinct offense categories and thus can be said to constitute nine distinct subsets of guidelines. The presumptive ranges are narrow, but 1988 legislative changes permit judges to "bump up" or "bump down" one cell, thus creating a three-cell "permitted range" and greater discretion for sentencing judges. Florida has also created exceptions to the guidelines in the form of minimum mandatory prison terms for some crimes and habitual offender provisions that permit prosecutors to gain access to penalties totally outside guidelines coverage. This brings up the matter of how effective these schemes are in imposing some order or uniformity on the "anarchy" of sentencing.

The Problem of Coherence

Determinate sentencing and sentencing guidelines systems are controversial among criminal justice practitioners because their fundamental tenet is the reduction, though not elimination, of discretion (Tonry, 1991; Holten & Handberg, 1990). Prosecutors and judges see such restrictions as interfering with their ability to do their job successfully. Therefore they make strenuous efforts to recapture the earlier degree of discretion or at least to loosen the restrictions. On the one hand, they seek loopholes or ways to manipulate the system. On the other, prosecutors especially lobby for changes or exceptions from the legislature.

State legislators have their own agenda, which usually emphasizes responsiveness to constituents' fears and anxieties. The crime problem has long been a staple of American politics but has achieved especial potency over the past 30 years. Determinate sentencing schemes were in fact one response to an earlier surge in public fear of crime and a rise in the crime rate. The heightened severity of most determinate sentencing proposals made them very attractive to politicians seeking to respond to public demands for action (Casper, 1983; Tonry, 1991). Over time, however, even determinate sentencing begins to appear less effective or suited for the needs of society (or at least as those needs are interpreted by legislators). Greater harshness is identified as the solution to the crime problem.

Therefore, the attack upon the policy coherence of determinate sentencing strategies and, by extension, sentencing guidelines takes place at two levels: the legislature and the court system itself.

The legislature's role comes in two forms, depending upon the state and its particular sentencing approach. First, the penalties for certain offenses are adjusted to reflect legislators' responses to specific incidents. A brutal or particularly publicized crime or series of crimes leads to demands and often legislative actions that increase punishments for certain crimes. This is often done by establishment of mandatory minimum sentences for those offenses—usually drug-related or sex offenses. Such laws often reduce severely the practitioners' flexibility in dealing with the crime, although, as we will see, that discretion is usually recaptured over time. By picking and choosing in an almost haphazard fashion which crimes are more harshly punished, the legislature can destroy the link between crime and punishment. For example, California's much ballyhooed determinate sentencing reform of the 1970s was reduced to ineffectualness by the late 1980s due to unplanned legislative changes and voter initiatives (Dubber, 1990). The system has become riddled with anomalies and special cases to the point that judges are severely hamstrung in deciding what sentence should be imposed (Tonry, 1991). Clearly, the legislature was responding to what it saw as an out of control crime problem, but because that intervention was episodic in nature and not thought out over the long haul, the result was an unplanned expensive prison population explosion.

Such changes, though dramatic, are not the only changes made by legislatures that have an impact upon sentencing disparity. Guidelines systems can also be affected by such changes as mandatory minimum sentences, although often the guidelines suffer by exclusions. That is, legislatures can withdraw offenses from the guidelines' jurisdiction. More usually, guidelines are picked to death by a series of relatively minor adjustments in point totals or changes in the "in-out" line (that is: whether prison is or is not a sentencing option for the judge for a particular offense). Such adjustments over time disrupt the guidelines' consistency, reintroducing disparity back into the system (Holten & Handberg, 1990).

The second impact of the legislatures comes not in the sentencing process itself but in the more usual legislative function of providing revenues and deciding budget priorities. Determinate sentencing systems can often increase average sentence length, meaning that the state's prison population increases. If the state legislature is reluctant or unable to provide sufficient budgetary resources, prisoners are released early to cope with the overload. The resulting sentence reduction is purely arbitrary and capricious, based on the budgetary considerations of the day rather than any systematic decision as to who is to be released. This effect of the legislature's actions upon sentencing disparity often goes unrecognized, but the consequences are real. For example, within Florida, sentences were reduced to a third of the expected length, the bulk of the reductions tied directly to prison overcrowding and the requirement that some prisoners be released in order to stay under court-mandated population caps.

The other pressure leading to a return in sentence disparity comes as a consequence of the growing familiarity of judges and especially prosecutors with the revised penal code. Their objective is to maximize the potential discretion available to them in order to achieve justice for society. That translates into the ability to punish deserving criminals more harshly and beyond the limits mandated by the sentencing code or guidelines. Therefore manipulations of the process begin at an early stage. One is to multiply counts or to insist that even where several offenses are being disposed at one time, those occurring earlier should be treated as "priors" for scoring purposes. Defense attorneys are not powerless, but are disadvantaged in that their posture is largely reactive to the activities of the prosecutors. Judges (many of whom were former prosecutors) are often sympathetic to such prosecutorial efforts because they perceive that many defendants get off much too lightly.

Discretion and its exercise are inherent in the criminal justice process. Successful reforms do not attempt to abolish it, but rather to channel its exercise in socially acceptable directions. The struggle to keep it confined within proper bounds is a continuing struggle. Because prosecutors normally dominate the plea bargaining process from the beginning, given their discretion in charging, disparity can be introduced almost immediately into the system. That phase is probably beyond effective control because professional judgments have to be made as to what offense should be charged. For example, Florida has a mandatory 3-year minimum sentence for commission of a felony using a firearm. In fact, prosecutors often "eat the gun" as part of the plea bargaining process, thus reducing the defendant's sentence. But prosecutors can draw advantages from that position because the score sheet itself may become the focus of bargaining efforts. For example, an individual's point total is influenced by prosecutor assessments of the seriousness of victim injury. On paper, the guidelines meet their objective of like punishments for similar offenses and equivalent prior records. A cooperative defendant may benefit from these transactions while other defendants suffer from overcharging and a more weighty prior record.

Whither Determinate Sentencing?

The concern for fairness or equity that motivated much of the movement toward determinate schemes has given way to an essentially conservative or hard-line approach to criminal justice issues. As we have pointed out, harshness or punitiveness and fairness or uniformity are not necessarily inconsistent goals. The cosponsors of the bill that created the federal sentencing guidelines were Senators Ted Kennedy, the liberal Democrat, and Strom Thurmond, the conservative southern Republican—two individuals who could never be accused of being ideological soul mates. The federal guidelines scheme that resulted and was implemented in 1988 is considered very punitive in addition to being very rigid.

The 1980s are marked by two major developments: (a) sentencing "reforms" and (b) rapidly increasing incarceration rates and prison populations. For many states, "reform" did not mean across the board presumptive sentencing schemes, but instead involved minimum mandatory and/or habitual or career criminal laws. These laws had the clearly intended effect of adding to imprisonment rates for felony offenders and generating higher populations for their institutions.

Even in those states in which schemes were devised to even out punishments and not necessarily to make them more harsh, prison population rates have grown faster than crime rates (Rackmill, 1991). The overcrowding that has resulted has spun off two responses: (a) huge building programs have been instituted to increase available prison capacity (estimates are that over 800,000 new beds are being added or planned in the next decade) and (b) "back door" early releases have accelerated, effectively reducing the prison terms many offenders are serving. At the same time, fiscal conservatism and its "no new taxes" principle restrain states' ability to fulfill their building plans or prevent them from opening and operating prisons already built (as happened in Florida in 1992). Thus the pressure increases to speed up early releases even more. The degree to which determinate sentencing schemes contribute to this dilemma, or conversely offer a way out of it, remains a hotly debated subject. Nevertheless, the recurrent conflict between ideological conservatism and fiscal conservatism over this issue seems to have swept aside the concerns about fairness and reducing disparities with which reformers were preoccupied in the 1970s and early 1980s.

Discussion Questions

1. Sentencing practices can be placed on the determinate-indeterminate continuum. Briefly describe what an indeterminate sentence means and compare that with what is termed a determinate sentence.

2. What are the differences between a "legal justice" approach and a "justice of dispensation" approach to handling criminal defendants?

3. Rehabilitation as a goal drove the penal system for many years. How did that approach handle individual prisoners in terms of deciding they were ready for parole? How successful were those predictions of future parolee behavior?

4. Controlling disparity of sentences is the goal of most determinate sentencing systems. Various methods have been identified as available for achieving that goal. What are those methods and how successful have they been in practice?

5. Define what is meant by the term *sentencing guidelines*. How do guidelines sentencing schemes determine what punishment to impose on the convicted defendant? What degree of discretion is left to the sentencing judge, and how is that discretion monitored?

6. Determinate sentencing approaches have had the problem of coherence. What factors operate that undermine the strictness inherent in such sentencing approaches? Is there anything that can be done to prevent such activities from occurring, or are they the normal processes of politics?

References

Blumstein, A., Cohen, J., Martin, S. E., & Tonry, M. (Eds). (1983). *Research on sentencing: The search for reform,* Vol. 1. Washington: National Academy Press.

Casper, J. D. (1983). The California Determinate Sentence Law. *Criminal Law Bulletin, 19,* 405-433.

Dubber, M. D. (1990). The unprincipled punishment of repeat offenders: A critique of California's Habitual Criminal Statute. *Stanford Law Review, 43,* 193-240.

Holten, N. G., & Handberg, R. (1990). Florida sentencing guidelines: Surviving but just barely. *Judicature, 73,* 259-267.

Holten, N. G., & Lamar, L. L. (1991). *The criminal courts.* New York: McGraw-Hill.

Lein, L., Richards, R., & Fabelo, T. (1992). The attitudes of criminal justice practitioners toward sentencing issues. *Crime and Delinquency, 38,* 138-203.

Palmer, T. (1992). *The re-emergence of correctional intervention.* Newbury Park, CA: Sage.

Rackmill, S. J. (1991). The impact of determinate sentencing ideology upon prison overcrowding. *Criminal Law Bulletin, 27,* 230-246.

Rich, W. D., Sutton, L. P., Clear, T. D., & Saks, M. J. (1982). *Sentencing by mathematics: An evaluation of the early attempts to develop sentencing guidelines.* Williamsburg, VA: National Center For State Courts.

Tonry, M. (1991). The politics and processes of sentencing commissions. *Crime and Delinquency, 37,* 307-329.

Tonry, M. (1988). Structuring sentencing. In M. Tonry & N. Morris (Eds), *Crime and Justice* (Vol. 10). Chicago: University of Chicago Press.

von Hirsch, A., Knapp, K., & Tonry, M. (1987). *The sentencing commission and its guidelines.* Boston: Northeastern University Press.

13

Plea Bargaining

A Necessary Evil?

PATRICIA A. PAYNE

If you were to ask the members of your community what opinion they had formed about plea bargaining, it would be my educated guess that people would react with great distaste, much as they do when people argue about all the "technicalities" that are available to defendants in the criminal justice system. The public abhors injustice, and when the system lets a guilty person squeak through simply because a little mistake occurred the public is up in arms. A similar conclusion is reached by many concerning the wholesomeness of the plea bargain. Questions are raised like this:

1. Why in the world would the prosecutor agree to a lesser charge when she knows the defendant is guilty of the standing charge?
2. What kind of conscience does defense counsel possess when they bargain to get the charges lessened or dropped after the client has admitted guilt?
3. Is the system actually rewarding those who plead guilty? Is it better to admit guilt for a crime immediately because your chances of acquittal on most charges increase tenfold?
4. Just what exactly is the point behind this legal oxymoron called plea bargaining?

Definitions and Legal Precedents

In the legal world recent attempts have been made to upgrade the term *plea bargaining* by referring to it as *plea negotiation.* The word *bargain* suggests that perhaps someone is receiving something they most likely do not deserve and now has possession of this item due to a bit of conniving, convincing, and coercing.

In fact, there really is nothing conniving about the "bargaining." The defendant actually gives up the Sixth Amendment right to a trial. There really is nothing mysterious about waiving a constitutional right for the sake of justice, now is there?

Procedurally, we formally recognize the plea bargain most often at the arraignment stage. It is at this point that the plea is entered into and the parties involved attempt to avoid a trial at whatever cost by negotiating the compromise of guilt. Constitutionally the practice was recognized in a 1970 United States Supreme Court case, *Brady v. United States,* wherein the court endorsed the use of plea bargaining in order to create a mutual advantage for both sides of the adversarial process. Later safeguards were imposed regarding the requirement of voluntariness and knowledge on the part of the defendant when the agreement is struck. The court also took an extreme step in the case of *Bordenkircher v. Hayes* (1978) when it declared that the state could essentially rule with an iron hand and threaten the defendant with potentially harsher charges if the accused refused to acquiesce to the terms set down in negotiations.

The Players

It is no secret that if we didn't have some shortcuts incorporated into the system it would overflow like a clogged drain and defendants would wait until their old age to stand trial. But one state in the union has outlawed plea bargaining, and the citizens of that state, Alaska, have no complaints about its loss. Is plea bargaining really a necessary evil, or is it an overused, abused part of our legal system?

Let us focus on the parties involved, for each plays a significant role in plea negotiation. The defendant, who is most likely guilty, is usually ready and willing to "cut a deal" unless he or she is vehemently professing innocence; the "fight" does not usually evolve from him or her. However, the attorneys are the ones facing the most pressures. The prosecutor needs convictions because convictions measure the rate of the state's success. Defense counsel desires a clear calendar; as every great criminal trial attorney will attest to, a closed file is a good file. The judge wants his or her courtroom to run smoothly, without any long, detailed trial situations arising unexpectedly. And remember—most defendants know that the chance of receiving a longer sentence post-trial, as opposed to "cutting it short" and accepting "the deal," is an almost frightening constant in the system. Certainly our forefathers never envisioned a system where if the accused elects to invoke his or her constitutional right to trial, the odds are completely against him or her regarding the sentencing, and it is better to gamble in plea bargaining negotiations that more likely result in a winning hand.

One amazing fact about plea bargaining is that it hasn't been around forever. It's a relatively new idea that our system allows attorneys to induce a defendant into a transaction for the "betterment of the community." At one time our nation's goal was to protect the civil liberties of the accused, not to think of the quickest way out of an unpleasant affair. And why should anyone want to disturb a matter agreed to and accepted by all parties concerned? Wouldn't James Madison and Alexander Hamilton be appalled at this lackadaisical attitude toward justice?

Plea bargaining falls far short of the intentions that our founding fathers had when drafting the United States Constitution. We need to energetically examine the present system and figure out what works and what doesn't.

We are all well aware that a successful plea negotiation avoids trial. The trial is avoided because the state has secured a guilty plea without the "inconvenience" and dilatory tactics prosecutors complain of when defense counsel is brought onto the scene. Any experienced criminal defendant will tell you that the first bit of advice that counsel gives them upon apprehension is not to talk openly and freely with the prosecutor or police for fear of judicial reprisal. The benefits of the *Miranda* rights are oft repeated to clients to remind them that anything they say can be used *against* them—not used to benefit their defense—and that if a confession is given it must be done so voluntarily and intelligently. As a matter of fact, every time a plea bargain is reached, the judge asks the accused a series of inquiries regarding the issue of voluntariness before accepting the plea as a matter of law. Is plea bargaining truly voluntary, or is it the fastest, least painful and least costly way to run around the adjudicatory process?

Abuse of Power?

One highly complicated factor in this plea negotiation business is the power of the prosecutor and the potential for abuse. My younger brother was an assistant prosecutor in a southern New Jersey county for a few years after he graduated from law school. He would be the first one to tell you that he was the fellow wearing the "white hat"; he was like the sheriff in the Wild West who had the power to round up the posse and call all of the shots. Defense attorneys had to come in and grovel and whine and moan on their clients' behalf, hoping to catch him in a good mood. He said it was always *his* call: *he* decided whether to send the matter to the grand jury; *he* decided how many charges were appropriate; *he* decided if the case merited discussion with defense counsel at all; *he* essentially decided the fate of each defendant brought before him. The power to control and destroy is some kind of power.

Gershman (1991) believes that the prosecutor is the most dominant figure in today's criminal justice system. He reminds us that the prosecutor not only has the powers mentioned above, but in a death penalty state literally decides who lives or dies. Gershman points out that the unfettered discretion exercised in the prosecutor's charging power is "tyrannical" and "lawless" and that the courts almost always defer to the prosecutor's discretion. He reminds us of what I would call a bone-chilling egregious abuse: prosecutorial retaliation in the form of increased charges after defendants raise statutory or constitutional claims.

In his article "Abuse of Power in the Prosecutor's Office," Gershman (1991) recalls a film entitled *The Thin Blue Line*: the sad, true story of Randall Dale Adams, whose murder conviction was eventually vacated because the prosecutors hid crucial evidence that would have proven the defendant's innocence. Adams was convicted in 1977 of murdering a police officer in Texas. His conviction and death sentence were predicated largely upon the testimony of a hardened juvenile delinquent who cut a "secret deal" with the state to implicate Adams. The juvenile had actually done the killing, but at the trial of Adams the prosecutor suppressed information about the "deal" and also withheld other crucial evidence that would have exonerated Adams. Fortunately, after a long, legal battle, a Texas court finally freed Adams, and he was luckily spared the death penalty.

In 1990 the U.S. Department of Justice, reporting from its Bureau of Justice Statistics, concluded generally that more than 90% of all guilty pleas are a direct result of plea bargaining. As a result of the study, Inciardi (1993, pp. 355-359) indicates that for every 100 felony arrests 18 were rejected by the prosecutor at screening and another 20 were automatically dismissed. Of the remaining 57 cases, 54 pleaded out, with only 2 reaching the point of the actual guilty verdict. As Inciardi notes, that raises the percentage to an astonishing 98% of guilty pleas having been negotiated.

It is not only the prosecution who wants a speedy solution to the problems confronted in the criminal justice system. Defense attorneys, judges, politicians, and civic leaders also seek the "quick fix" to satisfy the many constituents to which they are held accountable.

Some critics have called for the abolition of plea bargaining because it is such an imperfect solution and is therefore judicially intolerable. But Walker (1989) still embraces the concept of plea bargaining as an integral component in the manufacturing and maintenance of justice. He believes that hard-core criminals do not routinely use plea bargaining to beat the system. He attributes the bad press factor to political consequences such as the highly publicized and most famous plea bargain of all time—that of former Vice President Spiro Agnew. Walker advises us not to overreact to such unique occurrences. He genuinely believes that the majority of felony cases are handled with a "profound sense of bureaucratic regularity." Are we to believe that "bureaucratic regularity" is one of our judicial goals? It sounds like something to be treated with an over the counter drug at the local five and dime!

Abolition Versus Screening

In 1975 the attorney general of Alaska banned plea bargaining throughout the state. Walker (1989) claims that Alaska is unique in that the local prosecutors are appointed by the state attorney general, which in turn gives the attorney general power to wipe plea bargaining out of the system. Contrary to what many believed would happen, the Alaskan criminal justice system did not collapse. Defendants pleaded guilty just as often as they had before abolition, and trial numbers did increase, but only by a very small percentage. One very interesting comment was that police officers who knew prosecutors no longer had unfettered discretion in prosecutorial matters were somewhat more careful as to what charges were brought against which particular defendants.

Kipnis (1976) has argued that there is far too much coercion for the choice of the bargain to be voluntary and that the system is inherently unjust. Kipnis views the system as containing the element of duress. He refers to the authors of the *Restatement of Contracts,* adopted in 1932 by the American Law Institute, speaking on the power of the prosecutor:

A threat of criminal prosecution . . . ordinarily is a threat of imprisonment and also . . . a threat of bringing disgrace upon the accused. Threats of this sort may be such compelling force that acts done under their influence are coerced, and the better foundation there is for the prosecution, the greater is the coercion.

Kipnis ends with the truism that even the most desperate are free to reject the terms offered, but that is opposite of the view we hold as evidence of judicial freedom.

The real issue at hand is how to ensure the quality of the terms reached as a result of the bargain entered into. Attorneys are craftpersons empowered with the gift of judicial representation. They take an oath to uphold the law and seek out justice and we take them at their word. Is that asking too much of defendants? Is that asking too much of the criminal justice system? It is my belief that we can never ask for enough.

Problems and Remedies

On July 23, 1993, two teenagers in the sleepy North Carolina town of Lumberton set out to rob someone. Never in their wildest dreams could they have imagined the victim would be the father of the famous basketball superstar Michael Jordan. Apparently the elder James Jordan had pulled off to the side of the road to rest in his luxury automobile and was attacked and shot in the chest and killed. The teenagers realized who their victim was after they rummaged through his belongings and found the championship ring that Michael had given his father. Both the accused are 18 years of age and have a history of violent crime. Each has been in and out of prison. Each has been charged with first degree murder, armed robbery, and conspiracy. Authorities claim this was a random act of violence and probably a carjacking incident. Last year the FBI reported 31,303 carjackings, up from 19,000 in 1991.

If you were the prosecutor in this case, would you consider a possible plea negotiation? Would you even entertain the thought of a bargain in such a violent, high-profile situation? How much pressure is on the prosecutor to "get the big win"?

We must look for real solutions to the dilemmas left to us as a result of the now-adopted concept of plea bargaining. Work must be done to ensure a productive and secure screening process at the initial adjudicatory stage, and that particular responsibility falls within the purview of the state prosecutor's offices. The prosecutor decides whether to send the case to the grand jury for indictment or whether to dismiss all or some of the designated charges. If each office utilized a highly effective screening process and thoroughly examined each case at this early preindictment stage, much of the routine plea negotiations going on today could be eliminated. Naturally, some cases, like capital offense situations, could not be judicially screened out of the system, but if more cases such as the inumerable amount of theft cases were in fact screened out, it would leave more valuable time to be spent by both attorneys to negotiate pleas in the truly important situations. The grand jury is the sole tool of the prosecutor, and effective screening could essentially clean up the tangled mess that most of the nation's grand jury systems are in at the current time. Prosecutors need to send the murder cases, the rape cases, and the robbery cases straight to the grand jury so those cases receive the proper media coverage for the benefit of the citizenry to feel safer. But the other, less heinous crimes that eat up our valuable court resources should be negotiated from the outset, and those files can be closed in a much quicker fashion than they are today.

Prosecutors are under a great deal of pressure to win the big cases. They face pressure from the community, who demand to be free of the fear of crime. The intention of streamlining plea bargaining should never maintain the underlying goal of instilling ignorance upon the people. People need to be informed so that they feel safe in their neighborhoods and safe in their schools. It is the prosecutor's job to ensure safety in the community and therefore open lines of communications that are essential to a functioning criminal justice system.

Summary

In a 1970 United States Supreme Court opinion, the court in *North Carolina v. Alford* ruled that a judge could accept a guilty plea from a defendant who said that he was innocent, as long as it was voluntary and there was substantial evidence to show guilt. Haven't the courts gone a bit too far in respect to the guidelines of plea bargaining?

Our system will not function without plea bargaining. Our judiciary is not willing to accept the change that the Alaskan court system has embraced. People feel good when they reach finality. When both sides in our adversarial system of law can finally agree upon the terms of a bargain, each is happy at the prospect of closure. But if defendants are cutting deals and admitting guilt for crimes in which they were not involved in order to avoid severe judicial reprisals, the system is being abused.

Discussion Questions

1. Could the criminal justice system survive if we abolished the procedure of plea bargaining?
2. What attempts should be made to curtail the powers of the prosecution in regard to the plea bargaining process?
3. Compare jurisdictions that have abolished or limited plea bargaining with those that have not done so yet. Discuss the pros and cons of each system.

4. Are we guilty of rewarding those criminal defendants who plead guilty. Do we "punish" people who actually invoke their Sixth Amendment right to trial by issuing longer sentences?

5. What types of pressures do both the defense counsel and the prosecutor face when confronted with a plea bargaining issue?

6. Watch the film called *The Thin Blue Line*. Critique the movie and discuss what happened to Randall Adams.

References

Bordenkircher v. Hayes, 434 U.S. 357 (1978).

Brady v. United States, 397 U.S. 742 (1970).

Bureau of Justice Statistics. 1990. *The Prosecution of Felony Arrest.* Washington, DC: Government Printing Office.

Gershman, B. L. (1991). Abuse of power in the prosecutor's office. In B. L. Gershman, *The world and I* (pp. 472-487). The Washington Times Corporation.

Inciardi, J. A. (1993). *Criminal justice* (4th ed.). Orlando, FL: Harcourt Brace Jovanovich.

Kipnis, K. (1976). Criminal justice and the negotiated plea. *Ethics, 86.*

North Carolina v. Alford, 400 U.S. 25 (1970).

Walker, S. (1989). *Sense and nonsense about crime: A policy guide* (2nd ed.). Pacific Grove, CA: Brooks/Cole.

14

Court Responses to Battered Women and Reform Legislation

ALBERT R. ROBERTS

The physical battering of women is a long-hidden problem that has been recognized by the public, journalists, legislators, and criminal justice professionals in recent years. Police, court intake workers, judges, and probation officers become involved because someone has been injured, harassed, or given death threats. Some cases lead to a restraining order against the batterer, criminal charges because of physical assaults resulting in injuries, or misdemeanor charges when no injuries are sustained as a result of the abuse. This chapter examines the latest policies and court-based programs aimed at reducing, intervening, and eliminating woman battering.

We have come a long way during the past two decades. Responsive prosecutors, judges, and legislators have begun to recognize family violence as a serious crime. All 50 states have passed civil and/or criminal statutes to protect battered women. Prosecutors' offices are beginning to implement efficient systems of screening and prosecuting cases. Police

AUTHOR'S NOTE: This chapter is an expanded version of my article, "Domestic Violence and Family Court" in R. Corsini (Ed.): ENCYCLOPEDIA OF CRIMINOLOGY (forthcoming). Copyright © by Macmillan Publishing Company. Used by permission of Macmillan Publishing Company.

and courts in a small yet growing number of jurisdictions have set up a round-the-clock method of issuing temporary restraining orders, as well as providing advocacy as the cases move through court. Although court-mandated, probation-operated batterers' counseling programs have been developed on a limited basis, more of these programs are needed.

The court system is still plagued with many problems in its handling of family violence cases, including:

- Judges, trial court administrators, case managers and intake officers who tend to minimize the dangers that abused women encounter and who discourage women from following through with criminal or civil complaints
- Overloaded dockets and overworked judges in large cities, resulting in the court's inability to schedule a hearing and a trial date in a timely manner
- A lack of specialized training on family violence for court personnel
- Abused women who fail to call the police or go to court because they believe that the criminal justice system will not be able to protect them
- A lack of counseling programs to which the court can refer the batterer and the victim.

From time to time, there are the tragic circumstances in which the court system does all it can to issue and enforce a restraining order, but the batterer flies into a rage as a result of the court involvement and murders the woman who had sought the court's protection. Occasionally the court itself has been the site of violence, when an enraged batterer has taken a concealed weapon into the courthouse and shot his partner while she was seeking protection from the court.

What are the statutory provisions for the effective handling of domestic violence by prosecutors, judges, and the courts? What changes were made at the end of the 1970s and the decade of the 1980s in state laws, family law remedies, and criminal assault statutes to benefit battered women? Under what circumstances can a woman obtain a restraining or protective court order against her abusive partner in most states? This chapter attempts to answer these questions related to changes in the legislative and judicial responses to the crime of domestic violence.

The Response of the Courts and Judges

Family courts and criminal courts are unique American institutions. The primary function of these courts is to provide a public forum for resolving legal disputes of a criminal or family nature. The powers and organizational structures of courts vary from state to state. For the most part, statutes from the many states are uniform with regard to the responsibilities of judges, prosecutors, and attorneys. The overwhelming majority of criminal and family law cases are settled without a trial. A family court judge often has courtroom administrative responsibilities; he or she may also preside over bail hearings, probation revocation hearings, and child custody hearings, and may issue search warrants, restraining orders, and protective orders.

The availability and commitment of judges to protect the legal rights of battered women vary from state to state and within states. For example, during the mid-1980s Cook County, Illinois, followed by Marion County (Indianapolis), Indiana, developed a special court with a specially trained magistrate to hear all domestic violence cases.

Court Orders

Judicial intervention on behalf of battered wives is a recent phenomenon. In 1976, Pennsylvania took the lead as the first state to pass legislation recognizing wife battering as a crime. By 1980, 44 states had enacted legislation that dealt with family violence. But it was not until 1988 that all 50 states took family violence laws seriously and passed acts that created civil and criminal remedies for victims of family violence.

Temporary restraining orders (TROs) became one of the most frequently used legal options for battered women during the decade of the 1980s. The protection order is known by different names across the country; it is most commonly referred to as an order of protection, a restraining order, or a temporary injunction. An order of protection can stay in effect for up to 1 year. The purpose of these court orders has been to prevent violence by one family member against another. These court orders usually forbid the alleged abuser from making contact with the victim. In some cases, the court order specifies the distance the abuser must maintain from the individual who requested the order. Depending on the state law, the court order may mandate that the abusive spouse move out of the house, refrain from terroristic threats of abuse or further physical abuse, pay support for the victim and minor children, or participate in a counseling program aimed at ending the violence or chemical dependency (both the batterer and the victim may be required to enter counseling).

In the past, in most jurisdictions, the battered woman needed a lawyer to prepare documents for a civil (family or domestic relations) court order. In most states, abused women may now file a petition in the appropriate court and represent themselves in the hearing. The batterer is given reasonable notice of the hearing and is asked to be present. He can hire an attorney to represent him, but legal representation is not required. The hearing for the temporary and permanent order of protection is before a judge; there is no jury.

The fearful and endangered victim needs to convince the judge that she was physically or sexually abused. Some judges have been very compassionate and sensitive to the needs of battered women. Other judges have the tendency to blame women for provoking the assaults. The judge usually has complete discretion over whether to grant a temporary restraining order and, 7 to 14 days later, a permanent restraining order. If the judge does not believe that the woman is in danger of further abuse, the case may well be dismissed.

The most serious drawback to "orders of protection" is that they are extremely difficult to enforce. Police cannot be available 24 hours a day, seven days a week. The courts and police rely on the victim to call them if the batterer violates the court order. If the batterer violates any of the conditions of the protection order (e.g., tries to get into the victim's apartment), he is in contempt of court or guilty of either a misdemeanor or criminal offense (depending on the state code).

There is wide variation in the penalties designated for the violation of restraining orders from one state code to another. Abusers can receive from 15 days to 6 months in jail, probation and mandated counseling, or up to a $500 fine. An additional drawback of the court order is that instead of constraining the abuser, it may provoke him into retaliating against the victim with more intense violence (Gondolf & Fisher, 1991, p. 280).

Judges need specialized training on the myths, dynamics, and effects of domestic violence as well as the court-mandated treatment needs of abusers. In the early 1990s, several statewide judicial conferences focused on family violence issues and policies. In addition, the National Council of Family and Juvenile Court Judges initiated two demonstration projects in 1990. The first project, funded by the U.S. Bureau of Justice, focused on improving family court practices with abused women through technical assistance. The second nationwide project, funded by the Conrad Hilton Foundation, is developing training materials for court personnel, judges, district attorneys, and probation officers.

Probation

County and city probation departments can play an important role in optimizing the delivery of services to batterers and their victims. Unfortunately, to date only a very small number of probation departments have provided any assistance to abusers, battered women, or their children.

Probation officers can provide early identification of serious cases, provide presentence reports on batterers (including detailed psychosocial history, criminal history, and relationship problems), monitor batterers' restitution orders, and either conduct or refer batterers to 6-month court-mandated group counseling programs.

Two illustrations of these types of programs are components of the San Francisco Probation Department and the Ocean County Probation Department in New Jersey.

Law Students Providing
Legal Services to Battered Women

Unfortunately, many attorneys are only interested in representing clients with substantial financial resources. Many battered women do not have the savings to draw upon to hire an attorney from either a large prestigious law firm or a small one-person law office. Because of the scarcity of legal services available to battered women, several law schools have established Clinical Practicum Programs on Battered Women's Rights. Third-year law students have the opportunity to help poor battered women, who often are single parents and sometimes are homeless. Three law schools that have led the way with this program are Yale Law School, Catholic University School of Law, and the City University of New York's Law School at Queens College (CUNY).

Prosecution of Family Violence Cases

In the past, it was very rare for batterers to be held accountable and punished for abusing their spouse or girlfriend. As was discussed in the previous section, judges in different parts of the country are beginning to receive training on the enforcement of protection orders and the necessity of sentencing violent batterers to jail or court-mandated counseling or both. Judges are viewed as the supreme authorities of their courtroom, and as such they wield significant power. When a batterer who breaches probation or a restraining order is given a stern lecture or a short-term jail sentence, it gives the perpetrator as well as the community an important message, namely that domestic violence will not be tolerated by the criminal justice system.

Prosecutors also have the potential to break the cycle of violence. Most victim advocates believe that more domestic violence cases should be actively prosecuted, particularly those acts involving alleged abusers with prior criminal histories. Although other advocates believe that the vast majority of abusive men are generally law-abiding citizens and that the first- or second-time abuser has the potential to change, the victim still needs to be protected. Therefore deferred prosecution pending the outcome of a 6-week, 12-week, or 6-month batterers' counseling program is the preferred prosecutorial alternative. The least useful approach is to encourage plea agreements (plea bargains) with the sole intent of reducing the prosecutor's caseload and clearing the court's calendar rather than protecting the victim. See Chapter 13 for information on plea bargaining.

Responsive prosecutors have been instituting promising strategies and policies with family violence. These recent policies have improved the different stages of the prosecution process. The first innovative stage has been the early identification of abuse cases and the filing of criminal charges by the prosecutor's office. The victim/witness assistance units in prosecutor's offices conduct a phone interview with each violently battered woman within a few hours after arrest. If they determine that the alleged abuser has caused serious bodily harm to the victim or that the abuser has been convicted of any assaultive crime, the advocate helps to prepare the victim to testify and collects eyewitness testimony from neighbors or photographs and x-rays of injuries. The other model was developed in Duluth and Minneapolis. In these Domestic Abuse Intervention (DAI) programs, staff interview and counsel victims after an arrest is made. A staff member then meets with prosecutors before the arraignment hearing to make sure that the prosecutors have all the necessary information and background evidence to prosecute the case.

In order to prevent batterers from intimidating and pressuring victims to drop charges or restraining orders, a growing number of prosecutors sign the criminal complaints themselves or file charges based on the arresting officer's signed complaint. When prosecutors take official responsibility by signing and filing charges themselves, they are giving the important message that domestic violence is a serious crime against the state, not a personal matter. Several prosecutors, (e.g., Madison, Wisconsin, and South Bend, Indiana) do not allow the battered women to drop charges unless there exists some extraordinary circumstances. However, in the majority of domestic violence arrests, neither the prosecutor nor the police will sign a criminal complaint. And in those cases when victims sign the complaint, most change their mind after the spouse apologizes and swears never to hit them again.

Sentencing options include traditional probation; pretrial diversion; probation and intensive supervision in a biweekly counseling program; Stipulated Order of Continuance pending completion of a diversion program; and presumptive sentence of 30 to 60 days in jail, with the sentence suspended for 1 year pending compliance with an agreement that the batterer have no contact with the victim and complete a counseling program. The main problem with these innovative sentencing options is that most courts and prosecutors have limited staff resources and refuse to assign enough staff to carefully screen applicants and monitor abusers' attendance and cooperation at the diversion program. Even when three to five full-time staff are assigned to these projects, they often fail because the community does not have enough alcohol rehabilitation, drug treatment, or group counseling programs for the hundreds of batterers in need of treatment. Nevertheless, some jurisdictions have assigned adequate staff to operate a comprehensive domestic violence treatment program. The Minneapolis Project employs 13 full-time staff members and is augmented by close to 50 trained volunteers. In both Minneapolis and Duluth when the civil courts determine that abuse has taken place, the batterer is required to participate in educational and counseling groups. A chemical dependency and psychological evaluation can also be ordered by the court. Abusers are required to sign contracts stipulating their responsibility to participate in the court-ordered treatment programs. The staff regularly monitors compliance with all aspects of the court order, including limited or no contact between the defendant and the victim. In the small number of cases where the abuser violates the court order, the prosecutor has the documentation to obtain a conviction.

Conclusion

Legal reforms aimed at protecting battered women and constraining the abusive partner have taken place in every state and the District of Columbia. Changes in state codes have occurred in such areas as civil protection orders, injunctions against further violence, the authorization of awards of child custody or visitation rights, authorization of no-contact or no-harassment provisions to be granted after a hearing, mandating police officers to make warrantless arrests if there is probable cause to believe that the perpetrator has violated a court order, and rules of evidence for battered women defendants (Hart, 1992).

Ideally, legal modifications and new domestic violence codes should reduce and eventually eliminate domestic violence. However, there is still ample room for improving the court administrative policies and practices so that domestic violence cases are handled swiftly, efficiently, and responsibly.

Several states have made significant changes in their criminal codes. In addition, state and county task forces and commissions have been established in order to begin implementation of a coordinated community response. In the states of Illinois, Massachusetts, New Jersey, Tennessee, and Washington, Domestic Violence Task Forces have developed policies and procedures for law enforcement, criminal and civil courts, prosecutors, defense attorneys, and victim advocates.

In order to ensure that the legal rights of battered women are protected, more needs to be done. Every court clerk, case manager, legal advocate, and judge in state and county courts throughout the United States needs specialized training on the handling of battered women and their abusive partners. All courts need systematic guidelines, simplified mandatory forms, and step-by-step instructions for processing protection orders, no-contact orders, restraining orders, and antiharassment orders. Police and court clerks should have a brochure available for dissemination to all victims of domestic violence. This brochure should describe the legal rights and options of battered women, instructions on how to obtain a court order or restraining order, and a list of local community resources. Navigating the court system is generally a time-consuming and overwhelming ordeal for victims of violent crime. But for a woman who has been a victim of repeated physical abuse, degradation, and terroristic threats by a spouse or boyfriend, "the thought of going to court may be so intimidating that no effort is made to get legal protection" (Roberts, 1981, p. 97).

Discussion Questions

1. Identify and discuss the purpose of a restraining order/order of protection for battered women.
2. Delineate specific penalties designated by county courts for the violation of restraining orders.
3. In what ways can probation officers help to eliminate violent behavior patterns among abusive partners?
4. Discuss prosecutorial policies and programs that hold batterers accountable while preventing the batterer from further intimidating his victim.
5. List the most innovative sentencing options for batterers and the limitations of these options and programs.

References

Buzawa, E. S., & Buzawa, C. G. (1990). *Domestic violence: The criminal justice response.* Newbury Park, CA: Sage.

Finn, P., & Colson, S. (1990). *Civil protection orders: Legislation, current court practice, and enforcement.* Washington, DC: Department of Justice.

Gondolf, E. W., & Fisher, E. (1991). Wife battering. In R.T. Ammerman & M. Hersen (Eds.), *Case studies in family violence* (pp. 273-292). New York: Plenum.

Hart, B. J. (1992). State codes on domestic violence. *Juvenile and Family Court Journal, 43*(4).

New Jersey Statutes, Annotated, 2C: 25-29 (b) (3) 1991.

Pence, E. (1983). The Duluth Domestic Abuse Intervention Project. *Hamline Law Review, 6,* 247-275.

Roberts, A. R. (1981). *Sheltering battered women: A national study and service guide.* New York: Springer.

Roberts, A. R. (1990). *Helping crime victims.* Newbury Park, CA: Sage.

Schmidt, J., & Steary, E. H. (1989). Prosecutorial discretion in filing charges in domestic violence cases. *Criminology, 27*(3), 487-510.

Sherman, L. W. (1992). Attacking crime: The police and crime control. In N. Morris & M. Tonry (Eds.), *Modern policing, Vol. 15: Crime and justice: A review of research.* Chicago: University of Chicago Press.

Sherman, L. W., & Berk, R. A. (1984). The specific deterrent effects of arrest for domestic assault. *American Sociological Review, 49,* 261-272.

PART V

CORRECTIONAL SYSTEMS

15

Jail Overcrowding

Social Sanitation and the Warehousing of the Urban Underclass

MICHAEL WELCH

On Being Warehoused in an Overcrowded Jail

Immediately after being arrested and booked on drug charges or any similar offense, most white, middle-class persons are detained only as long as it takes for a family member to arrive with the cash needed to secure their release. In cases such as these, bail may be set at $1,000: high enough to ensure the defendant's court appearance, but certainly not high enough to prevent his or her release from jail.

But for an unemployed person from the lower class facing similar charges, the same $1,000 bail might readily prevent his release. Therefore he will remain in jail until his court appearance, a wait that may last weeks or even months.

During this wait, he will experience the horrific aspects of pretrial detention, which are exacerbated by jail overcrowding. For instance, every day for the next number of weeks or months, he will wait in line to use the telephone for nearly one hour before he can call his family, as well as his court-appointed lawyer whom he will not actually meet until moments before he appears before the judge. In fact, because most pretrial detainees have such difficulty calling their family and reaching their attorney, they eventually realize that waiting in line for the telephone is a waste of time.

Due to overcrowded jail conditions, a pretrial detainee may have to sleep on the floor for several days or weeks before a bed becomes available. However, the actuality of being able to sleep should not be taken for granted. Loud voices of other inmates can be heard at all hours of the day and night. Thoughts of release become an obsession, especially when it is painfully clear that being held in jail means being denied even the most basic elements of outside living.

Pretrial detention also means eating cold institutional food, wearing dirty clothes reeking of body odor, and having to shower and go to the bathroom without privacy. In overcrowded jails, the plumbing cannot keep pace with the demands placed on the toilets; hence clogged toilets and flooding create an unbearable stench. These nauseating odors are worsened by the summer heat, which generates a permanent stench of urine that permeates the living units. As one develops a heightened sense of vigilance, the insufferable conditions eventually fade into the background. One continuously maintains close surveillance over the other inmates to ward off any potential threats of physical and sexual assault.

Understandably, pretrial detention in an overcrowded jail is a punishing experience. And this form of punishment raises two serious issues. First, being forced to undergo this punishment *before* trial violates the "innocent until proven guilty" principle of criminal justice. Second, this form of pretrial punishment is often reserved for those who cannot financially secure their release by meeting the bail. In other words, even at the early stages of determining one's guilt or innocence, the criminal justice system treats persons differently on the basis of their social class. Upper- and middle-class persons are more likely to spend time in the community while awaiting trial, whereas those who are poor face months of detention in an overcrowded jail.

An Introduction to Jails

During the summer of 1989, the election campaign for mayor of New York City was heating up. At this point, most of the political rhetoric had mirrored national political strategies by targeting street crime as society's most pressing issue. Most mayoral candidates in New York City spent several months exaggerating their "tough on crime" promises. Candidate Ronald S. Lauder amplified his disdain for street crime by visiting Rikers Island, the largest penal colony in the world, located off the banks of New York City.

Lauder was outraged at what he saw at Rikers Island: Inmates were allowed to watch television and had access to recreational facilities. Lauder proclaimed that he would remove televisions and close the recreational facilities, which he believed helped criminals strengthen their bodies for their return to the streets. Regarding jails, Lauder quipped, "It says that, hey, it is not so bad. If it were up to me, I would have them breaking stones to pebbles" (Barbanel, 1989, p. B1).

Although Lauder's condemnation of the jail system may have earned him some votes from those equally fed up with street crime, it is clear that Lauder himself did not know the fundamental differences between jails and prisons. What he failed to realize is that Rikers Island is a jail complex in which 65% of the population are pretrial detainees. Moreover, according to the Correctional Association of New York (1989), most of these pretrial detainees are held there because they are too poor to meet their bail, which is sometimes as low as $250 to $500.

Corrections officials at Rikers Island responded to Lauder's misinformed remarks by pointing out that exercise and television are essential to managing the inmate population by easing tensions and relieving stress. Furthermore, the policy at Rikers Island that grants inmates 1 hour of recreation per day is consistent with the minimum standards of incarceration that are also observed by federal penitentiaries (Barbanel, 1989).

Even though we might expect politicians to be aware of the basic differences between jails and prisons, Lauder's level of confusion is common among many persons who are uneducated about the various components of the criminal justice system. In brief, although jails and prisons differ in numerous ways, the distinction has traditionally been drawn along the lines of the legal status of their inmates. For example, whereas prisons house convicted felons (those serving sentences for 1 year or more), jails hold pretrial detainees, convicted misdemeanants (those serving sentences of less than 1 year), and convicted felons who are awaiting transfer to their assigned prison. Furthermore, jails are usually local and county institutions, whereas prisons are governed by state or federal authorities. Due to these basic differences, jails and prisons are destined to remain distinct institutions that face problems unique to their respective roles in the criminal justice system (Welch, 1992a).

The purpose of this chapter is to promote a heightened awareness of how jails differ from prisons. As we explore the use of jails, particularly in major urban settings, we will learn that jails also serve a distinct function in society known as *social sanitation*. Moreover, we will examine jail overcrowding in light of correctional *warehousing:* the practice of incarcerating massive numbers of inmates with the sole institutional goal of securing custody. Human storage, not rehabilitation or reform, is the primary objective in warehousing, and it is society's *urban underclass* who are most likely to undergo this form of incarceration. In this chapter, we will focus on the problems associated with jail overcrowding and proposed solutions, and because urban jails have the highest concentration of inmates, particular attention will be paid to the jail systems in New York City, Chicago, Los Angeles, Houston, and Miami.

Correctional Overcrowding: The Scope of the Problem

The United States is the world's leader in the number of persons it holds in prisons and jails, and its lead continues to widen over second-place South Africa and third-place Soviet Union. At an annual cost of $20 billion, taxpayers have inherited the burden of incarcerating more than 1 million Americans in prisons and jails. This massive warehousing effort in the United States is almost 4 times the incarceration rate of most European and Asian nations (Mauer, 1992a).

During the 1980s the prison and jail population more than doubled, and although considerable deliberation has focused on the crisis of prison overcrowding, less attention has been placed on jails, whose population increased by 77% between 1983 and 1989 (Bureau of Justice Statistics, 1989). While state prisons continue to absorb more inmates than they can reasonably manage, large urban jails take on a proportionately higher influx of admissions. New York State's prison population has jumped 160% over the past 12 years. By comparison, the inmate population in New York City jails has tripled during the same period (Mauer, 1992b).

Perhaps the most disturbing contradiction in this pattern of warehousing is that crime rates increased by only 2% in the period 1979-1988 (Mauer, 1992a). For those suggesting that Americans are soft on crime, it must be pointed out that our nation has "become more punitive than at any other time in our history" (Austin & Irwin, 1990, p. 2).

Jail Overcrowding

Overcrowding is considered the most pressing problem facing jails; in fact, in a widely cited survey, Guynes (1988) found that jail overcrowding poses a more serious problem than prison overcrowding. The "War on Drugs" has contributed to booming populations in both prisons and jails, and the unique role of the jail within the criminal justice system adds to the perennial problem of having to admit more inmates than there is space (see Klofas, Stojkovic, & Kalinich, 1992; Welsh, Leone, Kinkade, & Pontell, 1991).

The jail has been viewed as a "strange correctional hybrid" because it is used as a detention center for suspects, a correctional facility for misdemeanants, and a refuge to hold social misfits (Clear & Cole, 1990, p. 205). Throughout history, the poor have disproportionately occupied jails. Hence jails live up to their reputation as being the "poorhouses of the twentieth century," the "ultimate ghettos," and "storage bins for humans," as well as social "garbage cans" used to discard society's "rabble" (Clear & Cole, 1990; Goldfarb, 1975; Glaser, 1979; Irwin, 1985; Moynahan & Stewart, 1980; Welch, 1991a). Much like the persons detained there, jails are the most neglected institutions within the criminal justice system.

As of June 1990, the average daily jail population in the United States was 408,075, which constitutes a 5.5% increase from 1989. (This figure is significantly lower than the increase recorded between 1988 and 1989, which reached 15%.) Overall, the number of inmates exceeded available space in jails: occupancy was 104% of the rated capacity (Bureau of Justice Statistics, 1991a).

Unlike their prison counterparts, which hold a relatively stable population in terms of admissions and releases, the jail operates more like a "people-processing station" distinguished by a constant flow of traffic with around the clock activity. From June 1989 to June 1990, there were nearly 20 million jail admissions and releases; clearly, jails have more contact with the general population than do prisons.

Who Goes to Jail?

Unlike the board game Monopoly, one does not end up in jail by mere chance; there is a clear pattern of detention. The jail population does *not* represent a cross-section of the general population; rather, its inmates are disproportionately black, Hispanic, and most significantly, poor, uneducated, and unemployed. According to the Bureau of Justice Statistics, the percentages of black and Hispanic jail inmates increased substantially between 1983 and 1989. "With the increase in drug offenders, the jail population was generally older, less likely to have been incarcerated in the past, and less likely to be serving time for a violent offense in 1989 than in 1983" (Bureau of Justice Statistics, 1989).

In an attempt to help answer the question "Who goes to jail?" let us examine the following findings from the most recent (1989) profile survey on jail inmates (Bureau of Justice Statistics, 1991b, pp. 1-2).

- In 1989 nearly 1 in every 4 jail inmates was in jail for a drug offense, compared to 1 in every 10 in 1983.
- More than a third of all Hispanic inmates and a quarter of black non-Hispanic inmates were in jail for a drug violation, compared to less than a sixth of the white non-Hispanic inmates.
- During the month before their offense, more than 4 of every 10 convicted inmates had used a drug, and at least 1 of every 4 was a current user of a major drug.
- More than half of all jail inmates said they were under the influence of drugs or alcohol at the time of their current offense—12.1% under the influence of both drugs and alcohol, 15.4% under the influence of only drugs, and 29.2% under the influence of only alcohol.
- More than three quarters of the jail inmates had a prior sentence to probation or incarceration. At least a third were in jail for a violent offense or had a prior sentence for a violent offense.
- Among those inmates sentenced to jail, half had received a sentence of 6 months or less. The median time that the inmates sentenced to jail would serve before release was 4.8 months.
- Approximately 39.1% of all jail inmates had grown up in a single parent household, and an additional 10.5% lived in a household without either parent.

Characteristics of Jail Inmates

To further our understanding of who goes to jail, it is important to consider additional research findings. We have already established that jail inmates are disproportionately young (age 18 to 34) black men from the inner city with a history of drug abuse. But looking at Tables 15.1 and 15.2 we can identify additional characteristics of jail inmates. For example, more than half (53.8%) of the jail inmates have not completed high school: 38.2% report having some high school education and 15.6% have achieved an eighth grade education or less. Another 33.1% are high school graduates and 13.1% report some college.

Prearrest employment status figures in Table 15.2 shed additional light on the population characteristics of jail inmates. At the time of arrest, 53.1% of jail inmates were employed full time, 11.4% were employed part time, and 35.5% were unemployed and either looking or not looking for work.

Prearrest income among those jail inmates who were free for at least 1 year prior to arrest is provided in Table 15.2. More than one fourth (26.5%) of the jail inmates reported annual incomes of less than $3,000 per year. Even more alarmingly, though, about 78% of all jail inmates earned less than $15,000 a year.

TABLE 15.1 Selected Characteristics of Jail Inmates, by Conviction Status, 1989 and 1983

| Characteristics | Percentage of Jail Inmates in 1989 | | | 1983 |
	Convicted	Unconvicted	Total	Total
Sex				
Male	90.0	91.5	90.5	92.9
Female	10.0	8.5	9.5	7.1
Race/Hispanic origin				
White non-Hispanic	42.5	33.5	38.6	48.4
Black non-Hispanic	37.1	48.2	41.7	37.5
Hispanic	17.5	16.7	17.4	14.3
Other[a]	2.9	1.6	2.3	1.8
Age				
17 or younger	1.1	2.0	1.5	1.3
18-24	30.9	35.1	32.6	40.4
25-34	44.0	41.2	42.9	38.6
35-44	17.0	16.5	16.7	12.4
45-54	5.0	4.0	4.6	4.9
55 or older	2.0	1.2	1.7	2.4
Marital status				
Married	20.1	17.3	19.0	21.0
Widowed	1.2	.7	1.0	1.4
Divorced	15.8	14.2	15.1	15.7
Separated	8.2	8.4	8.2	7.9
Never married	54.8	59.4	56.7	54.1
Education				
8th grade or less	16.0	15.1	15.6	17.7
Some high school	38.1	39.0	38.2	41.3
High school graduate	32.2	34.3	33.1	29.2
Some college or more	13.7	11.7	13.1	11.8
Military service				
Veterans	15.7	15.2	15.5	21.2
Vietnam era	3.2	3.3	3.2	9.2
Other	12.5	11.9	12.3	12.0
Nonveterans	84.3	84.8	84.5	78.8
Number of jail inmates	218,797	162,441	395,554	223,552

SOURCE: *Profile of Jail Inmates, 1989*, by the Bureau of Justice Statistics, 1991, Washington, DC: Government Printing Office.
NOTES: Total includes jail inmates with an unknown conviction status or no offense. Data were missing for marital status on 0.2% of the inmates; for education, on 1.7% of the inmates; and for military service, on 1.2% of the inmates.
a. Includes Asians, Pacific Islanders, American Indians, Aleuts, Eskimos, and other racial groups.

TABLE 15.2 Prearrest Employment and Income for Jail Inmates, 1989 and 1983

| | Percentage of Jail Inmates | |
	1989	1983
Prearrest employment	100.0	100.0
Employed	64.5	53.2
Full time	53.1	40.9
Part time	11.4	12.3
Not employed	35.5	46.8
Looking for work	21.4	32.9
Not looking	14.1	13.9
Prearrest income		
Annual income[a]		
(Free at least 1 year)	100.0	100.0
Less than $3,000[b]	26.5	33.1
$3,000-$4,999	12.2	13.7
$5,000-$9,999	23.3	24.2
$10,000-$14,999	15.5	13.7
$15,000 or more	22.4	15.3
Number of jail inmates	285,599	170,393
Monthly income[c]		
(Free less than 1 year)	100.0	100.0
Less than $300[b]	22.4	36.3
$300-$499	15.5	17.1
$500-$999	25.3	28.0
$1,000-$1,449	17.4	8.4
$1,500 or more	19.4	10.2
Number of jail inmates	65,677	38,566

SOURCE: *Profile of Jail Inmates, 1989* by the Bureau of Justice Statistics, 1991, Washington, DC: U.S. Government Printing Office.
NOTES: Prearrest employment data were available for approximately 99% of jail inmates in 1989 and 1983. Income data were available for 89% of the inmates in 1989 and 93% in 1983.
a. Annual income figures based on inmates who reported being free at least 1 year prior to the offense for which they were sent to jail.
b. Includes inmates reporting no income.
c. Monthly income figures for inmates who were free less than 1 year prior to the offense for which they were sent to jail.

Perhaps the most accurate interpretation of the education, employment, and income figures is that jail inmates generally represent two segments of the lower class: They are either members of the working poor or permanent members of the underclass. Moreover, if one considers their educational background, it is clear that many of them have limited means to survive economically.

We have already established that those who are charged with drug offenses now make up 1 in 4 jail inmates. Table 15.3 presents the other changes in current offense data. As indicated by the data, those in jail for a violent offense (e.g., murder, rape, robbery, assault) decreased from 30.7% in 1983 to 22.5% in 1989. It is important to note that this decrease is expressed as a percentage: The total number of inmates charged with a violent offense actually increased from an estimated 67,439 in 1983 to 85,532 in 1989, an increase of 26.8%. In other words, there has been an overall increase in violent offenders, but their percentage drops because of an increase in two other offense categories. In addition to an increase of the percentage of drug offenses (from 9.3% in 1983 to 23% in 1989), there was also an increase of those charged with public order offenses (from 20.6% in 1983 to 22.8% in 1989). Yet those charged with driving while intoxicated account for almost all of the change in this category. Finally, the percentage of property offenses (e.g., burglary, larceny/theft, fraud) also decreased, from 38.6% in 1983 to 30% in 1989.

The Jail: Managing the
Underclass in American Society

The aforementioned research findings on the profile of jail inmates provide us with ample evidence indicating that jail populations are disproportionately poor, young, black, Hispanic, uneducated, and unemployed persons who have drug abuse problems and reside in the lower class neighborhoods of our nation's major cities. Considering these socioeconomic characteristics, the issue of social class is simply too important to ignore. As mentioned, those in jail occupy one of two segments of the lower class: the working poor and the underclass. Whereas the jail experience adversely affects both groups, those who are considered the working poor appear to be less disrupted because, at the very least, they possess some skills and the opportunity to survive economically upon their release. In contrast, the underclass, by its very definition, are those who have limited means to survive: They are uneducated, possess virtually no job skills, and have little or no work experience. For them, the jail experience reinforces their inability to lead a productive and economically independent life (see Gibbs, 1982; Weisheit and Klofas, 1989; Welch, 1989, 1991b; Wilson, 1987).

John Irwin has greatly contributed to the discourse of the social function of jails and the underclass in his book entitled *The Jail: Managing the Underclass in American Society* (1985). Irwin contends that jails are used in American society to manage the underclass. In his analysis of jails, he

TABLE 15.3 Most Serious Offense of Jail Inmates by Conviction Status, 1989 and 1983

Most Serious Offense	Percentage of Jail Inmates in 1989			1983
	Convicted	Unconvicted	Total	Total
Violent offenses	16.6	30.4	22.5	30.7
Murder[a]	1.2	5.1	2.8	4.1
Negligent manslaughter	0.7	0.3	0.5	0.6
Kidnapping	0.3	1.5	0.8	1.3
Rape	0.7	1.0	0.8	1.5
Other sexual assault	2.7	2.4	2.6	2.0
Robbery	5.0	9.1	6.7	11.2
Assault	5.1	10.0	7.2	8.6
Other violent[b]	1.0	1.2	1.1	1.3
Property offenses	29.2	31.2	30.0	38.6
Burglary	9.8	12.0	10.7	14.3
Larceny/theft	8.5	7.1	7.9	11.7
Motor vehicle theft	2.8	2.9	2.8	2.3
Arson	0.5	0.9	0.7	0.8
Fraud	4.2	3.6	4.0	5.0
Stolen property	2.2	2.6	2.4	2.5
Other property[c]	1.2	2.1	1.6	1.9
Drug offenses	22.5	23.8	23.0	9.3
Possession	10.7	8.4	9.7	4.7
Trafficking	10.7	13.7	12.0	4.0
Other/unspecified	1.0	1.6	1.3	0.6
Public-order offenses	30.2	12.9	22.8	20.6
Weapons	2.2	1.5	1.9	2.3
Obstruction of justice	2.4	3.4	2.8	2.0
Traffic	4.1	0.9	2.7	2.2
Driving while intoxicated[d]	13.8	2.0	8.8	7.0
Drunkenness/morals[e]	2.0	1.3	1.7	3.4
Violation of parole/probation[f]	3.7	2.1	3.0	2.3
Other public-order[g]	2.0	1.6	1.8	1.6
Other[h]	1.4	1.8	1.6	0.8
Number of jail inmates	218,303	161,858	380,160	219,573

SOURCE: *Profile of Jail Inmates, 1989,* by the Bureau of Justice Statistics, 1991, Washington, DC: Government Printing Office.
NOTES: Excludes an estimated 15,393 jail inmates whose conviction status or offense was unknown.
a. Includes non-negligent manslaughter.
b. Includes blackmail, extortion, hit-and-run driving with bodily injury, child abuse, and criminal endangerment.
c. Includes destruction of property, vandalism, hit-and-run driving without bodily injury, trespassing, and possession of burglary tools.
d. Includes driving while intoxicated and driving under the influence of drugs or alcohol.
e. Includes drunkenness, vagrancy, disorderly conduct, unlawful assembly, morals and commercialized vice.
f. Includes parole or probation violations, escape, AWOL, and flight to avoid prosecution.

has identified a specific economically subordinate social group that he classifies as the *rabble*. The rabble are socially detached (not belonging to any conventional social network), disorganized, disorderly, and viewed by the conventional world as *offensive* to their middle-class sensibilities. Irwin claims that most persons who occupy jails (the rabble) are detained for minor offenses and do not fit the stereotype of the dangerous and threatening criminal. Whereas one might believe that jail inmates are detained for the purpose of protecting society while they await trial, Irwin found that many jail inmates represent various types of "disreputables" such as petty hustlers, derelicts, and junkies. These "disreputables" are generally detained for nonviolent and minor offenses (for example, drug possession) and are simply too poor to meet their bail. Moreover, by the very nature of their economic standing, the rabble are unable to adequately defend themselves legally. Therefore, from the moment of arrest, they are at the mercy of the police, the jail staff, their court-appointed attorney, and the courts.

In light of the issues surrounding social class, Irwin places his findings in a larger social context. He concludes that the jail functions as an extension of the welfare state and becomes a means by which society manages and controls the underclass. Similar arguments have been developed by other researchers, such as Piven and Cloward in *Regulating the Poor: The Functions of Public Welfare* (1971). In their work, Piven and Cloward assert that throughout contemporary history, welfare has been used to reduce social unrest and reinforce the poor's social position in a class society.

According to Irwin, criminal justice resources are likely to continue placing disproportionate emphasis on managing the underclass instead of pursuing more serious offenders. Such forms of law enforcement, he asserts, serve as a "political diversion" that draws attention from the apparent lack of success in dealing with the serious offenders (Irwin, 1985, p. 112). Although critics argue that Irwin overstates his case by "claiming that jailed persons are less involved in serious criminality than is the case," there is agreement with him "regarding the broader issues of public policy toward members of the rabble class who get caught up in lawbreaking, and in many cases, who get sent to jails" (Backstand, Gibbons, & Jones, 1992, p. 228). (Also refer to Table 15.3 for current offense data.)

In taking a closer look at the jail experience, Irwin learned that the rabble undergo a distinct form of socialization by which they are stigmatized and kept constrained within the underclass. Inspired by the work of Erving Goffman in *Asylums* (1961), Irwin outlined various passages of the jail experience that comprise four stages: disintegration, disorientation, degradation, and preparation.

Disintegration

Unlike white, employed, middle-class persons, who are perceived as being reputable and thus generally released on their own recognizance or are able to meet bail, disreputable persons (the rabble) are detained. This denotes the outset of the disintegration stage because it tends to destroy the few social ties the rabble might have. Simply being denied convenient access to telephones makes it difficult to contact one's family, friends, and court-appointed attorney. Moreover, being detained prevents one from "taking care of business," such as calling one's employer or paying bills.

Although having convenient access to telephones while in jail is often rare, sometimes there are circumstances that make this problem worse. For example, in New York City's Rikers Island jail complex, there are reports that black inmates monopolize one telephone while the Hispanic inmates dominate the other, leaving white inmates (who represent only 5% of the pretrial detainee population) without regular access to telephones.

Obviously, without regular contact with family, friends, and lawyers, jail inmates undergo considerable disintegration. Upon release inmates have the stressful task of "picking up the pieces." Irwin notes,

> Unlike released convicts and mental patients, they [jail inmates] have received no official preparation for their release. And when they do get out, city, county, and private agencies rarely offer them any help in coping with the problems of reentering society. In trying to pick up the pieces of their shattered lives, most of them will be working alone, with virtually no resources and many handicaps. (1985, p. 52; see also Weisheit & Klofas, 1989).

Disorientation

Among the psychological effects of being arrested and detained is a profound sense of internal disorganization and demoralization. Subsequent to months of detention, released inmates understandably reenter society in a state of confusion similar to "being in a fog." This degree of disorientation is compounded by the replacement of one's personal routine by the institution's. For example, one eats according to a schedule organized by the staff, and assuming one can actually sleep, that too is dictated by the institution. Eventually, one's sense of independence is replaced by feelings of powerlessness, which are further compounded by the humiliation inherent to being in jail. Moreover, Irwin reminds us that in jail one eats, urinates, defecates, washes, changes clothes, and bathes without privacy. Inmates are continuously subjected to stares, comments, insults, and threats.

"Persons who are arrested and thrown in jail experience a sudden blow that hurls them outside society. It not only unravels their social ties; it stuns them and reduces their capacity and their resolve to make the journey back into society" (Irwin, 1985, p. 66). Irwin concedes that being detained once or twice does not lead to permanent social isolation, but because many inmates are rabble who are detained rather frequently, their ability to "bounce back" is strained. "The jail is not the only expelling process, of course; economic misfortune and drug abuse are others" (p. 66).

Degradation

As might be expected, the jail experience also involves relentless humiliation as inmates are continuously stripped of their dignity. Inmates are met with unyielding hostility from police officers, deputies, guards, and other detainees. Under routine surveillance by the staff, inmates are subjected to frisks, strip searches, and body cavity examinations. Irwin provides us with a glimpse of the humiliation one feels during a "kiester search" as described by a deputy:

> "Now bend over and spread your cheeks," I ordered. The kid bent over and grabbed his buttocks, pulling them apart. The plastic bag [of narcotics] inserted into his rectum had broken. The red pills had partially melted from this body heat, and his anus was a flaming scarlet color. The intestinal pressure had forced some of the pills out through his sphincter where they remained matted in his anal hair. We began to laugh with black humor at the grotesque sight. When the cops became bored with the game, the kid was ordered to dig the narcotics out of his rectum. (1985, p. 77)

In some jails, inmates are required to wear orange jump suits instead of their own clothes, which might help preserve whatever sense of personal identity that can be salvaged. Additional aspects of the degradation process are the loss of privacy and being forced to live in an environment where the human density is intolerable; indeed, inmates are literally *warehoused.*

While in jail, inmates also endure a barrage of insults. They are routinely called slime balls, dirt balls, pukes, scum, kronks, and the most popular reference, assholes. Following months of detention, their outward appearances are likely to change: Because shaving is not always easy, many inmates grow beards, and their hair becomes long and straggly. Not only is this an extension of degradation, but at their court appearance, inmates are judged not solely or even primarily in terms of crimes, but rather for their character, which is generally assessed by their physical appearance (Irwin, 1985).

Preparation

Irwin points out that a great majority of those arrested and those detained are not sentenced to serve a jail or prison term. Considering the humiliation and degradation experienced at the hands of the criminal justice system, however, all those arrested are subjected to some form of punishment, even those whose charges are dismissed. Indeed, one way to view this pattern of social disgrace is to recognize it as "process as punishment."

Whereas reputable persons are likely to "pick up the pieces" and move forward with their lives, the rabble are less likely to do so. With limited means to survive and few resources and economic opportunities at their disposal, the rabble fall victim to the self-fulfilling prophecy constructed by the criminal justice system. For many, accepting the labels of "loser" or "asshole" and dropping out of society becomes the inevitable option. Considering this, the rabble become even more defeated and more socially disintegrated or marginalized, and, as Irwin asserts, "The jail experience prepares them for an acceptance of the rabble life" (1985, p. 84).

Social Sanitation

So why is the jail in the business of locking up poor and disreputable persons? What larger social purpose is served by warehousing the rabble, especially when it is clear that these persons are *not* dangerous and do *not* pose an imminent threat to the community? One objective is *social sanitation,* the process by which police remove socially offensive (disreputable) persons from specific urban zones, thereby creating the illusion that certain sections of a city are indeed reputable.

Every medium to large city in the nation has a so-called "good" section and a so-called "seedy" section. Among the many tasks expected of city police is to keep the "good" section free of "riffraff" or disreputable persons: those who offend the middle-class sensibilities of the conventional world, such as street-walking prostitutes, the homeless, bums, junkies, and drug peddlers. Again, it is important to emphasize that the rabble are not regarded by the police as dangerous, but rather as offensive to society at large. Whereas the truly dangerous go to prison, the merely offensive are sent to jail for a temporary stay (Irwin, 1985, p. 3; also see Klofas, 1987; McCarthy, 1990; Spitzer, 1975). In this sense, social sanitation is a form of *social control* more than it is a form of *crime control* because it emphasizes sweeping the urban streets of those persons deemed offensive but not necessarily dangerous.

Therefore the jail should always be contextualized within the concept of social sanitation. As mentioned, the role of the jail in social sanitation has historical precedents. As early as the 16th century in Europe, as feudalism was unraveling and more vagabonds, beggars, prostitutes, "gonophs" (petty thieves), and peasants were drifting into the urban centers, jails were constructed for the purposes of social sanitation (Chesney, 1972).

The Effects of Jail Overcrowding

Not only is overcrowding itself a problem, but it becomes a source of other institutional problems as well. For example, it places enormous strain on classification, sorting, housing assignments, food, medical services (especially in light of AIDS and TB), security, and various programs, such as substance abuse counseling. Overcrowding also disrupts the daily routine of the facility and places additional pressure on budgetary allowances. But the consequences of overcrowding reach beyond institutional operations by affecting both inmates and staff. The social psychological effects of overcrowding can be traced primarily to the stress it creates, resulting in anger, hostility, violence, anxiety, and depression. Jails are by their very nature stressful environments; overcrowding merely compounds pre-existing problems that result from warehousing too many persons in too little space.

More specifically, recent studies have documented the effects of overcrowding on staff in terms of increased sick call and disciplinary violation rates, as well as higher mortality rates (Werner & Keys, 1988; see also Leger, 1988; Paulus, Cox, McCain, & Chandler, 1975). This places additional stress not only on the staff and inmates, but also on the jail as an institution, which must respond to the requirements of health care, security, and maintaining internal order.

The degree of disruption caused by overcrowding is far greater in jails than in prisons owing to a number of factors. First, because jails are designed for short-term confinement, there is little emphasis on long-range routines for inmates. Consequently, there are few programs and services available that can occupy and pacify the inmates. In fact, many violent incidents can be traced directly to inmates' resorting to fist fights to relieve the boredom caused by idleness. Again, this is a feature of warehousing, whereby inmates are merely tossed into jails until their court appearances. Additionally, the inmates' relatively short stay in jail makes it difficult for staff to keep sorting out the troublemakers who are responsible for aggravating the already volatile conditions. Moreover, corrections officers have the ominous task of ensuring that fist fights do not escalate to large-scale disturbances and riots (see Sechrest, 1989).

Civil Suits and Court Orders

As noted in *Cook v. City of New York* (1984), inmates do not forfeit all of their constitutional rights when they are incarcerated, even though the facility may limit some inmate rights in order to meet reasonable institutional needs (*U.S. v. Lewis,* 1975). Yet among the numerous consequences of overcrowding are civil and class-action suits filed by attorneys representing jail inmates against the jail administrators (see Champion, 1991; Embert, 1986). Figures from the latest Bureau of Justice Statistics (1991a) survey show that in 1990, 508 jurisdictions were under court order to reduce population or to improve conditions of confinement. More specifically, 28% of the jurisdictions had at least one jail under court order to limit population, and 30% were under court order to improve one or more conditions of confinement.

In 1979, a landmark case known as *Bell v. Wolfish* was filed in federal court. This case challenged the double-bunking practices of the Metropolitan Correctional Center (also known as the MCC), which serves as a federal jail in New York. The doublebunking policy was initiated when the pretrial detainee population dramatically increased, thus inducing the Federal Bureau of Prisons to assign sentenced and unsentenced inmates to single-occupancy accommodations. The class-action suit alleged violations of constitutional rights (such as undue length of confinement, improper searches, and inadequate employment, recreational, and educational opportunities). The U.S. Supreme Court rejected the allegations that these conditions violated inmates' constitutional rights. More important, because nearly all pretrial detainees were released within 60 days, doublebunking was not regarded as unconstitutional.

Despite the *Bell v. Wolfish* ruling, sheriffs and jail wardens remain alert because the courts are capable of holding them personally liable for damages in cases filed by inmates who allege violations of their constitutional rights. Even if the courts rule in favor of the jail administrators, the time and effort involved in litigation become a major distraction to jail management. In light of these developments, many of the large urban jails, which are described in the next section, face similar law suits and court orders.

Solutions and Remedies:
How Five Major City Jails
Cope With Overcrowding

Due to the possibility of litigation, jail administrators stay continuously aware of their jail's conditions, especially if their facility is under court order to limit population. As we have mentioned throughout this chapter, the highest concentrations of inmates are held in large urban jails. Moreover, the nation's largest cities also have the highest concentrations of the underclass (the rabble), many of whom also come into contact with the criminal justice system. As mentioned, the majority of inmates held in these large jails are disproportionately young, black or Hispanic, of low socioeconomic status, poorly educated, and unemployed, report poly-substance-abuse problems, and are arrested for nonviolent offenses such as drug violations (possession and/or sales) as well as property offenses that often relate to drug violations. Considering this, it is instructive to examine how the following jail systems cope with overcrowding: New York City, Chicago, Los Angeles, Houston, and Miami. It should be noted that the selection of these cities is intended to target some of the nation's largest cities and to feature different geographic regions: the Northeast, Midwest, West, Southwest, and Southeast, respectively.

New York City

The jail system in New York City consists of 18 facilities, including the Rikers Island jail complex and the borough jails. As of May 1992, the inmate population was more than 21,690, and the operating budget had increased from approximately $100 million a year to nearly $800 million. Approximately 65% of the city's jail population consists of pretrial detainees, most of whom are confined not because they have been judged dangerous but because they are too poor to make the relatively low bails (sometimes as low as $500 or even $250) that have been set for them (Correctional Association of New York, 1989).

It should be pointed out that New York City's jail population is further bloated by the number of convicted felons who are awaiting transfer to state prisons, which do not expedite transfer because of overcrowding there as well. In fact, this is a national problem that jails are continuously forced to deal with: Of the 37,965 jail inmates nationwide held for other authorities in 1990, 24,238 were being held because of overcrowding elsewhere, especially in state prisons (Bureau of Justice Statistics, 1991a).

Though many jail systems nationwide have experimented with make-shift jails—the conversion of existing structures such as old buildings for correctional purposes—New York City has introduced jail barges, which constitute one of the most unique and controversial applications of make-shift jails. Jail barges are literally floating jails, and a small fleet of them is located at the river banks surrounding the city. Two of these barges in particular have an interesting history. Known as the Bibby Resolution and the Bibby Venture, they were purchased from England for the purposes of alleviating overcrowding at Rikers Island, but years before they had served as troop barracks for the British navy during the Falklands Island War with Argentina (Welch, 1991a).

After their conversion to jails, the Bibby Venture and Bibby Resolution, also known as the "Love Boats" by the inmates, were moored on the banks of the Hudson and East Rivers to house minimum security, low-risk, nonviolent inmates who were enrolled in substance abuse treatment and work release programs. Because they were docked next to middle-class neighborhoods, residents engaged in a "not in my backyard" dispute with the city, forcing the barges to be moved to other locations, where similar protests also occurred (Welch, 1991a).

The Bibby Venture formerly held inmates involved in work-release and substance abuse programs (380 capacity), but it has been temporarily vacated due to increased capacity in other facilities within the system. However, as of May 1992, the Bibby Resolution houses 280 work-release inmates (capacity is also set at 380). The third barge in this fleet of floating jails is the Vernon Bain, currently being prepared for operation, whose capacity is set at 800.

To appreciate the extent to which the city has gone to create additional capacity, it should be noted that two refurbished Staten Island ferries, holding 162 inmates each, are also moored at Rikers Island. Furthermore, a series of *sprungs* have been installed on Rikers to house 1,900 inmates (50 beds per unit). Sprungs are another form of makeshift jails that resemble large bubble-like structures commonly used elsewhere as indoor tennis courts. At Rikers, the sprungs are used as dormitories for inmates from the general population and inmates enrolled in substance abuse and shock incarceration programs. Soon a few sprungs will be converted into medical units for inmates suffering from contagious diseases.

Another strategy designed to alleviate overcrowding at Rikers Island is the shock incarceration program, a quasimilitary boot camp regiment for young first-time offenders. The primary institutional benefit of the shock incarceration program is that it imposes a shorter, although more intense, sentence, thereby making more beds available sooner.

In addition to a number of substance abuse programs, the city also has a proposed plan to introduce electronic monitoring. According to James Bennett of the Board of Correction for the City of New York (a correctional watchdog group), the strategy to deal with jail overcrowding in the 1990s is fundamentally different from that of the 1980s. During the 1980s, the city attempted to "build their way out of the crisis" by constructing more facilities. The lesson learned was that officials had subsequently placed themselves on the "correctional treadmill," meaning that construction did not keep pace with increased admissions. By contrast, in the 1990s, the city is placing renewed emphasis on programs and other alternatives to incarceration.

Finally, many of the administrative policies dealing with overcrowding are monitored by the federal courts in an effort to compliance with court orders. In 1989, Judge Morris E. Lasker of the Federal District Court in Manhattan handed down a court order that specified that each new inmate be assigned a bed and given a medical examination within 24 hours of being taken into the department's custody. In 1990, a fine for noncompliance was established in which inmates who were not assigned a bed would be paid $150. To complicate matters, in May 1992, 21 jail supervisors and officers were charged with falsifying records to conceal such violations. The city's investigator claimed that the department falsified or made errors in the records of about 650 inmates (Raab, 1992).

Chicago/Cook County

Chicago's Cook County Jail is the largest single-site detention facility in the nation. The jail, which was designed to house 6,217 inmates, was in fact holding approximately 9,000 inmates as of May 1992. The jail employs more than 2,700 corrections officers, administrators, and staff members, and its annual operating budget is in excess of $98 million. The jail complex is made up of eight divisions, and the oldest division was built in 1929 (Sheriff's Office of Cook County, Illinois).

To better understand the overcrowding problem in the Cook County Jail, it is important to address its contemporary history in the context of inmate litigation. In 1974, pretrial detainees filed a class-action suit protesting the conditions of confinement, citing them as a violation of their constitutional rights. The suit, *Duran v. Elrod,* led to a consent decree handed down in 1982 that stated that each pretrial detainee is entitled to a permanent bed in a cell. But less than 1 year later, jail officials were charged with violating that consent decree by allowing inmates to sleep on the floors. Following numerous debates about which government branches should be responsible for decision making and inmate management, the court ordered that inmates with the lowest bail amounts who had been incarcerated the longest be released on their own recognizance.

This practice led to the formal introduction of Administrative Mandatory Furlough (AMF), which has since functioned as one of the primary mechanisms of dealing with overcrowding. It should be pointed out, however, that overcrowding and the practice of allowing inmates to sleep on floors, in dayrooms, and under stairwells remained a problem. According to the John Howard Association (a prison reform, advocacy, and watchdog organization), in September 1989 the jail was in violation of the consent decree, resulting in fines exceeding $270,000 paid by the county officials to the Inmate Welfare Fund (expended for goods directly benefiting inmates).

Because pretrial detainees represent about 95% of the inmate population, various measures installed to deal with overcrowding were designed with this in mind. For example, the specific strategies now in place include AMF, work furlough program (periodic imprisonment), and electronic monitoring. The electronic monitoring program began in 1989 and currently involves more than 1,100 detainees. The idea is to keep detainees under virtual house arrest by strapping a tamperproof bracelet to them, allowing the authorities to monitor them in their residences. In some cases, detainees are allowed to leave their homes to attend school, receive job training, or continue their regular employment; hence the program sets out to avoid expensive incarceration while maintaining nonviolent detainees as productive members of society.

Los Angeles County

The city/county jail system in Los Angeles is the largest in the nation. As of April 1992, the inmate population exceeded 22,790, which placed the jail complex of 10 facilities 136% over capacity. Consequently, city and county officials have cooperated with the Sheriff's Department and the Countywide Criminal Justice Coordination Committee to develop a series of mechanisms and programs to alleviate overcrowding. Such efforts have led to the implementation of nearly 50 mechanisms and programs countywide. The following are brief descriptions of a few of these criminal justice strategies, presented in the *1990 Programs Affecting Courts and Jails Report* published by the Countywide Criminal Justice Coordination Committee (1990).

Early Release Program
    The Sheriff's Department under the authority of a May 1988 federal court order, instituted this program in June 1988. Eligible inmates qualifying for this program include all sentenced inmates with a County jail sentence. The inmates are released after a discretionary number of days and are credited to the original sentence by the Sheriff. (p. 95)

Pretrial Supervised Release Program
    This program is partially funded by a grant through the Bureau of Justice Assistance (BJA). The remainder is funded through the County. The program is offered by the Pretrial Services Division of the Superior Court and is aimed at providing an alternative release mechanism for the courts that, in turn, positively

impacts jail overcrowding. All defendants are supervised and may be involved in the following additional components:
— Drug Testing
— Treatment Referral
— Electronic Monitoring. (p. 103)

Regimented Inmate Diversion
    Also known as RID or BOOT CAMP, this program includes youthful non-violent offenders who are given reduced sentences for participation in a rigid military style basic training program. The goals of the program are to reduce jail overcrowding, cut costs, deter recidivism, and improve control. (p. 105)

Other programs and mechanisms include Own Recognizance, Community Service Sentencing, Bail Deviation Program, Weekend Commitment to Local Jails, Work Furlough, and Work Release.

Houston/Harris County

As of May 1992, the jail system in the city of Houston and Harris County held more than 13,000 inmates. In contrast to Chicago, the overcrowding problem in Houston is not caused by an excess number of pretrial detainees, but rather by an excess number of state-ready felons. That is, Houston's jail population is bloated by the enormous number of convicted felons awaiting transfer to the state prison system—again, a problem facing jails nationwide.

To understand how the Houston jail system inherited this problem of housing inmates who belong to the state prison system, we turn to the recent correctional history of the state of Texas. In 1972, a landmark lawsuit known as *Ruiz v. Estelle* filed by inmates against the state prison system led to sweeping changes on how the state prison system would manage inmates. Among the numerous modifications affecting the prison system was the agreement that the state prisons would not exceed 95% capacity. Consequently, the county jails throughout Texas were forced to hold state-ready inmates until there were openings in the state prisons. The jail system in Houston, much like the jail systems in Dallas, Fort Worth, and San Antonio, found itself confronting overcrowding effected by the state prison system. In this case, prisons overcrowding creates a *hydraulic effect:* "when pressure is alleviated at one point in the correctional system, it is increased at another" (Champion, 1991, p. 214).

Fortunately, the jail system in Houston does a fairly good job detaining only those inmates who really belong in the system. This is achieved by a number of screening mechanisms that keep many pretrial detainees out of the system while awaiting trial. Yet the degree of overcrowding has forced the jail system to look elsewhere for additional jail space. At this time, 1,600 inmates who belong to the Houston/Harris County jail system are held at neighboring county jails on a contract basis. This strategy, also known as "farming out," is supported by the state of Texas which compensates the participating county's expenditures. Nevertheless, due to the problems stemming from overcrowding in the state prisons, contracting has emerged as a costly and logistically awkward procedure.

Finally, the city of Houston and Harris County offer additional programs to deal with jail overcrowding. For example, adult probation services help alleviate jail crowding by supervising more than 49,000 probationers, and at this time there are more than 380 inmates enrolled in their Boot Camp Program.

Miami/Dade County

The Miami jail complex in Dade County comprises seven facilities holding more than 6,200 inmates as of May 1992. The problem in the Miami system also features litigation, in that the jail currently operates under a state lawsuit limiting overcrowding. The conditions of this court order have led to the construction of an additional 1,000 beds, which have allowed the jail system to discontinue use of makeshift jails (a series of trailers housing as many as 400 inmates).

In addition to the construction of a new facility, the Miami system utilizes such programs as Release on Own Recognizance (for nonviolent detainees), Pretrial Release and Diversion, and Work Furloughs. Overall, the Miami/Dade County jail complex resembles many other jail systems throughout the nation. It is generally a well-functioning system despite being enormously overburdened. Again, a major problem with jail overcrowding is that it generates other institutional problems by placing undue stress on resources and staff (see Kalinich, 1986; Thompson and Mays, 1991).

In sum, the strategies, mechanisms, and programs implemented to alleviate jail overcrowding can be classified into two policy categories: those accommodating social sanitation and those resisting social sanitation. Strategies designed to reduce overcrowding by constructing additional jails (building new facilities or renovating old facilities) accommodate social sanitation by expanding capacity needed to warehouse the underclass. However, those strategies developed to return the inmate into the community run counter to, or resist, social sanitation.

Large urban jails experience similar difficulties, especially problems related to poverty and substance abuse. These problems are further exacerbated when we take into consideration that jails are also dealing with problems previously handled by other human service agencies and mental health systems (Jerrell & Komisaruk, 1991; Kalinich, Embert, & Senese, 1991; Lawrence, 1989). For instance, today jails have to deal more with the homeless mentally ill than ever before (Abram, 1990; Belcher, 1988). Therefore strategies that merely alleviate jail crowding by releasing detainees do not necessarily address the underlying social problems, and it is these social problems that contribute to larger numbers of persons being processed by the criminal justice system.

Conclusions

In this chapter, we have examined jail overcrowding in a larger social context by drawing attention to the urban underclass and social sanitation. By exploring the various ways in which large city jails cope with overcrowding, we have learned that jail policy tends to swim against the tide of complex social problems such as poverty, unemployment, homelessness, substance abuse, inadequate education, and inaccessible heath care, each of which directly or indirectly contributes to street crime and jail overcrowding (Welch, 1992b).

In light of the interconnection between jail policy and social forces, it is important that we expand our awareness of social problems facing our cities and demand more ambitious social policies. For example, we have noted throughout this chapter that drug arrests account for the latest surge in jail populations. As mentioned, it makes more sense to treat drug abuse as a public health problem than as a criminal justice problem. Clearly, treatment upon demand is more cost effective and goal oriented than mere warehousing.

Other areas of social policy requiring additional development are employment and educational programs. Indeed, serious investment in such programs is actually a crime control strategy. According to Mauer, "Studies of the Head Start program, for example, have shown that every $1 invested in early intervention resulted in savings of $4.75 in remedial education, welfare, and crime costs" (1992b, p. 82; see also Currie, 1985). Such educational and employment programs are particularly relevant in light of the problems facing the urban underclass. Moreover, such interventions also cut to the root of the problem instead of relying on warehousing as a form of social sanitation.

Finally, Irwin (1985) argues that social reforms must be addressed before jail reform "because no progress at all can be made on reforming the jail until we begin to reform our fundamental societal arrangements.

Until we do, the police will continue to sweep the streets of the rabble and dump them in the jails" (p. 118).

Discussion Questions

1. How does a person's social class (socioeconomic status) determine how he or she will be processed in the criminal justice system? For a nonviolent offense, such as a drug violation, are middle-class persons more likely to avoid jail detention than lower-class persons? Why?

2. What is meant by warehousing in corrections, and why have jails resorted to such a practice?

3. How has the "war on drugs" impacted jail overcrowding, and what additional problems has it caused jail administrators?

4. What is meant by social sanitation, and besides drug peddling, what other social problems are subject to this practice?

5. Compare and contrast the strategies to reduce overcrowding in the five major city jails discussed in this chapter.

6. Explain the various stages of the jail experience developed by John Irwin (1985).

7. What are the common characteristics of those detained in large urban jails?

8. How should jails be reformed, and how can they be used more efficiently and fairly in the criminal justice system?

References

Abram, K. M. (1990). The problem of co-occurring disorders among jail detainees: Antisocial disorder, alcoholism, drug abuse, and depression. *Law and Human Behavior, 14,* 333-344.

Austin, J., & Irwin, J. (1990). *Who goes to prison.* San Francisco: National Council on Crime and Delinquency.

Backstand, J. A., Gibbons, D., & Jones, J. F. (1992). Who is in jail? An examination of the Rabble hypothesis. *Crime & Delinquency, 38,* 219-229.

Barbanel, J. (1989, June 15). Lauder likes TV but at Rikers Jail it's an 'outrage.' *New York Times*, p. B-1.

Belcher, J. R. (1988). Are jails replacing the homeless health system for the homeless mentally ill? *Community Mental Health Journal, 24*(3), 185-194.

Bell v. Wolfish, 441 U.S. 520 (1979).

Bureau of Justice Statistics. (1989). *1989 survey of inmates in local jails.* Washington, DC: Government Printing Office.

Bureau of Justice Statistics. (1991a). *Jail inmates, 1990.* Washington, DC: Government Printing Office.

Bureau of Justice Statistics. (1991b). *Profile of jail inmates, 1989.* Washington, DC: Government Printing Office.

Champion, Dean J. (1991). Jail inmate litigation in the 1990s. In J. A. Thompson & G. L. Mays (Eds.), *American jails: Public policy issues* (pp. 197-215). Chicago: Nelson-Hall.

Chesney, K. (1972). *The Victorian underworld.* New York: Schocken.

Clear, T., & Cole, G. F. (1990). *Introduction to corrections* (2nd ed.). Monterey, CA: Brooks/Cole.

Cook v. City of New York, 578 F. Supp. 179 (1984).

Correctional Association of New York. (1989). *Basic prison and jail fact sheet.* New York: Author.

Countywide Criminal Justice Coordination Committee (1990). *1990 programs affecting courts and jails.* Subcommittee on Court Process. County of Los Angeles, California.

Currie, E. (1985). *Confronting crime: An American challenge.* New York: Pantheon.

Duran v. Elrod, 74 C. 2949 (1974).

Embert, P. S. (1986). Correctional law and jails. In D. B. Kalinich & J. Klofas (Eds.), *Sneaking inmates down the alley: Problems and prospects in jail management* (pp. 63-84). Springfield, IL: Charles C Thomas.

Gibbs, J. J. (1982). The first cut is the deepest: Psychological breakdown and survival in the detention setting. In R. Johnson & H. Toch (Eds.), *The pains of imprisonment* (pp. 97-114). Prospect Heights, IL: Waveland.

Glaser, D. (1979). Some notes on urban jails. In D. Glaser (Ed.), *Crime in the city.* New York: Harper & Row.

Goffman, E. (1961). *Asylums.* Garden City, NY: Doubleday.

Goldfarb, R. (1975). *Jails: The ultimate ghetto.* Garden City, NY: Doubleday.

Guynes, R. (1988). *Nation's jail managers assess their problems.* Rockville, MD: National Institute of Justice.

Irwin, J. (1985). *The jail: Managing the underclass in American society.* Berkeley: University of California Press.

Jerrell, J., & Komisaruk, R. (1991). Public policy issues in the delivery of mental health services in a jail setting. In J. A. Thompson & G. L. Mays (Eds.), *American jails: Public policy issues* (pp. 100-115). Chicago: Nelson-Hall.

Kalinich, D. (1986). Overcrowding and the jail budget: Addressing dilemmas of population control. In D. B. Kalinich & J. Klofas (Eds.), *Sneaking inmates down the alley: Problems and prospects in jail management* (pp. 85-100). Springfield, IL: Charles C Thomas.

Kalinich, D., Embert, P., & Senese, J. (1991). Mental health services for jail inmates: Imprecise standards, traditional philosophies, and the need for change. In J. A. Thompson & G. L. Mays (Eds.), *American jails: Public policy issues* (pp. 79-99). Chicago: Nelson-Hall.

Klofas, J. (1987). Patterns of jail use. *Journal of Criminal Justice, 15,* 403-411.

Klofas, J., Stojkovic, S., & Kalinich, D. A. (1992). The meaning of correctional crowding: Steps toward an index of severity. *Crime and Delinquency, 38*(2), 171-187.

Lawrence, J. E. (1989). Substance abusers in jail: Health service breakdown in five New York jails. *American Journal of Criminal Justice, 14*(1), 122-134.

Leger, R. (1988). Perception of crowding, racial antagonism, and aggression in a custodial prison. *Journal of Criminal Justice, 16,* 167-181.

Mauer, M. (1992a). *Americans behind bars: One year later.* Washington, DC: The Sentencing Project.

Mauer, M. (1992b, February 11). "Lock 'em up" is not key to crime control. *New York Newsday,* pp. 44, 82.

McCarthy, B. R. (1990). A micro-level analysis of social structure and social control: Intrastate use of jail and prison confinement. *Justice Quarterly, 7,* 325-340.

Moynahan, J. M., & Stewart, E. K. (1980). *The American jail: Its growth and development.* Chicago: Nelson-Hall.

Paulus, P. B., Cox, C. V., McCain, G., & Chandler, J. (1975). Some effects of crowding in a prison environment. *Journal of Applied Social Psychology, 1,* 86-91.

Piven, F. F., & Cloward, R. A. (1971). *Regulating the poor: The functions of public welfare.* New York: Vintage.

Raab, S. (1992, May 16). Charges filed in crackdown at corrections: Altered inmate records prompt hearings for 21. *New York Times,* pp. 25-26.

Ruiz v. Estelle, F. 2d 115 (5th Cir. 1982).

Sechrest, D. K., & Collins, W. C. (1989). *Jail management and liability issues.* Miami: Coral Gables.

Spitzer, S. (1975). Toward a Marxian theory of deviance. *Social Problems, 22,* 638-651.

Thompson, J. A., & Mays, G. L. (1991). Paying the piper but changing the tune: Policy changes and initiatives for the American jail. In J. A. Thompson & G. L. Mays (Eds.), *American jails: Public policy issues* (pp. 240-246). Chicago: Nelson-Hall.

U.S. v. Lewis, 400 F. Supp. 1046 (1975).

Weisheit, R. A., & Klofas, J. M. (1989). The impact of jail on collateral costs and affective response. *Journal of Offender Counseling, Services and Rehabilitation, 14*(1), 51-66.

Welch, M. (1989). Social junk, social dynamite and the rabble: Persons with AIDS in jail. *American Journal of Criminal Justice, 14,* 135-147.

Welch, M. (1991a). The expansion of jail capacity: Makeshift jails and public policy. In J. A. Thompson & G. L. Mays (Eds.), *American jails: Public policy issues* (pp. 148-162). Chicago: Nelson-Hall.

Welch, M. (1991b). Persons with AIDS in prison: A critical and phenomenological approach to suffering. *Dialectical Anthropology, 16*(1), 51-61.

Welch, M. (1992a, July/August). How are jails depicted by corrections textbooks? A content analysis provides a closer look. *American Jails: The Magazine of the American Jail Association,* pp. 28-34.

Welch, M. (1992b). Social class, special populations, and other unpopular issues: Setting the jail research agenda for the 1990s. In G. L. Mays (Ed.), *Setting the jail research agenda for the 1990s* (pp. 17-23). Washington, DC: National Institute of Corrections.

Welsh, W., Leone, M. C., Kinkade, P., & Pontell, H. (1991). The politics of jail overcrowding: Public attitudes and official policies. In J. A. Thompson & G. L. Mays (Eds.), *American jails: Public policy issues* (pp. 131-147). Chicago: Nelson-Hall.

Werner, R. E., & Keys, C. (1988). The effects of changes in jail population densities on crowding, sick call, and spatial behavior. *Journal of Applied Social Psychology, 18*(10), 852-866.

Wilson, W. J. (1987). *The truly disadvantaged: The inner city, the underclass and public policy.* Chicago: University of Chicago Press.

16

Public Policy and
Prison Industries for the 1990s

DIANE C. DWYER

ROGER B. McNALLY

Each weekday morning, male and female inmate-employees in work clothes board a former school bus at the Kansas Correctional Institution at Lansing to ride to their jobs. The bus, driven by a correctional officer, takes the inmates over public roads and delivers them to work by 7:30 a.m. They arrive for work at the same time as civilian employees.

Once Zephyr's workday begins, inmates perform tasks typically required of sheet metal workers. Some of the inmates bolt together valve assemblies that will funnel grain into bulk bins used to feed pigs and chickens. Two other inmate-employees unload 4 by 8-foot sheets of metal from trucks. Others shear the sheet metal to size. One inmate punches holes in the sheet metal where bolts will fasten the valve assemblies to grain bins. Some inmate-employees bend the sheet metal into a funnel shape. After these tasks are completed, inmates place the valve assemblies in boxes with the necessary nuts and bolts. The boxes are shipped to the company's warehouse to await purchase. They are not opened until a farmer is ready to attach the valve assemblies to a grain bin at the farm.

Still other inmates weld together a steel chassis for saws used to cut concrete. They begin with bulk steel purchased directly from a steel mill. They cut, punch, and bend numerous pieces of steel into various forms before welding them together. The saws are featured in the contracting company's catalogues under the titles Super Concrete Saw and PRO-3511.

While working, little conversation is heard between employees except when a civilian supervisor corrects a work related error or reminds an inmate-employee about a change in company policy or a new safety measure. During mid-morning or mid-afternoon breaks or at lunch time, conversation centers around current profit and loss figures, job deadlines, the evening's softball or basketball game, or a weekend visit.

At 4:00 p.m., the workday ends and the inmate-employees reboard the bus for the ride back to their "off-work residence." Their driver is the same uniformed correctional officer who brought them. He remained at the factory throughout the day but was hardly noticed amid the moving machines and the constant activity. (Callison, 1989, pp. 2-3)

If the rapid changes of the early 1990s are any indication of what is to come, then we must brace ourselves for the turbulent decade ahead! We have witnessed the fall of communism, the reduced threat of world war, the shrinking of our planet through satellite technology, and the emergence of a global economy. In this country, we are seeing demographic shifts in age and ethnicity. As we approach the 21st century, our shrinking and less educated labor pool will affect our ability to compete globally. The implications of this are increasing geometrically. The challenge is one that government must embrace responsively and prudently. Perhaps it is time to reexamine the mission, goals, and fiscal ramifications of government's various public policy responsibilities.

Researchers and policy analysts have long argued about the "politically correct" mission of prisons in our society. Proponents of the punishment model see retribution as the appropriate end-product of corrections, whereas others espouse rehabilitation as the goal. Regardless of where one stands on the continuum of philosophical approaches to corrections, it is obvious to even the casual observer that public policy has been unsuccessful in the area of imprisonment. This failure has had major social and economic repercussions.

With the proliferation of drug abuse and violence we are incarcerating more people, 455 per 100,000 ("Comparative Incarceration Rates," 1992, p. 1) than any other country (see Figure 16.1). In reality we have an expensive prison system at the local, state, and federal level that simply incapacitates. Additionally, there are clear social consequences to these aptly called "schools of crime." They "teach" violence, dependence and irresponsibility; "skills" are learned with no apparent correlation to even marginal adjustment in the real world. As noted in recent research, our current practices threaten "the possibility of writing off an entire generation of black men from leading productive lives" (Mauer & Kline, 1990, p. 1).

By all traditional measures this is a failing system. It impacts negatively on communities around the country. Escalating correctional budgets take

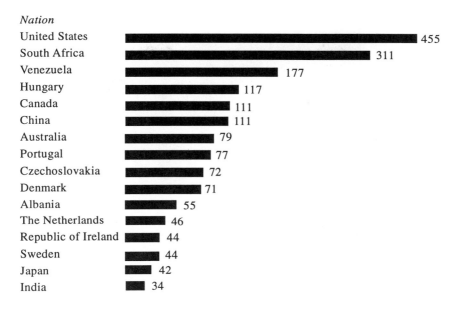

Figure 16.1 Comparative Incarceration Rates in 16 Countries
SOURCE: "Comparative Incarceration Rates," 1992 (January 16), *Criminal Justice Digest,* p. 4.

an ever-increasing portion of fiscally constrained state and local budgets, thereby reducing the already scarce resources available for other necessary governmental expenditures, such as education, social programs, and the infrastructure. In essence, social and economic costs associated with incarceration are holding businesses, taxpayers, and other necessary publicly funded programs hostage in the 1990s.

There is an alternative to maintaining the status quo in corrections. It calls for a reexamination of the basic philosophy of correctional programming and the implementation of a strategy to restructure prisons so that they more closely replicate "real life." Work programs that generate revenues (defraying prison costs) and create real jobs (mandating inmate responsibility) must become the cornerstone of such a change. This philosophy must embrace the changing milieu of the 1990s and incorporate basic American values of a work ethic, productivity, and fiscal responsibility.

Within the criminal justice system, prison industries have been and continue to be very controversial. Critics, generally business and labor unions, traditionally opposed prison industry programs from the perspective of unfair competition and abusive labor practices. This resulted in restrictive legislation curtailing its development. However, just as contemporary developments have given rise to the present social, economic, and political trends, these same forces have had an impact on corrections and the reemergence of a role for prison industries. This past decade alone has witnessed the resurrection of partnerships formed between the private sector and correctional industrial programs, for example, in Minnesota and in Stafford County, New Hampshire (Miller, Sexton, & Jacobsen, 1991, p. 5).

Although the problem of crime is complex and no single solution will emerge, what is likely to occur during this decade is the development of alternative methods to manage offender populations in a more cost-effective manner. A change in correctional philosophy from a purely incapacitative approach to one that employs a work ethic model is necessary. This will ". . . parallel the private industrial world and provide inmates with knowledge, skills, practice, and experience necessary to live in the general social environment" (Miller & Grieser, 1986, p. 8). As prison populations continue their unprecedented growth, this shift will become significant to budget planners in search of deficit reduction measurers. Moreover, an entrepreneurial approach operating on a businesslike basis will allow policy makers to view the incarcerated not solely as economic liabilities but as potential economic assets.

The purpose of this article is to present a review of the role of prison industries in American corrections from a historical and contemporary perspective. Discussion will focus on the description and analysis of several models of prison work programs. The framework will address the issues central to business, labor, and correctional philosophy. Legislative and policy issues will be considered and alternatives proposed.

Evolution and Metamorphosis
of Prison Work Programs

From a historical perspective, inmate labor has always been a part of correction's serving both philosophical and economic goals. A sentence to "hard" labor addressed the need to punish as well as to help defray the costs of imprisonment. An examination of inmate labor (prison industries) from its origin through the present reflects the following five periods, embracing varying correctional philosophies:

1. Pre-Civil War—Developmental Period
2. Post-Civil War—Expansionism
3. Demise and Restriction of Prison Industries
4. Post-Depression—Emergence of the Rehabilitation Model
5. Resurgence of the Work Ethic and Decline of the Medical Model

Pre-Civil War—Developmental Period

The roots of inmate labor date back to Europe and the beginnings of workhouses in England in 1576. These workhouses (Bridewells) were created for housing London's destitute and were based on a work ethic model. Work was perceived as virtuous and as a way of paying for one's keep (Allen & Simonsen, 1992, p. 23). Moreover, the emergence of the Classical School of criminology (Cesare Beccaria) and the reform-minded ideas of John Howard began to supplant capital punishment as the preferred response to law violation.

During the late 18th century (in the United States), the Quakers introduced the notion of imprisonment with hard labor as an alternative to the existing penalties of corporal and capital punishment; hence the Walnut Street Jail of 1790. This Quaker influence became the dominant theme embodied in the Pennsylvania/Auburn period of corrections (Clear & Cole, 1990, p. 74). As the Civil War commenced, inmate labor was an accepted component of American corrections and thus the forerunner of what became known as prison industries.

Post-Civil War—Expansionism

As America approached the 19th century, the construction of prisons and the expansion of prison industries became the hallmark of corrections. The notion of inmate labor on a "for-profit" basis was perceived not only as a reform measure (inmates being productively busy) but as economically sound.

The evolving configuration of prison industries generally centered on the search for ways to eliminate inmate idleness and simultaneously to make prisons self-sustaining. Systems that favored either private or public benefit tended to emerge. The distinction was largely the degree of private involvement, that is, the contracting or leasing of inmate labor to the private sector.

Although these new market systems were considered successful, they became victims of their own success. Shifting philosophies in corrections moved toward a medical model approach, and other forces (public, labor, business, government, etc.) rejected the exploitation of inmate labor. The reformation movement and opposition to prison industries began to gain ground.

Demise and Restriction of Prison Industries

Opposition to prison industries came from a variety of fronts and ultimately resulted in the passage of restrictive legislation. The concern of the private manufacturer was that goods produced in prison utilized cheap labor and made fair competition impossible. The labor unions that emerged in the late 1800s expressed similar concerns. Unfair competition took on the added dimension of taking jobs away from law-abiding citizens. In 1905, President Theodore Roosevelt signed Executive Order 325A barring the use of state inmate labor on all federal contracts.

The impact of attitudes opposing prison industries was intensified by the effects of the Great Depression on the American economy. With high unemployment and the perception that this was being exacerbated by cheap inmate labor, the foundation for controlling legislation was laid. Significant legislation virtually halting prison industries included the Hawes-Cooper Act of 1929, the Ashurst-Summers Act of 1935, the Prohibitory Act of 1940, and the Walsh-Healey Act of 1935 (Miller & Grieser, 1986, p. 6). The climate supporting the work ethic as a viable correctional philosophy was short-lived.

Post-Depression—Emergence of the Rehabilitation Model

With the exception of limited goods to be produced for and sold to governmental agencies, and the war effort during World War II, inmates were relegated to idleness. The impact on corrections was major. At the beginning of the 20th century approximately 85% of all inmates worked; by 1940, however, less than 45% were employed in prison industries (Miller & Grieser, 1986, p. 6). This forced idleness contradicted the American work ethic and served to heighten inmate irresponsibility and dependence.

Concurrently, a new correctional philosophy came into favor, one viewing the offender as ill and needing treatment and rehabilitation. This "medical model" philosophy supplanted the work ethic as the prevailing approach, and influenced correctional thinking for the next three decades.

Ironically, despite restrictive legislation and a new correctional philosophy, the Federal Bureau of Prisons (BOP) established UNICOR in 1934. This is the trade name for the Federal Prison Industries (FPI), a wholly owned government corporation created by Congress. UNICOR employed federal prisoners in federal prisons to produce goods and services that were sold for a profit to other federal agencies. This program kept the door open and became the forerunner to the reemergence of prison industries in the 1950s.

Resurgence of the Work Ethic
and Decline of the Medical Model

The rekindling of the work ethic in corrections was precipitated by a number of events. First, prison populations grew in the early 1950s, as did idleness, prison riots, and the costs of incarceration. Second, the social revolution of the 1960s challenged all traditional institutions of life, and a trend toward community-based corrections emerged, integrating a work release approach. Third, a growing cynicism developed toward rehabilitation and the medical model. Robert Martinson's (1974) "nothing works" findings and a ground swell from a conservative electorate dealt a final blow to the rehabilitation philosophy. This new conservatism brought with it a concomitant shift in public attitude toward a more punitive ("get tough") approach to crime and criminality.

Two additional events brought prison industries to the forefront of correctional thinking. They were the liberalizing of inmate-labor-related legislation, and former Chief Justice Warren Burger's 1981 speech on "prisons as factories with fences," in which he advocated

a) conversion of prisons into places of education and training and into factories and shops for production; b) a repeal of statutes which limit prison industry production; c) an affirmative limitation against any form of discrimination against prison products; and d) a change in attitudes of organized labor and in the leaders of business towards the use of prison inmates to produce goods or parts. (Burger, 1982, pp. 111-120)

Reinvolvement of Congress and the Executive Branch

A series of congressional acts supported by the executive branch removed some of the long-standing restrictions on interstate commerce of prison made goods. This new era began in the 1960s with the U.S. Labor Department's Manpower Development Training Act (MDTA) allowing prisoners (like underemployed civilians) the opportunity for education, training, and meaningful work. At the same time, the nation was again experiencing rising crime rates, more incarceration, prison overcrowding, and ultimately prison riots, such as the Attica riot of 1971. The result was a rethinking of the rehabilitation model and the reintroduction of the work ethic philosophy.

By 1979, President Carter signed the Prison Industries Enhancement Act, which was amended in 1984 and became the Justice Assistance Act. This continued to exempt prison industries from federal restraints and also encouraged private sector involvement. These two acts resulted in the certification of a limited number (23) of pilot prison programs working in a partnership with the private sector. By 1992, 23 states participated in the Prison Industry Enhancement (P.I.E.) project (see Table 16.1). The

TABLE 16.1 Private Sector/Prison Industry Enhancement Certification Program, as of February 1, 1992

Certified Agencies	
Alaska Dept. of Corrections	Minnesota Dept. of Corrections
Arizona Dept. of Corrections	Missouri Dept. of Corrections
Belknap County Dept. of Corrections, NH	Nebraska Dept. of Correctional Services
	Nevada Dept. of Prisons
California Youth and Adult Corr. Agency	New Mexico Dept. of Corrections
	Oklahoma Dept. of Corrections
Colorado Dept. of Corrections	So. Carolina Dept. of Corrections
Idaho Dept. of Corrections	So. Dakota Dept. of Corrections
Iowa Dept. of Corrections	Strafford County Dept. of Corrections, NH
Kansas Dept. of Corrections	Utah Dept. of Corrections
Maine Dept. of Corrections	Washington Dept. of Corrections

Applications Pending	
Delaware Dept. of Corrections	Red River County, Texas
Hawaii Dept. of Public Safety	Texas Dept. of Criminal Justice
Illinois Dept. of Corrections	Vermont Dept. of Corrections
Indiana Dept. of Correction	Wisconsin Dept. of Corrections
Massachusetts Dept. of Corrections	Wood County, Ohio

SOURCE: "Justice Department Raises Eyebrows With Focus on Need for Prisons," 1992 (April 1), *Criminal Justice Newsletter*, p. 3.

project required agreeing to certain limitations (Deloitte & Touche, 1991, p. 65):

- A portion of inmate wages must go to supporting programs that provide aid to crime victims.
- Representatives of organized labor and private industry must be consulted when inmate work programs are established.
- Inmate workers must be paid commensurate with those in the private sector.
- State labor officials must certify that private-sector workers will not be displaced, or existing labor contracts infringed upon.
- Inmates must participate voluntarily, and must receive standard benefits (including workers' compensation).
- Each program must incorporate a substantial role for the private sector.

This recent change in the stance of the federal government has opened the door to a new era for prison industries. The new programs rely strongly on an alliance with private enterprise and at the same time allay the fears of organized labor. They incorporate a businesslike approach to the operation of prison industries and the development of a variety of industrial models.

Contemporary Models

With the reappearance of private sector involvement in prison industries, several organizational models have evolved. The strength of the alliance between the private sector and the correctional institution varies from model to model, as does the locus of power, risk, and reward. Additionally, there are clear advantages and disadvantages to each.

In the traditional *governmental use* model, prison industries produce products whose sale is restricted to state and local governmental markets. Private sector involvement is minimal, usually centering on a consultant role in the provision of management advice or technical assistance. Such programs are financed through appropriations from correctional services budgets with profits, where generated, being returned as revenues to those budgets. Inmates are typically paid a small stipend for their labor, and some programs include production incentives.

This model maintains control within the public sphere; therefore it can more easily accommodate correctional goals, such as maximizing inmate employment and reducing idleness. Though public risks are minimal, so are fiscal rewards. Markets tend to be limited but secure. Bureaucratic policies inherent in governmental institutions frequently impact negatively on the efficiency and effectiveness of governmental use industries. Nevertheless, these continue to be the most prevalent form of prison industries (Grieser, 1987, p. 1). Examples of this model can be found in the correctional services programs of Illinois, Maryland, and Louisiana.

The *joint venture* model entails prison industries' contracting with a private sector business. This expands upon the previous model by opening up opportunities for prison production of private firm products or purchase of a product name and design for sales within the existing governmental use markets.

Control, in this model, is shared between the public and the private sector. The correctional agency is typically in charge of organizational structure, industry goals, wage scales, and inmate hiring. Private sector involvement in the areas of design, production, marketing, and distribution are greater than in the previous model. Corcraft, the New York State Correctional Services Prison Industry, exemplifies a joint venture project.

The next level of privatization of prison industries is the *Corporate* model, wherein the prison industry is a relatively freestanding, semi-independent organism. In organizational structure and control, it emulates a private sector business. The influence of the correctional agency is generally limited to issues of security, promulgating its goals of maximum inmate involvement and providing inmates with work skills. However, even these may become secondary to profitability. Hence correctional influence decreases as the control and rewards shift to the private sector.

Several states have experimented with variations of this model. One of the more successful examples is Florida's PRIDE (Prison and Rehabilitative Industries and Diversified Enterprises). It is noted that "as a legislatively created non-profit entity, any benefits that accrue to PRIDE are enjoyed by the Florida taxpayer, state government and the prison laborer, not the corporation" (Goldberg & Breece, 1990, p. 25). UNICOR, the Federal Prison Industry, is another example of the corporate model.

The most independent model of private sector prison industry is the *free enterprise* model. Projects spurred by the Prison Industries Enhancement Certification project fall within this category. Business and employment decisions are made by the private sector employer, and public sector risk is reduced. Minimum or market wages are paid to the inmate, who is typically charged for room, board, and, where relevant, restitution.

Two of the most notable examples of free enterprise prison industries are the telephone reservation center operated by Best Western International inside the Arizona (Phoenix) Correctional Institute for Women, and Zephyr Products, Inc., which operates a manufacturing facility just outside the Lansing, Kansas, correctional facility. In both cases, the prison industry is a totally freestanding, profit-making organization utilizing inmate labor because it meets specific needs, such as being readily accessible (often on a stand-by basis, as in the Best Western case). In a 1986 interview, an inmate employee commented,

> Zephyr employment is a chance to become a taxpayer again, to replace empty days, and to prepare ourselves for a successful return to society. I don't want to mess up this program for everybody else who's worked hard to make it go. (Callison, 1989, p. 65)

Clearly, such programs have potential benefits to private enterprises, correctional institutions, taxpayers, and offenders.

Prisons at a Crossroad: Current Concerns

As the 20th century closes its final chapter, we might question just how far we have advanced in corrections and, more specifically, what we, the public, expect from prisons. There are many trends and patterns repetitious of those of previous decades, such as increased prison populations, over-crowding, idleness, escalating costs, the call for more prison construction, and the call for more punishment.

By the mid-1990s, at the present incarceration rate, the U.S. prison population will exceed 1 million. Furthermore, the Attorney General has sounded an alarm that calls for the construction of more jails and prisons, citing national average costs of $53,000 per bed for construction plus another $21,000 per bed per year for operation ("Justice Department," 1992, p. 2). During 1990, the number of prisoners under federal and state jurisdiction reached a year end high of 771,243, translating to a need for approximately 1,100 prison bedspaces per week (Cohen, 1991, p. 1).

To comprehend the totality of this, one must consider the regional ramifications. In New York State this translates to $130,000 per new cell with an annual upkeep of $26,413. This means it will take 17 New Yorkers paying an average tax of $1,519 *each* to pay for the upkeep of one inmate, not including the cost of construction! (See Figure 16.2.) Viewed from another perspective, the state of Washington spends $4,000 per child on elementary and secondary education, yet it requires an expenditure of $26,000 per year to maintain each prison inmate ("Justice Department," 1992, p. 2).

Consequently, with the prison population's continued growth, state legislatures are forced to reallocate resources from other vital programs, such as public education, health care, and housing, to support the demands of correctional budgets. Hence the public is being victimized twice: first as the victims of the criminal activity and second as taxpayers, who support the offender and possibly his or her family during this period of incarceration.

Prison Industries in the 21st Century:
The Entrepreneurial Spirit

Without question, it is crucial to reconsider the purpose of incarceration and adopt a pragmatic philosophy to guide us through the turn of the century. It is quite evident that a correctional philosophy of pure punish-ment is responsible, in a large part, for bringing state budgets closer to the brink of bankruptcy. Perhaps the public's frustration with crime and the soaring costs of incarceration can be addressed through a reintegrative philosophy, one that combines the need for punishment (incarceration) and productivity (employing the offender) through the resurrection of prison industries.

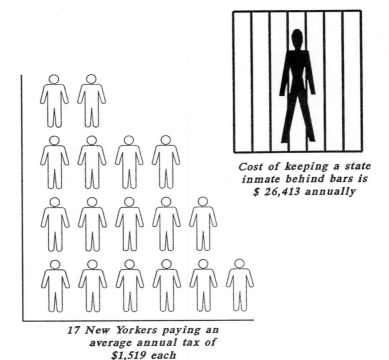

Cost of keeping a state
inmate behind bars is
$ 26,413 annually

17 New Yorkers paying an
average annual tax of
$1,519 each

Figure 16.2 Cost of Incarceration to the Taxpayer
SOURCE: *New York State Correctional Services Report, 1992* (pp. 14 and 16) by the New York State
Department of Corrections, 1992, Albany, NY: New York State Department of Corrections.

The contemporary period of prison industries' embracing a work ethic
model was heralded in the 1967 President's Commission Task Force
report. Given that over 95% of all inmates will be released eventually
("Justice Department," 1992), the report recommended that inmates be
provided with real work experience that will prepare them for the outside
world. Additionally, it was noted that prison industries should operate on
a businesslike basis, relying on the private sector without the exploitation
of inmate labor or unfair competition problems of previous decades.

A recent study (Auerbach, Sexton, Farrow, & Lawson, 1988) indicated
that the use of prison industries is increasing. Forty-five prison work
projects were in operation, and 28 of these entailed significant private
sector involvement, that is, adoption of a joint venture, corporate, or free
enterprise model. (See Table 16.2.) Moreover, legislation has been intro-

TABLE 16.2 Products and Services Produced by Private Sector Prison Industries in 1989

Products	*Services*
airline wheel chocks	auto repair
airline shipper frames	data entry
auto parts	envelope stuffing
automobiles (customized)	grommet modification
boat docks	industrial cleaning
commercial display cases	industrial drafting
computer interface cables	inspection & sorting
crutches	microfilming
dog runner chains	packaging
drapes	record distribution
electronic components	travel reservations
farm machinery	telemarketing
furniture (home & office)	
garments	
hydraulic vacuum pumps	
industrial heating elements	
medical testing equipment	
oil burner parts	
optical lenses	
printed forms	
radon test kits	
sheet metal products	
stone tiles	
sugar cane	
timber products	
toys and toy blocks	
vegetables	
vinyl binders	
waterbed mattresses	
wood garden planters	

SOURCE: *Developing Private Sector Prison Industries: From Concept to Start-Up* (p. 18) by G. Sexton, 1990, Philadelphia: Criminal Justice Associates.

duced in Congress to conduct pilot projects testing the feasibility of putting inmates to work producing goods that are not currently manufactured in the United States. The legislation would pose no threat to organized labor and business because inmates would not produce goods that are currently manufactured in this country ("Bill," 1992, p. 6).

A Crisis in the Making or Alternatives

From 1973 to 1991, the number of felons in state and federal prisons has more than quadrupled, from 204,000 to 823,414. This represents an increase of 300% (Bureau of Justice Statistics, 1992). Ironically, this increase in the prison population has not reduced crime rates. With most states and the federal prison system operating beyond capacity (18-29%) and exacerbated by court orders to improve prison conditions, many states have opted for early release mechanisms (Cohen, 1991, p. 1). Others have addressed the overcrowding issue by experimenting (pilot projects) and expanding work opportunities for offenders while also using these to reduce the costs of incarceration to the taxpayer.

This renewed interest in putting imprisoned persons to work should yield additional dividends by reducing the potential for violence that often results from enforced idleness and overcrowded conditions. It is evident that we can no longer afford to simply warehouse prisoners and allow them to revictimize the taxpayer!

It becomes apparent that prison industry programs must be enhanced throughout the nation. Moreover, no single model can offer a panacea to address the multitude of problems. However, any combination of models utilizing private partnerships will have the benefits of employing inmates in real work experiences while *not* competing with private sector companies.

Benefits of Pilot Programs

As we proceed with this new-found commitment to the development and expansion of prison industries, it is necessary to recognize the benefits. An independent market study (Deloitte & Touche, 1991, p. 10) on the Bureau of Prison's (BOP's) federal prison industries (FPI) forecasts:

1. Private sector businesses will have increased opportunity to compete in the federal marketplace. FPI's growth in labor-intensive manufacturing will be directed away from federal markets that are the last domain of some U.S. businesses. The potential exists for the repatriation of offshore business and creation of new private sector business opportunities. Within the federal market, recommended changes should level the playing field and make FPI more predictable, while reflecting the realities of prison industry production.

2. Labor will benefit by having FPI meet a portion of its inmate employment requirements in activities that are currently performed outside of the U.S. The potential exists for job creation in supplier industries.

3. Federal departments and agencies will have an increased ability to select among competing sources, and increased assurance that prices reflect cost of production.
4. The public will continue to benefit from the lower cost of maintaining prison systems, and from the increased likelihood that inmates who work in FPI are less likely to return to prison.
5. The Bureau of Prisons will be able to avoid inmate idleness and the risk of disruption. FPI will be positioned to remain self-sufficient.

Furthermore, in an attempt to determine the relationship between work in prison industries and post-release success, the federal BOP collected data that showed that the experience of working while imprisoned has beneficial effects on post-release employment, earnings, and the successful completion of community supervision—even though inmates in FPI programs had a more serious criminal record and longer sentences than the overall BOP inmate population (see Table 16.3).

Creating Employment in Other Countries

The issue of foreign-produced products and cheap labor is germane to the growth and development of prison industries. Despite tariffs and other trade barriers, countries with wages significantly lower than in this country (e.g., Hong Kong, Mexico, Philippines, and the Caribbean countries), have been able to assemble and produce products (with U.S. components) and sell them back to American markets. Considering the emerging global economy, it is reasonable to assume that the United States is losing significant business opportunities to foreign competitors.

The possibility of promoting prison-based labor forces as an alternative to offshore competition becomes significant. If inmate labor were perceived by U.S. corporations as a viable, cost-effective alternative to offshore labor, the number of companies that might consider domestic prison-based operations could increase significantly and therefore recapture enterprises that have gone to foreign competitors (Will, 1989).

Epilogue

We have seen prison industries come nearly full cycle during the past 150 years. Without question, industrial programs can and should be the dominant correctional theme of the 1990s. It is imperative they become

TABLE 16.3 Summary of Bureau of Prisons Postrelease Study Findings: Comparison of Inmates in Federal Prison Industries Program (FPI) Versus Control Group

Percentage of Inmates With	FPI Inmates	Control Group	Baseline Average (13,760 Inmates)
Offense of "high" or "greatest" severity	27.6%	24.2%	17.5%
Prior offense record	50.5%	51.9%	49.5%
Projected length of incarceration greater than 60 months	5.4%	3.1%	2.6%

Outcome	FPI Inmates	Control Group
Percentage revoked from supervision after 12 months	6.6%	10.1%
Percentage under supervision and employed at month 12	71.7%	63.1%
Average wage earned in month 12 by those supervised and employed	$821	$769
Sample size	2,013	2,855

SOURCE: *Independent Market Study of UNICOR Federal Prison Industries, Inc.: Report to Congress on Study Findings and Recommendations* (p. 60) by Deloitte and Touche, 1991, Washington, DC: DRT International.

more entrepreneurial and self-sustaining. Self-supporting prison industry programs can play a major role in assisting state legislatures to reallocate financial resources for other necessary governmental expenditures.

Within the decade of the 1990s it would seem prudent to reexamine society's expectations of imprisonment. With the recurring trends of the past decades—overcrowded conditions, idleness, inmate violence, the exorbitant costs of prisons, and so forth—a correctional crisis seems inevitable. Perhaps it is one that can be avoided. But this can only occur if policy makers at the state and federal level assume a proactive role by furthering the demand for self-supporting prisons.

The following enumerates some of the benefits that accrue to all parties when private sector prison enterprises become integrated with corrections:

- *Taxpayers*—when inmates are productively employed and thereby contributing to their imprisonment, supporting dependents, and paying restitution and taxes, there will be more public interests served by reallocated savings.

- *Business*—by forming partnerships with correctional institutions, companies increase the opportunity to recapture businesses lost to foreign markets; enhance the work skills of the inmate population, thereby enhancing their employability upon release; and have a resource of available employees to fill fluctuating service demands.
- *Prisons*—by adopting a work ethic philosophy, the mission of corrections becomes more purposeful. Employing inmates should result in less violence and a more manageable population. Equally important, prisons will become schools of "trade" versus schools of "crime."
- *Labor*—if programs pay inmates market wages comparable to the civilian workforce and adhere to federal regulations preventing the displacement of civilian workers, the inmate population has the potential for augmenting a shrinking skilled labor force.
- *Offenders*—when offenders begin to value the fundamental work ethic that is necessary for success in the "real" world, that is, when they are paid wages and when they pay support, restitution, and taxes, their sense of self-worth will be enhanced. Moreover, with employable skills they decrease their chances of recidivating. Lastly, they can begin to contribute to a pension plan in preparation for retirement and ultimately break the welfare cycle of dependence.

In sum, if we are to make progress in corrections as we approach the next century, then spending money on mortar and steel for prison construction is simply anachronistic. Alternatives must be given serious consideration. Perhaps the statement of the International Association of Residential and Community Alternatives says it best: "In the past few years . . . prison building sounded fine, but states are now spending so much . . . it's coming down to prisons versus schools" ("Justice Department," 1992, p. 3). As former Chief Justice Burger noted, we need prison industries with incentives for good performance that will accomplish the dual objectives of training inmates for gainful occupations while taking them off the backs of American taxpayers! The need for and the opportunity to create self-supporting prisons is here, and long overdue.

Discussion Questions

1. Discuss the advantages of private sector involvement in prison industry programs.
2. Who are the traditional opponents of private sector involvement in prison industries, and why do they hold these positions?
3. Discuss the historical origin of prison industries.
4. Make a case for prison industry programs based upon cost effectiveness that is nonthreatening to business and labor interests.

5. What factors have precipitated the current interest in private sector prison industry programs?

6. What is the relationship between recidivism rates and prison industry programs?

7. Identify the four contemporary models of private sector/prison work programs. Discuss the advantages and disadvantages of each.

References

Allen, H., & Simonsen, C. (1992). *Corrections in America*. New York: Macmillan.

Anderson, W. (1985). *UNICOR products: Federal prison industries can further ensure customer satisfaction*. Washington, DC: General Accounting Office.

Auerbach, B. (1982, Spring). New prison industries legislation: The private sector re-enters the field. *Prison Journal, 18*(2), 28-34.

Auerbach, B., Sexton, G., Farrow, F., & Lawson, R. (1988). *Work in American prisons: The private sector gets involved*. Washington, DC: National Institute of Justice.

Bernstein, A. (1992, February 17). There's prison labor in America too. *Business Week,* pp. 42-43.

Bill would increase options for federal prison industries. (1992, February 18). *Criminal Justice Newsletter,* pp. 5-6.

Bureau of Justice Statistics. (1992). *Prisoners in 1991*. Washington, DC: Department of Justice.

Burger, W. E. (1982, Winter). More warehouses or factories with fences? *New England Journal of Prison Law, 8*(1), 111-120.

Callison, H. (1989). *Zephyr products: The story of an inmate-staffed business*. Washington, DC: American Correctional Association.

Chi, K. S. (1985). *The private sector in state correctional industries: Control Data Program in Minnesota*. Lexington, KY: Council of State Governments.

Clear, T., & Cole, G. (1990). *American corrections*. Pacific Grove, CA: Brooks/Cole.

Cohen, R. L. (1991, May). *Prisoners in 1990*. Bureau of Justice Statistics Bulletin No. NCJ 129198. Washington, DC: Department of Justice.

Comparative incarceration rates. (1992, January). *Criminal Justice Digest*.

Deloitte & Touche. (1991). *Independent market study of UNICOR Federal Prison Industries, Inc.: Report to Congress on study findings and recommendations*. Washington, DC: DRT International.

Federal Bureau of Prisons. (1991, June). *Post Release Employment Project: Summary of preliminary findings*. Unpublished manuscript. Available from the Office of Research and Evaluation, Federal Bureau of Prisons, U.S. Department of Justice, Washington, DC 20534.

Funke, G. (Ed.). (1986). *National Conference on Prison Industries: Discussions and recommendations*. Washington, DC: National Center for Innovations in Corrections.

Goldberg, K., & Breece, Y. (1990, Fall). An overview: The history of prison industries. *Correctional Industries Association Newsletter, 5*(3).

Grieser, R. C. (1987, November). *Organizational models of prison industries*. Paper prepared for the American Correctional Association's Conference of Prison Industries, Chicago.

Grieser, R. C. (1988). *The economic impact of Corcraft Correctional Industries in New York State*. Alexandria, VA: Institute for Economic and Policy Studies.

Grieser, R. C. (1989, March). Do correctional industries adversely impact the private sector? *Federal Probation, 53*(1), 18-24.

Ingley, G. (1989, October). Working for a livin'. *Police, 13*(1), 41-44, 71-73.

Justice Department raises eyebrows with focus on need for prisons. (1992, April 1). *Criminal Justice Newsletter,* 1-4.

Kennedy, B. (1990, August 15). Federal prisoners are unfair competition. *Wall Street Journal,* p. 11.

Klayman, D. (1990, June). *The economic impact of prison industry: A summary of current studies.* In-house paper available from the Institute of Policy Studies Inc., 815 King St., Alexander, VA 22314.

Martinson, R. (1974). What works?—Questions and answers about prison reform. *The Public Interest, 35,* 22-54.

Mauer, M., & Kline, G. (1990, February). *Young black men and the criminal justice system: A growing national problem.* Report available from the Sentencing Project, 918 F Street NW, Washington, DC 20004.

Miller, N., & Grieser, R. (1986). *A study of prison industry: History, components and goals.* College Park, MD: American Correctional Association.

Miller, R., Sexton, G., & Jacobsen, V. (1991). *Making jails productive.* National Institute of Justice Research in Brief, Monograph No. NCJ 132396. Washington, DC: Department of Justice.

President's Commission. (1967). *Task Force Report: Corrections.* Washington, DC: Government Printing Office.

Prison Industries Information Clearinghouse. (1989). *Key issues in foreign production: Perspectives for correctional industries.* Working paper. Available from the American Correctional Association, 4321 Hartwick Road, College Park, MD 20740.

Sexton, G. (1988). *A guide to private sector prison industries: Identifying, screening, and contacting companies.* Philadelphia: Criminal Justice Associates.

Sexton, G. (1990). *Developing private sector prison industries: From concept to start-up.* Unpublished manuscript. Available from Criminal Justice Associates, 48 E. Chestnut Hill Ave., Philadelphia, PA 19118.

Sexton, G., & Openheim, L. (1988). *Private sector prison industries: Steps for future action.* Philadelphia: Criminal Justice Associates and the Wharton Center for Applied Research.

Will, J. (1989). *Offshore assembly of U.S. made components: Can correctional industries bring jobs home?* Laurel, MD: Correctional Industries Clearinghouse.

17

Changing Patterns and Trends
in Parole Supervision

CHERYL L. RINGEL

ERNEST L. COWLES

THOMAS C. CASTELLANO

During the 1970s and 1980s, parole practices underwent significant recon-ceptualization and modification nationwide. The vast bulk of attention, criticism, and policy reform during this time frame focused on parole as a mechanism of discretionary release from prison. However, parole super-vision, the "other parole" as it has been described (Flanagan, 1985; Wilson, 1977), which involves the postprison supervision of inmates conditionally released to the community, has also been undergoing dramatic change in the United States during the last 20 years. Unfortunately, relatively little scholarly attention has been paid to this phenomenon (see Bottomly, 1990, for a recent example).

To help remedy this situation, this chapter provides an overview of the forces that have led to an increasingly more complex and turbulent envi-ronment in which parole supervision is provided, and describes the results for parole supervision. Policy makers have been experimenting with a multiplicity of parole supervision strategies in recent years in response to a variety of forces: altered sentencing and correctional philosophies, altered organizational structures for the delivery of correctional services, explosions in the size of correctional populations resulting in acute fiscal and workload constraints, and critical evaluations of parole supervision effectiveness. For instance, 20 years ago one could go to any state in the nation and find a public agency charged with supervising parolees that would be quite similar in name, function, and structure to an analogous agency operating on the other side of the nation. This is no longer the case, as a patchwork of diverse parole strategies and program designs have emerged throughout the nation. In this chapter we discuss the variety of adaptive strategies that are being employed in response to changing environmental conditions.

In the first section of this chapter, the historical evolution of parole supervision is described. It examines the extent to which parole supervision has or has not been linked to early and discretionary parole release from prison, and the extent to which the emergence of parole supervision has been rooted in rehabilitative ideology.

In the second section of the chapter, we examine three major forces considered to be responsible for the changing patterns of parole supervision. They include the organizational restructuring of correctional agencies, the pronounced attack on rehabilitation during the last 20 years and related questions of whether parole supervision achieves purported utilitarian aims, and the explosion in correctional populations which has resulted in increased experimentation with community-based sanctions. Available published data illustrative of these forces (e.g., the volume of persons released to differing models of postrelease supervision, parole populations, and caseload figures) are presented. These data provide a portrait of the changing face of parole supervision between the late 1970s and the current day.

Throughout the chapter, attention is given to parole reform in a number of states. Certain states have been selected to illustrate what appear to be common adaptive strategies. Parole supervision in New York State and Texas exemplify how states that have not abandoned discretionary parole release but continue to face bulging parole populations and fiscal distress have responded to public demands for offender accountability. The states of Maine and Florida illustrate how the adoption of determinacy in sentencing and the abolition of parole supervision have resulted in the creation of little-known functional equivalents to parole supervision. Finally, the states of California and Illinois indicate how determinacy and the formal abolition of parole have resulted in label changes—mandatory supervised release or conditional supervised release—but not public demands for the supervision of parole releasees in the community. Innovations in supervision structures are also highlighted.

A final section summarizes the major themes from the foregoing sections and concludes that the parole supervision landscape will likely become more variegated during the coming decade. Coupled with doomed attempts to reinvent wheels that have never been shown to work, it is likely that promising intervention strategies will be discovered. It is unlikely, however, that in the near future the field of parole will coalesce its efforts around a program strategy based on a coherent ideological position.

Origins of Parole Supervision

Most standard discussions of parole supervision treat it as emanating directly from rehabilitative ideology: that early release from prison should be accompanied by the provision of services and assistance to ease the offender's gradual and lawful transition to the community. Thus an "assistance" model of supervision is enunciated, a model implemented as a result of the benevolent actions of progressive rehabilitationist reformers (Rothman, 1980). This model was compromised over time to accommodate the organizational convenience of newly created bureaucracies and public demands for offender control, but the origins of parole have been largely unquestioned—until recently, that is.

In examining the origins and objectives of parole supervision, Flanagan ties its development to the "desire to cushion the 're-entry shock' . . . a key factor in the post-release experience of offenders" (1985, p. 169). His discussion of parole supervision's original tie to reintegration is tempered by the reminder that control of the offender was also considered important—that, in effect, parole supervision serves many functions. Thus the single pure motive of rehabilitation and "cushioning the re-entry shock" became the dual motive of "simultaneously protecting community safety and promoting the reintegration of the offender into the community" (Flanagan, 1985, p. 169). Indeed, both of these functions are clearly stated in California's parole statute's preamble.

In general, parole supervision evolved slowly and unevenly in the United States. A historical antecedent involved volunteers (masters of indentured children from houses of refuge and members of prison societies) playing the role of supervisor for persons recently released from newly developed correctional institutions, or at least being held accountable for the offenders' conduct in the community (Cromwell, Killinger, Kerper, & Walker, 1985). Not until 1845 were there public employees whose job it was to assist released prisoners (Cromwell et al., 1985). The commonly described antecedent of parole in the United States, the British ticket-of-leave system as applied in the Australian penal settlements, did not initially require a supervision component, and the stringent supervision associated with the Irish ticket-of-leave system implemented by Sir Walter Crofton was not received with enthusiasm by early American penal reformers (Killinger & Cromwell, 1974, pp. 412-414), who at the time felt it "un-American to place any individual under the supervision of the police" (Abadinsky, 1991, p. 170). This has led Bottomly (1990) to conclude that "[parole] supervision was not seen as an essential component of many of the parole schemes that mushroomed across America at the end of the nineteenth century" (1990, p. 323).

This admittedly limited historical review of the origins of parole illustrates that the parole supervision function cannot be assumed to be premised on a particular coherent or tightly defined correctional philosophy. As Bottomly has written, "It is doubtful whether it [parole] ever really operated consistently in the United States either in principle or practice according to the true canons of the rehabilitative model" (1990, p. 326). Rather than focusing on some "ideal type" by which to assess parole practices, the search for an informed understanding of what is happening to parole supervision in the contemporary era must be shaped by a knowledge of the specific contexts in which penal practices emerge. For as Messinger, Berecochea, Rauma, and Berk remind us, "penal reforms, like parole, are sufficiently malleable to permit their adoption [and probably their alteration] for quite different reasons" (1985, p. 103). Thus as parole and especially parole supervision undergoes change it is important to examine and understand these changes in relation to contemporaneous developments in correctional philosophies and policies, as well as organizational problems and system constraints facing correctional entities. Though the "chronological development of the many functions of contemporary parole is not helpful in deciding the contemporary retention/abolition debate" (Flanagan, 1985, p. 169), it is helpful in deciphering what level of explanatory power should be attributed to the factors seemingly associated with the contours and patterns of contemporary reform movements.

The Contexts of Parole Supervision Reform: Driving Forces

In recent years, the parole supervision function has come under attack from many quarters. Crime control advocates have denounced parole supervision as largely nominal and ineffective; due process advocates have criticized parole revocation as arbitrary and counterproductive; social welfare advocates have decried the lack of meaningful and useful rehabilitation services. These criticisms have acquired added force as the number of offenders under criminal justice supervision reaches new heights, thereby straining even further what many already viewed as inadequate system resources. States have responded to this situation in a variety of ways. Some jurisdictions have abolished parole supervision altogether. Other jurisdictions have attempted to remedy the deficiencies of the parole system in patchwork fashion. Still other jurisdictions have called into question the traditional philosophies and premises of parole supervision and have undertaken a total reorganization of parole services. We suggest that three major and interrelated forces have most directly shaped these changes.

Organizational Restructuring

First, there was a coalescence of criminal justice entities into larger functional groupings. Part of this movement was brought about by the recommendations for criminal justice agency reform made by numerous commissions and study groups established during this time. Many of these recommendations were based on assumptions of a need for cohesion among the parts of corrections and criminal justice that were increasingly being viewed as systems (Smykla, 1984, p. 87). This led in many instances to a move away from an independent model of paroling authority, in which the paroling entity was an autonomous body with sole authority over parole release and parole supervision. Rather, a consolidated model was implemented, where the paroling authority was incorporated into a larger correctional agency as a subunit, or where the paroling authority remained an autonomous unit but the supervision of those on community release was performed by staff of a larger corrections department. For example, and as illustrated in Figure 17.1, in 1966 there were 31 independent parole boards responsible for parole supervision in the United States. By 1988, there were only 13 such parole boards, with the vast bulk of states (38) placing the responsibility for parole supervision within a consolidated correctional agency.

In general, although these changes were primarily intended to better serve the offender they were also undertaken to emphasize correctional efforts in providing public safety. One result of these changes for community corrections is that parole became less of a priority program within the total corrections system as its autonomous authority over releasees was diluted and emphasis was increasingly placed on adult institutional corrections. As seen in Figure 17.2, the proportion of correctional dollars devoted to community corrections relative to funding for institutions has shown significant declines during the contemporary era.

Number of States

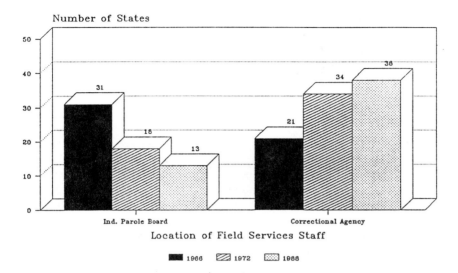

Location of Field Services Staff

■ 1966   ▨ 1972   ▥ 1988

Figure 17.1 Location of Administrative Control Over Parole Supervision
SOURCE: *Parole Authorities: Recent History and Current Practice* (p. 103) by E. E. Rhine, W. R. Smith, and R. W. Jackson, 1990, Laurel, MD: American Corrections Association.

A Reexamination of Correctional Philosophies

A second major pressure for changes in the parole system during this period was the growing disenchantment with the rehabilitative model and offender treatment in general. As Palmer notes,

> From the 1960s to 1970s there was a broad surge of confidence regarding rehabilitation's ability to change and control offenders on a short- as well as long-term basis. This high optimism was quickly followed by widespread pessimism from 1975 to 1981, a period that was triggered by Martinson's (1974) mid-1970s critique of rehabilitation's presumed effectiveness. (1992, p. 3)

This discontent with treatment effectiveness was accompanied by the presentation of David Fogel's (1975) *justice model* and Andrew von Hirsh's (1976) *just deserts model,* both of which sounded calls for the elimination of the indeterminate sentence and discretionary parole release.

These two thrusts, a perception of lack of effective treatment interventions and the call for determinate or flat-time sentences without parole release, had both popular and political support. In 1976, Maine became the first state to enact legislation to eliminate parole. The following year

California and Indiana joined Maine in establishing determinate sentencing legislation. In the ensuing 25 years, a number of states and the federal government have enacted various determinate sentencing structures, either eliminating or greatly diminishing the power of parole authorities to give discretionary release.

Parole Supervision Effectiveness

It was not surprising that parole supervision as well as discretionary parole release would come under attack. Yet as the effectiveness of parole supervision was questioned, it became apparent that there were woefully few sound research studies that addressed questions of parole supervision efficacy. Though studies existed, results were not easily pooled because differing definitions of parole failure, recidivism, and other key issues had been applied. Even the ultimate question of what should be considered "effective" in supervision—for example, lower recidivism for those supervised, ease of reintegration to the community, or the provision of services based on knowledge of offender need—was left unanswered.

Flanagan (1985) offers a succinct and extensive review of parole effectiveness literature. In summarizing the methodology and findings of these effectiveness studies, three studies are shown to have found positive effects of parole supervision in terms of recidivism: Gottfredson, 1975; Martinson and Wilks, 1977; and Lerner, 1977. Two studies show parole supervision to be ineffective (Nuttal et al., 1977; Stanley, 1976). And three studies present findings that are both positive and negative: Waller (1974), showing early effects on recidivism that disappear at 1 and 2 years after release; Gottfredson, Mitchell-Herzfeld, & Flanagan (1982), indicating a supervision effect that is tempered by both specific offender characteristics and the minuteness of effect size; and Sacks and Logan (1979, 1980), showing that supervision has at best a delaying effect on parolee recidivism. Thus the empirical research on the effectiveness of parole supervision as a method of reducing recidivism has been equivocal at best. The most that can be concluded from extant research is that traditional supervision practices may delay recidivism for a relatively short period of time for certain offenders. Thus experimentation with altered parole supervision strategies has not been constrained by knowledge about "what works" as it relates to the adjustment of released offenders into the community.

Soaring Correctional Populations

The third major force shaping the change in parole during this period was the growth in correctional populations and the overcrowding problem.

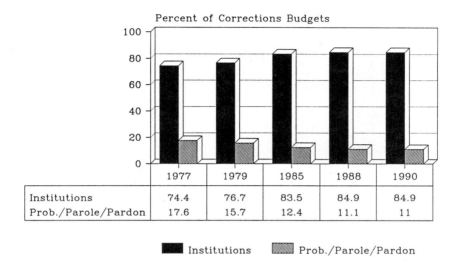

	1977	1979	1985	1988	1990
Institutions	74.4	76.7	83.5	84.9	84.9
Prob./Parole/Pardon	17.6	15.7	12.4	11.1	11

■ Institutions   ▨ Prob./Parole/Pardon

Figure 17.2 Direct Corrections Expenditures: Institutions Versus Community Supervision
SOURCE: *Sourcebook of Criminal Justice Statistics* by the Bureau of Justice Statistics, 1978, 1980, 1986, 1989, 1991, Washington, DC: Government Printing Office.

Nationally this has been attributed to an increasing number of convicted offenders incarcerated under mandatory sentencing provisions. As Blumstein noted in 1988, incarceration rates were relatively stable in the United States from the mid-1920s until the 1970s, then climbed dramatically, nearly tripling by 1988. Following this growth in prison populations was a proportional growth in releasee populations (see Table 17.1).

During the mid-1980s many state correctional systems embarked on ambitious prison construction programs to deal with the population growth and overcrowding. However, as these building programs gained momentum, many states also began facing shrinking revenues and budget shortfalls. This prompted the question, What should be done with the increasing parole population? This question was especially significant in that the parole supervision function in many states was at the same time witnessing significant budget cutbacks. The net consequence has been increasingly large parole caseloads. For instance Table 17.2 presents caseload data from the 10 states with the largest parole populations, as reported by those states as of February 1989.

The average caseloads in these states were all much higher than the recommended caseload of the American Correctional Association and

TABLE 17.1 U.S. Parole Populations and Rates

Year	Parole Population (as of Dec. 31st)	Rate (per 100,000 Adult Residents) of Persons on Parole
1978	185,100	138
1981	226,200	136
1984	266,992	155
1988	407,977	201
1990	531,407	287

SOURCE: *Sourcebook of Criminal Justice Statistics* by the Bureau of Justice Statistics, 1979, 1982, 1985, 1989, and 1991, Washington, DC: Government Printing Office.

larger than average caseloads in earlier years. It became clear that the traditional policy of treating most parolees similarly, that is, requiring supervision of most persons released from prison, was increasingly becoming untenable.

What Have Been the Results for Parole Supervision?

Palmer's (1992) recent discussion of the four traditional themes found in correctional intervention—personal or interpersonal change, external control/surveillance, life skills development, and focus on certain types of offenses or persistent patterns of behavior—presents a useful perspective by which to better understand the diverse adaptations parole supervision has witnessed in response to the driving forces discussed above. The first of these, personal or interpersonal change of the offender, would be most closely identified with the rehabilitative position.

As discussed earlier, the rehabilitative perspective has long been influential in shaping the delivery of parole services, even if it did not truly "father" parole, and although rehabilitative values certainly are still prominent in shaping correctional interventions, these values per se are not driving current reform efforts in parole. Rather, the theme of external control/surveillance has been predominant in structuring contemporary innovations in parole supervision programming. Following is a discussion of related trends and developments in a number of states.

TABLE 17.2 Ten Largest Parole Supervision Populations and Average Caseload Size as of 2/1/89

State	Parole Supervision Population	Average Caseload Size
Texas	91,294	74:1
California	57,508	53:1
Pennsylvania	47,702	81:1
New York	36,685	38:1[a]
New Jersey	20,062	73:1
Georgia	17,439	45:1
Illinois	14,550	261:1[b]
Tennessee	10,700	55:1
Michigan	9,890	82:1
Maryland	9,802	125:1[c]

SOURCE: *Determining Parole Officers' Average Caseload* (p. 9) by M. Eisenberg, 1990, Austin, TX: Texas Department of Criminal Justice, Pardons and Paroles Division.
a. Supervised at this ratio for first 15 months of supervision, then increases to 73:1 for remainder of supervision term
b. Reflects a situation relating to temporary parole officer layoffs
c. Probation and parole combined

Supervised Release Structures as External Control

The end of discretionary parole release in certain states has not been accompanied by a widespread abandonment of mandated terms of supervision for released offenders. The theme of external control/surveillance has played a dominant role in this regard: The perception among legislators that the public demands released offenders be supervised even if their prison sentences have expired has resulted in the common adoption of determinate sentencing structures with mandatory and/or conditional supervision provisions. For example, in 1978 when Illinois abolished discretionary parole, it mandated terms of supervision in the community of from 1 to 3 years for released offenders, depending on initial conviction charges. Further, the Illinois Prisoner Review Board is empowered to determine the conditions of release, impose sanctions for violations, and revoke an ex-prisoner's conditional release status (Ill. Stat. Rev. 1978, Chapt. 38, sec. 1003-3-1(a)(5)). Minnesota, which introduced sentencing guidelines in 1980, also retained community supervision upon an offender's release from prison, the duration of which equals the amount of good time that had been earned (Goodstein & Hepburn, 1985, p. 80). Certain states that had abolished postprison supervision altogether in their original determinate sentencing later reintroduced a mandated supervision component (e.g, Connecticut and Florida).

Such postprison supervision provisions satisfied the public perception that these forms of release provided for public safety, while control restrictions enhanced the notion that the offender was paying for his or her crime. The orientation of such release models consequently shifted from a primary focus on offender needs to a focus on offender risks. Conditional release mechanisms also brought added practical benefits to the correctional system. The shift in orientation from offender treatment needs to offender risk meant that scarce resources could be directed away from treatment programs without damage to the integrity of the model. No longer was there a strong implicit assumption that the correctional agencies providing such supervision had to provide extensive programs to bring about offender change. Such treatment became more the offenders' responsibility, as program participation became less often a condition of supervision and offenders were also more frequently called upon to pay the costs of such programs. The move to a primary theme of external control/surveillance thus satisfied two pragmatic concerns associated with prison crowding and the increased costs of imprisonment: It permitted a conditional release that was theoretically less likely to incur a return to incarceration while simultaneously reducing the costs of treatment associated with such release. Hence this orientation fit with concerns about prison overcrowding and costs while also filling the philosophical needs created by public sentiment mandating more emphasis on public safety.

How did this change in orientation and the well publicized abolition of parole in many states actually impact supervised release? As can be seen in Figure 17.3, the percentage of releasees unconditionally released from prison has actually decreased between 1978 (18.2%) and 1990 (14.1%). The major trend has been a drastic reduction in the percent of releases to parole in this time frame (70.4% in 1978 to 40.5% in 1990) and a parallel increase in the percentage of releases to mandatory supervised release (5.8% in 1978 to 29.6% in 1990). Also witnessed in this time frame were modest increases in the percentage of releases to probation and "other conditional release," both of which tend to include an explicit supervision component. Thus although parole supervision has nominally witnessed a major decline, functional equivalents in terms of basic supervision components have emerged. The framework of release has changed to accommodate the practical and philosophic shifts discussed above.

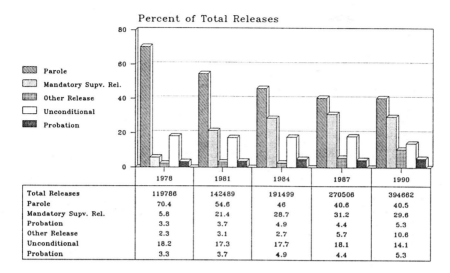

		1978	1981	1984	1987	1990
Total Releases		119786	142489	191499	270506	394662
Parole		70.4	54.6	46	40.6	40.5
Mandatory Supv. Rel.		5.8	21.4	28.7	31.2	29.6
Probation		3.3	3.7	4.9	4.4	5.3
Other Release		2.3	3.1	2.7	5.7	10.6
Unconditional		18.2	17.3	17.7	18.1	14.1
Probation		3.3	3.7	4.9	4.4	5.3

Figure 17.3 Releases From State Prisons by Method of Release, 1978-1990
SOURCE: *Probation and Parole* by the Bureau of Justice Statistics, 1990, Washington, DC: Department of Justice.

State-Level Adaptations

The above conclusions can be further illustrated by looking at the experience of a number of states. Table 17.3 presents changes in the frequency distributions of method of prison release for selected states from 1978 to 1990. The table illustrates the dramatic impact that altered statutory provisions have had on the mechanisms by which inmates are released from prison, and the attempts of public officials to create new legal structures that allow for the continued supervision of inmates after their release from prison. For instance, when California and Illinois abolished discretionary parole release in the late 1970s, "mandatory supervised release" replaced "parole supervision." The result is that a relatively modest number of inmates in each state are unconditionally released to the community (more so in California than Illinois).

Release patterns have also been relatively stable in New York, which has retained discretionary parole release and parole supervision. However, forced to handle bulging parole populations in the face of fiscal distress, parole in New York State has responded to public demands for offender accountability by utilizing a variety of innovative case management

TABLE 17.3 Method of Release From Selected State Prison Systems: 1978, 1981, 1984, 1988, 1990

	Total Released	Total Unconditional Release	%	Total Conditional Release	%	Type of Conditional Release (Percent)			
						Parole	Probation	Mandatory Supervised Release	Other
California:									
1978	9,422	212	(2.2)	9,210	(99.7)	100.0	0.0	0.0	0.0
1981	12,781	415	(3.2)	12,366	(96.8)	0.0	0.0	100.0	0.0
1984	24,781	219	(.1)	24,562	(99.9)	0.0	0.0	100.0	0.0
1988	63,197	1,180	(1.8)	62,017	(98.1)	0.0	0.0	100.0	0.0
1990	80,758	1,348	(1.7)	79,410	(98.3)	0.0	0.0	100.0	0.0
Florida:									
1978	6,011	1,154	(19.2)	4,857	(80.8)	63.2	0.0	36.8	0.0
1981	8,754	3,019	(34.5)	5,735	(65.5)	67.2	10.7	17.2	4.9
1984	11,637	7,767	(66.7)	3,870	(33.3)	74.5	25.5	0.0	0.0
1988	32,516	21,559	(66.3)	10,957	(33.7)	4.0	20.8	0.0	75.1
1990	38,088	12,282	(32.2)	25,806	(67.7)	1.0	21.4	0.0	77.6
Illinois:									
1978	6,596	107	(1.6)	6,489	(98.4)	89.1	0.0	10.9	0.0
1981	7,370	1,171	(15.9)	6,199	(84.1)	14.0	0.0	86.0	0.0
1984	8,307	642	(7.7)	7,665	(92.3)	3.5	0.0	96.5	0.0
1988	9,454	630	(6.7)	8,824	(93.3)	0.4	0.0	99.5	0.0
1990	15,045	1,501	(10.0)	13,544	(90.0)	0.4.	0.0	99.5	0.0

Maine:									
1978	439	255	(58.1)	184	(41.9)	57.1	42.9	0.0	0.0
1981	349	247	(70.8)	102	(29.2)	18.6	81.4	0.0	0.0
1984	462	302	(65.4)	160	(34.6)	5.6	94.3	0.0	0.0
1988	626	216	(34.5)	410	(65.5)	1.9	93.9	0.0	4.1
1990	815	324	(39.8)	491	(60.2)	0.0	91.9	0.0	8.1
New York:									
1978	7,469	480	(6.4)	6,989	(93.6)	71.7	0.0	28.3	0.0
1981	8,126	590	(7.3)	7,536	(92.7)	66.4	0.0	33.6	0.0
1984	11,300	407	(3.6)	10,893	(96.4)	82.7	0.0	17.3	0.0
1988	17,978	709	(3.9)	17,269	(96.1)	87.6	0.0	12.4	0.0
1990	24,021	1,086	(4.5)	22,935	(95.5)	87.0	0.0	13.0	0.0
Texas:									
1978	9,954	3,771	(37.9)	6,183	(62.1)	96.3	0.6	2.2	0.7
1981	13,436	1,735	(12.9)	11,701	(87.1)	69.0	0.3	30.1	0.6
1984	21,726	1,203	(5.5)	20,523	(94.5)	41.5	9.1	49.0	0.4
1988	32,484	128	(.4)	32,356	(99.6)	77.0	2.3	20.6	0.0
1990	39,229	126	(.3)	39,103	(99.7)	88.2	3.2	8.5	0.0

SOURCE: *Sourcebook of Criminal Justice Statistics*, 1979, 1982, 1985, 1989, 1991, Washington, DC: Government Printing Office.

techniques. Importantly, New York now uses a differential case supervision strategy in which the bulk of parole resources is allocated to offenders "who pose the greatest risk to the community, those recently released from prison" (New York State Division of Parole, 1990).

More interesting release patterns with more dramatic consequences for supervision strategies are evident for Maine, Florida, and Texas. For instance, Maine is often discussed as a state that has eliminated parole supervision altogether without witnessing increasing crime as a result (Morris & Tonry, 1990). Beyond the absolute small number of offenders released from prison on an annual basis, Table 17.3 reveals that through the latter half of the 1980s less than 40% of Maine's prisoners were unconditionally released into the community. The vast majority of those conditionally released were placed on probation after their term of imprisonment expired (i.e., judicial parole). Thus an adaptation was made subsequent to the abolishment of parole supervision to ensure the continuance of at least some of the functions of parole supervision (Krajick, 1983, p. 31; see also Bottomly, 1990, p. 341).

Florida typifies the problems faced by a populous state with a large and overcrowded prison system that is trying to balance a determinate sentencing framework with the need to provide acceptable prison release mechanisms. In 1983, sentencing guidelines were established in Florida and the state abolished the Parole Commission as a discretionary releasing authority, retaining it only for jurisdiction over those offenders sentenced before the effective date of the legislation (Rhine, Smith, & Jackson, 1991, p. 88). Parole supervision was in effect abolished with this legislation. Prior to 1983, about 80% of all Florida releasees were released conditionally through either parole (63%) or mandatory supervised release (37%).

By 1984, the number of unconditional releasees from prisons had surpassed the number of conditional releasees, and "mandatory supervised release," which had accounted for 18% of the state's conditional releasees in 1981, had been effectively eliminated. In its place, the "split" probation sentence, consisting of a period of incarceration followed by a term of probation supervision, had become the sentence of 25% of those conditionally released. A court-ordered prison population "cap" and the unremitting growth in prison populations prompted a commission to recommend a return to an early release mechanism in Florida. In response, in 1989 the state established the Controlled Release Authority, a body comprised of the same members of the previous parole board (Rhine et al., 1991, p. 89).

By 1990, once again conditional release resumed its predominance as the primary mode of prison release: about 70% of releasees were released conditionally. However, a bit of a twist was introduced, a twist that has also been found elsewhere. Florida's Controlled Release Program includes "supervised" and "unsupervised" releasee statuses. Among conditional releasees, about a quarter of the individuals are released without supervision being required. Thus demands for releasee accountability persist in Florida, and innovative adoptions have been introduced to assure that although at least some releasees are supervised in the community, scarce supervision resources are not extended to those not considered in need of supervision.

Differing patterns of adjustment have occurred in Texas, adjustments that to a large extent have also been driven by dire prison overcrowding levels in that state. In Texas, parole release has been used as a safety valve to manage prison crowding, resulting in a 260% increase in the number of parole releases between 1985 and 1991 (Texas Criminal Justice Policy Council, August 1992, p. 2). In Texas, however, the community supervision of prison releasees takes a number of forms. It includes the supervision of parolees released through traditional discretionary parole release mechanisms, the mandatory supervision (MS) of prisoners who have not been paroled but who are released when their calendar time served plus any accrued good conduct time equals the maximum term to which they were sentenced, the supervision of inmates who were within 6 months of their mandatory release date and who have been released at the discretion of the parole board, and the assignment of split sentences. Taken together, these forms of conditional release accounted for well over 99% of the prison releases in 1988 and 1990. In contrast, in 1978 almost 40% of releasees were unconditionally released into the community upon the expiration of their sentence. When looked at in light of the numbers of inmates released to these various forms of conditional supervision, it becomes clear that the Pardons and Paroles Division of the Texas Department of Criminal Justice, which is responsible for the supervision of the vast majority of prison releases in Texas, has a hefty mandate to fulfill.

Intensive Parole Supervision and Electronic Monitoring

Another correctional strategy suggested by Palmer (1992) to be reflective of the new nature of correctional interventions focuses limited resources upon targeted offender groups considered particularly problematic due to their perceived dangerousness or persistent pattern of offense behavior. This strategy often employs "intensive" supervision. Although parole supervision's effectiveness is still under question, supervision has taken a new turn with the emergence of many "intensive" supervision programs (ISPs) being implemented across the country in parole since the 1980s. Intensive supervision has been seen as a way to insure the treatment of high-risk offenders (e.g., drug abusers, sex offenders) and to maintain strict surveillance over those offenders most likely to slip up. Offenders are often mandated to participate in specialized treatment, such as sexual offender therapy or drug treatment, while receiving a concentrated form of control supervision such as being confined in a community release center, being placed on electronic monitoring, or having frequent visits from a supervising officer. Intensifying surveillance has also been seen as a possibility for reducing the revocation rate of parolees, which has been perceived as steadily increasing compounding the existing problems of institutional crowding. Figure 17.4 presents some figures on the number of parolees on intensive supervision and electronic monitoring devices in 1990.

The state of Texas has been a leader in the intensive supervision and electronic monitoring movement within parole. Included is an electronic monitoring program that is designed to service 1,366 clients a month and a bifurcated intensive supervision program. Intending to promote public safety by closely monitoring high-risk offenders on reduced caseloads (25:1 releasee/officer ratio), one program focuses on offenders who have exhibited difficulty adjusting to regular supervision (ISP), and the other focuses on individuals whose assessment scores indicate the need for enhanced supervision (SRC). In 1991, 1,600 releases were supervised under ISP and 3,850 were supervised under SRC.

Associated with the increased emphasis on intensive parole programs, the research on parole supervision effectiveness has begun to focus on ISP programs. A 1988 study conducted by RAND exemplifies some of the issues of ISP's effectiveness. A randomized experiment was set up to compare, among other things, the recidivism of intensive versus regular supervision parolees in Texas. The results show ISP to be effective both in insuring more treatment and implementing more surveillance (Turner, Petersilia & Deschenes, 1992). However, ISP serves to increase rather than decrease recidivism, mainly because ISP offenders are revoked for more technical violations, especially drug use (Turner et al., 1992; Turner & Petersilia, 1992). It was shown that almost twice as many ISP offenders were sentenced to prison as regular parolees—35% versus 21% (Texas Criminal Justice Policy Council, 1991). Ironically, though implemented to ensure added surveillance and enhance public safety, intensive parole has been shown to increase the correctional costs that they were meant to reduce and to exacerbate the problem of parole revocations they were meant to alleviate. Unfortunately, the assumed direct benefits of intensive supervision for public safety have not been found: There is little to indicate that such programs reduce the recommission of new crimes by parolees.

However, early studies that examined intensive supervision and mandated treatment of drug offenders continue to shed a glimmer of hope in this latter regard. The California Civil Addict Program, a program that

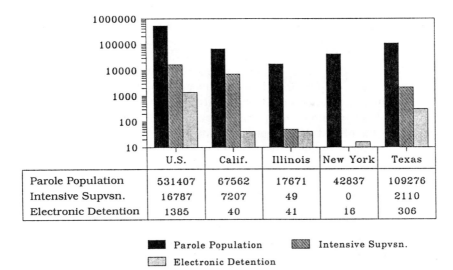

	U.S.	Calif.	Illinois	New York	Texas
Parole Population	531407	67562	17671	42837	109276
Intensive Supvsn.	16787	7207	49	0	2110
Electronic Detention	1385	40	41	16	306

■ Parole Population ▨ Intensive Supvsn.
▢ Electronic Detention

Figure 17.4 Use of Intensive Supervision Strategies: Number of Parolees on Intensive Supervision and Electronic Detention
SOURCE: *Probation and Parole* by the Bureau of Justice Statistics, 1990, Washington, DC: Department of Justice.

lasted 7 years and involved a period of incarceration followed by parole or monitored release for committed addicts, has been extensively evaluated. One of the major studies of this program considered the impact of different types of supervision on parolees' behavior and found that intensive supervision combined with urine testing was more effective in reducing parolees' drug use and criminality than either regular supervision without urine testing or no supervision (see Anglin & McGlothin, 1984). Coupled with studies on the effectiveness of intensive probation supervision that suggest probationers who received more treatment as part of their probation performed better on probation than those who received less treatment (Turner et al., 1992), there is some reason to believe that intensive parole supervision programs that demand offender treatment may promote some beneficial results in terms of reduced recidivism.

Life Skills Development/Special Populations

The other two correctional intervention themes identified by Palmer (1992), that of life skills development and a focus on specific offender groups and types of behavior, helped shape the specific direction taken by those jurisdictions that were moving their primary orientation away from offender change toward external control/surveillance. The first of these seemed to promote an image not so much of remolding the offender into a law abiding citizen, but of fabricating a citizen. It took a deficit perspective, that is, that the offender was missing certain vital parts that were necessary for the person to function appropriately within the community. "Treatment" strategies in this orientation could essentially replicate or even use existing skill development programs in the community. The emphasis focused on providing the offender with employability skills, social interaction techniques, and daily living knowledge presumed absent, while still simultaneously surrounding the individual with the larger framework of monitoring and control.

The state of Texas can serve as an example for states attempting to develop innovative programming for special populations. Since the mid-1980s Texas has introduced a variety of special programs to (1) most efficiently target resources on specific areas of need and (2) to enhance the prospect of successful rehabilitation through special treatment modes (Texas Department of Criminal Justice, 1991, p. 43). In contrast to intensive supervision and electronic monitoring programs, which are designed primarily for risk control purposes, other Texas programs explicitly seek rehabilitative and treatment goals. Included is Project RIO, which involves an Interagency Cooperation Contract with the Texas Employment Commission. Funded by the legislature at over $4 million dollars for FY 91, the program is designed to provide releasees with employment assessment, training, referral, and placement. It has been reported that in FY 91, 70% of those who requested assistance found jobs through the program (12,591 releasees) and that program participants exhibited a 5% lower recidivism rate than comparable groups that did not participate in the program (p. 45).

In Texas, specialized caseloads are in place for sex offenders, who are required to attend sex offender therapy sessions; mentally impaired offenders, who are sought out and diverted from the criminal justice system for treatment; and mentally retarded offenders, who are placed in educational, vocational, or job readiness programs and who receive financial, residential, and counseling support. All of the client groups are placed on smaller, specialized caseloads that require enhanced levels of client/officer contacts and referrals to community-based agencies. Plans are in place to expand current specialized substance abuse programming (currently 14 substance abuse officers supervise 350 high-need substance abusers in a 180-day program).

The above discussion illustrates some of the major changes in parole supervision practices that have been occurring throughout the United States in response to changing sociopolitical and economic constraints. The state of Illinois, however, has recently radically transformed its parole supervision philosophy and practice. The following section presents an overview of what has been happening in that state.

Radical Restructuring of Parole in Illinois

Since 1977 and the adoption of a determinate sentencing law that ended discretionary parole release mechanisms for newly convicted offenders, Illinois has mandated supervised release of inmates released from prison. Supervision models remained similar to those found under earlier parole models, with offenders being supervised from 1 to 3 years based on the seriousness of the original conviction charge (Goodstein & Hepburn, 1985).

Facing significant budget constraints in the mid to latter part of the 1980s, the Illinois Department of Corrections (IDOC) gave greater priority to institutional corrections and began to downscale its community correctional supervision division, which administers the mandatory supervision release program.

Due to population growth and concerns with maintaining the safety of prisoners and institutional staff, the Illinois Department of Corrections' operational spending budget has more than tripled since 1975, even when accounting for inflation. However, within the agency an increasing portion of the budget has been devoted to adult institutional corrections. For instance, total appropriations for FY 92 were $567 million, nearly 80% of which goes toward operating adult institutions. By contrast, less than 60% of the Department's operating budget in FY 75 went toward adult prisons (Illinois Task Force on Crime and Corrections, 1992, pp. 11-12). Expenditures for community supervision remained relatively stable throughout the 1980s, going from $4.2 million in 1979 to $4.46 million in 1989 (Illinois Department of Corrections, 1979; Illinois Department of Corrections, 1989) despite the tremendous increase in IDOC's overall budget.

From 1980 to 1987, the increase in parole populations was accompanied by a gradual decrease in the number of parole agents, culminating in 1987 when more than half of the parole staff was laid off due to budget cuts. The number of parole agents gradually increased afterward up until 1991, but not at a fast enough rate to bring average caseloads to levels found in the early 1980s. In fact, the average caseload in 1991 was more than twice the caseload in 1982, and almost 4 times the recommended caseload of the American Correctional Association. If one considers variation in caseload size within regions of the state, the numbers are even more staggering, with some Chicago-based parole agents carrying caseloads of over 300. For the most part, this situation continued until mid-1991, when Illinois introduced an innovative and unique structure of post-release services and supervision termed PreStart.

With the introduction of the Prestart program, which began operations on July 1, 1991, Illinois has basically introduced a bifurcated system into its mandatory supervised release program. Radically different from most parole supervision structures, PreStart separates the surveillance and supervision functions of parole from integrative social service provision functions. After mandated specialized institutional preparation for release (termed Phase I programming), the vast majority of releasees are allowed to voluntarily utilize community resources brokered through a system of newly developed Community Service Centers. The Service Centers are designed to be information and resource brokerage facilities, intended to promote the abilities of releasees to develop and implement effective employment, residential living, and treatment plans.

For releasees who present specific needs, Illinois has planned the implementation of specialized service delivery mechanisms: (a) four Community Drug Intervention Programs, which will provide services and drug testing for releasees posing manifest substance abuse needs; (b) contracted services for specialized interventions with selected sex offenders, which will be available under the PreStart program; and (c) PreStart's Special Intensive Supervision Unit, to which certain releasees who are thought to pose enhanced risks to public safety, along with those released from the Dixon Springs Shock Incarceration Program, will be assigned. The Special Intensive Supervision Unit is the only component of the PreStart program that retains the traditional surveillance function of parole supervision. The total package of services and programs available for releasees in the community is termed Phase II programming.

It is too early to tell what the consequences of PreStart are for public safety and the delivery of services to parolees in the state of Illinois, but clearly the philosophical and structural changes represented by the program stand in marked contrast to traditional philosophies and structures. It does not appear that what has happened within Illinois will be limited to just that state. For instance, in California a Blue Ribbon Commission on Inmate Population Management has recommended an overhaul of parole operations along similar lines (Schiraldi, 1991). The commission's recommendations included the following:

1. Minimize or eliminate the supervision/revocation function of parole. Postrelease supervision would be abolished or shortened for all or mostly all parolees. Unsupervised parolees would be revoked and returned to prison only if apprehended by the police.

2. Reallocate the funds that were previously spent on supervision functions to pay for rehabilitative services. The community-based treatment programs

would offer a variety of services including drug rehabilitation, job training, and housing assistance.

3. Increase the use of prerelease programs in prison in order to equip inmates with basic skills for successful functioning in the community.

Although these recommendations were rejected by Governor Wilson, California has taken a number of more modest initiatives in altering parole practices and the costs they generate. Included prominently are a variety of policies that serve to reduce technical violation rates (The quiet shift in prison policy, 1992).

The above developments in parole indicate that what is happening in Illinois with regard to parole supervision reflects a variety of factors evident nationwide that have resulted in a broad questioning of traditional parole supervision structures and in a good level of related experimentation and innovation.

Summary and Conclusions

The changing realities of the correctional environment in the 1990s, including the organizational restructuring of corrections and the loss of faith in rehabilitative ideals, led to a serious reconsideration of the role of parole in both release and supervisory functions. The need for parole as discretionary release ceased to exist in the federal system and in various states adopting determinate sentencing structures. Further, the end of parole as a release mechanism raised basic questions of efficacy for parole supervision in general. As such questions were considered, it became clear that there were no strong arguments for the effects of parole (intensive or otherwise) on recidivism. Moreover, the problems caused by the increasing flow of revoked parolees (often for technical violations versus new felony convictions) were adding to the difficulties of already overcrowded institutions. Fiscal constraints seem, in many states, to have been the "final nail in the coffin" for traditional parole supervision structures.

States have responded to both the fiscal cuts and the increasing call for public safety in various ways. One adaptation has been the creation of mandatory supervised release structures to replace former parole functions as a method of external control. These structures have deemphasized the delivery of services and assistance while emphasizing offender accountability and issues of risk control, both of which reflect pragmatic correctional concerns. Second, some states have continued traditional parole supervision practices but have allocated increasingly scarce resources for those considered most likely to compromise public safety. Operationalizations of this adaptation in states fitting this broad category have varied, ranging from a focus on those most recently released from prison to those objectively classified as high risk. Finally, the delivery of treatment-related services has been minimized for the vast bulk of releasees and has been targeted toward special classes of individuals considered to have significant treatment needs (e.g., sex and drug offenders).

A major theme underlying all these adaptations is that parole supervision cannot be all things for all people. The nature of postrelease supervision must instead be individualized to meet the specific risks and needs presented by offenders. Although the situation will probably lead to the discovery of promising interventions, the lack of a clear and coherent correctional ideology upon which parole supervision practices are premised warns of a tenuous and unstable upcoming decade for parole supervision.

Discussion Questions

1. Parole supervision in often addressed as inherently tied to rehabilitative ideology. This paper presents historic information showing that this is not always the case. Discuss the historical origins of parole and parole supervision in terms of how it is or is not inherently tied to rehabilitation. How might this affect parole policy/programming?

2. What are the major driving forces influencing changes in contemporary parole supervision? Which of these forces seems to have had the greatest impact on current postrelease supervision strategies?

3. Discuss some of the major obstacles in drawing conclusions from parole supervision effectiveness research. Given the inherent problems with parole supervision effectiveness research, what implications does the existing research hold for policy makers?

4. Given the discussion of experimentation in parole strategies, what are the basic forms of supervision that have emerged across the nation in the 1980s and 1990s?

5. What is the future for parole supervision and postrelease supervision in this country?

References

Abadinsky, H. (1991). *Probation and parole: Theory and practice* (4th ed.). Englewood Cliffs, NJ: Prentice Hall.

Anglin, M. D., & McGlothin, W. H. (1984). Outcome of narcotic addict treatment in California. In F. M. Tims & J. P. Ludford (Eds.), *National Institute on Drug Abuse*

Research Monograph No. 51 (pp. 106-128). Rockville, MD: U.S. Department of Health and Human Services, National Institute on Drug Abuse.

Blumstein, A. (1988). Prison populations: A system out of control. In M. Toney & N. Morris (Eds.), *Crime and criminal justice: A review of research, Vol. 10* (pp. 231-266). Chicago: University of Chicago Press.

Bottomley, K. A. (1990). Parole in transition: A comparative study of origins, developments, and prospects for the 1990s. In M. Tonry & N. Morris (Eds.), *Crime and justice: A review of research* (pp. 319-374). Chicago: University of Chicago Press.

Bureau of Justice Statistics. (1978). *Sourcebook of criminal justice statistics 1977.* Washington, DC: Government Printing Office.

Bureau of Justice Statistics. (1979). *Sourcebook of criminal justice statistics 1978.* Washington, DC: Government Printing Office.

Bureau of Justice Statistics. (1980). *Sourcebook of criminal justice statistics 1979.* Washington, DC: Government Printing Office.

Bureau of Justice Statistics. (1982). *Sourcebook of criminal justice statistics 1981.* Washington, DC: Government Printing Office.

Bureau of Justice Statistics. (1985). *Sourcebook of criminal justice statistics 1984.* Washington, DC: Government Printing Office.

Bureau of Justice Statistics. (1986). *Sourcebook of criminal justice statistics 1985.* Washington, DC: Government Printing Office.

Bureau of Justice Statistics. (1989). *Sourcebook of criminal justice statistics 1988.* Washington, DC: Government Printing Office.

Bureau of Justice Statistics. (1991). *Sourcebook of criminal justice statistics 1990.* Washington, DC: Government Printing Office.

Cromwell, P. F., Jr., Killinger, G. C., Kerper, H. B., & Walker, C. (1985). *Probation and parole in the criminal justice system* (2nd ed.). New York: West.

Flanagan, T. (1985). Questioning the other parole: The effectiveness of community supervision of offenders. In L. F. Travis (Ed.), *Probation, parole, and community corrections* (pp. 167-183). Prospect Heights, IL: Waveland.

Fogel, D. (1975). *We are the living proof.* Cincinnati: Anderson.

Goodstein, L., & Hepburn, J. (1985). *Determinate sentencing and imprisonment: A failure of reform.* Cincinnati: Anderson.

Gottfredson, D. (1975, November). *Some positive changes in the parole process.* Paper presented at the Annual Meeting of the American Society of Criminology, Tucson, AZ.

Gottfredson, M. R., Mitchell-Herzfeld, S. D., & Flanagan, T. J. (1982). Another look at the effectiveness of parole supervision. *Journal of Research in Crime and Delinquency, 16,* 218-231.

Illinois Department of Corrections. (1979). *Plan for human services, fiscal year 1979.* Springfield, IL: Bureau of the Budget.

Illinois Department of Corrections. (1989). *Human services plan fiscal years 1989-1991.* Springfield, IL: Author.

Illinois State Legislature. (1978). Illinois Statute, Revised; Chapter 38, 1003-3-1 (a) (5).

Illinois Task Force on Crime and Corrections. (1992). *Report of the Task Force on Crime and Corrections.* Unpublished manuscript. Springfield, IL.

Killinger, G. G., & Cromwell, P. F. (Eds.). (1974). *Corrections in the community: Alternatives to imprisonment.* St. Paul, MN: West.

Krajick, K. (1983, June). Abolishing parole: An idea whose time has passed. *Corrections Magazine,* pp. 32-40.

Lerner, M. J. (1977). The effectiveness of a definite sentence parole program. *Criminology, 15,* 211-224.

Martinson, R. (1974). What works? Questions and answers about prison reform. *The Public Interest, 35,* 22-54.

Martinson, R., & Wilks, J. (1977). Save parole supervision. In K. C. Haas & G. P. Alpet (Eds.), *The dilemmas of corrections: Contemporary readings* (pp. 421-428). Prospect Heights, IL: Waveland.

Messinger, S. L., Berecochea, J. E., Rauma, D., & Berk, R. A. (1985). The foundations of parole in California. *Law and Society Review, 9,* 69-106.

Morris, N., & Tonry, M. (1990). *Between prison and probation: Intermediate punishments in a rational sentencing system.* New York: Oxford University Press.

New York State Division of Parole. (1990). *Annual report, 1986-1989: Decades of dedication.* Albany, NY: State of New York Executive Department, Division of Parole.

Nuttall, C. P., et al. (1977). *Parole in England and Wales.* Home Office Research Study no. 38. London: H.M. Stationery Office.

Palmer, T. (1992). *The re-emergence of correctional intervention.* Newbury Park, CA: Sage.

The quiet shift in prison policy. [Editorial] (p. B6). (1992, June 6). *Sacramento Bee.*

Rhine, E. E., Smith, W. R., and Jackson, R. W. (1991). *Paroling authorities: Recent history and current trends.* Laurel, MD: American Corrections Association.

Rothman, D. J. (1980). *Conscience and convenience.* Boston: Little, Brown.

Sacks, H. R., & Logan, C. H. (1979). *Does parole make a difference?* West Hartford, CN: University of Connecticut School of Law Press.

Sacks, H., & Logan, C. (1980). *Parole: Crime prevention or crime postponement?* Storrs, CT: University of Connecticut Law School Press.

Schiraldi, V. (1991). Parole violators in California: A waste of money, a waste of time. *Overcrowded Times, 2*(6), 5-11.

Smykla, J. O. (1984). *Probation and parole: Crime control in the community.* New York: Macmillan.

Stanley, D. (1976). *Prisoners among us: The problem of parole.* Washington, DC: The Brookings Institution.

Texas Criminal Justice Policy Council. (1992, May 29). *Recidivism in the Texas criminal justice system: Sentencing dynamics study, report 5.* Austin, TX: Author.

Texas Department of Criminal Justice. (1991). *Annual report 1991.* Austin, TX: Author.

Turner, S., & Petersilia, J. (1992). Focusing on high-risk parolees: An experiment to reduce commitments to the Texas department of corrections. *Journal of Research in Crime and Delinquency, 29,* 34-61.

Turner, S., Petersilia, J., & Deschenes, E. P. (1992). Evaluating intensive supervision probation/parole (ISP) for drug offenders. *Crime and Delinquency, 38,* 539-556.

Von Hirsh, A. (1976). *Doing justice: The choice of punishments.* New York: Hill & Wang.

Waller, I. (1974). *Men released from prison.* Toronto: University of Toronto Press.

Wilson, R. (1977). Supervision (the other parole) also attacked. *Corrections Magazine, 3*(3), 56-59

About the Editor

Albert R. Roberts, D.S.W., is a Professor of Criminal Justice and Social Work at the School of Social Work, Rutgers University, New Brunswick, New Jersey. He is the Executive Director of the Institute of Criminal Justice and Security Administration at Rutgers. He previously taught at the Indiana University School of Social Work in Indianapolis, Seton Hall University, the University of New Haven, and Brooklyn College of the City University of New York. He received his doctorate in social work from the University of Maryland School of Social Work with a concentration in social work research and a minor in criminal justice. His M.A. degree is in sociology and criminology and was obtained from Long Island University.

He is a lifetime member of the Academy of Criminal Justice Sciences and an active member of N.A.S.W., the American Correctional Association, and the National Council of Juvenile and Family Court Judges. He is a member of the NJ Governor's Juvenile Justice and Delinquency Prevention Commission, as well as the New Jersey Supreme Court's Probation Advisory Board. Dr. Roberts has extensive experience in juvenile and criminal justice research. Over the past two decades, he has served as Project Director or consultant on several research and evaluation projects including: the New Jersey State Law Enforcement Planning Agency's Evaluation Projects, Research for Better Schools, Inc., (Philadelphia) Correctional Education Project, the American Correctional Association's National Study on the Utilization of Instructional Technology in Corrections, and the National Institute of Justice (N.I.J.) funded study on the

Effectiveness of Crisis Intervention with Crime Victims at Victim Services Agency in New York City.

He serves on the editorial board of *The Justice Professional* and is the Editor-in-Chief of the journal *Crisis Intervention and Time-Limited Treatment*. He has also authored and edited fifteen books, including *Helping Crime Victims* (Sage, 1990), *Juvenile Justice* (1989), *Criminal Justice in the 21st Century* (with Roslyn Muraskin, 1994), and *Crisis Intervention and Time-Limited Cognitive Therapy* (Sage, 1994). He has more than 90 publications to his credit.

About the Contributors

David M. Altschuler, Ph.D., is a Principal Research Scientist at The Johns Hopkins University's Institute for Policy Studies and holds a joint appointment in the Sociology Department. He has a doctorate in social service administration and a master's degree in urban studies from the University of Chicago. His work focuses on juvenile justice sanctioning and aftercare; community-based delinquency program design, implementation and assessment; privatization in corrections; and drug involvement and crime among inner city youth. In addition to acting as Project Director and Co-Principal Investigator on the Intensive Aftercare Project, he is also part of a three-person federal research team studying the federal government's juvenile justice and delinquency prevention formula grant program. He recently directed a statewide workload study of the Maryland Department of Juvenile Services. He also participated in two other recent studies: (1) drug involvement and crime in a sample of inner city teenage males in Washington, D.C., and (2) cost effectiveness of private and public secure treatment programs for youth in Massachusetts.

Troy L. Armstrong, Ph.D., is Professor in the Division of Criminal Justice at California State University, Sacramento, and is currently Co-Principal Investigator on the Office of Juvenile Justice and Delinquency Prevention (OJJDP)-funded Intensive Community-Based Aftercare Program. Trained as a social anthropologist, he began his career in juvenile justice as a juvenile parole officer in Chicago during the early 1970s. Over the past decade, he has served as a consultant on a variety of juvenile justice-related projects at the national, state, and local levels, including the

National Center for Juvenile Justice, the National Council of Juvenile and Family Court Judges, the Administrative Office of the Courts in New Jersey, and the Casey Family Program in Seattle. He has published widely on a number of programming issues including serious and violent offenders, restitution and community services, school crime, intensive probation supervision, and community-based alternatives to formal justice system processing. Most recently, he edited a volume on intensive interventions with high-risk juvenile offenders.

Mary Ellen Beekman is a Special Agent of the Federal Bureau of Investigation where she has been a member for 14 years. She has been assigned to the Joint Auto Larceny Task Force for 11 years. Agent Beekman came to the FBI after spending 5 years with the New York City Police Department where she earned a master's degree in Forensic Psychology from John Jay College of Criminal Justice.

She is the author of an article on automobile insurance fraud and coauthor of an article on the shipping of stolen vehicles out of the country. She has coordinated several major theft cases with the U.S. Custom Service, New York City Police Department, and several other FBI offices. As a coordinator for the National Center for the Analysis of Violent Crime, she provides training in Criminal Investigation Analysis and VI-Cap to local law enforcement and other criminal justice groups.

Bruce L. Berg received his Ph.D. in sociology from Syracuse University in 1983. For three years he served as the Internship Director and as Assistant Professor at the School of Criminology at Florida State University (now the School of Criminology and Criminal Justice). He has also served as a Visiting Assistant Professor in the Department of Sociology at the University of Massachusetts, Boston Harbor Campus, for two years. During that period he conducted extensive ethnographic research in police academies, attending seven full programs of training. Currently, he is an Associate Professor of Criminology at Indiana University of Pennsylvania. He has published numerous articles and presented many papers on police and criminology topics. He is the author of two books, one entitled *Qualitative Research Methods for the Social Sciences* and the other entitled *Law Enforcement: An Introduction to Police in Society.* He has also recently completed a book with Dr. Robert Mutchnick entitled *Research Methods for the Social Sciences: Applications and Practice.*

Mark Blumberg is a Professor of Criminal Justice at Central Missouri State University in Warrensburg, Missouri. He received his bachelor's and master's degrees from the University of Kansas, Lawrence, and an additional master's and a doctoral degree from the State University of New York at Albany. He has authored numerous book chapters and journal articles on police use of deadly force, the impact of AIDS on the criminal justice system, and other issues. His work has appeared in such publications as the *Criminal Law Bulletin, American Journal of Police, Justice Professional Crime and Delinquency, Criminal Justice Policy Review,* and the *Prison Journal.* He is the author of an edited book entitled *AIDS: The Impact on the Criminal Justice System* and the coauthor of a book entitled *The Mythology of Crime and Criminal Justice.*

Thomas C. Castellano is Associate Professor of Criminal Justice at the Center for the Study of Crime, Delinquency and Corrections at Southern Illinois University at Carbondale. He received his Ph.D. in criminal justice from the State University of New York at Albany in 1986. His research interests include the criminal justice policy formation and implementation process, sociopolitical factors influencing criminal sanctioning decisions, and the effectiveness of correctional sanctions. He is currently conducting an implementation and impact analysis of parole reform in Illinois and a nationwide study of the drug treatment and aftercare components of shock incarceration programs. He has recently contributed articles to the *Journal of Research in Crime and Delinquency,* the *Journal of Offender Rehabilitation,* the *Journal of Crime and Justice,* and the *American Journal of Police.*

Ernest L. Cowles is Assistant Professor of Criminal Justice at the Center for the Study of Crime, Delinquency and Corrections at Southern Illinois University at Carbondale. He received his Ph.D. in criminology from Florida State University in 1981. His background in the criminal justice field includes having served as an instructor, researcher, and correctional practitioner. He was the Director of the Division of Classification and Treatment for the Missouri Department of Corrections and Human Resources. He has served as a consultant to a number of criminal justice agencies, including the National Institute of Justice and National Institute of Corrections. He is currently working on a nationwide study of the drug treatment and aftercare components of shock incarceration programs. His most recent work includes a chapter entitled "Is there a next generation of shock incarceration facilities: The evolving nature of goals, program components, and drug treatment services" in the forthcoming book *Intermediate Sanctions: Sentencing in the '90s,* published by Sage.

Paul Cromwell is Professor of Sociology and Criminology at the University of Miami in Coral Gables, Florida. He received his Ph.D. in criminology from Florida State University. He is the author and coauthor of numerous articles and books, including *Community Based Corrections: Probation, Parole, and Intermediate Sanctions* (1994), *Probation and Parole in the Criminal Justice System* (1985), and *Breaking and Entering: An Ethnographic Analysis of Burglary* (Sage, 1991). He has extensive experience in the criminal justice system, including service as Chairman of the Texas Board of Pardons and Paroles.

Diane C. Dwyer, Visiting Assistant Professor of Social Work, has been a member of the State University of New York College at Brockport social work faculty since 1981. From 1977 until 1981, she was on the faculty of D'Youville College in Buffalo, New York. She teaches courses in social work methods, human growth and social environment, probation and parole, and domestic violence. She has previously collaborated with Professor Roger B. McNally on several research projects in the area of juvenile justice. Their work has been presented at several national conferences and published in numerous professional journals.

Roger Handberg is Professor of Political Science at the University of Central Florida. His publications include numerous articles on the United States Supreme Court, county sheriffs, criminal courts in Florida, the plea bargaining process, and a forthcoming book on the Florida Sentencing Guidelines with N. Gary Holten.

N. Gary Holten is Associate Professor of Criminal Justice and former Chair of the Department at the University of Central Florida. He has been extensively involved in researching the criminal justice system in Florida and has written *The Criminal Justice System* with Melvin Jones, *The Criminal Courts* with Lawson Lamar, and a forthcoming book on the Florida Sentencing Guidelines with Roger Handberg.

Barton L. Ingraham is an Associate Professor at the Institute of Criminal Justice and Criminology, University of Maryland, and has been a member of the faculty there since 1970. He was Acting Director of the Institute during the years 1979 and 1980 and was Dr. Charles F. Wellford's predecessor. He is a graduate of Harvard University (B.A., 1952), of Harvard Law School (J.D., 1957), and of the University of California (Berkeley) School of Criminology (D. Crim., 1972). Before his academic career, he was a lawyer for ten years, practicing law in Newark, New Jersey; New York City; Lovington, New Mexico; and Berkeley, California. He is the author of many journal articles and three books.

Roger B. McNally is an Associate Professor of criminal justice at S.U.N.Y. College at Brockport. He came to Brockport in 1979 after holding administrative positions in the New York State Division of Probation and the New York State Division for Youth. He teaches courses on corrections, juvenile justice, and family violence and coordinates the criminal justice internship program. He has previously collaborated with Professor Diane C. Dwyer on several research projects in the area of juvenile justice. Their work has been presented at several national conferences and published in numerous professional journals.

C. Aaron McNeece received his M.S.W. and Ph.D. at the University of Michigan. He has worked in both adult and juvenile corrections in probation as well as institutions. He has served as a consultant on drug and alcohol treatment programs for criminal offenders in the United States, Ireland, and England. His most recent research has been concerned with the apprehension, processing, and treatment of drug offenders. His most recent book is *Chemical Dependency: A Systems Approach* (coauthored with Diana M. DiNitto). He has been a Professor of Social Work at Florida State University since 1978, and he currently serves as director of FSU's Institute for Health and Human Services Research.

Patricia A. Payne, B.S., J.D., is the Coordinator of the Criminal Justice Program and Assistant Professor of Criminal Justice and Political Science at Middlesex County College in Edison, New Jersey, where she currently teaches courses in constitutional law, criminal justice, criminology, U.S. national government, juvenile justice, and justice in American society. She is also a licensed attorney in the state of New Jersey. For the past three years, she has been a Visiting Lecturer at Rutgers University in the Administration of Justice Program. Her current research interests center on the situation of Federal Habeas Corpus and its constitutional ramifications.

Cheryl L. Ringel is Research Assistant at the Center for the Study of Crime, Delinquency and Corrections at Southern Illinois University at Carbondale. Her interests include criminal justice policy formation, the interplay of public opinion and criminal justice policy, and feminist criminological theory. She is currently working on an implementation and impact analysis of parole reform in Illinois. She received her M.S. in Administration of Justice at Southern Illinois University at Carbondale in 1993.

John G. Robertson, M.S.W., is at present completing doctoral studies at the Columbia University School of Social Work, New York, NY, with a focus on noncustodial fathers, child support, employment, and economics. He has worked in drug treatment and HIV/AIDS treatment and prevention at Integrity, Inc., a therapeutic community in Newark, New Jersey. While there, he directed the Essex County, New Jersey, court diversion program for teenagers arrested for selling or using drugs and/or alcohol. For many years prior to his work in Newark, he worked with neighborhood organizations in Brooklyn and San Francisco.

Joseph F. Ryan, Ph.D., is an Associate Professor of Criminal Justice and Sociology at Pace University in White Plains, New York. He received his Ph.D. in criminology from Fordham University in the Bronx, New York. During the 1992-1993 academic year, he was a Visiting Fellow at the National Institute of Justice in Washington, D.C., where he conducted research on defining community policing. He is also a former detective with the New York City Police Department and was their expert on violence, especially as it relates to spouse, child, and elder abuse.

Lori Koester Scott, M.C., is the Administrator of Sex Offender Supervision for Maricopa County Adult Probation in Phoenix, Arizona. She received her B.S. in Sociology from St. Louis University and a Master's in Counseling from Arizona State University. She began her specialization in this field in 1981 as a sex offender therapist in the Arizona State Prison. As a trainer and consultant to probation departments throughout Arizona and other states, she is presently researching the recidivism factors of probationary sex offenders revoked to prison.

Donald J. Sears is a former New Jersey police officer as well as criminal investigator for the Public Defender Service, Washington, D.C. He holds a B.S. in criminology from the University of Tampa, and a J.D. from Rutgers University Law School, Newark, New Jersey. As an Assistant County Prosecutor, he obtained extensive criminal litigation experience in both trial and appellate courts. He also acted as a police legal advisor, lecturing on the use of deadly force and drunk driving laws. He is currently a practicing attorney with the law firm of Busch and Busch, North Brunswick, New Jersey, specializing in criminal defense cases. He is also an Adjunct Professor/Visiting Lecturer at Rutgers University in the Administration of Justice Department, New Brunswick, New Jersey. He has taught courses on issues confronting police officers as well as on the criminal justice system. He is the author of *To Kill Again: The Motivation and Development of Serial Murder* (1991). He is a member of the Society for Police and Criminal Psychology.

Judith E. Waters, Ph.D., received her degree from the Graduate Center of the City University of New York. She has taught at Brooklyn College and is presently Professor of Psychology and Co-Director of the Masters Program in Applied Social Science and Community Psychology at Fairleigh Dickinson University in Madison, New Jersey. She has just completed a new curriculum design to train people in the substance abuse area using a practitioner-research model. Her own research has focused on police stress, program evaluation in substance abuse, and studies of HIV prevention. Her contribution to this book is derived from her work at a residential drug therapeutic community in Newark, New Jersey.

Michael Welch received the Ph.D. in sociology from the University of North Texas, Denton. At present he is Associate Professor in the Administration of Justice Program at Rutgers University, New Brunswick, New Jersey. Previously an Associate Professor at St. John's University in Queens, New York, he also has correctional experience at the federal, state, and local levels. His research interests include corrections and social control. He has published numerous book chapters and articles that have appeared in the *American Journal of Criminal Justice*, the *Journal of Crime and Justice*, *Dialectical Anthropology*, and the *Journal of Offender Counseling, Services, and Rehabilitation.* He is also author of *Corrections: A Critical Approach.*

Charles F. Wellford, Ph.D., Associate Professor at the Institute of Criminal Justice and Criminology at the University of Maryland where he has been director since 1981. He serves on numerous state and federal advisory boards and commissions and was Vice-President Elect of the American Society of Criminology. From 1976 to 1981 he served in the Office of the United States Attorney General, where he directed the Federal Justice Research Program. During that time he directed research on federal sentencing and prosecution policies and on the state of civil justice in America. The author of numerous publications on criminal justice issues, his most recent research has focused on the determinants of sentencing, the development of comparative crime data systems, and the measurement of white-collar crime. He received his Ph.D. in 1969 from the University of Pennsylvania.